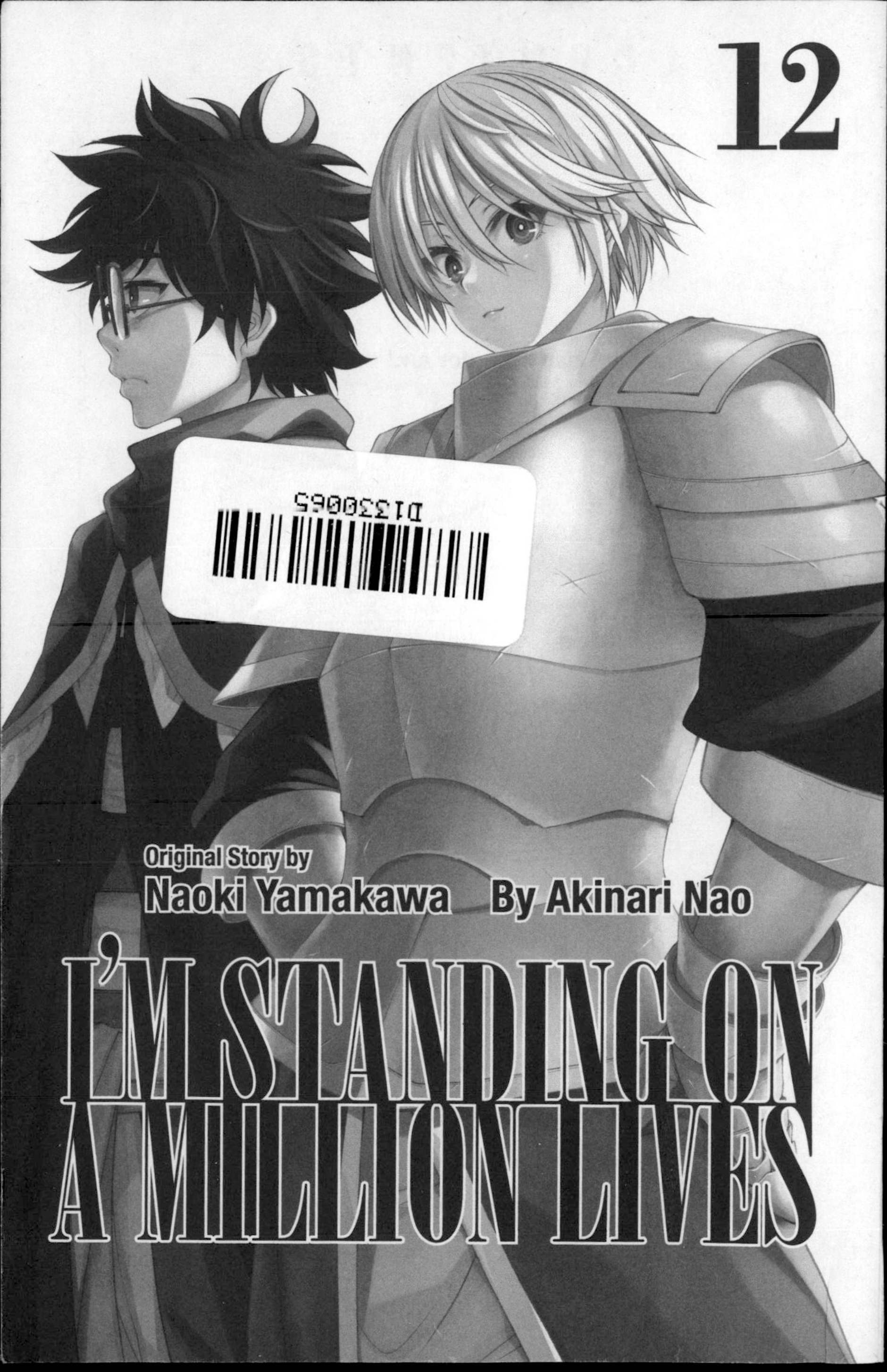
12
Original Story by
Naoki Yamakawa
By Akinari Nao
I'M STANDING ON
A MILLION LIVES

⚔ CONTENTS ⚔

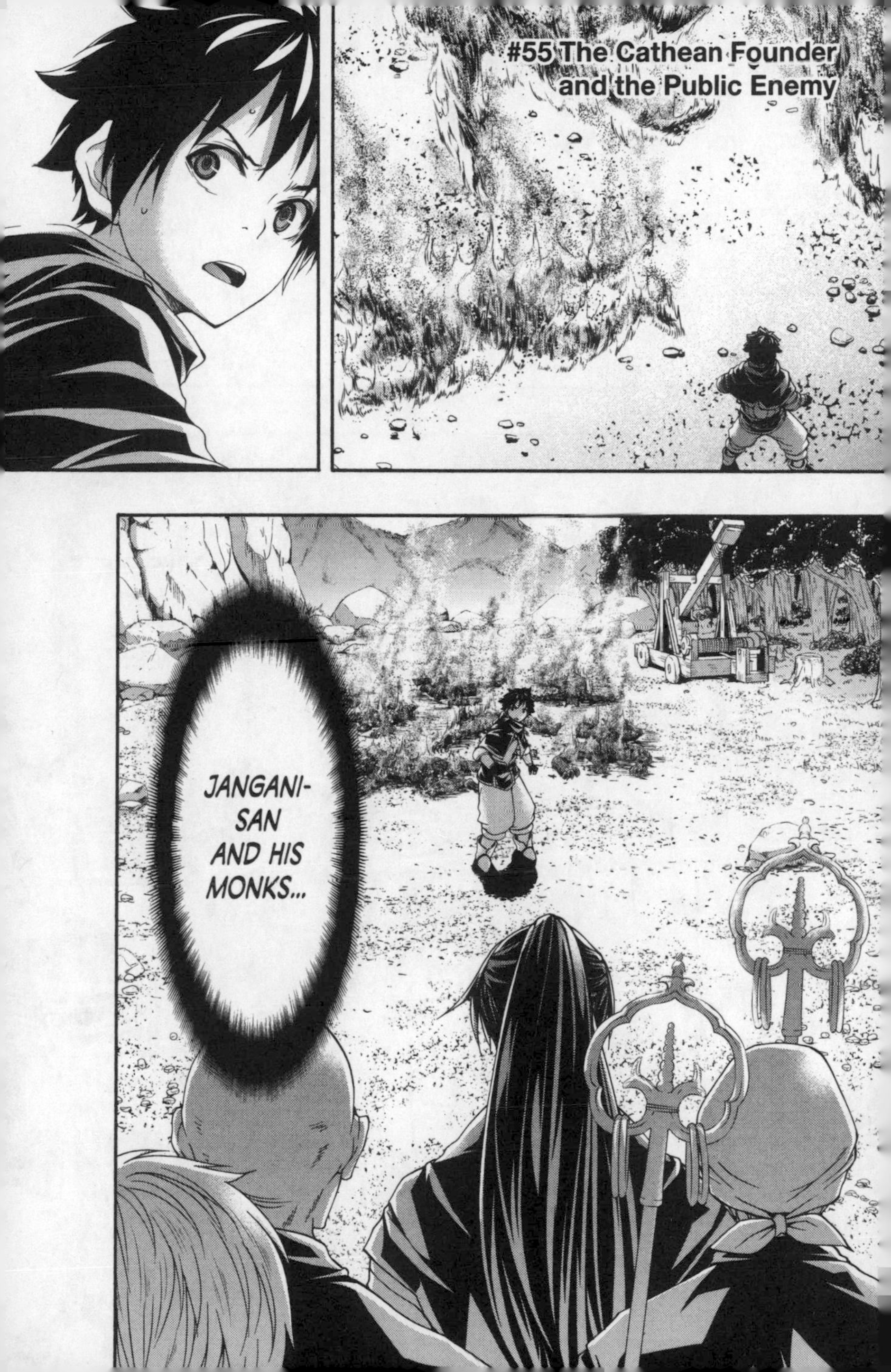
#55 The Cathean Founder and the Public Enemy
JANGANI-SAN AND HIS MONKS...

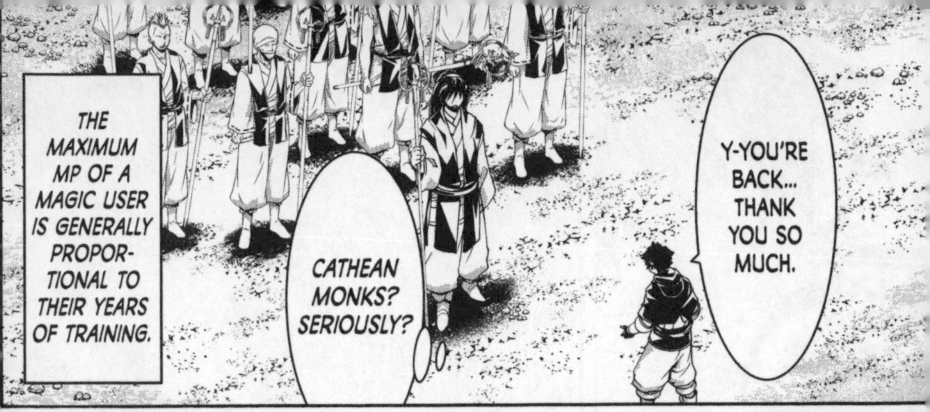
Y-YOU'RE BACK... THANK YOU SO MUCH.
CATHEAN MONKS? SERIOUSLY?
THE MAXIMUM MP OF A MAGIC USER IS GENERALLY PROPOR-TIONAL TO THEIR YEARS OF TRAINING.
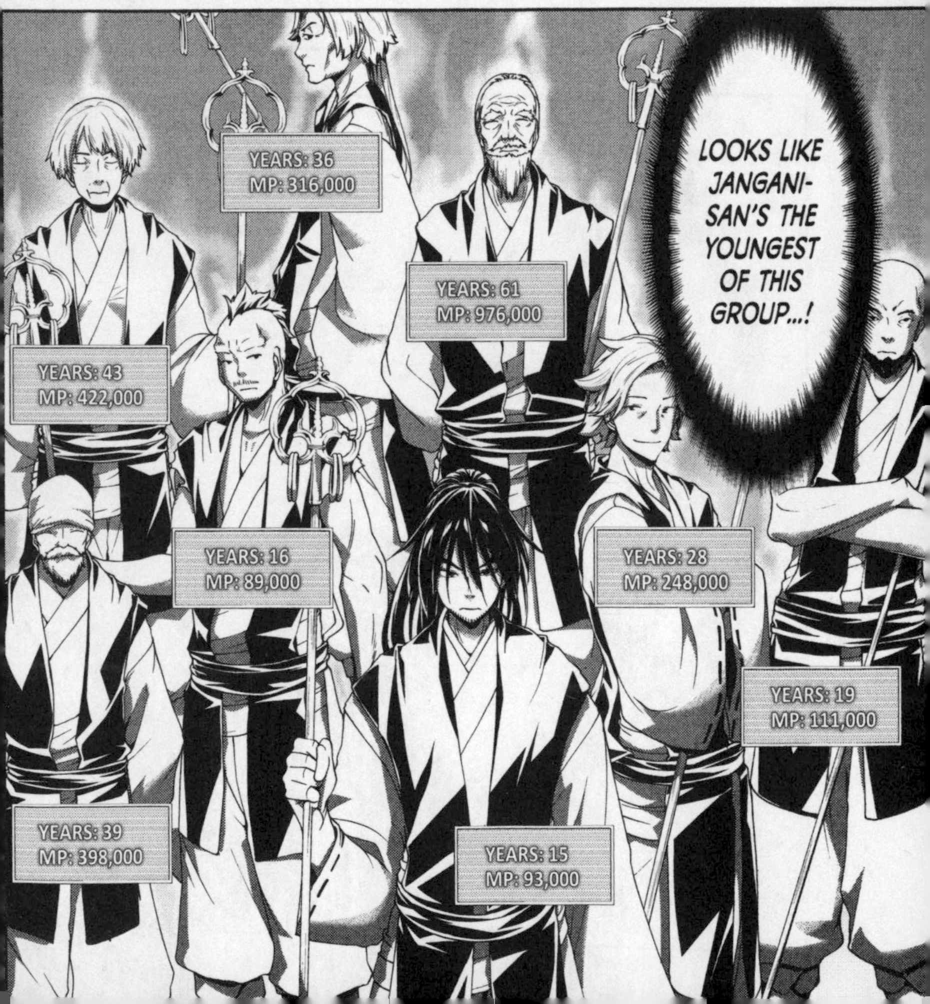
LOOKS LIKE JANGANI-SAN'S THE YOUNGEST OF THIS GROUP...!
YEARS: 61 MP: 976,000
YEARS: 36 MP: 316,000
YEARS: 43 MP: 422,000
YEARS: 19 MP: 111,000
YEARS: 28 MP: 248,000
YEARS: 16 MP: 89,000
YEARS: 15 MP: 93,000
YEARS: 39 MP: 398,000

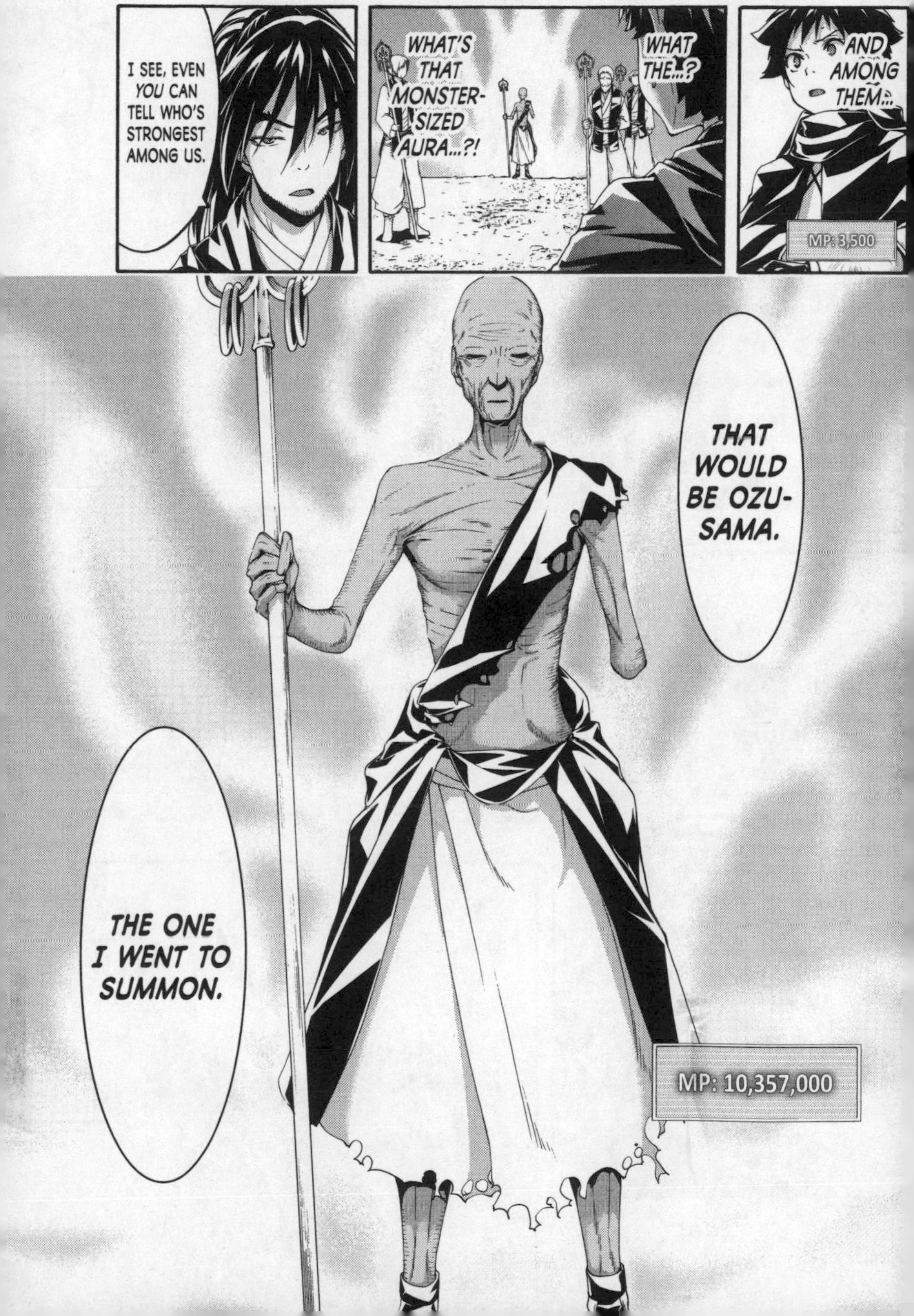

AND AMONG THEM...
MP: 3,500
WHAT THE...?
WHAT'S THAT MONSTER-SIZED AURA...?!
I SEE, EVEN *YOU* CAN TELL WHO'S STRONGEST AMONG US.
THAT WOULD BE OZU-SAMA.
THE ONE I WENT TO SUMMON.
MP: 10,357,000

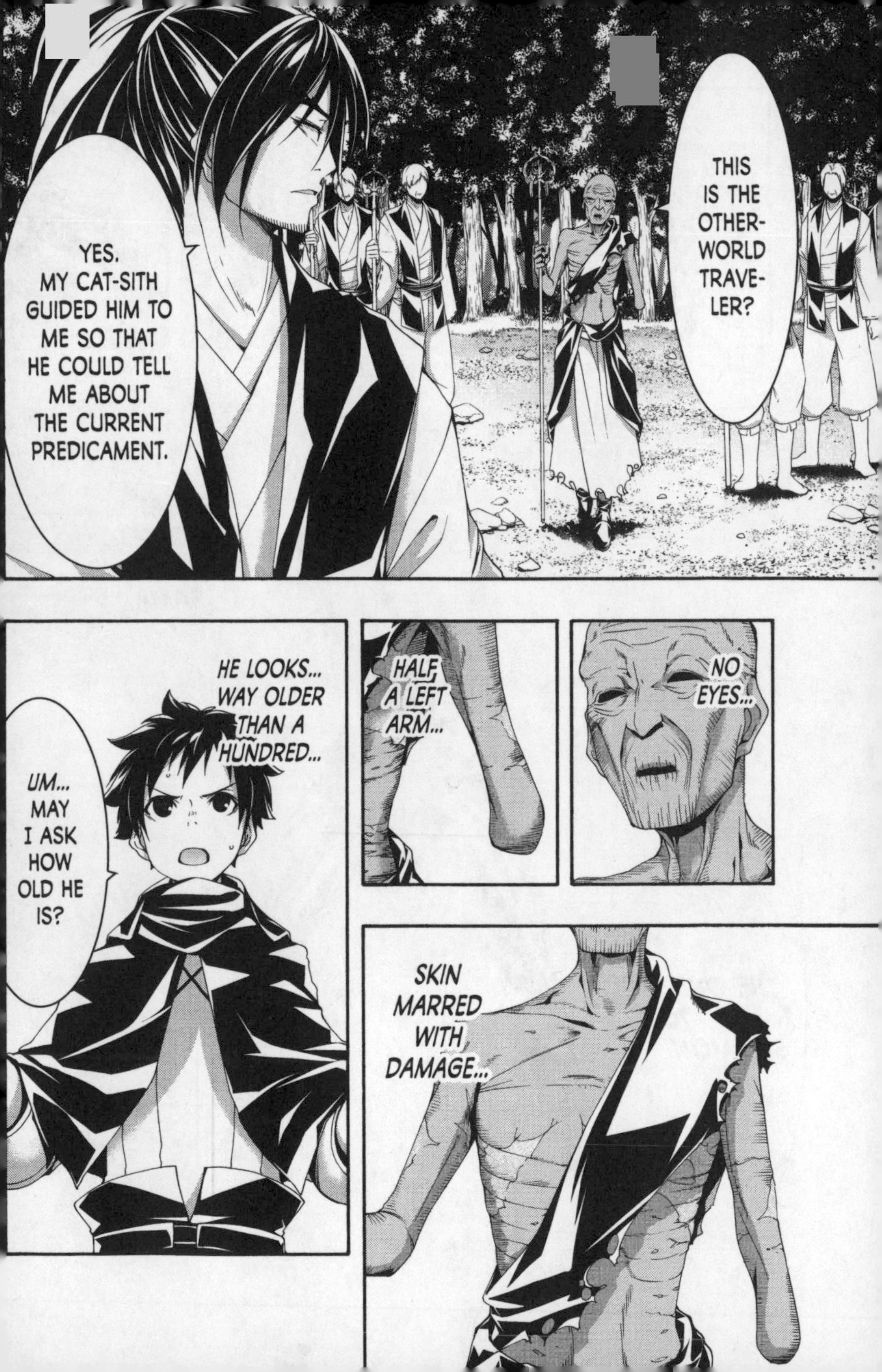
THIS IS THE OTHER-WORLD TRAVE-LER?
YES. MY CAT-SITH GUIDED HIM TO ME SO THAT HE COULD TELL ME ABOUT THE CURRENT PREDICAMENT.
NO EYES...
HALF A LEFT ARM...
SKIN MARRED WITH DAMAGE...
HE LOOKS... WAY OLDER THAN A HUNDRED...
UM... MAY I ASK HOW OLD HE IS?

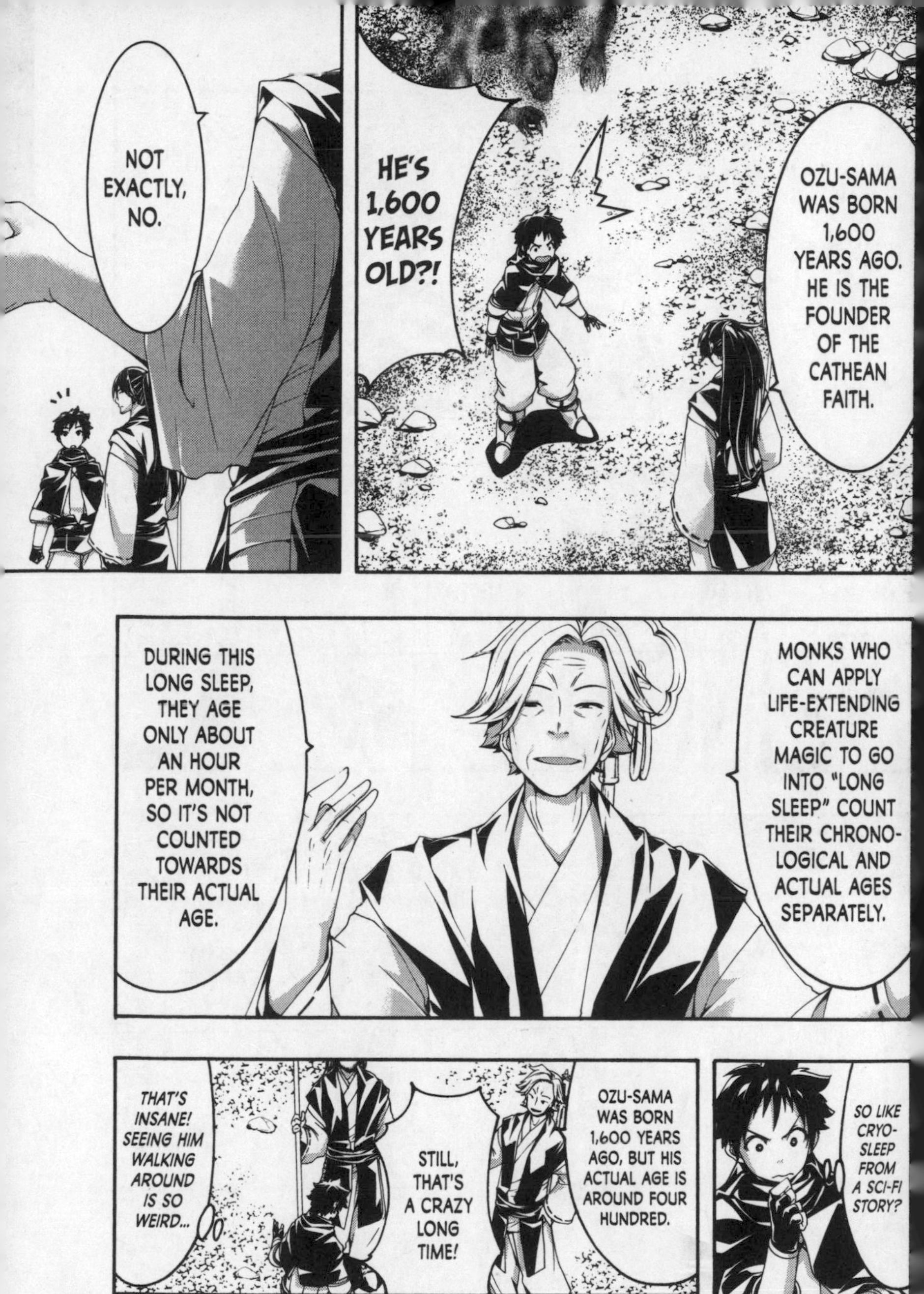
OZU-SAMA WAS BORN 1,600 YEARS AGO. HE IS THE FOUNDER OF THE CATHEAN FAITH.
HE'S 1,600 YEARS OLD?!
NOT EXACTLY, NO.
MONKS WHO CAN APPLY LIFE-EXTENDING CREATURE MAGIC TO GO INTO "LONG SLEEP" COUNT THEIR CHRONO-LOGICAL AND ACTUAL AGES SEPARATELY.
DURING THIS LONG SLEEP, THEY AGE ONLY ABOUT AN HOUR PER MONTH, SO IT'S NOT COUNTED TOWARDS THEIR ACTUAL AGE.
SO LIKE CRYO-SLEEP FROM A SCI-FI STORY?
OZU-SAMA WAS BORN 1,600 YEARS AGO, BUT HIS ACTUAL AGE IS AROUND FOUR HUNDRED.
STILL, THAT'S A CRAZY LONG TIME!
THAT'S INSANE! SEEING HIM WALKING AROUND IS SO WEIRD...

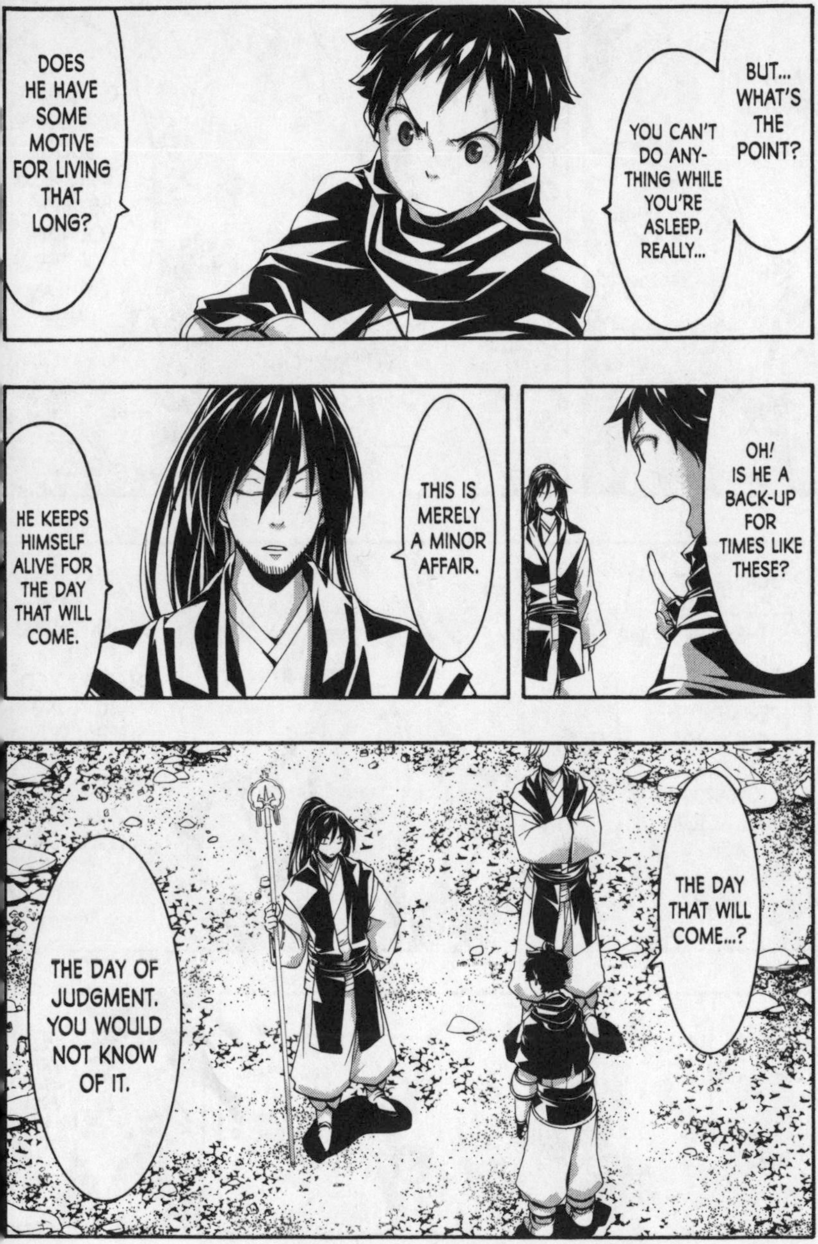
BUT... WHAT'S THE POINT?
YOU CAN'T DO ANY-THING WHILE YOU'RE ASLEEP, REALLY...
DOES HE HAVE SOME MOTIVE FOR LIVING THAT LONG?
OH! IS HE A BACK-UP FOR TIMES LIKE THESE?
THIS IS MERELY A MINOR AFFAIR.
HE KEEPS HIMSELF ALIVE FOR THE DAY THAT WILL COME.
THE DAY THAT WILL COME...?
THE DAY OF JUDGMENT. YOU WOULD NOT KNOW OF IT.

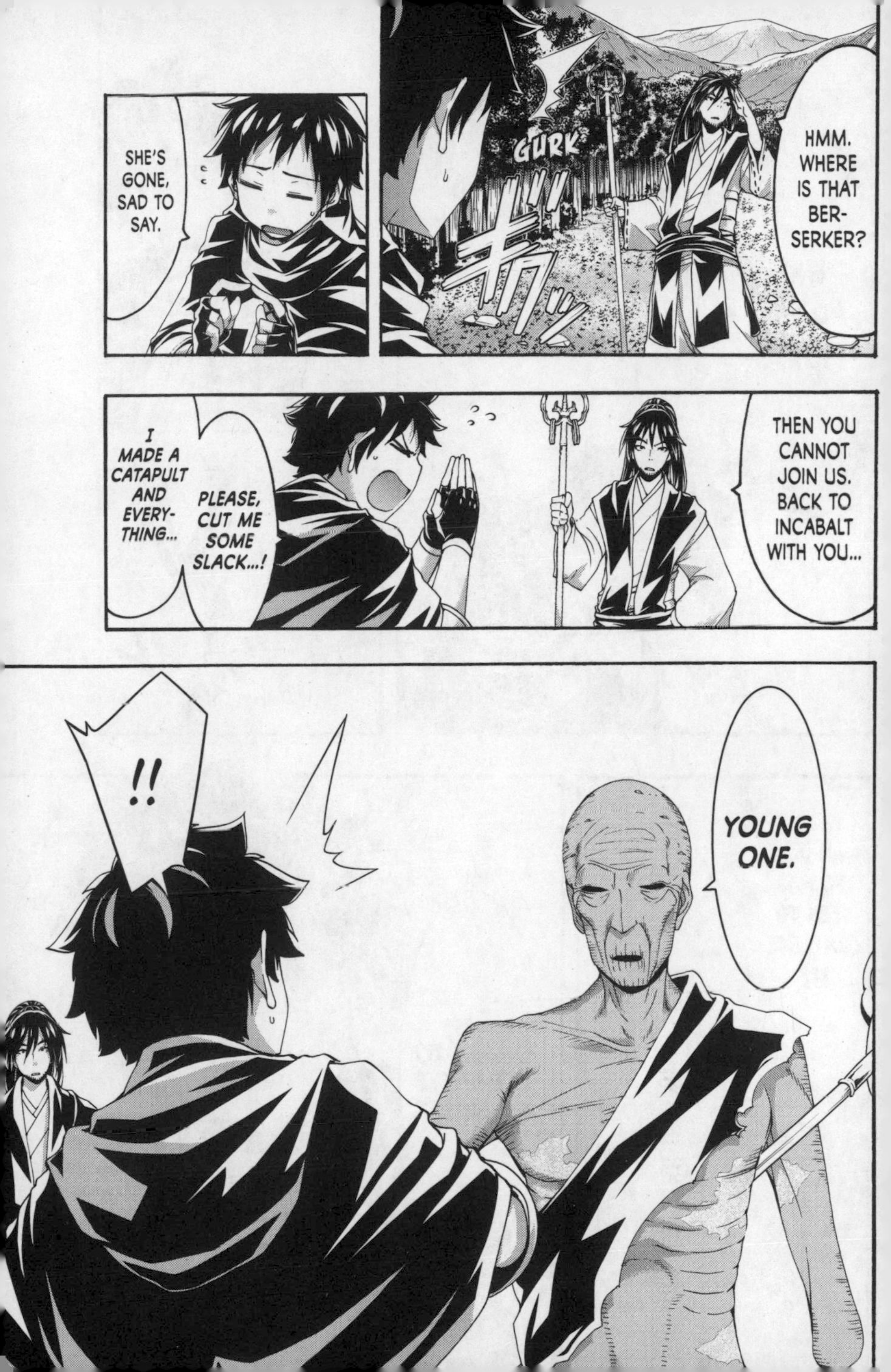
HMM. WHERE IS THAT BER-SERKER?
GURK
ギクッ
SHE'S GONE, SAD TO SAY.
THEN YOU CANNOT JOIN US. BACK TO INCABALT WITH YOU...
PLEASE, CUT ME SOME SLACK...!
I MADE A CATAPULT AND EVERY-THING...
YOUNG ONE.
!!

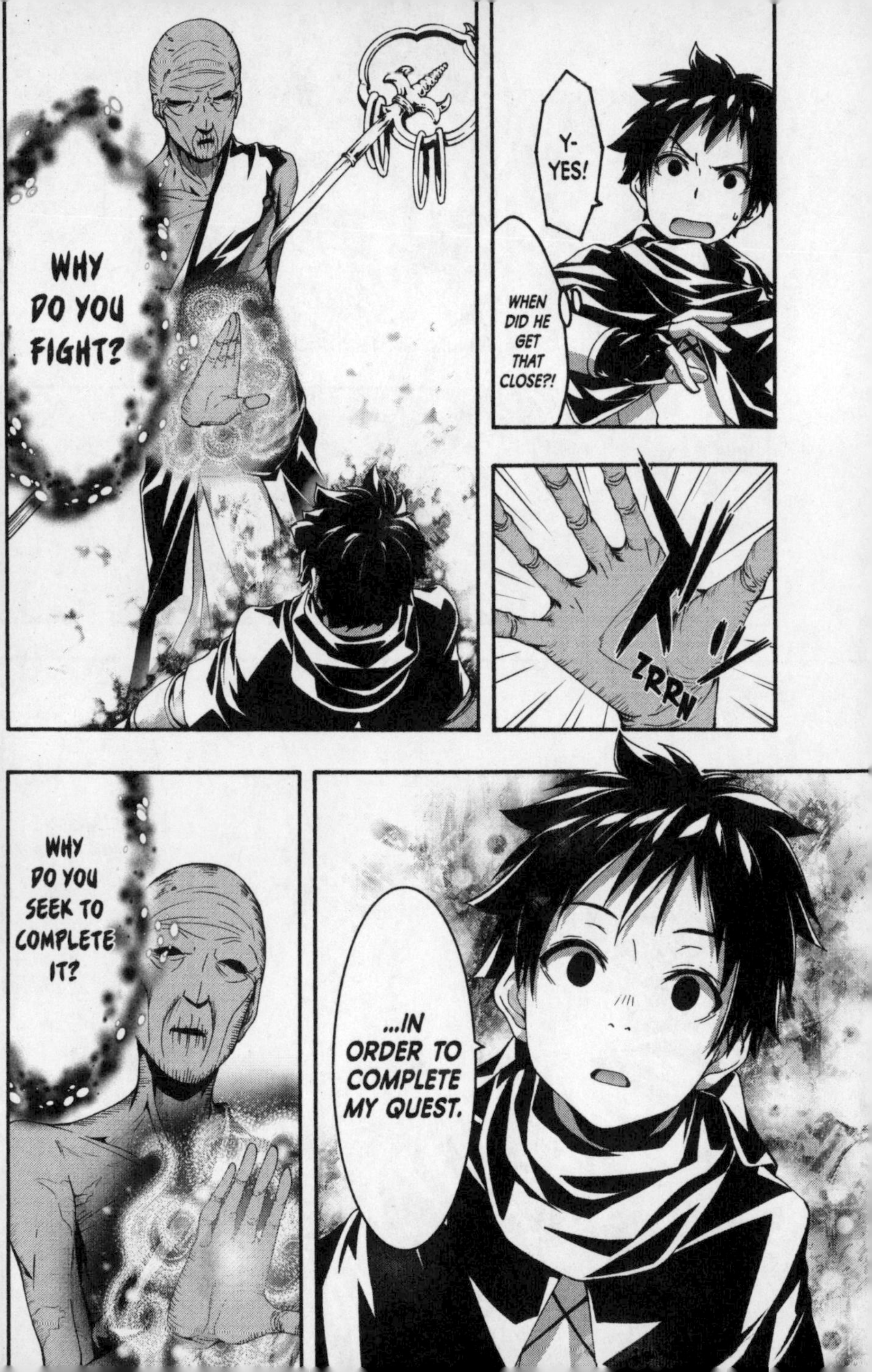
Y-YES!
WHEN DID HE GET THAT CLOSE?!
ZRRN
WHY DO YOU FIGHT?
...IN ORDER TO COMPLETE MY QUEST.
WHY DO YOU SEEK TO COMPLETE IT?

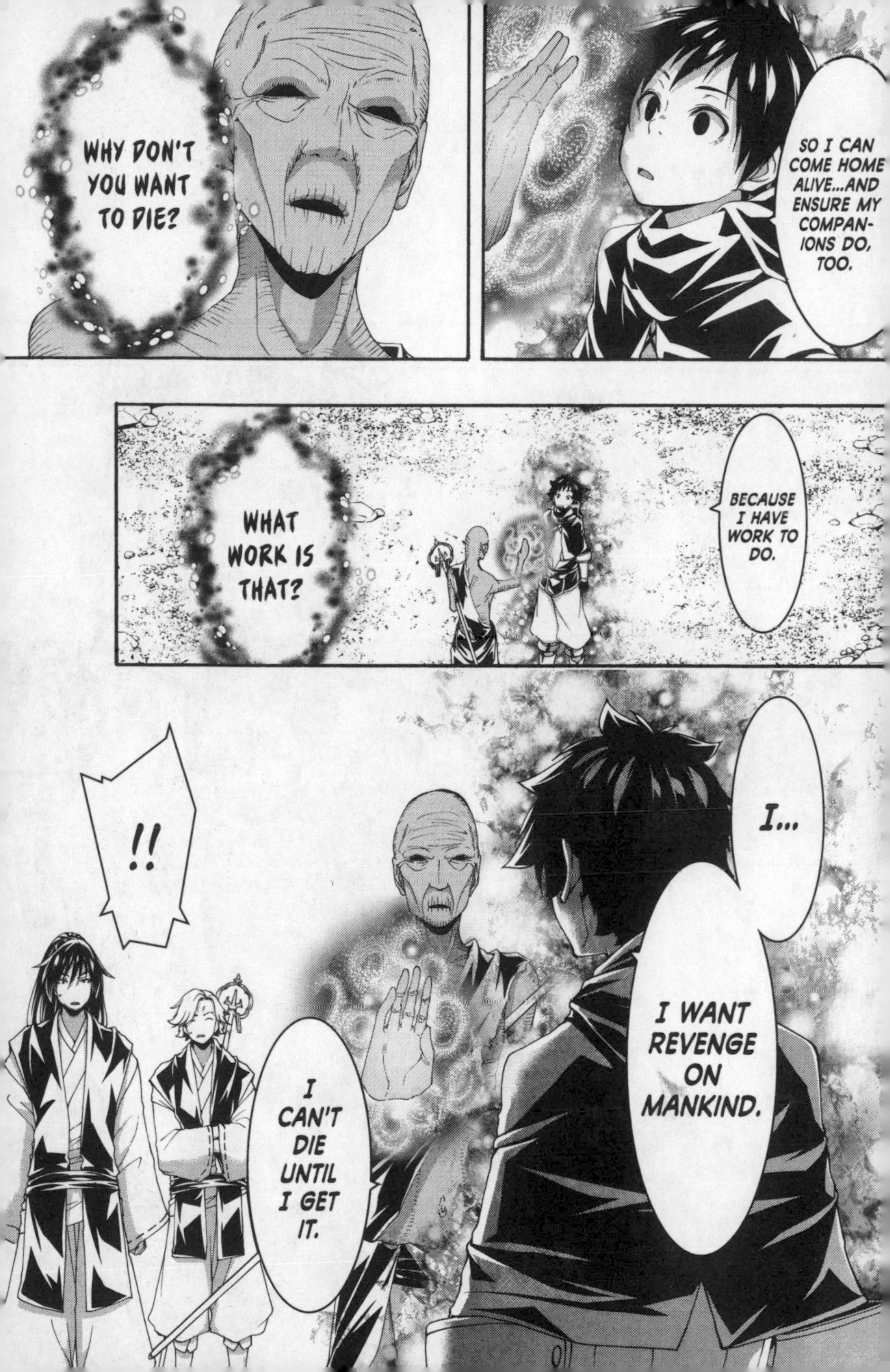
SO I CAN COME HOME ALIVE...AND ENSURE MY COMPANIONS DO, TOO.
WHY DON'T YOU WANT TO DIE?
BECAUSE I HAVE WORK TO DO.
WHAT WORK IS THAT?
I...
I WANT REVENGE ON MANKIND.
I CAN'T DIE UNTIL I GET IT.
!!

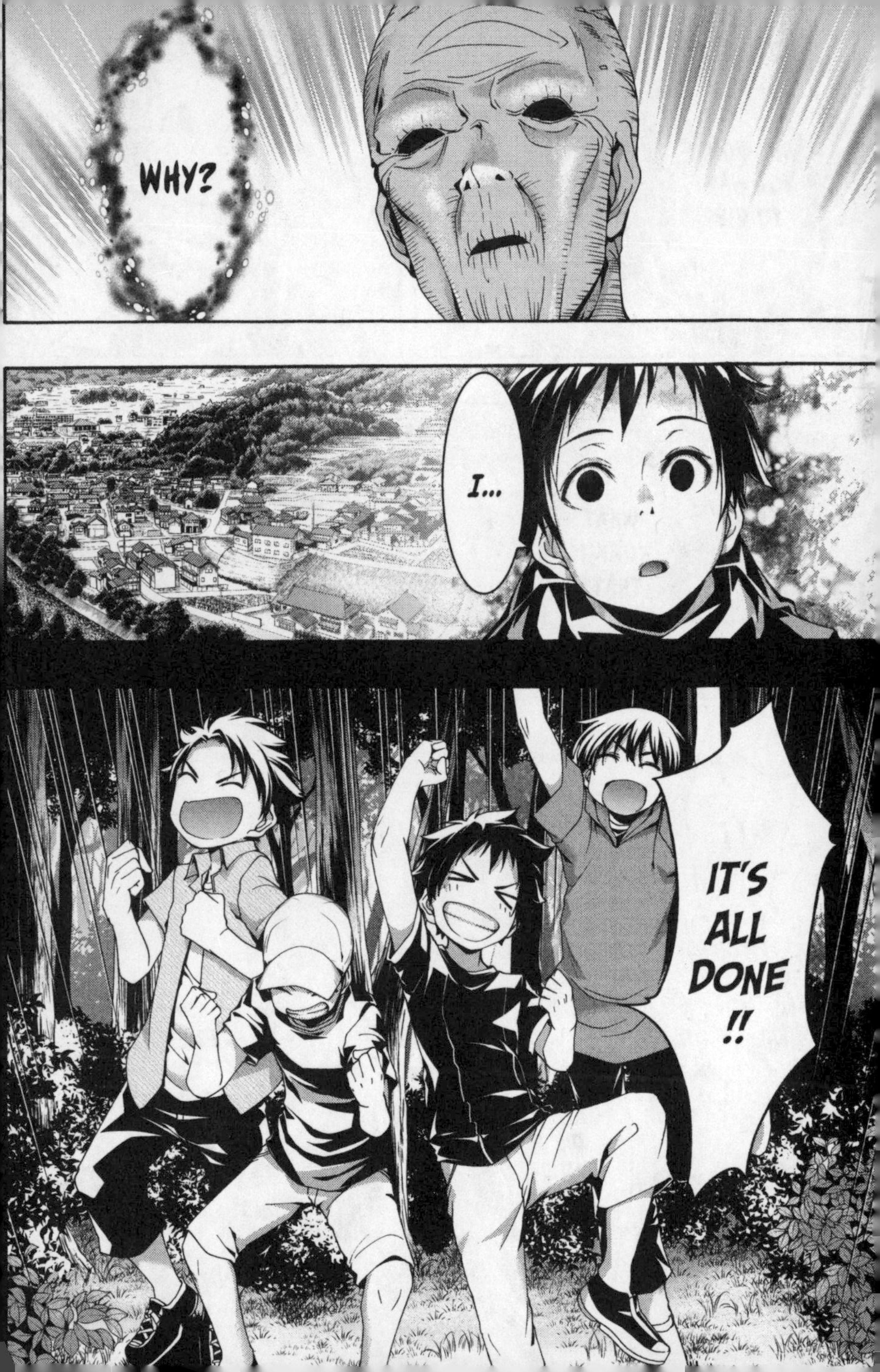
WHY?
I...
IT'S ALL DONE !!

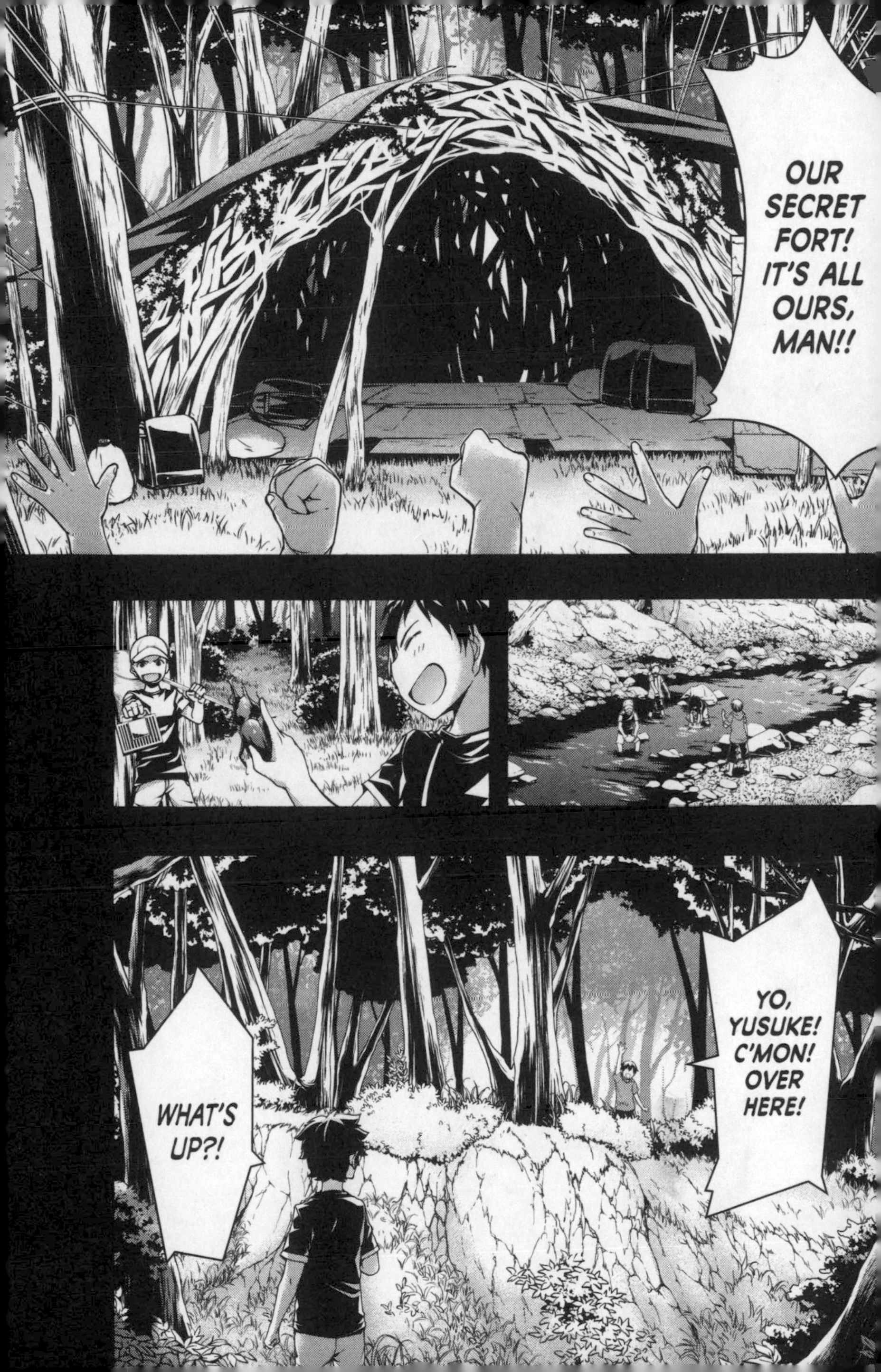
OUR SECRET FORT! IT'S ALL OURS, MAN!!
YO, YUSUKE! C'MON! OVER HERE!
WHAT'S UP?!

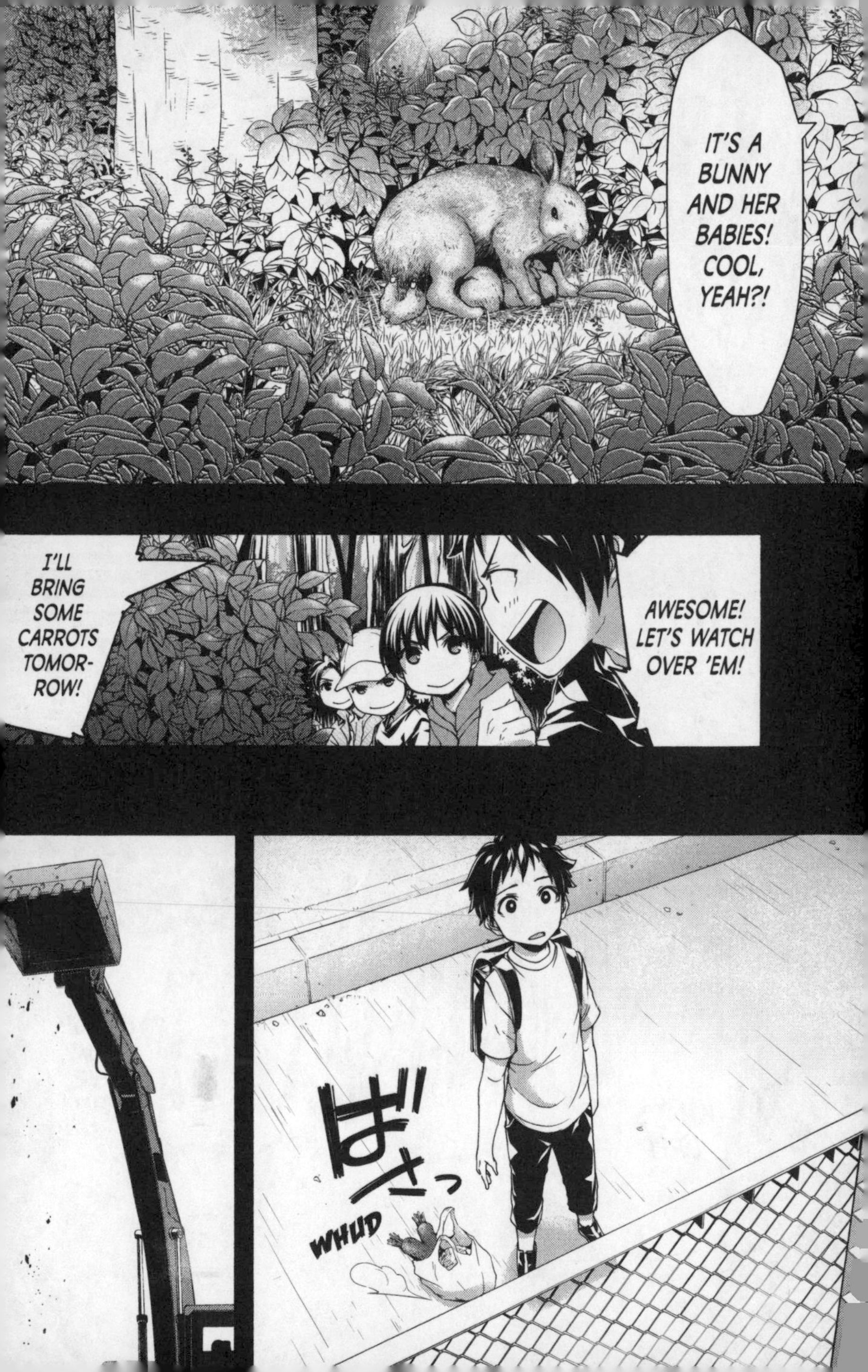
IT'S A BUNNY AND HER BABIES! COOL, YEAH?!
AWESOME! LET'S WATCH OVER 'EM!
I'LL BRING SOME CARROTS TOMOR-ROW!
ばさっ
WHUD

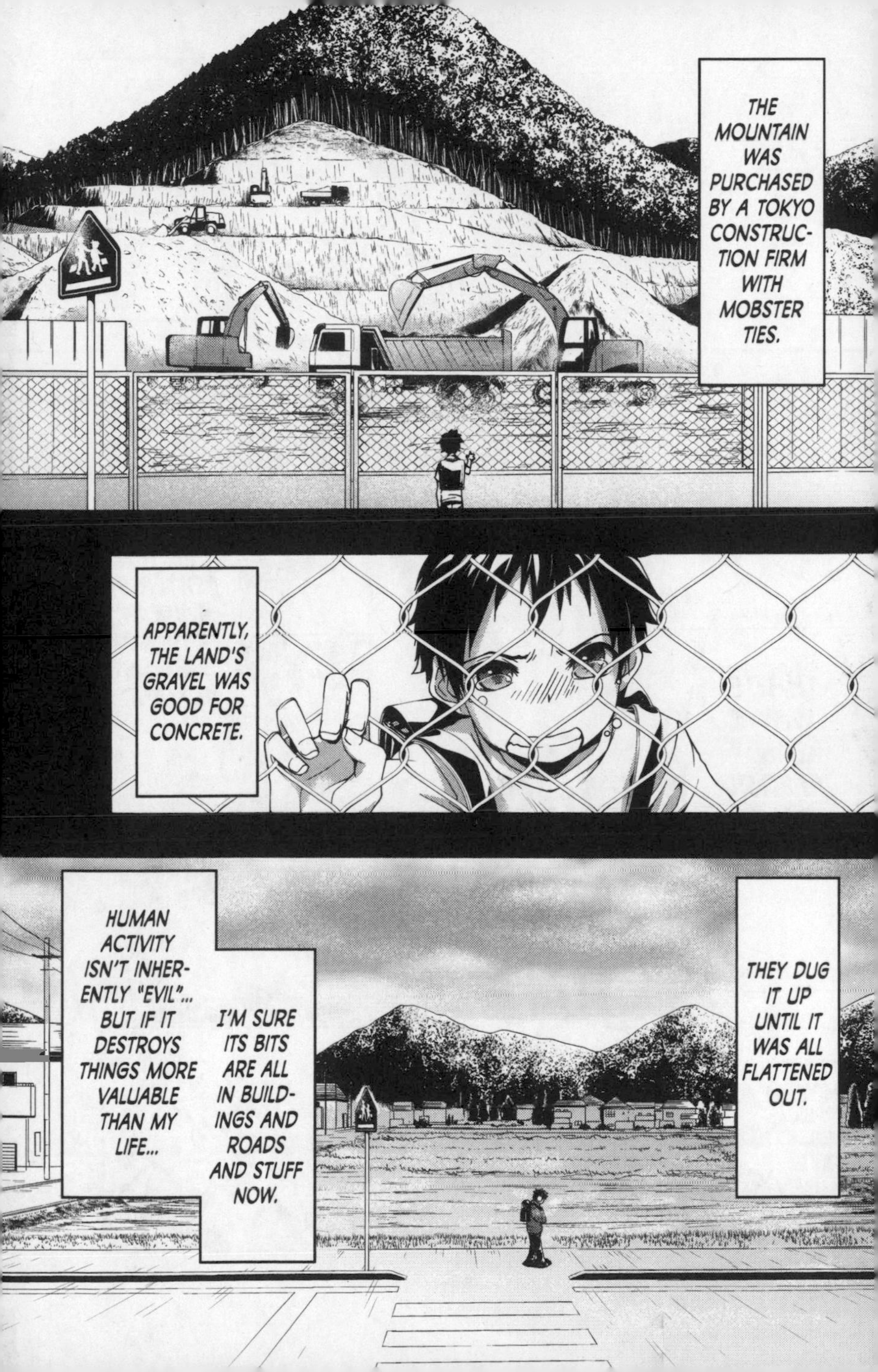
THE MOUNTAIN WAS PURCHASED BY A TOKYO CONSTRUCTION FIRM WITH MOBSTER TIES.
APPARENTLY, THE LAND'S GRAVEL WAS GOOD FOR CONCRETE.
THEY DUG IT UP UNTIL IT WAS ALL FLATTENED OUT.
I'M SURE ITS BITS ARE ALL IN BUILDINGS AND ROADS AND STUFF NOW.
HUMAN ACTIVITY ISN'T INHERENTLY "EVIL"... BUT IF IT DESTROYS THINGS MORE VALUABLE THAN MY LIFE...

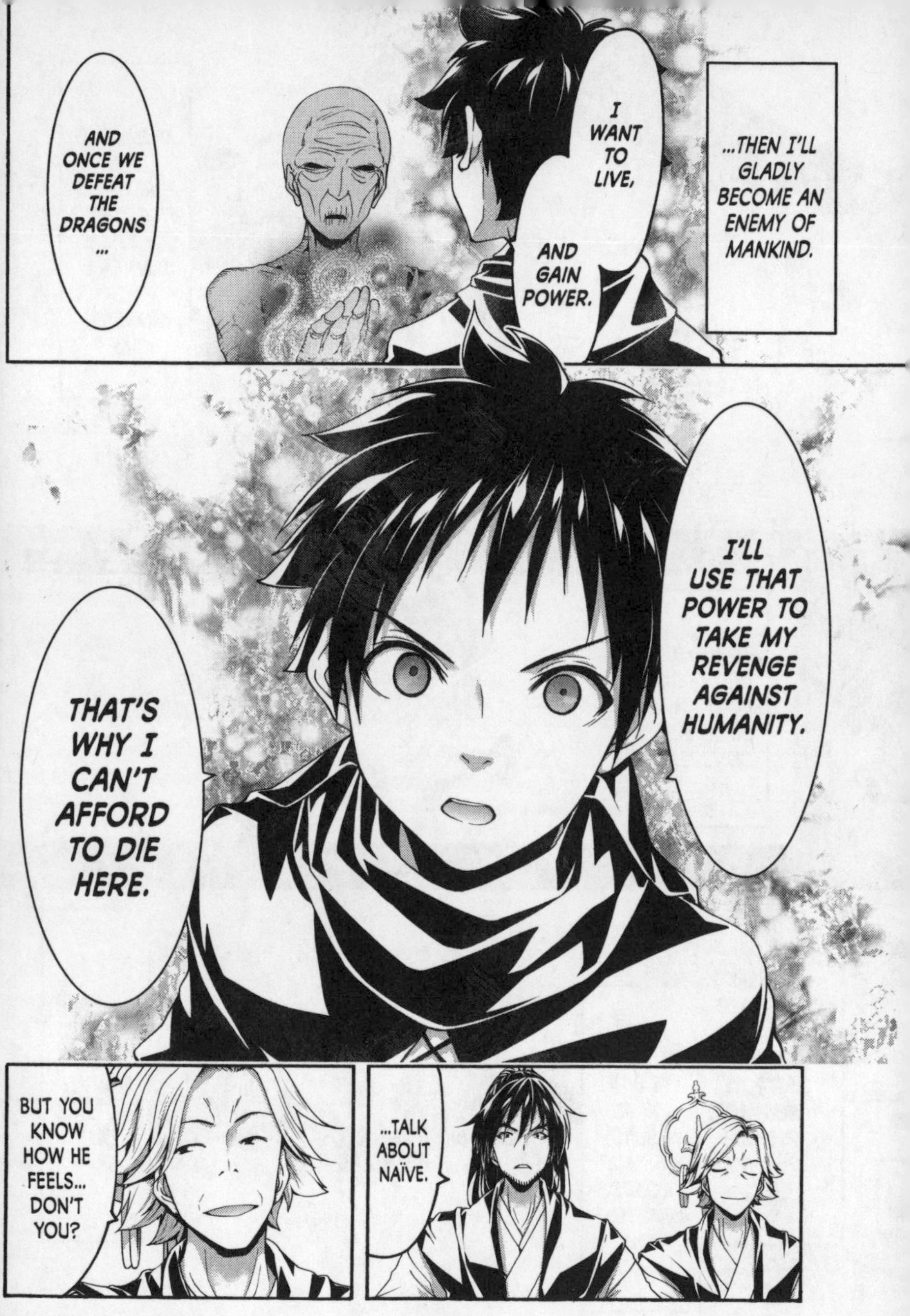
...THEN I'LL GLADLY BECOME AN ENEMY OF MANKIND.
I WANT TO LIVE,
AND GAIN POWER.
AND ONCE WE DEFEAT THE DRAGONS ...
I'LL USE THAT POWER TO TAKE MY REVENGE AGAINST HUMANITY.
THAT'S WHY I CAN'T AFFORD TO DIE HERE.
...TALK ABOUT NAÏVE.
BUT YOU KNOW HOW HE FEELS... DON'T YOU?

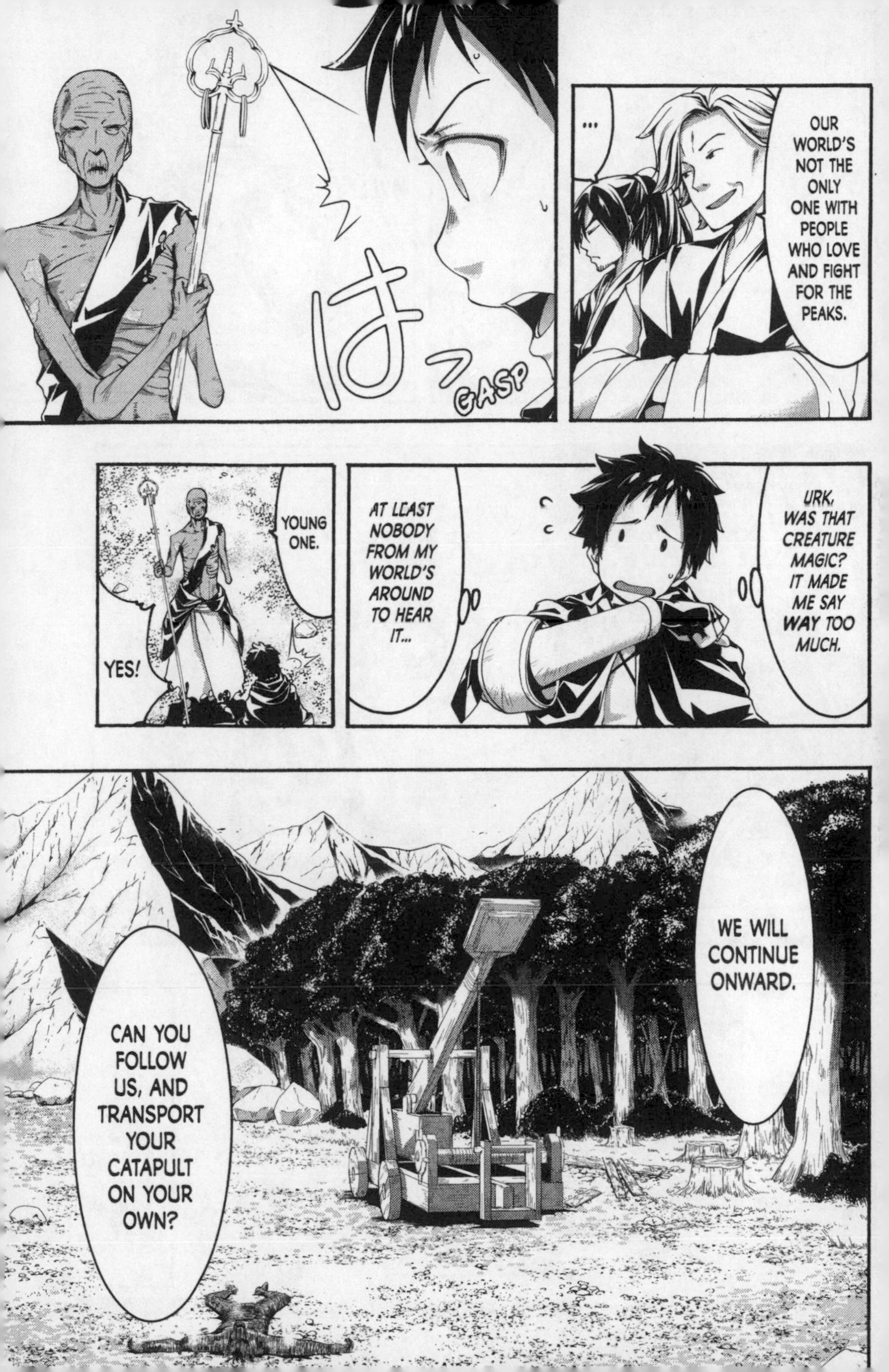
OUR WORLD'S NOT THE ONLY ONE WITH PEOPLE WHO LOVE AND FIGHT FOR THE PEAKS.
...
はっ
GASP
URK, WAS THAT CREATURE MAGIC? IT MADE ME SAY WAY TOO MUCH.
AT LEAST NOBODY FROM MY WORLD'S AROUND TO HEAR IT...
YOUNG ONE.
YES!
WE WILL CONTINUE ONWARD.
CAN YOU FOLLOW US, AND TRANSPORT YOUR CATAPULT ON YOUR OWN?

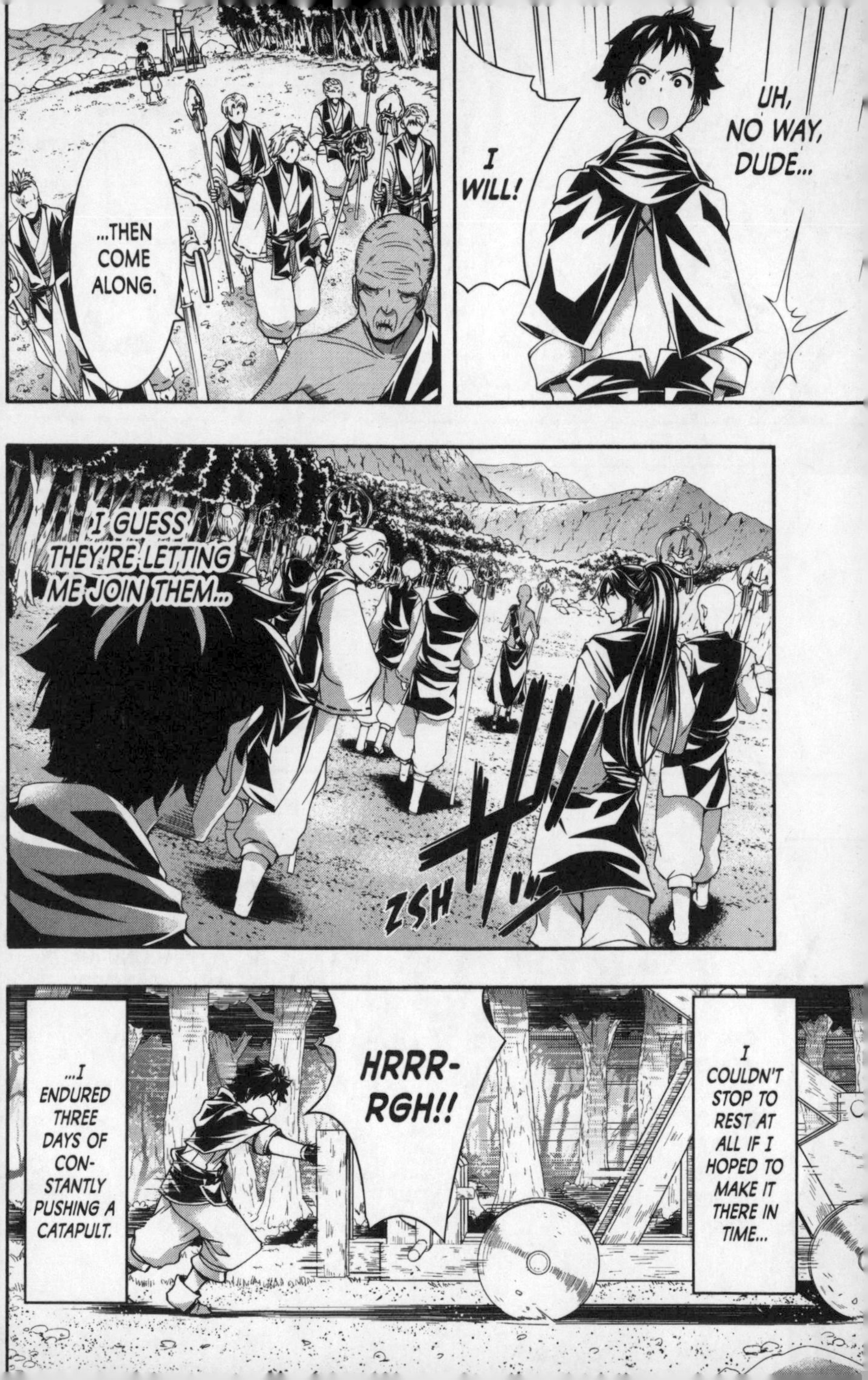
UH, NO WAY, DUDE...
I WILL!
...THEN COME ALONG.
I GUESS THEY'RE LETTING ME JOIN THEM...
ZSH
I COULDN'T STOP TO REST AT ALL IF I HOPED TO MAKE IT THERE IN TIME...
HRRR-RGH!!
...I ENDURED THREE DAYS OF CON-STANTLY PUSHING A CATAPULT.

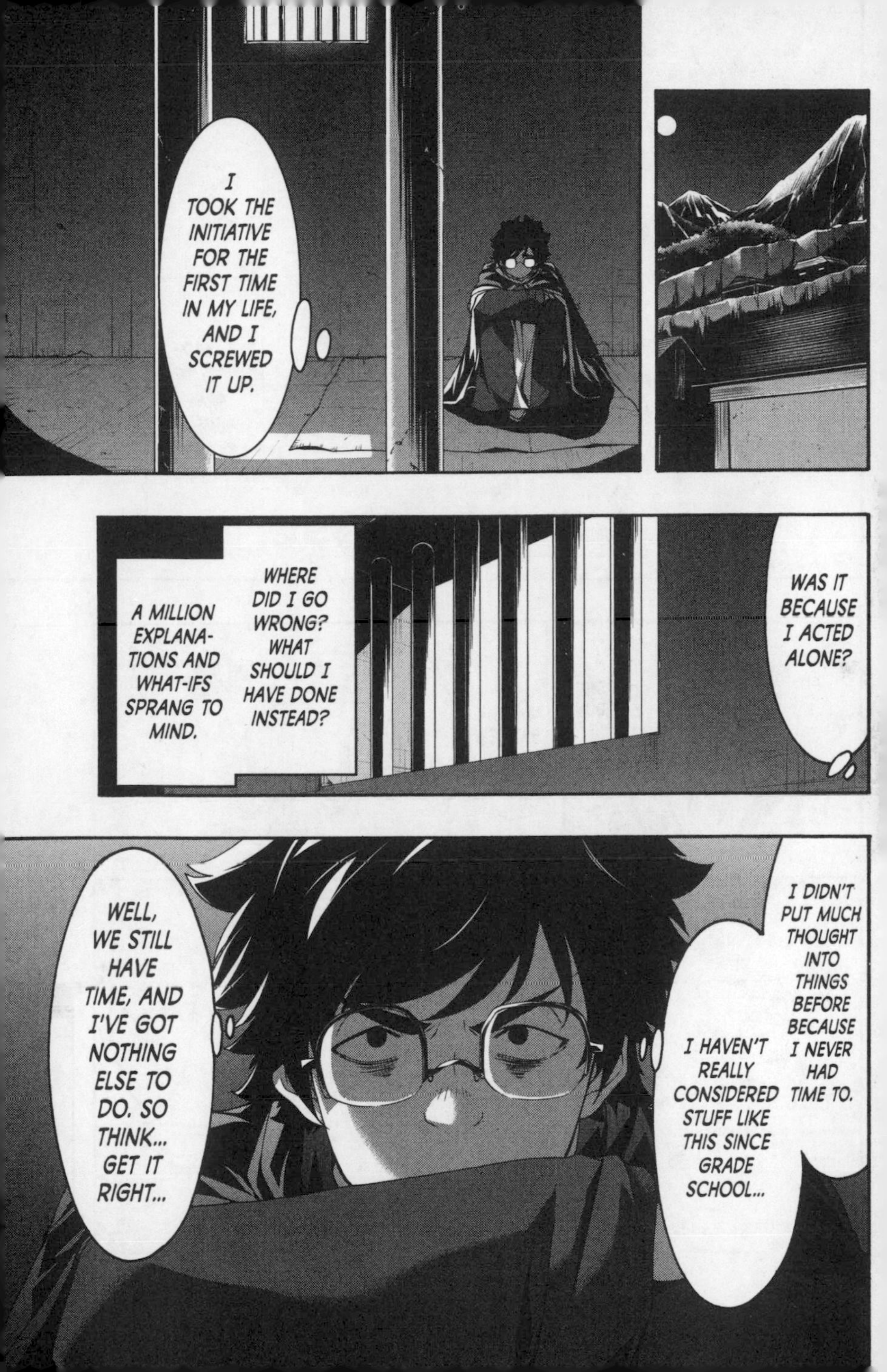
I TOOK THE INITIATIVE FOR THE FIRST TIME IN MY LIFE, AND I SCREWED IT UP.
WAS IT BECAUSE I ACTED ALONE?
WHERE DID I GO WRONG? WHAT SHOULD I HAVE DONE INSTEAD?
A MILLION EXPLANA-TIONS AND WHAT-IFS SPRANG TO MIND.
I DIDN'T PUT MUCH THOUGHT INTO THINGS BEFORE BECAUSE I NEVER HAD TIME TO.
I HAVEN'T REALLY CONSIDERED STUFF LIKE THIS SINCE GRADE SCHOOL...
WELL, WE STILL HAVE TIME, AND I'VE GOT NOTHING ELSE TO DO. SO THINK... GET IT RIGHT...

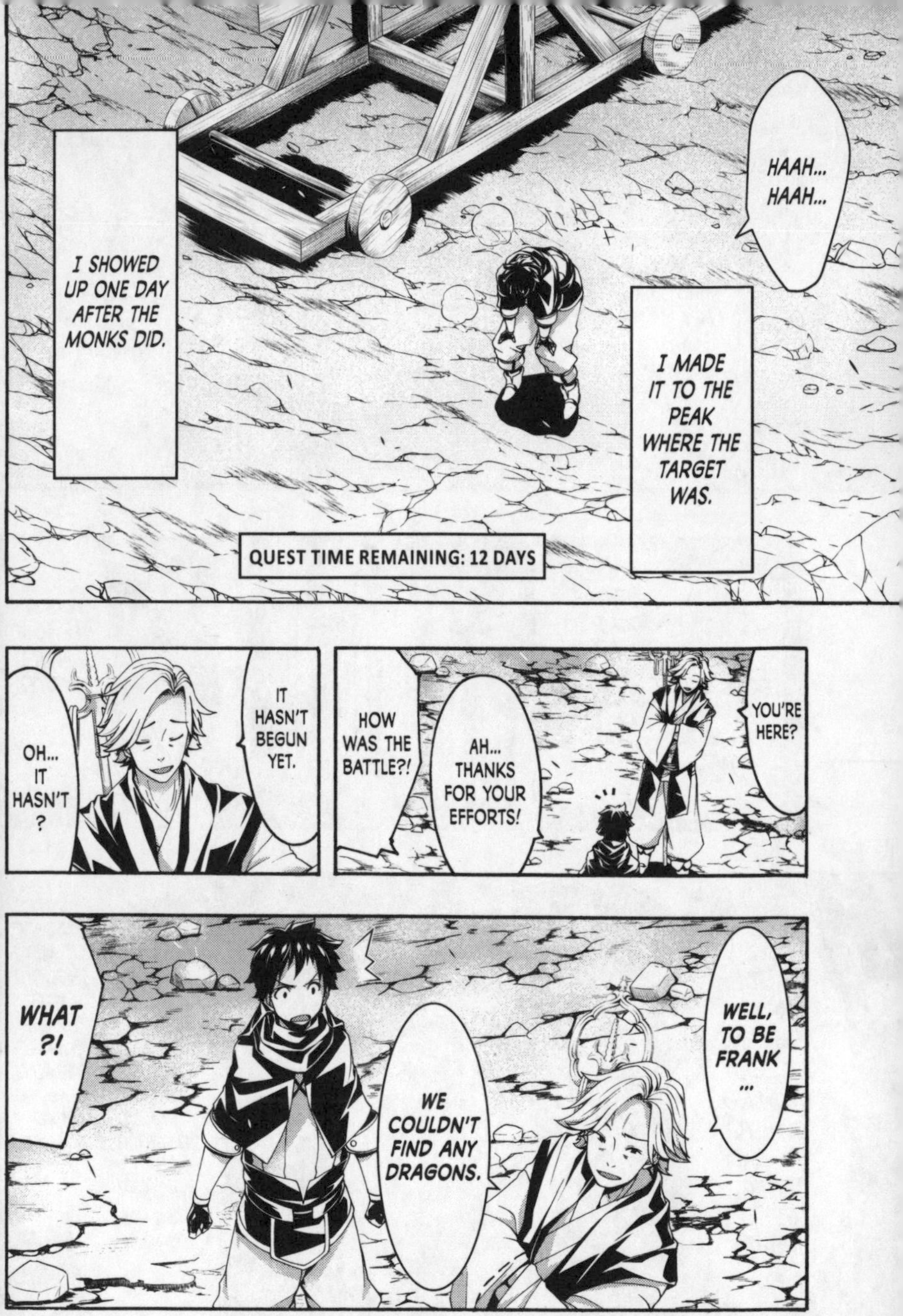
HAAH... HAAH...
I MADE IT TO THE PEAK WHERE THE TARGET WAS.
I SHOWED UP ONE DAY AFTER THE MONKS DID.
QUEST TIME REMAINING: 12 DAYS
YOU'RE HERE?
AH... THANKS FOR YOUR EFFORTS!
HOW WAS THE BATTLE?!
IT HASN'T BEGUN YET.
OH... IT HASN'T?
WELL, TO BE FRANK ...
WE COULDN'T FIND ANY DRAGONS.
WHAT ?!

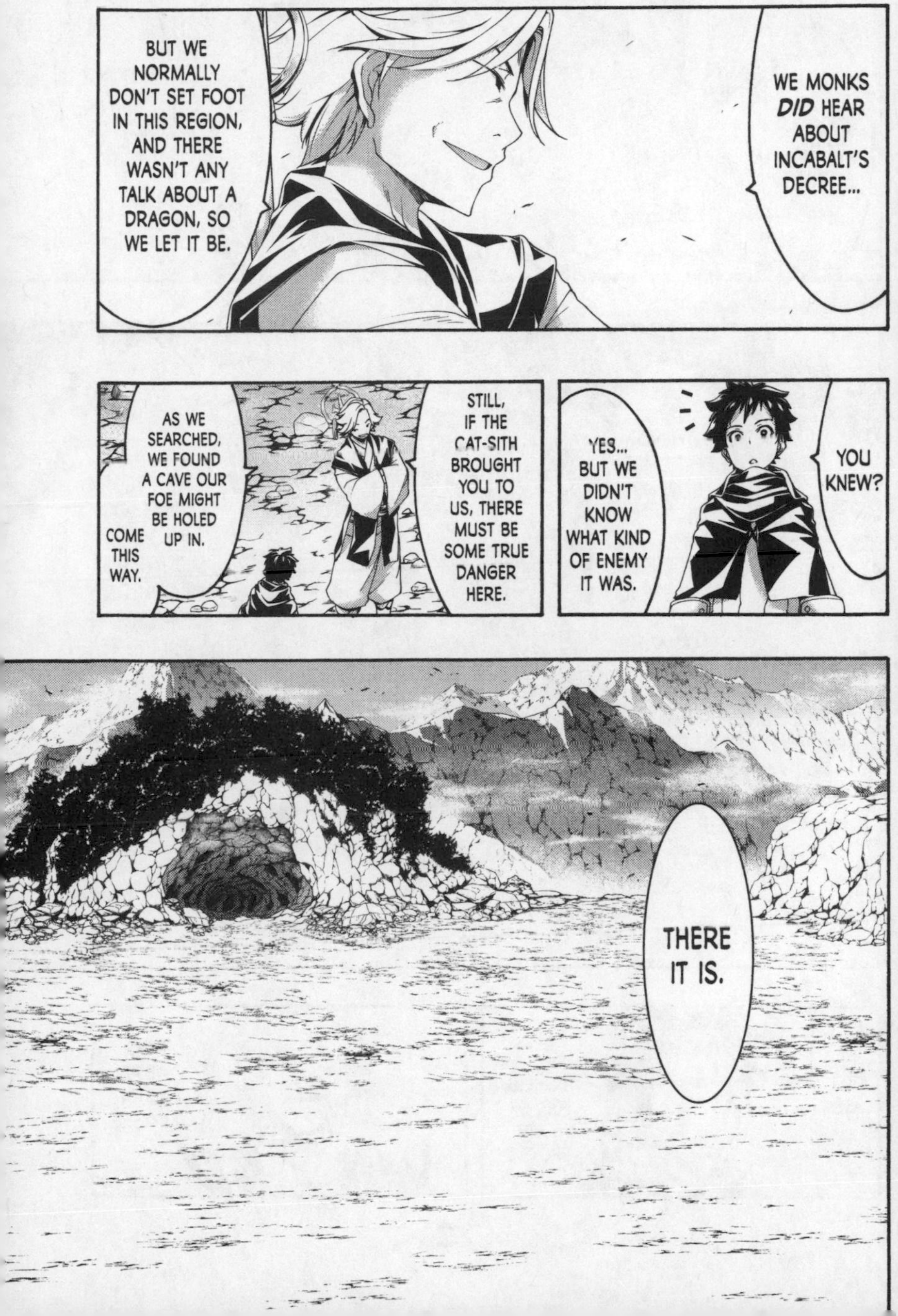
WE MONKS DID HEAR ABOUT INCABALT'S DECREE...
BUT WE NORMALLY DON'T SET FOOT IN THIS REGION, AND THERE WASN'T ANY TALK ABOUT A DRAGON, SO WE LET IT BE.
YOU KNEW?
YES... BUT WE DIDN'T KNOW WHAT KIND OF ENEMY IT WAS.
STILL, IF THE CAT-SITH BROUGHT YOU TO US, THERE MUST BE SOME TRUE DANGER HERE.
AS WE SEARCHED, WE FOUND A CAVE OUR FOE MIGHT BE HOLED UP IN.
COME THIS WAY.
THERE IT IS.

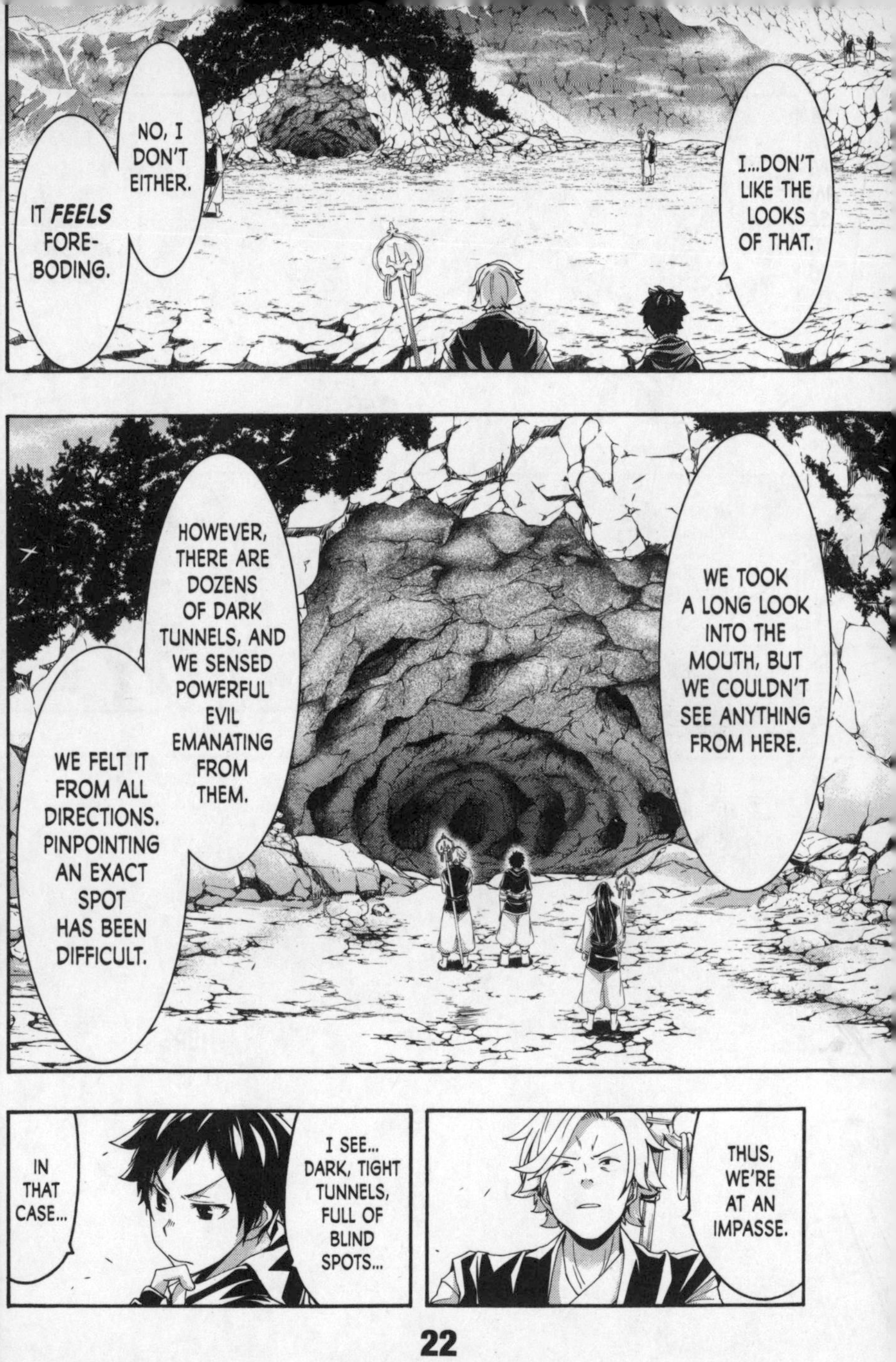
I...DON'T LIKE THE LOOKS OF THAT.
NO, I DON'T EITHER.
IT *FEELS* FORE-BODING.
WE TOOK A LONG LOOK INTO THE MOUTH, BUT WE COULDN'T SEE ANYTHING FROM HERE.
HOWEVER, THERE ARE DOZENS OF DARK TUNNELS, AND WE SENSED POWERFUL EVIL EMANATING FROM THEM.
WE FELT IT FROM ALL DIRECTIONS. PINPOINTING AN EXACT SPOT HAS BEEN DIFFICULT.
THUS, WE'RE AT AN IMPASSE.
I SEE... DARK, TIGHT TUNNELS, FULL OF BLIND SPOTS...
IN THAT CASE...

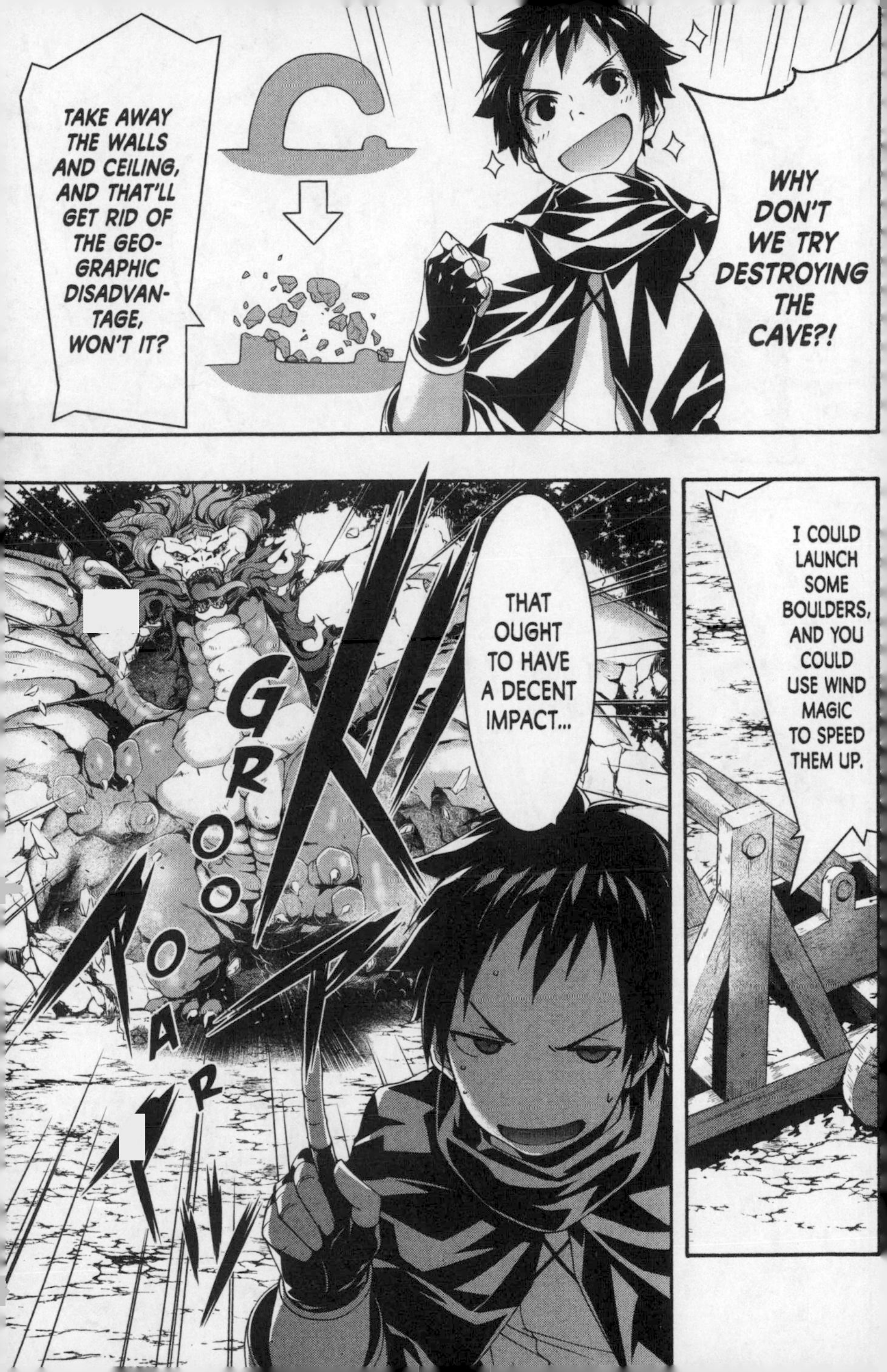
WHY DON'T WE TRY DESTROYING THE CAVE?!
TAKE AWAY THE WALLS AND CEILING, AND THAT'LL GET RID OF THE GEO-GRAPHIC DISADVAN-TAGE, WON'T IT?
I COULD LAUNCH SOME BOULDERS, AND YOU COULD USE WIND MAGIC TO SPEED THEM UP.
THAT OUGHT TO HAVE A DECENT IMPACT...
GROOOAR

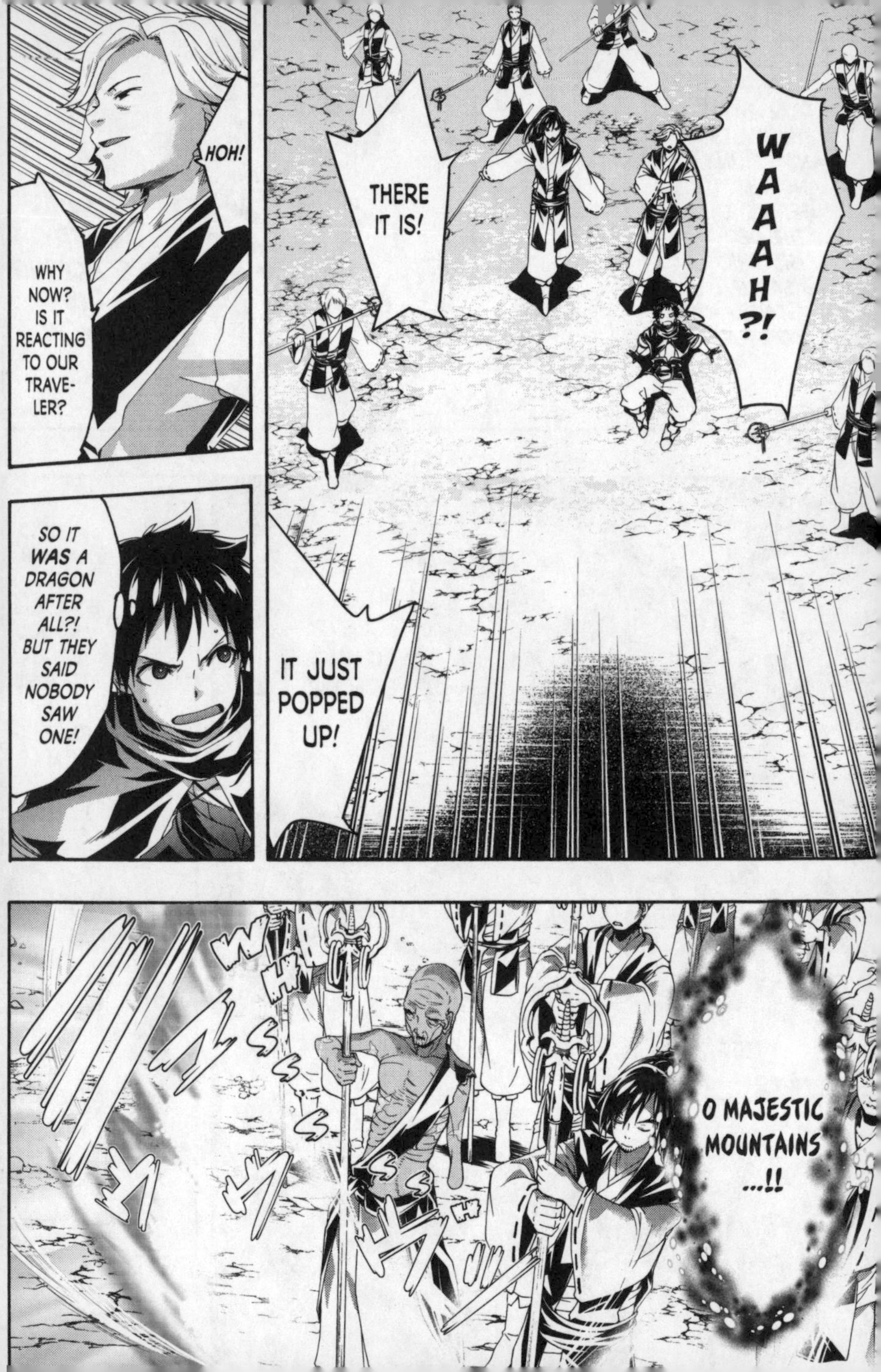
WAAAH?!
THERE IT IS!
IT JUST POPPED UP!
HOH!
WHY NOW? IS IT REACTING TO OUR TRAVELER?
SO IT WAS A DRAGON AFTER ALL?! BUT THEY SAID NOBODY SAW ONE!
O MAJESTIC MOUNTAINS ...!!

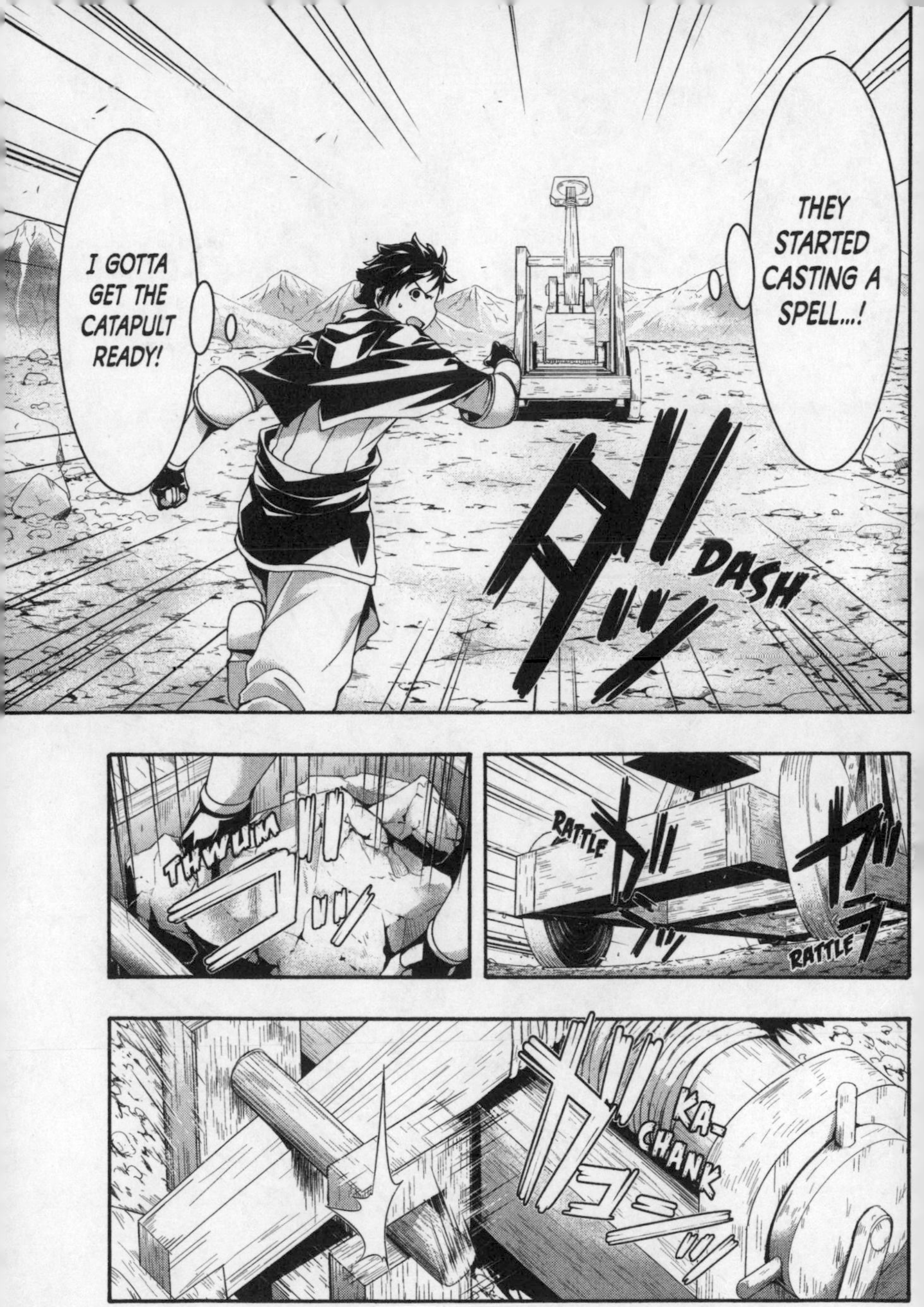
THEY STARTED CASTING A SPELL...!
I GOTTA GET THE CATAPULT READY!
DASH
RATTLE
RATTLE
THWUM
KA-CHANK

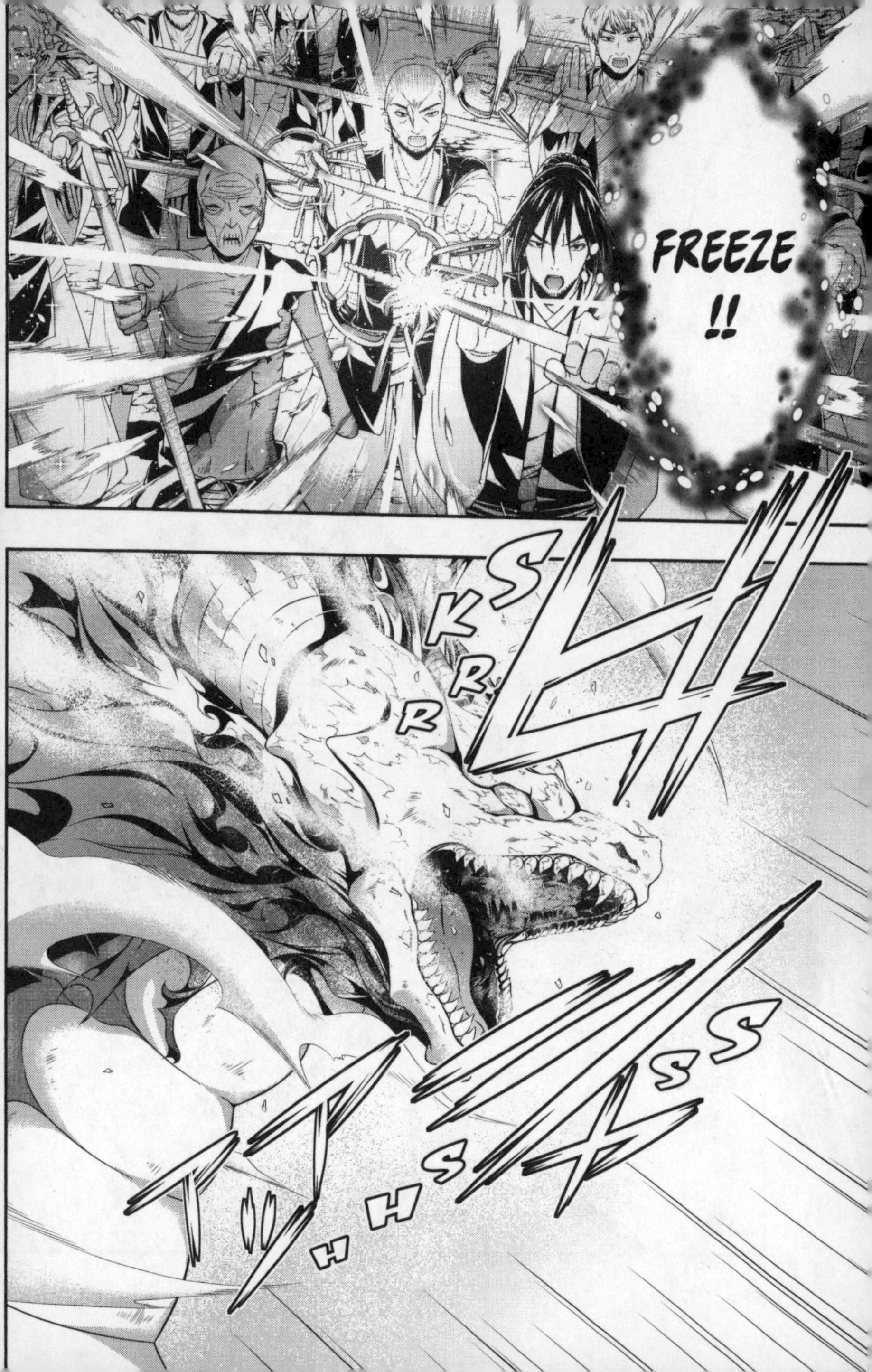
FREEZE !!
SKRR
HHSSS

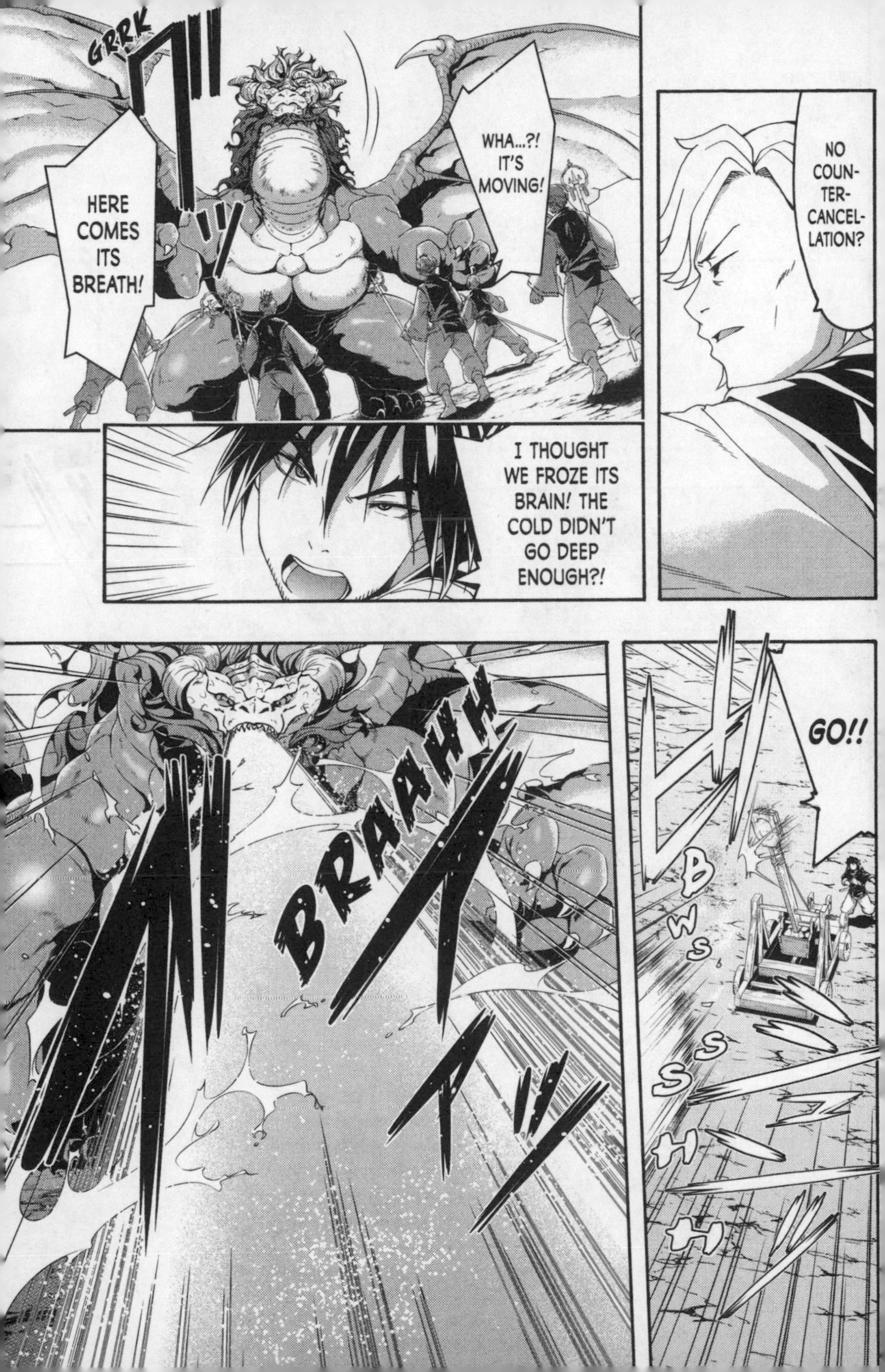
NO COUNTER-CANCELLATION?
WHA...?! IT'S MOVING!
GRRK
HERE COMES ITS BREATH!
I THOUGHT WE FROZE ITS BRAIN! THE COLD DIDN'T GO DEEP ENOUGH?!
GO!!
BWS
SSHH
BRAAHH

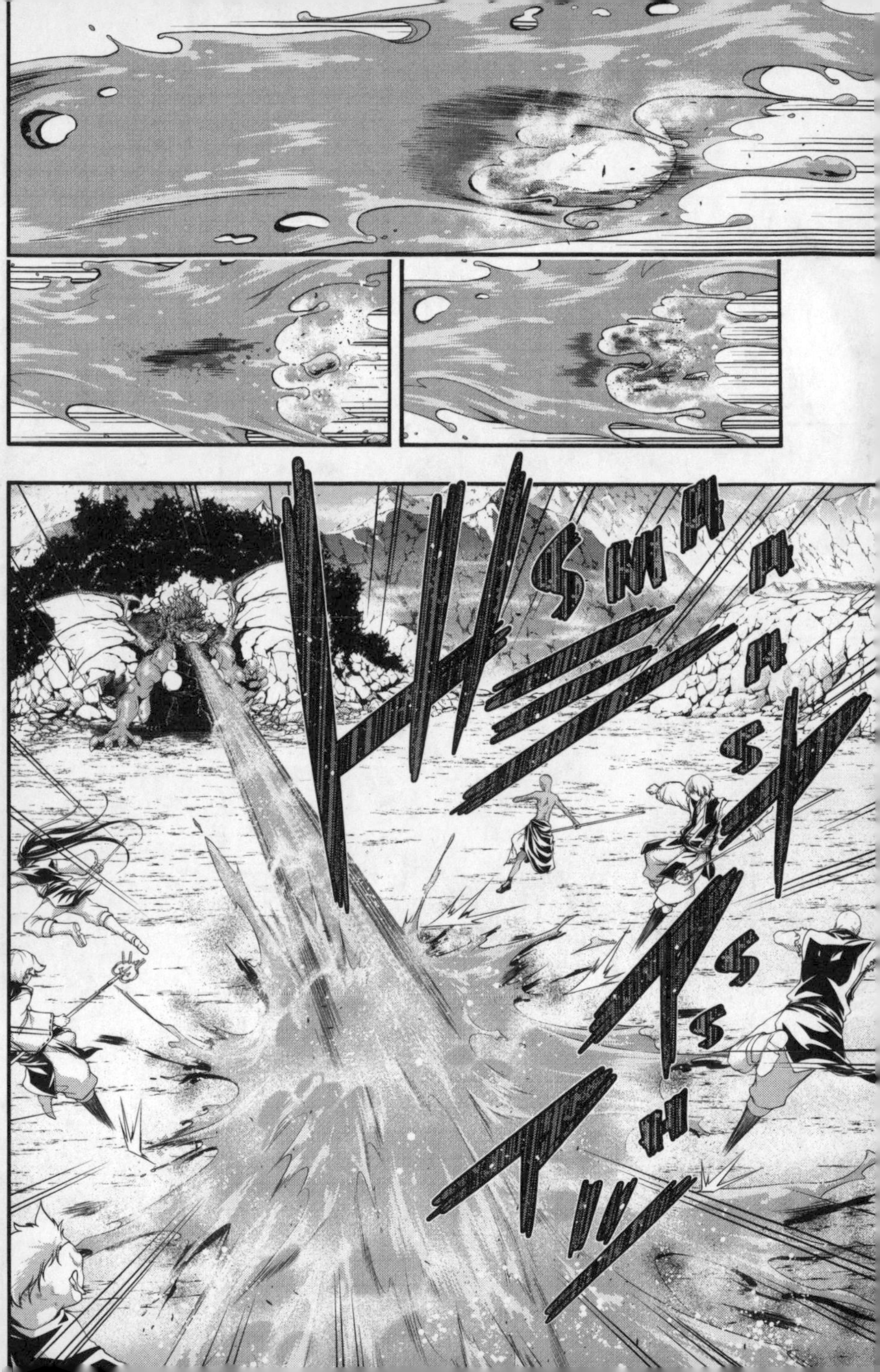
SHAAA
SSSH

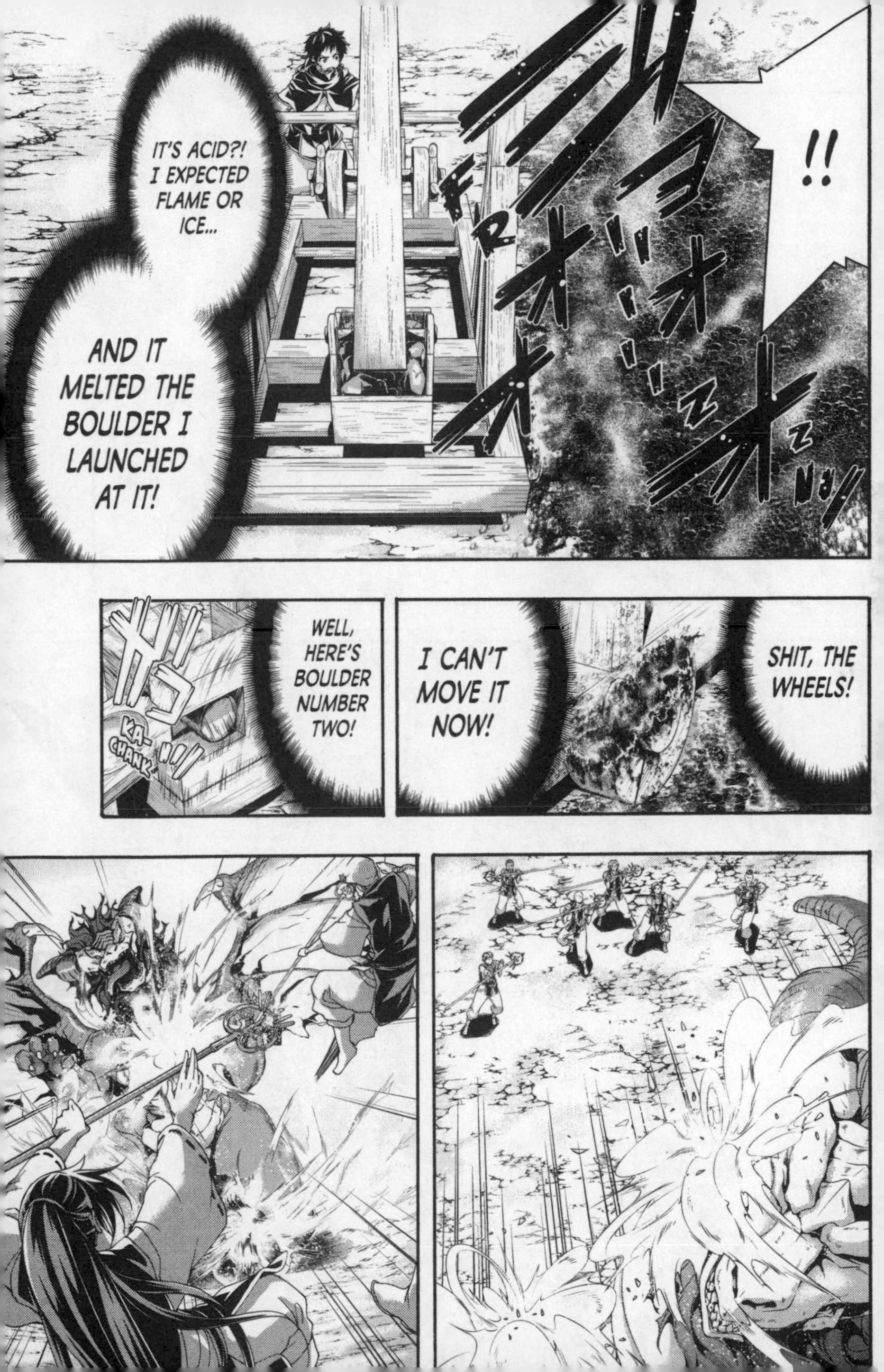
!!
IT'S ACID?! I EXPECTED FLAME OR ICE...
AND IT MELTED THE BOULDER I LAUNCHED AT IT!
SHIT, THE WHEELS!
I CAN'T MOVE IT NOW!
WELL, HERE'S BOULDER NUMBER TWO!
KA-CHANK

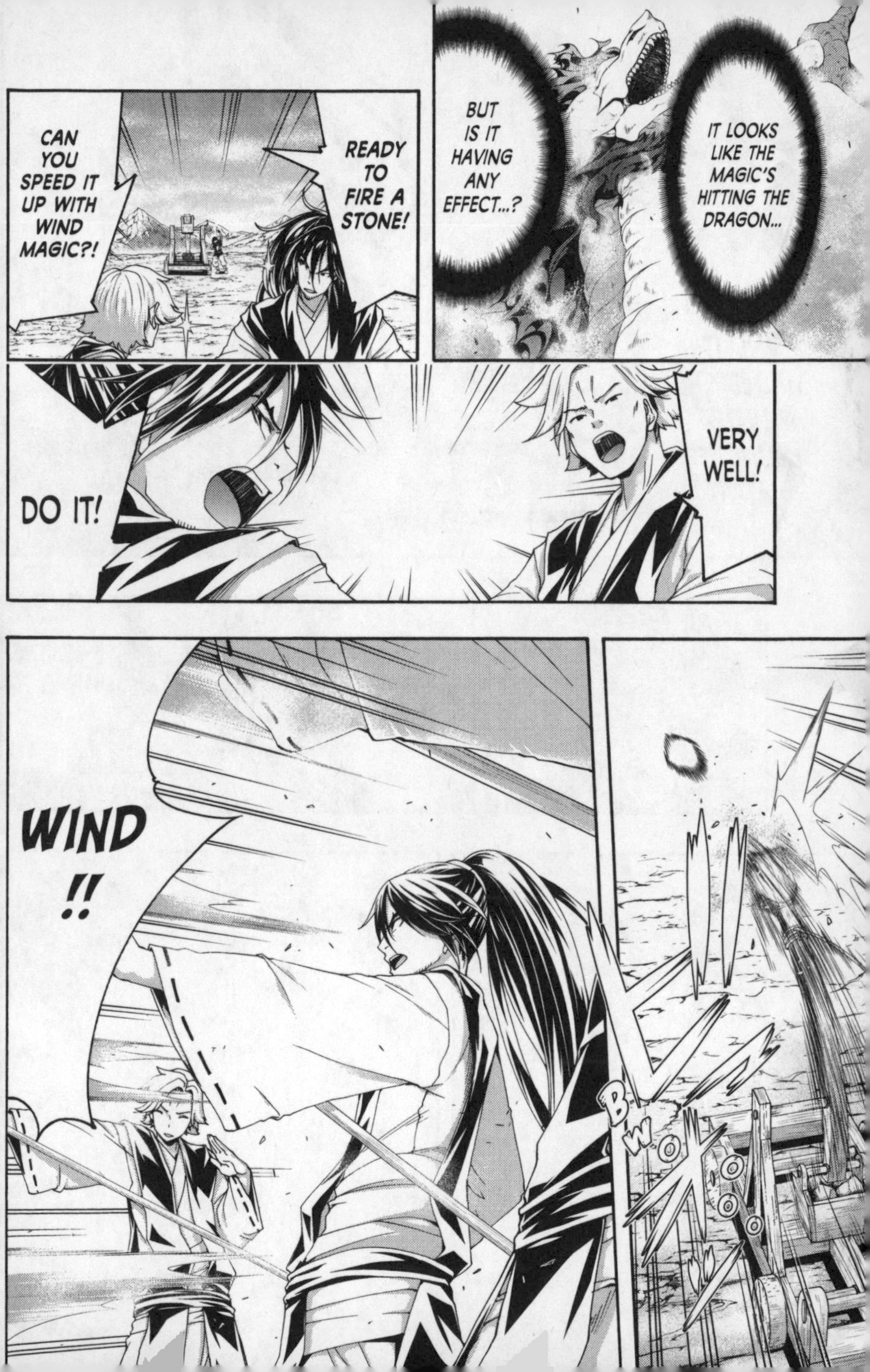
IT LOOKS LIKE THE MAGIC'S HITTING THE DRAGON...
BUT IS IT HAVING ANY EFFECT...?
READY TO FIRE A STONE!
CAN YOU SPEED IT UP WITH WIND MAGIC?!
VERY WELL!
DO IT!
BWOOOO
WIND!!

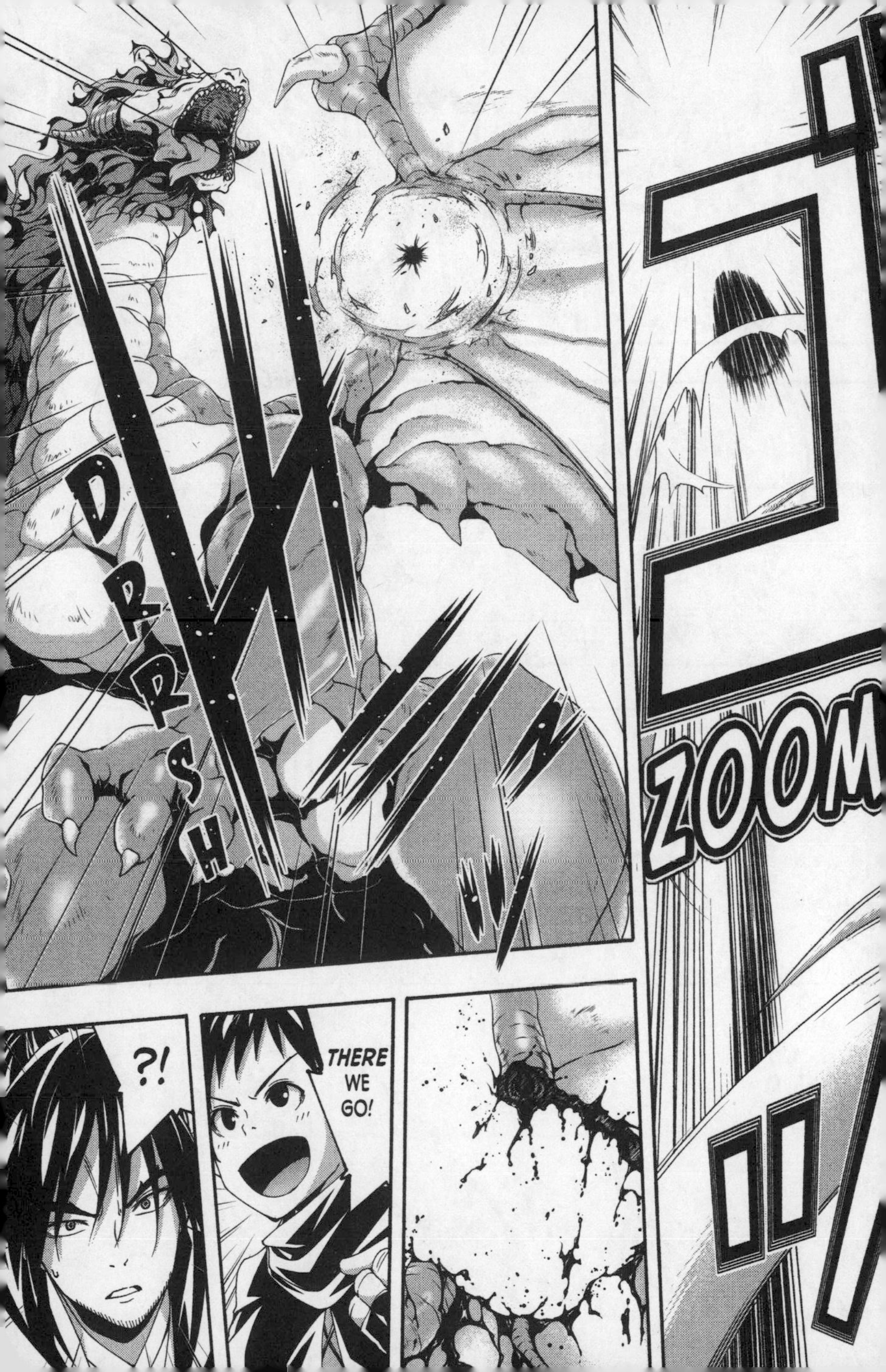
ZOOM
DRPRSH
THERE WE GO!
?!

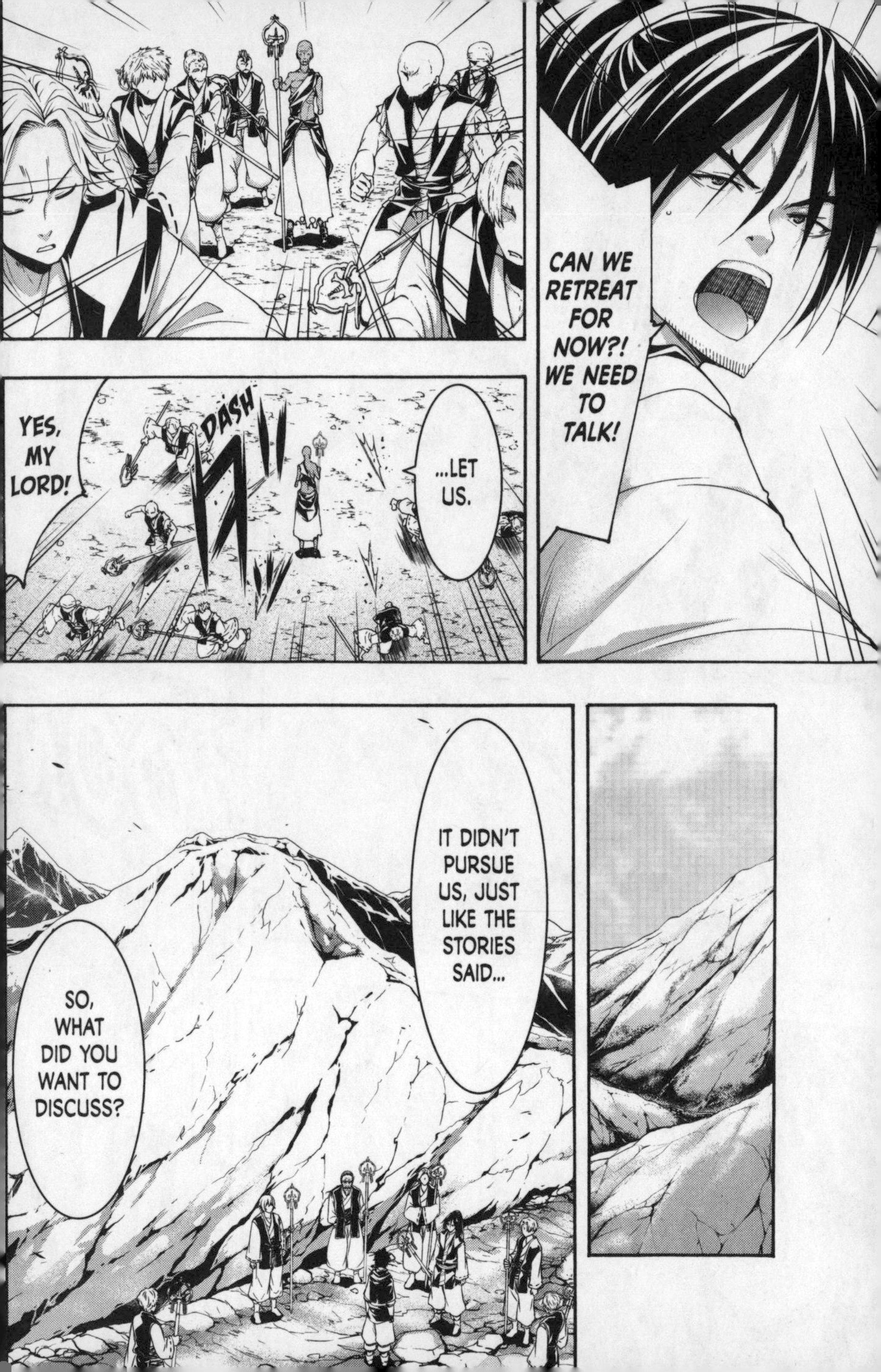
CAN WE RETREAT FOR NOW?! WE NEED TO TALK!
...LET US.
DASH
YES, MY LORD!
IT DIDN'T PURSUE US, JUST LIKE THE STORIES SAID...
SO, WHAT DID YOU WANT TO DISCUSS?

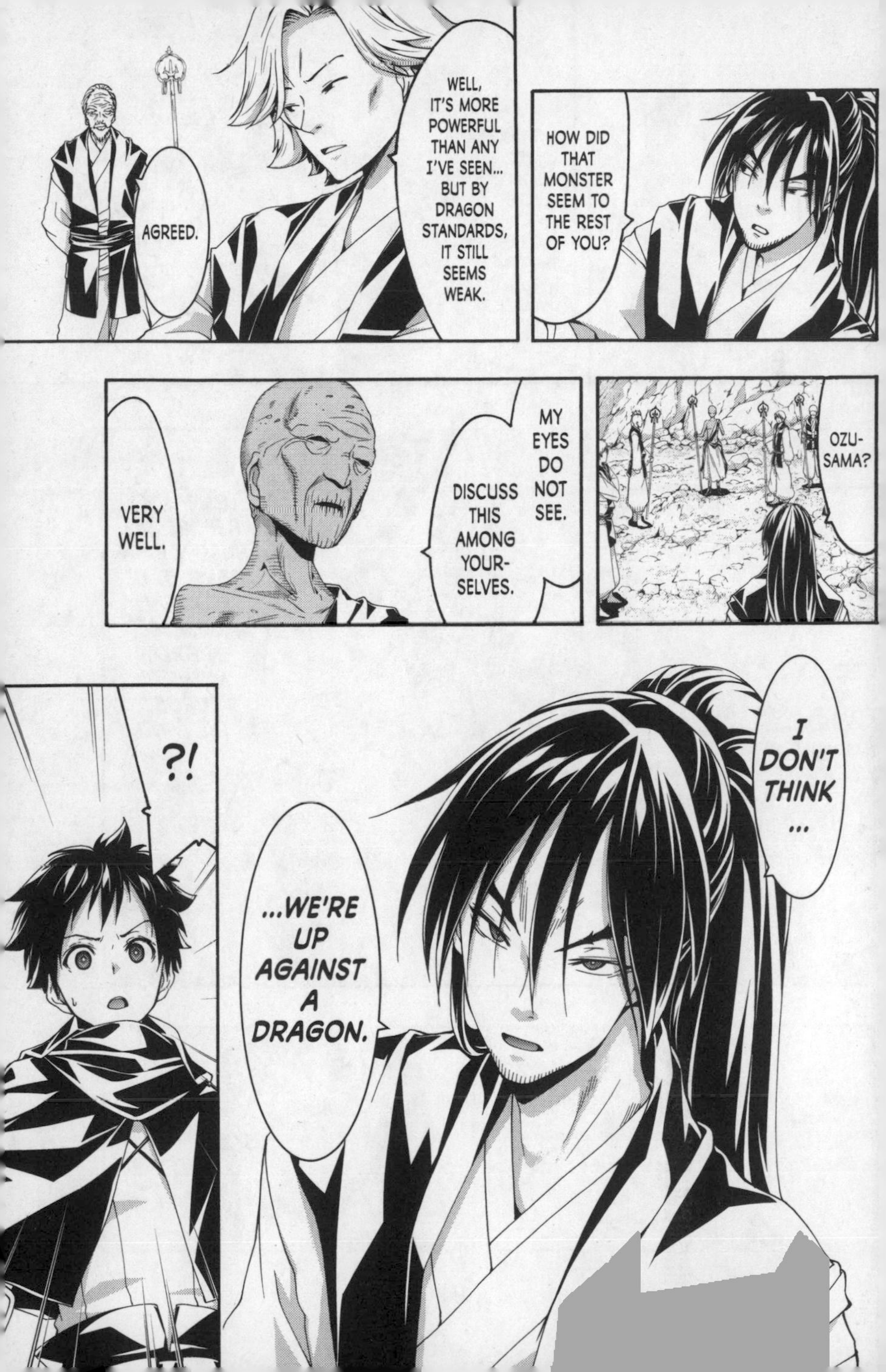
HOW DID THAT MONSTER SEEM TO THE REST OF YOU?
WELL, IT'S MORE POWERFUL THAN ANY I'VE SEEN... BUT BY DRAGON STANDARDS, IT STILL SEEMS WEAK.
AGREED.
OZU-SAMA?
MY EYES DO NOT SEE.
DISCUSS THIS AMONG YOUR-SELVES.
VERY WELL.
I DON'T THINK...
...WE'RE UP AGAINST A DRAGON.
?!

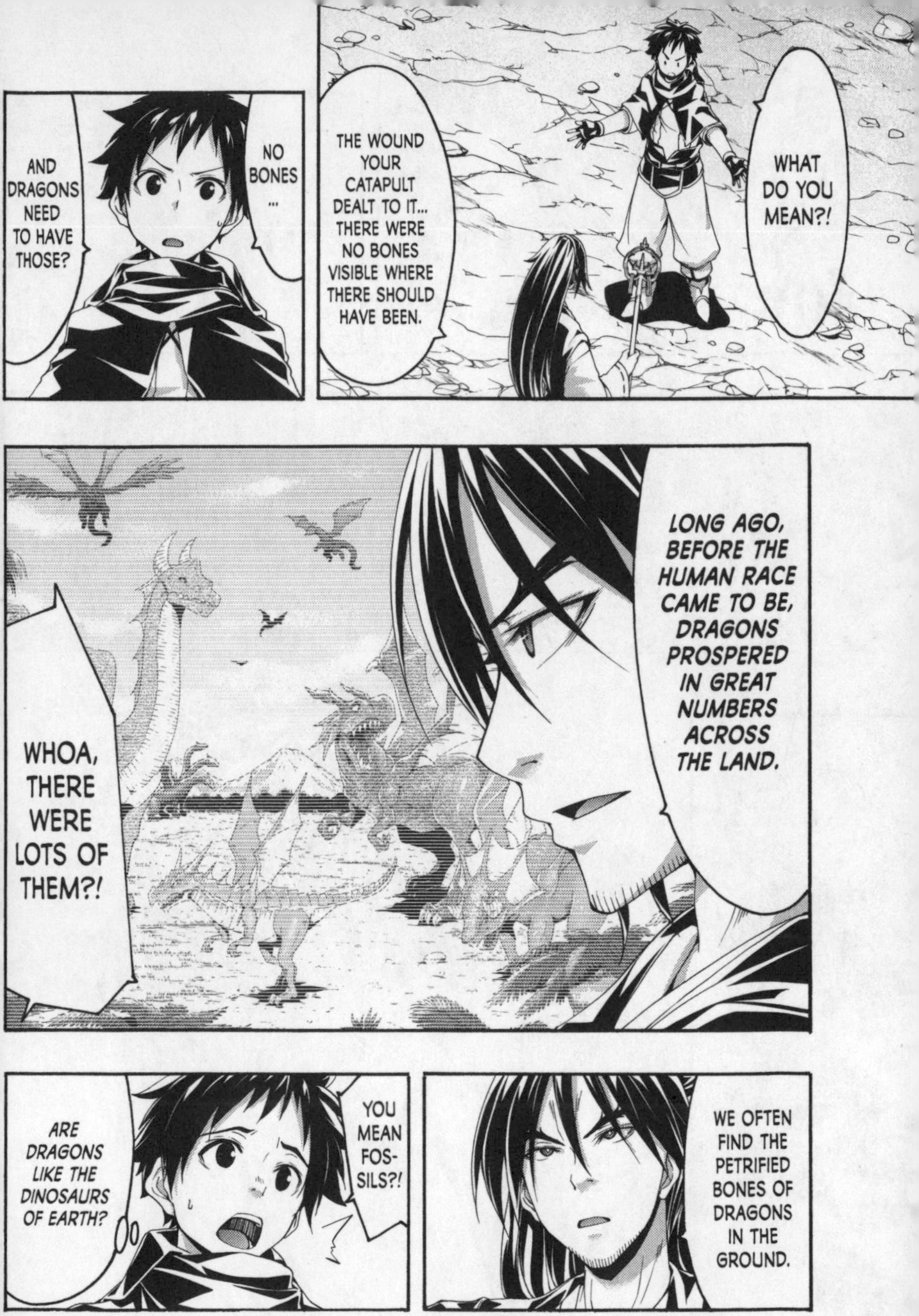
WHAT DO YOU MEAN?!
THE WOUND YOUR CATAPULT DEALT TO IT... THERE WERE NO BONES VISIBLE WHERE THERE SHOULD HAVE BEEN.
NO BONES ...
AND DRAGONS NEED TO HAVE THOSE?
LONG AGO, BEFORE THE HUMAN RACE CAME TO BE, DRAGONS PROSPERED IN GREAT NUMBERS ACROSS THE LAND.
WHOA, THERE WERE LOTS OF THEM?!
WE OFTEN FIND THE PETRIFIED BONES OF DRAGONS IN THE GROUND.
YOU MEAN FOS-SILS?!
ARE DRAGONS LIKE THE DINOSAURS OF EARTH?

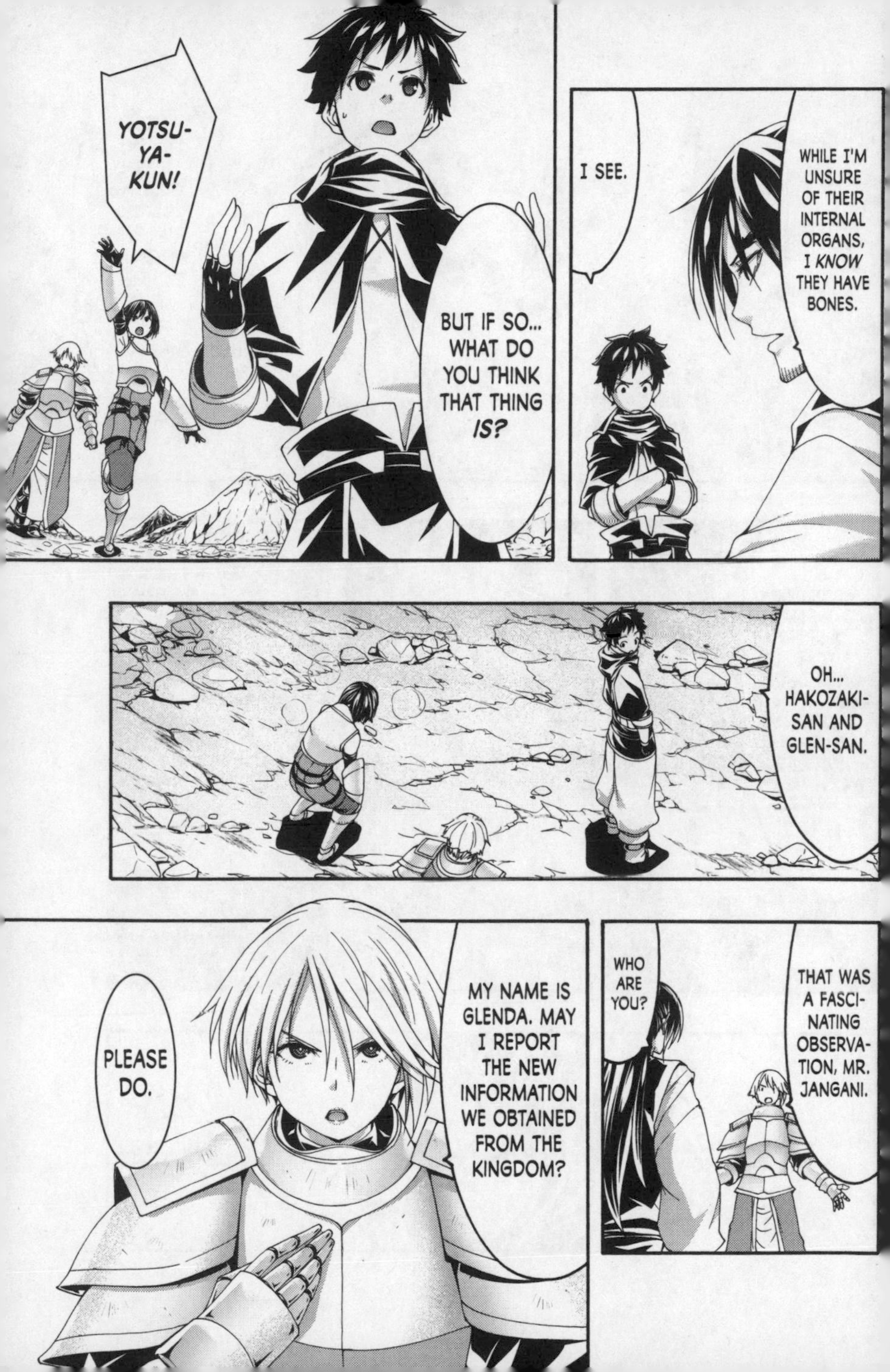
WHILE I'M UNSURE OF THEIR INTERNAL ORGANS, I *KNOW* THEY HAVE BONES.
I SEE.
BUT IF SO... WHAT DO YOU THINK THAT THING *IS?*
YOTSU-YA-KUN!
OH... HAKOZAKI-SAN AND GLEN-SAN.
THAT WAS A FASCI-NATING OBSERVA-TION, MR. JANGANI.
WHO ARE YOU?
MY NAME IS GLENDA. MAY I REPORT THE NEW INFORMATION WE OBTAINED FROM THE KINGDOM?
PLEASE DO.

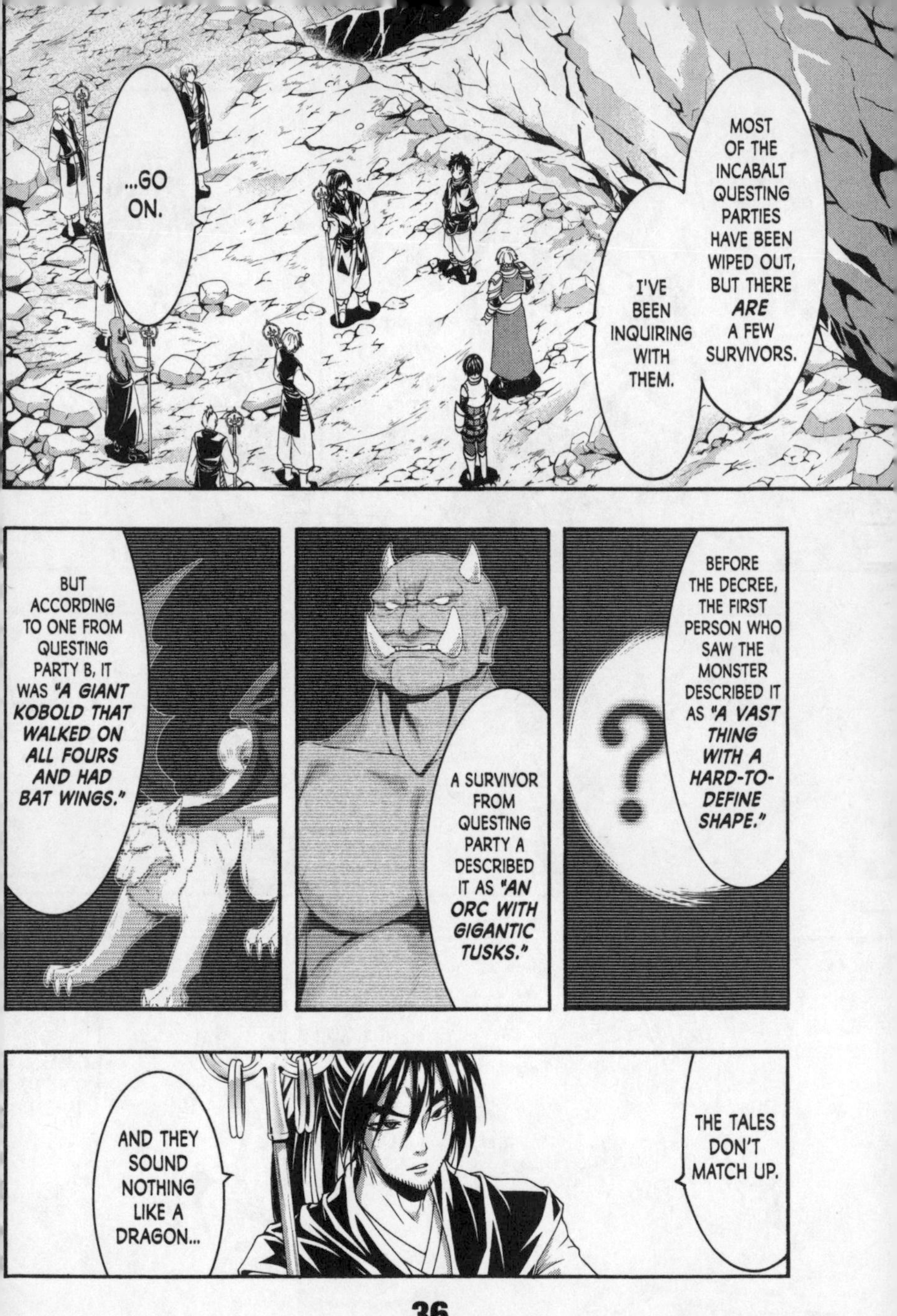
MOST OF THE INCABALT QUESTING PARTIES HAVE BEEN WIPED OUT, BUT THERE *ARE* A FEW SURVIVORS.
I'VE BEEN INQUIRING WITH THEM.
...GO ON.
BEFORE THE DECREE, THE FIRST PERSON WHO SAW THE MONSTER DESCRIBED IT AS *"A VAST THING WITH A HARD-TO-DEFINE SHAPE."*
?
A SURVIVOR FROM QUESTING PARTY A DESCRIBED IT AS *"AN ORC WITH GIGANTIC TUSKS."*
BUT ACCORDING TO ONE FROM QUESTING PARTY B, IT WAS *"A GIANT KOBOLD THAT WALKED ON ALL FOURS AND HAD BAT WINGS."*
THE TALES DON'T MATCH UP.
AND THEY SOUND NOTHING LIKE A DRAGON...

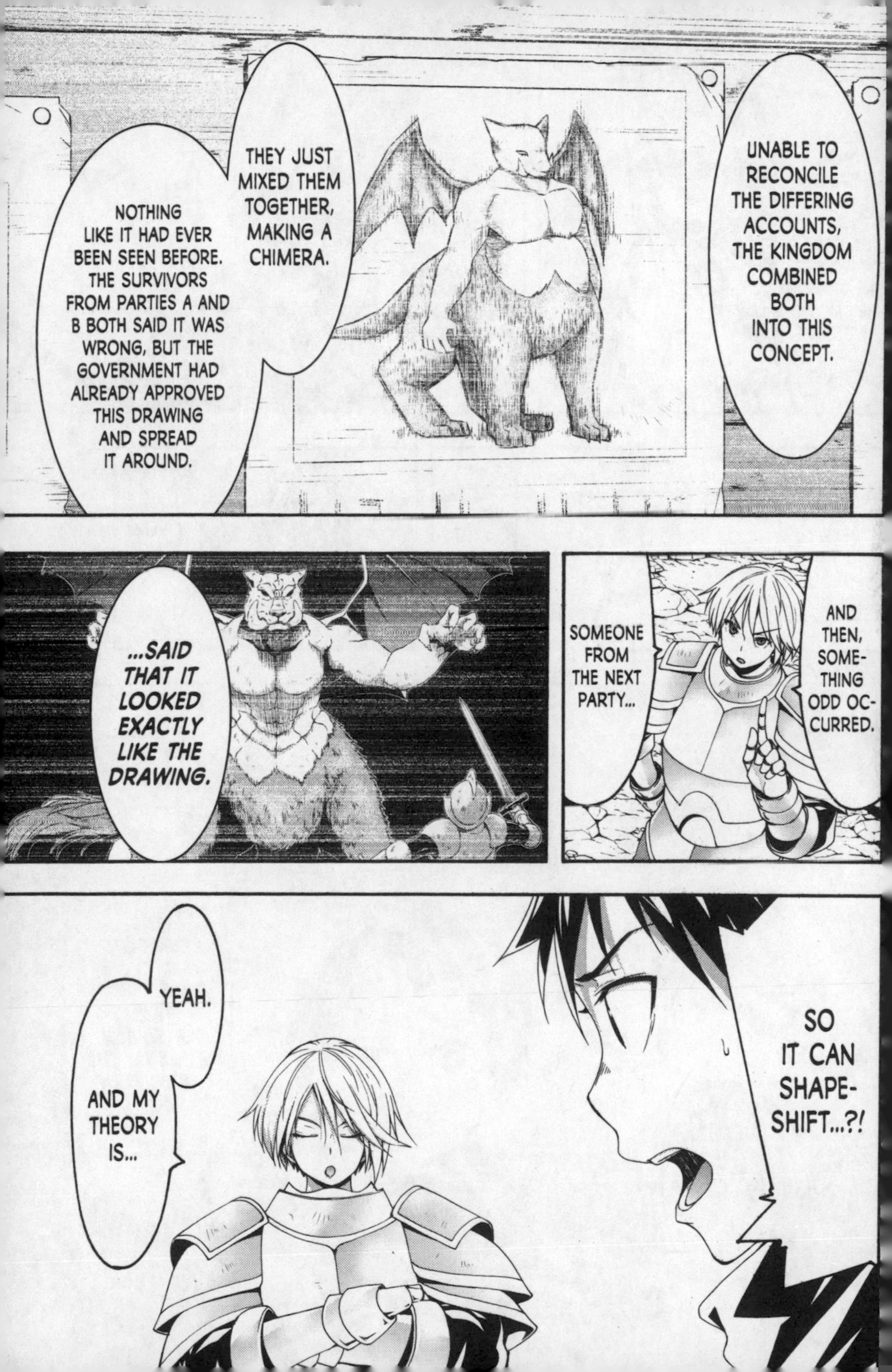
UNABLE TO RECONCILE THE DIFFERING ACCOUNTS, THE KINGDOM COMBINED BOTH INTO THIS CONCEPT.
THEY JUST MIXED THEM TOGETHER, MAKING A CHIMERA.
NOTHING LIKE IT HAD EVER BEEN SEEN BEFORE. THE SURVIVORS FROM PARTIES A AND B BOTH SAID IT WAS WRONG, BUT THE GOVERNMENT HAD ALREADY APPROVED THIS DRAWING AND SPREAD IT AROUND.
AND THEN, SOME-THING ODD OC-CURRED.
SOMEONE FROM THE NEXT PARTY...
...SAID THAT IT LOOKED EXACTLY LIKE THE DRAWING.
SO IT CAN SHAPE-SHIFT...?!
YEAH.
AND MY THEORY IS...

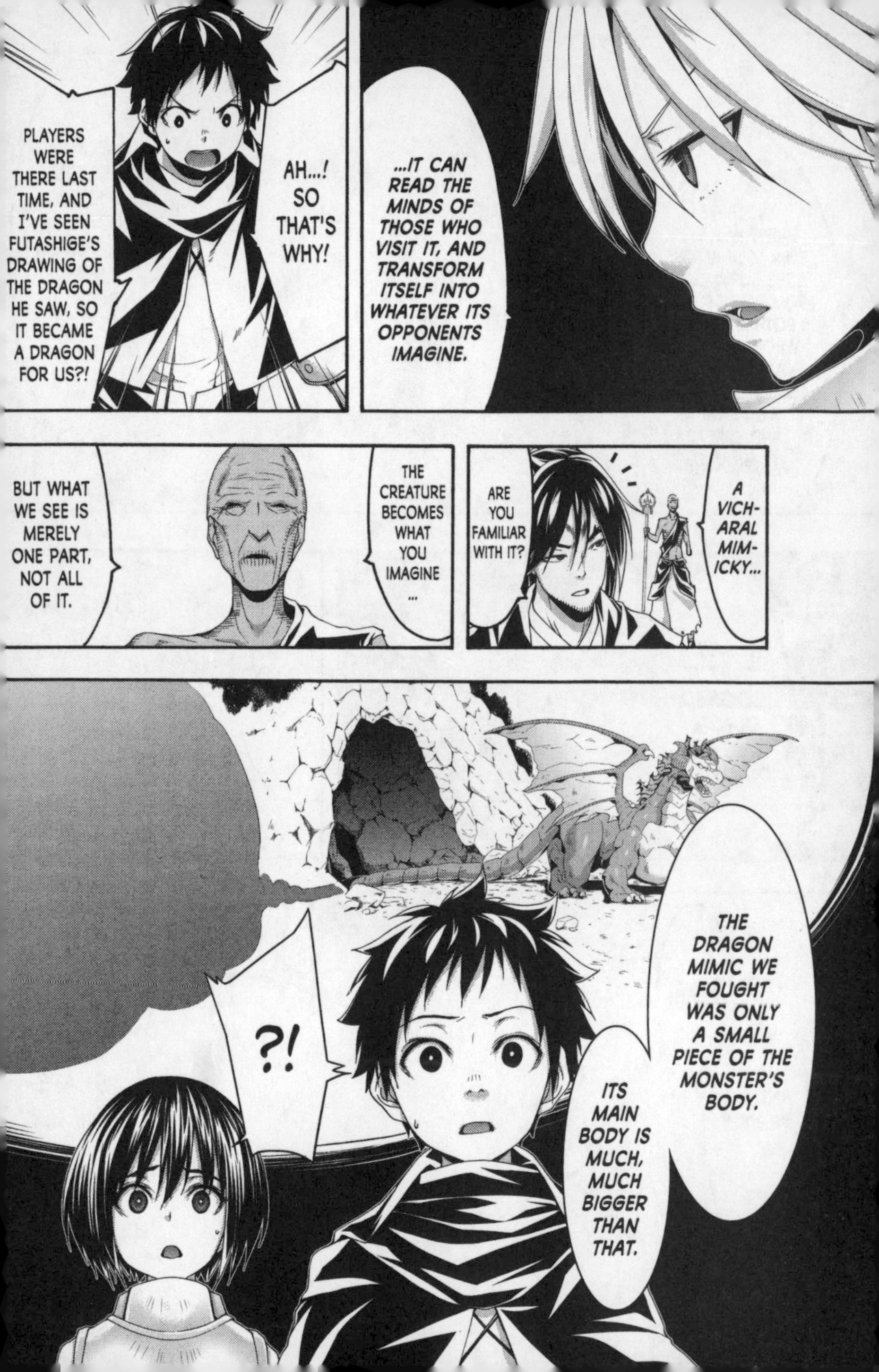
...IT CAN READ THE MINDS OF THOSE WHO VISIT IT, AND TRANSFORM ITSELF INTO WHATEVER ITS OPPONENTS IMAGINE.
AH...! SO THAT'S WHY!
PLAYERS WERE THERE LAST TIME, AND I'VE SEEN FUTASHIGE'S DRAWING OF THE DRAGON HE SAW, SO IT BECAME A DRAGON FOR US?!
A VICH-ARAL MIM-ICKY...
ARE YOU FAMILIAR WITH IT?
THE CREATURE BECOMES WHAT YOU IMAGINE ...
BUT WHAT WE SEE IS MERELY ONE PART, NOT ALL OF IT.
THE DRAGON MIMIC WE FOUGHT WAS ONLY A SMALL PIECE OF THE MONSTER'S BODY.
ITS MAIN BODY IS MUCH, MUCH BIGGER THAN THAT.
?!

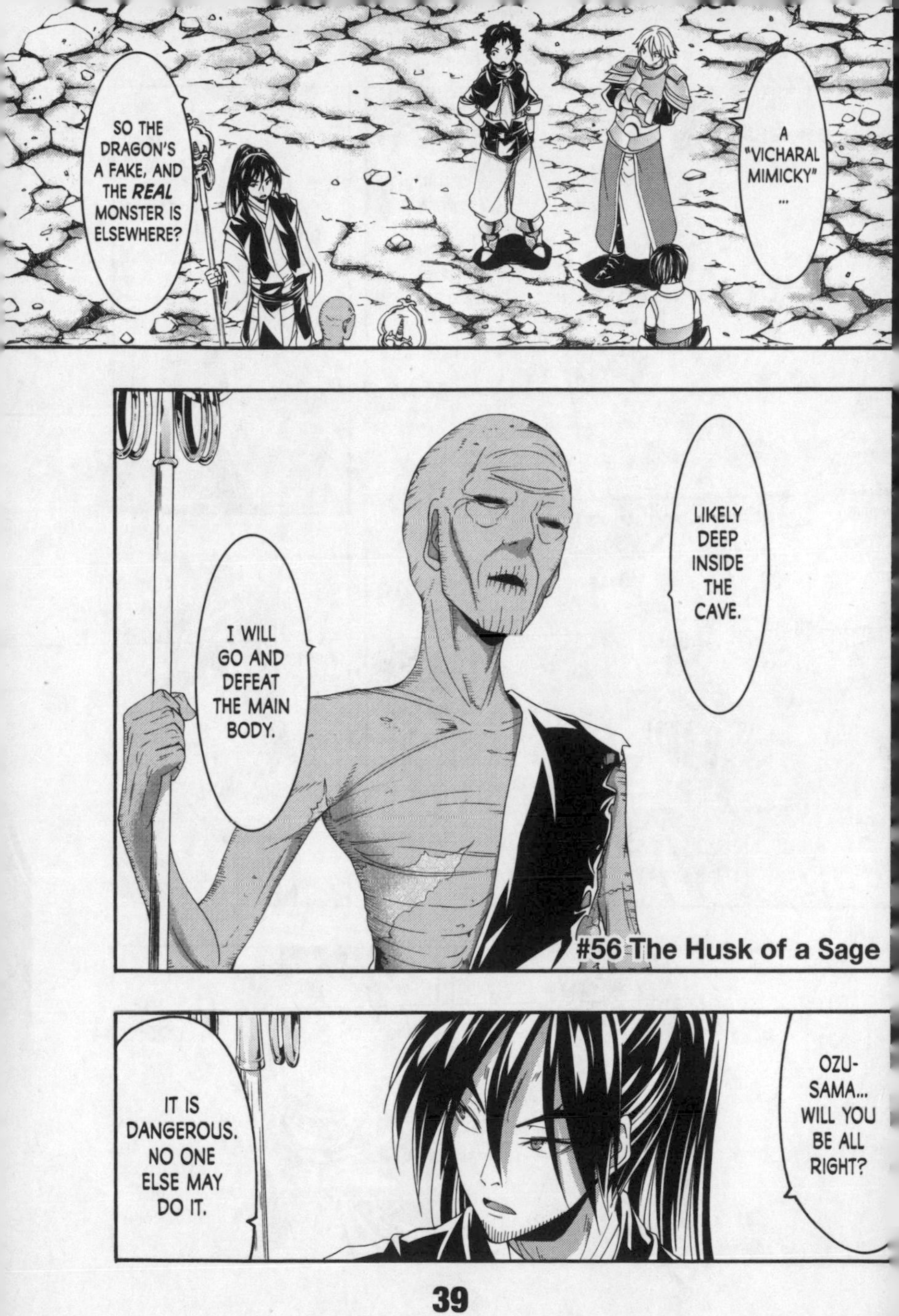
A "VICHARAL MIMICKY" ...
SO THE DRAGON'S A FAKE, AND THE *REAL* MONSTER IS ELSEWHERE?
LIKELY DEEP INSIDE THE CAVE.
I WILL GO AND DEFEAT THE MAIN BODY.
#56 The Husk of a Sage
OZU-SAMA... WILL YOU BE ALL RIGHT?
IT IS DANGEROUS. NO ONE ELSE MAY DO IT.

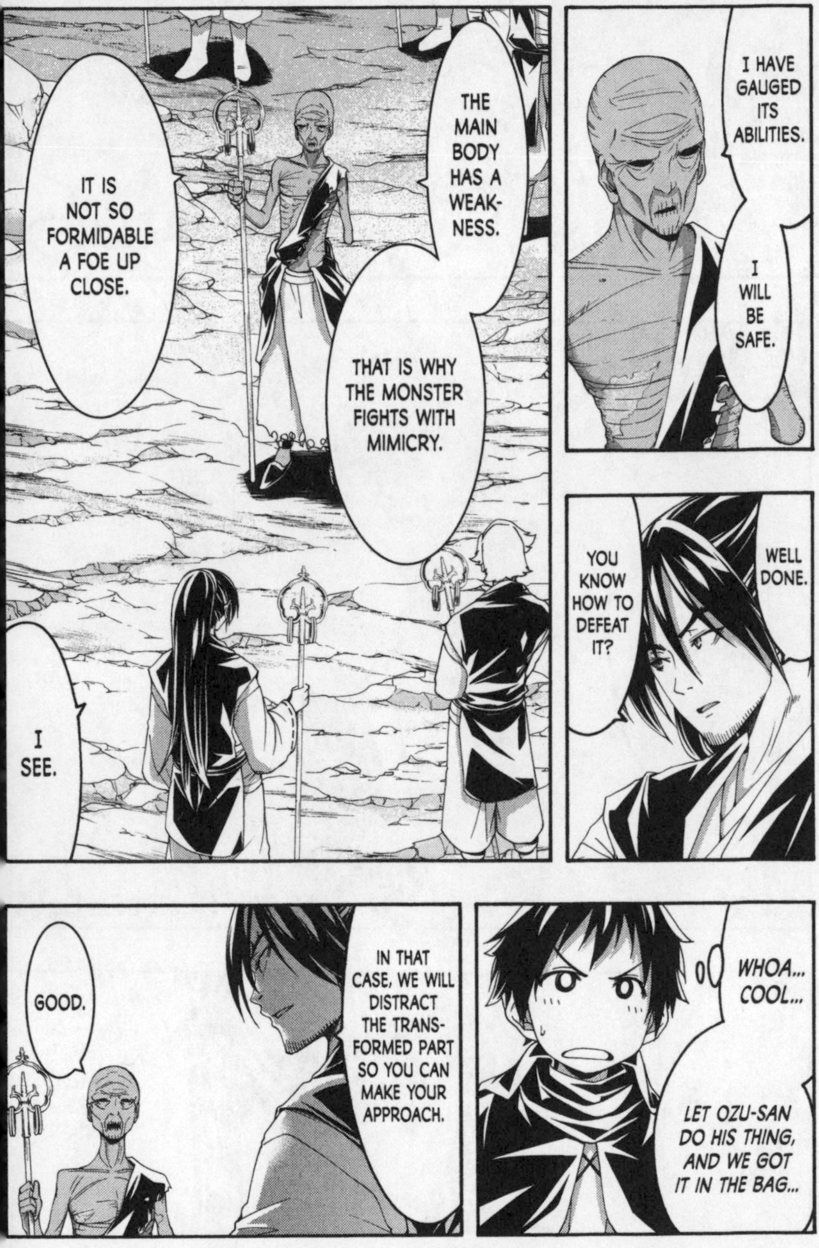
I HAVE GAUGED ITS ABILITIES.
I WILL BE SAFE.
WELL DONE.
YOU KNOW HOW TO DEFEAT IT?
THE MAIN BODY HAS A WEAKNESS.
IT IS NOT SO FORMIDABLE A FOE UP CLOSE.
THAT IS WHY THE MONSTER FIGHTS WITH MIMICRY.
I SEE.
WHOA... COOL...
LET OZU-SAN DO HIS THING, AND WE GOT IT IN THE BAG...
IN THAT CASE, WE WILL DISTRACT THE TRANSFORMED PART SO YOU CAN MAKE YOUR APPROACH.
GOOD.

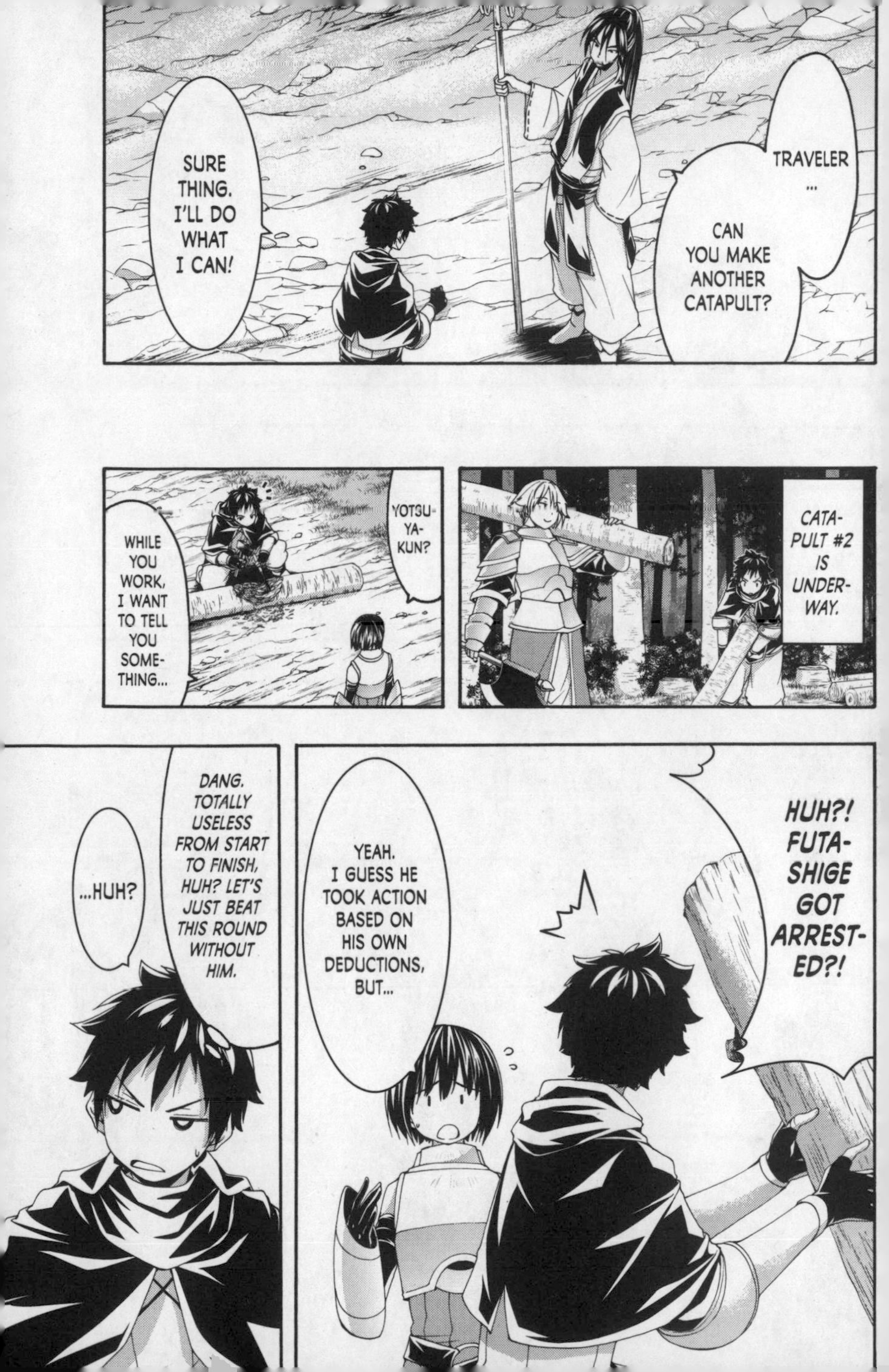

TRAVELER ... CAN YOU MAKE ANOTHER CATAPULT?
SURE THING. I'LL DO WHAT I CAN!
CATAPULT #2 IS UNDERWAY.
YOTSUYA-KUN?
WHILE YOU WORK, I WANT TO TELL YOU SOMETHING...
HUH?! FUTASHIGE GOT ARRESTED?!
YEAH. I GUESS HE TOOK ACTION BASED ON HIS OWN DEDUCTIONS, BUT...
DANG. TOTALLY USELESS FROM START TO FINISH, HUH? LET'S JUST BEAT THIS ROUND WITHOUT HIM.
...HUH?

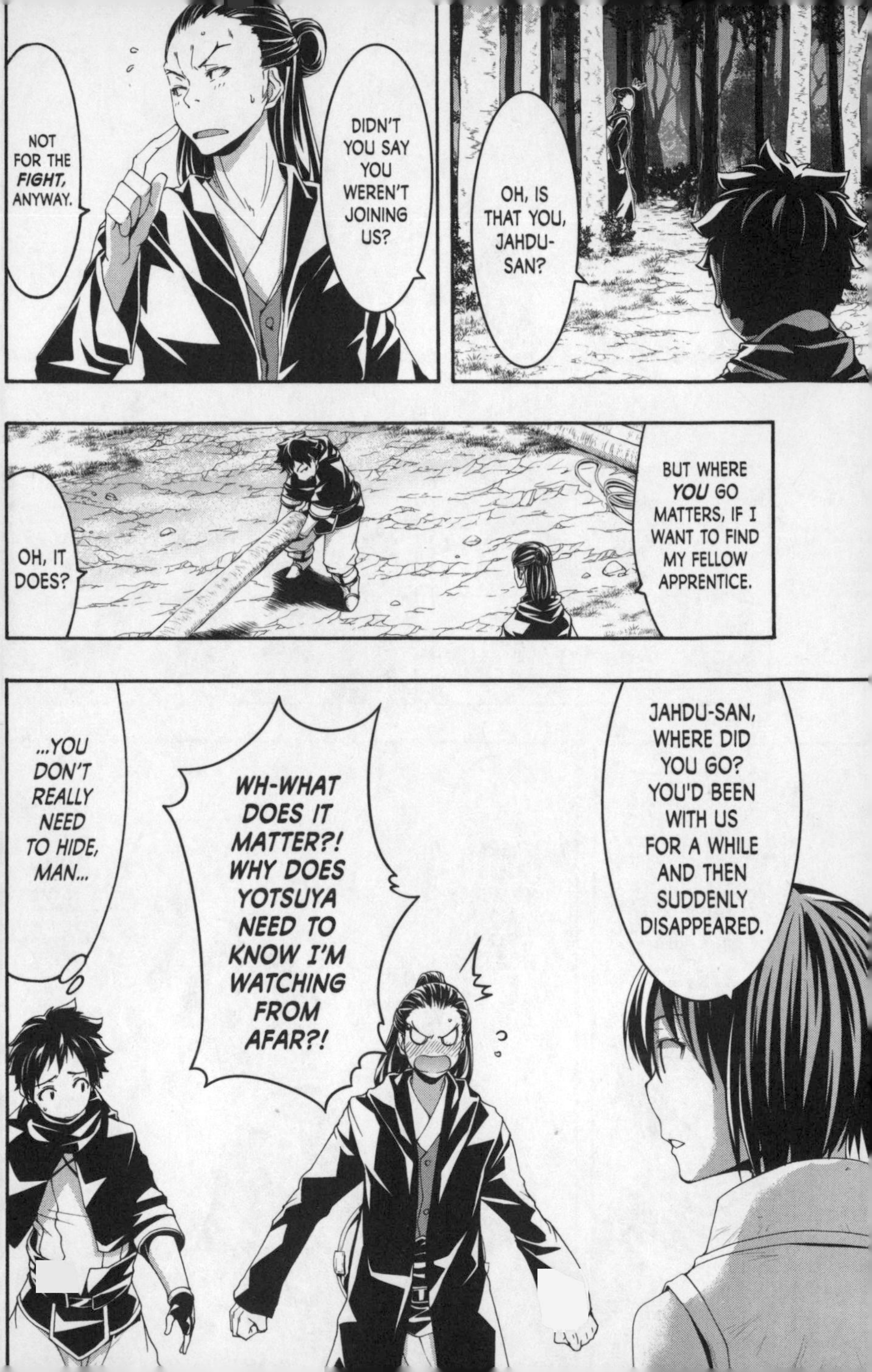
OH, IS THAT YOU, JAHDU-SAN?
DIDN'T YOU SAY YOU WEREN'T JOINING US?
NOT FOR THE FIGHT, ANYWAY.
BUT WHERE YOU GO MATTERS, IF I WANT TO FIND MY FELLOW APPRENTICE.
OH, IT DOES?
JAHDU-SAN, WHERE DID YOU GO? YOU'D BEEN WITH US FOR A WHILE AND THEN SUDDENLY DISAPPEARED.
WH-WHAT DOES IT MATTER?! WHY DOES YOTSUYA NEED TO KNOW I'M WATCHING FROM AFAR?!
...YOU DON'T REALLY NEED TO HIDE, MAN...

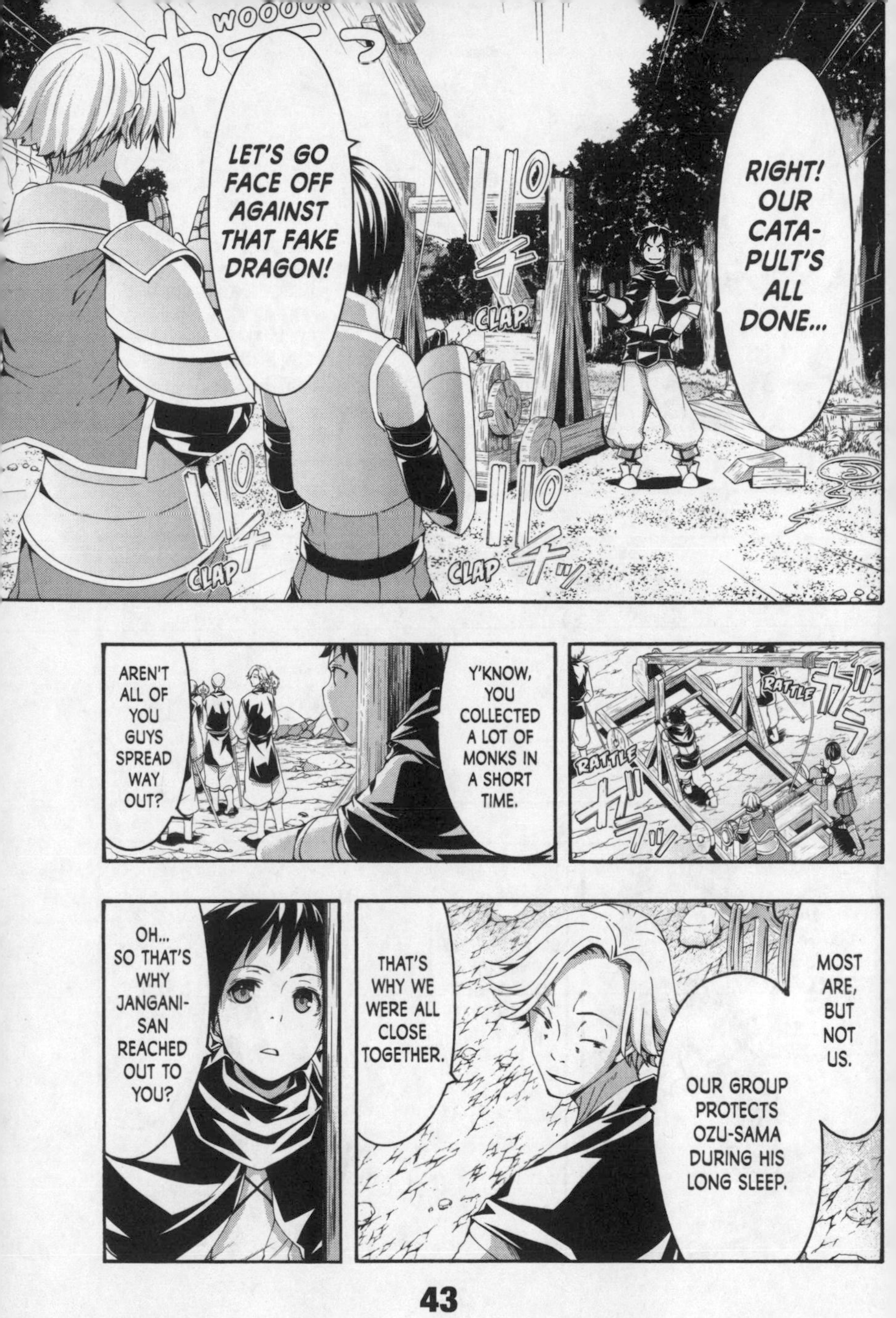
WOOOO!
RIGHT! OUR CATA-PULT'S ALL DONE...
LET'S GO FACE OFF AGAINST THAT FAKE DRAGON!
CLAP
CLAP
CLAP
RATTLE
RATTLE
Y'KNOW, YOU COLLECTED A LOT OF MONKS IN A SHORT TIME.
AREN'T ALL OF YOU GUYS SPREAD WAY OUT?
MOST ARE, BUT NOT US.
OUR GROUP PROTECTS OZU-SAMA DURING HIS LONG SLEEP.
THAT'S WHY WE WERE ALL CLOSE TOGETHER.
OH... SO THAT'S WHY JANGANI-SAN REACHED OUT TO YOU?

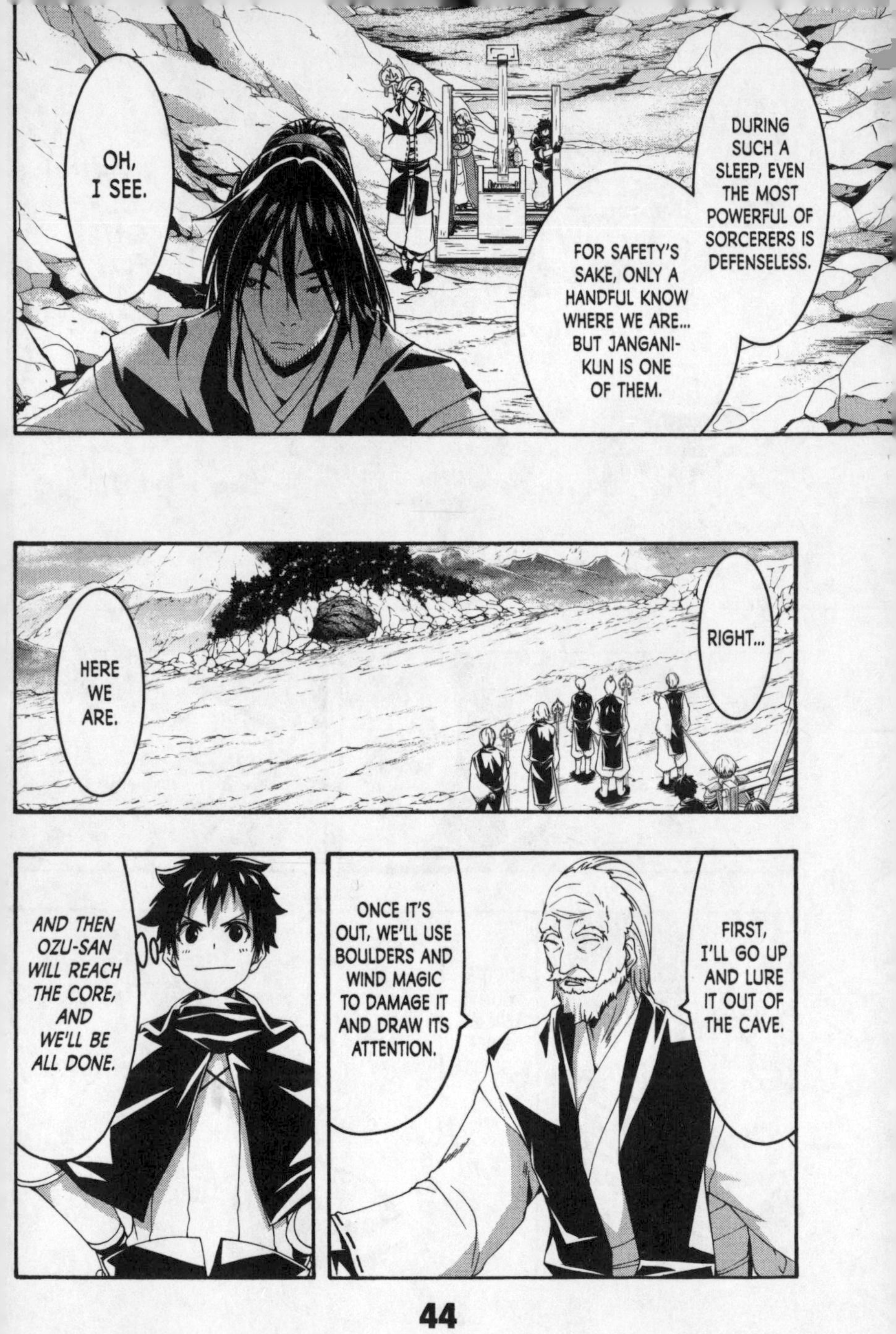
DURING SUCH A SLEEP, EVEN THE MOST POWERFUL OF SORCERERS IS DEFENSELESS.
FOR SAFETY'S SAKE, ONLY A HANDFUL KNOW WHERE WE ARE... BUT JANGANI-KUN IS ONE OF THEM.
OH, I SEE.
RIGHT...
HERE WE ARE.
FIRST, I'LL GO UP AND LURE IT OUT OF THE CAVE.
ONCE IT'S OUT, WE'LL USE BOULDERS AND WIND MAGIC TO DAMAGE IT AND DRAW ITS ATTENTION.
AND THEN OZU-SAN WILL REACH THE CORE, AND WE'LL BE ALL DONE.

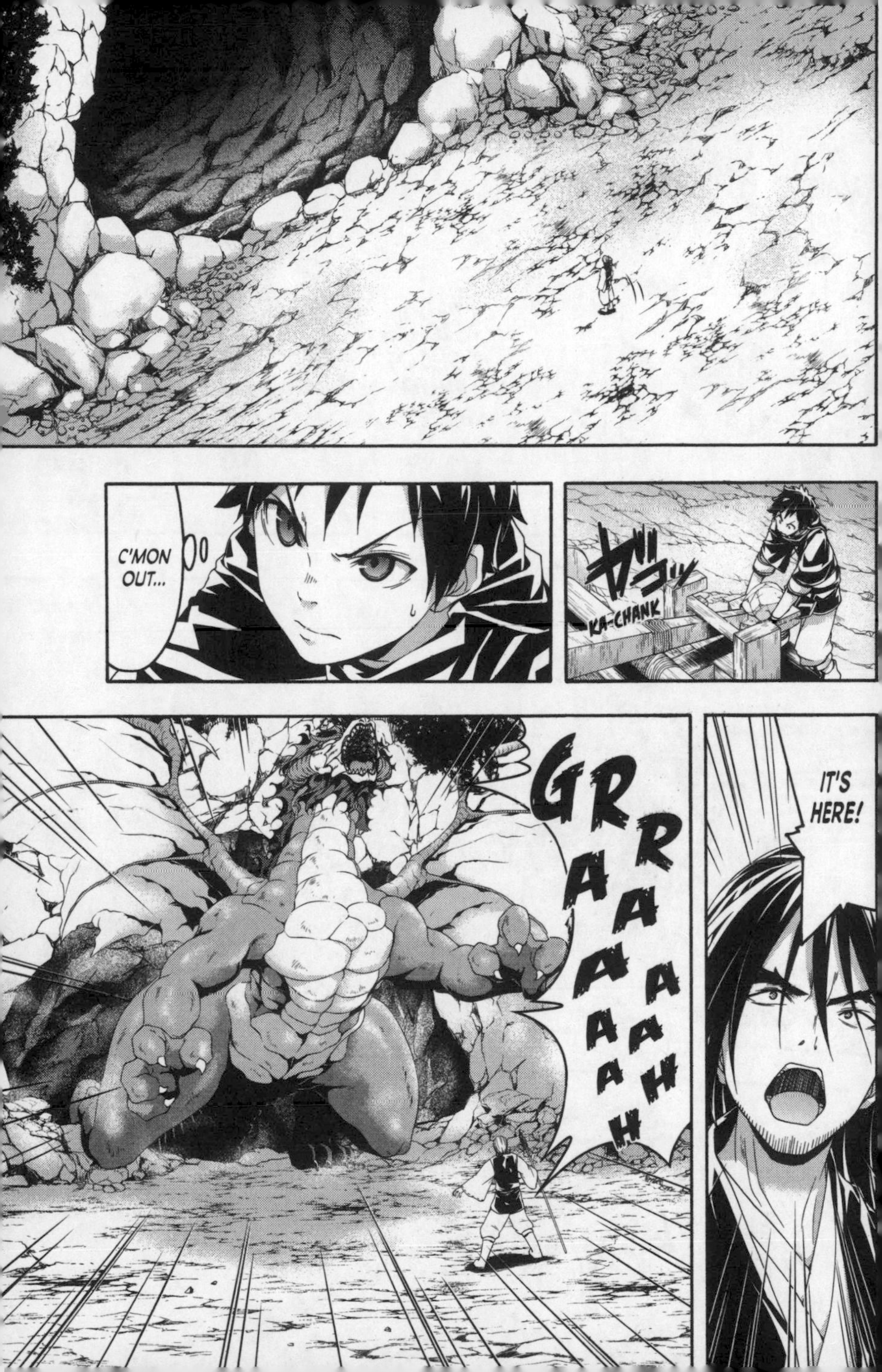
ヤリコッ
KA-CHANK
C'MON OUT...
IT'S HERE!
GRAAAAH
RAAAH

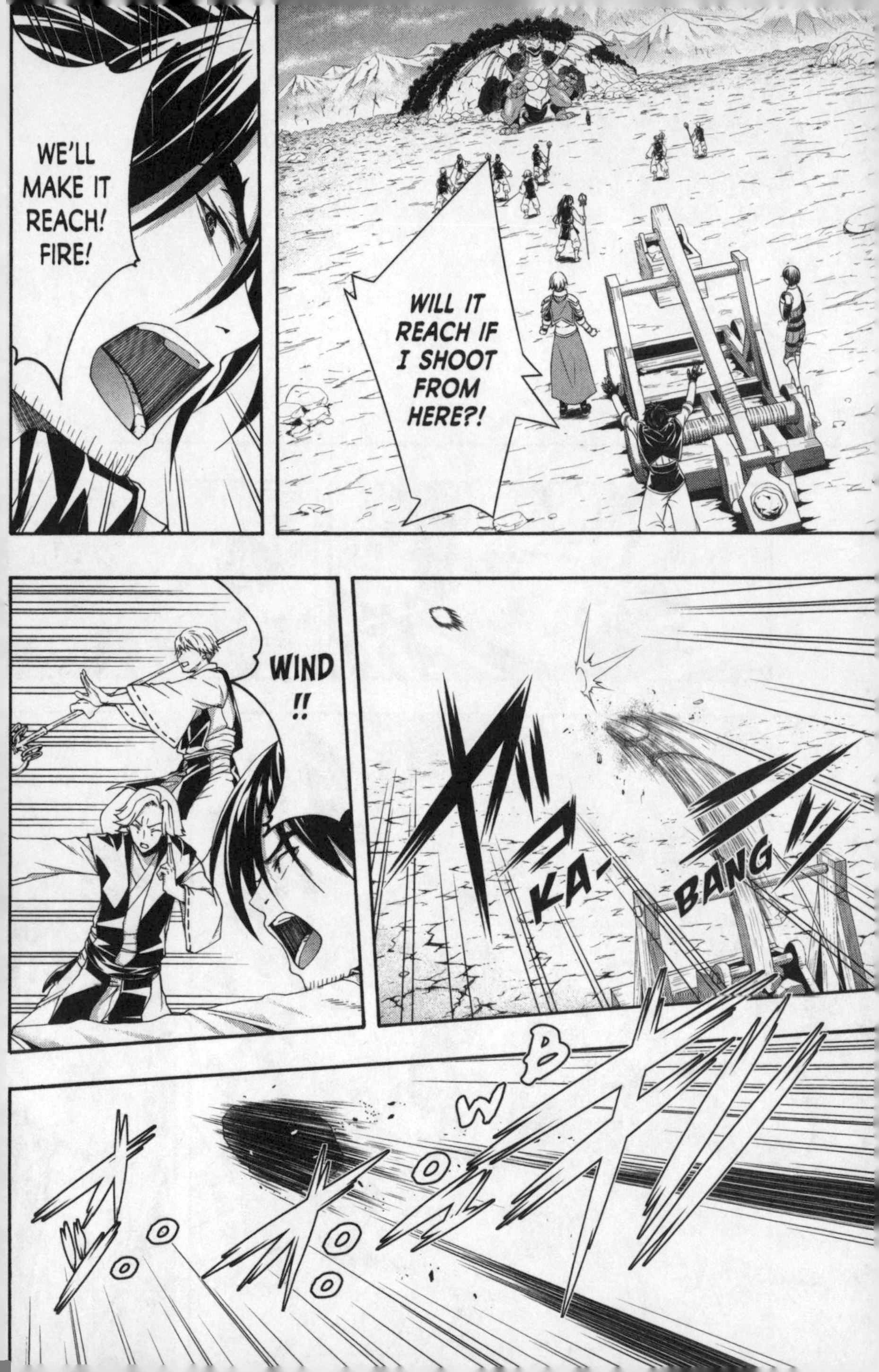
WILL IT REACH IF I SHOOT FROM HERE?!
WE'LL MAKE IT REACH! FIRE!
KA-BANG!!
WIND!!
BWOOOOO

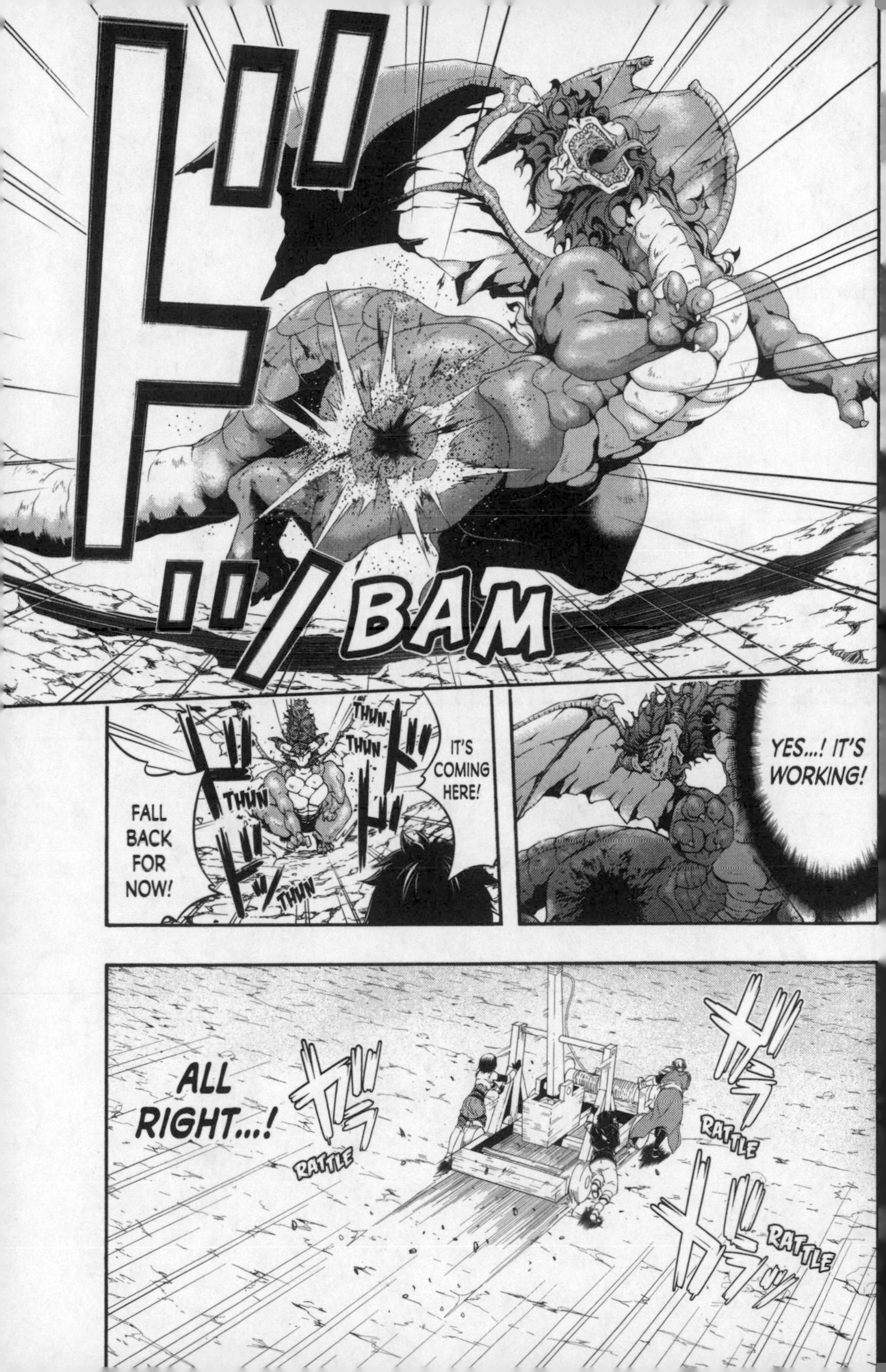
BAM
YES...! IT'S WORKING!
THUN THUN
IT'S COMING HERE!
THUN
FALL BACK FOR NOW!
THUN
RATTLE
RATTLE
ALL RIGHT...!
RATTLE

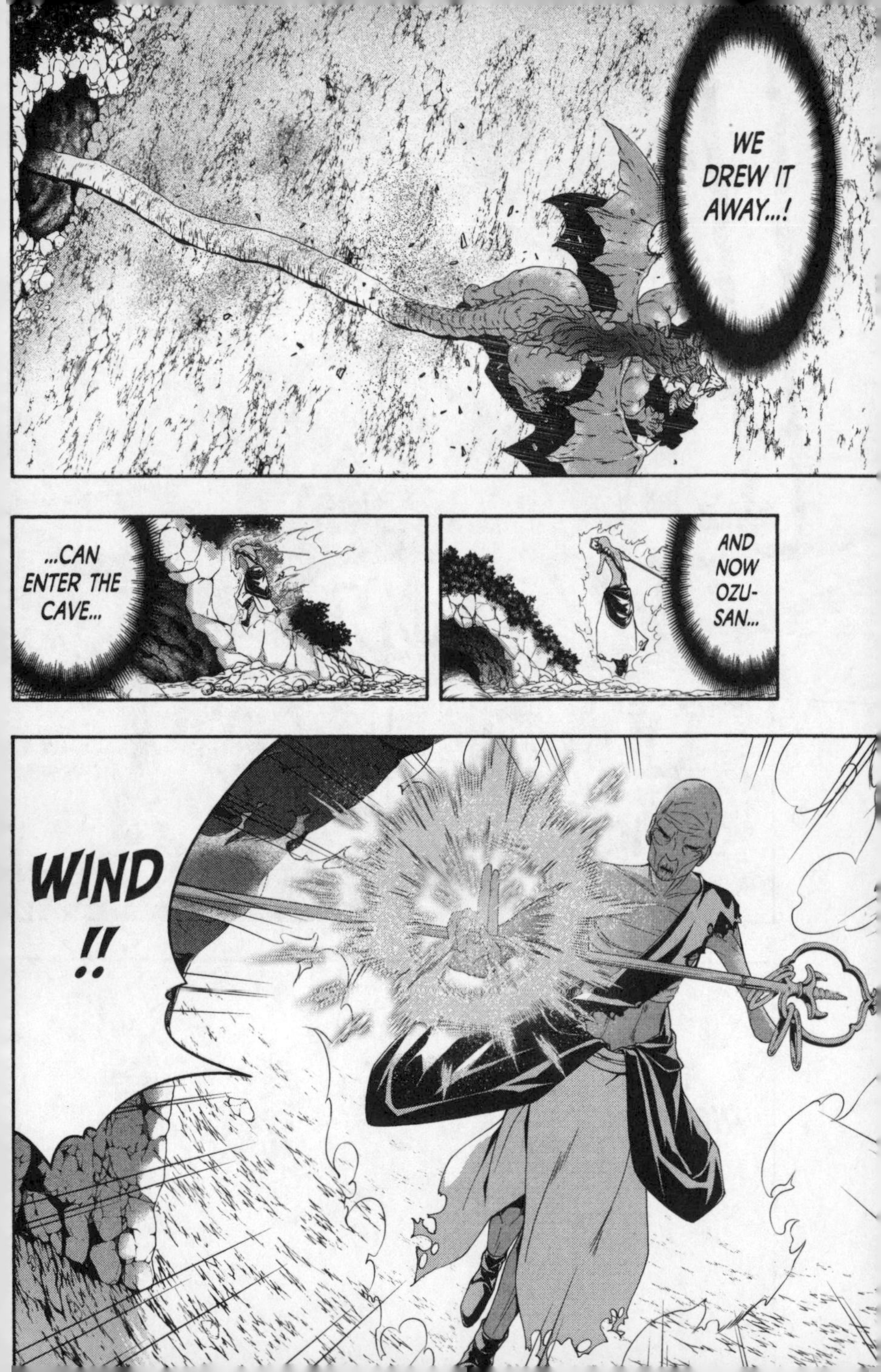
WE DREW IT AWAY...!
AND NOW OZU-SAN...
...CAN ENTER THE CAVE...
WIND !!

...AND END THIS FIGHT!!

IT'S LOSING FORM... WE WON!

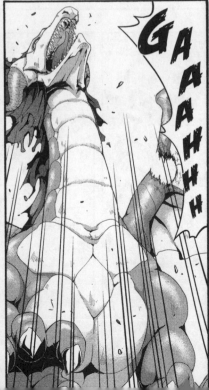

GAAAHHH

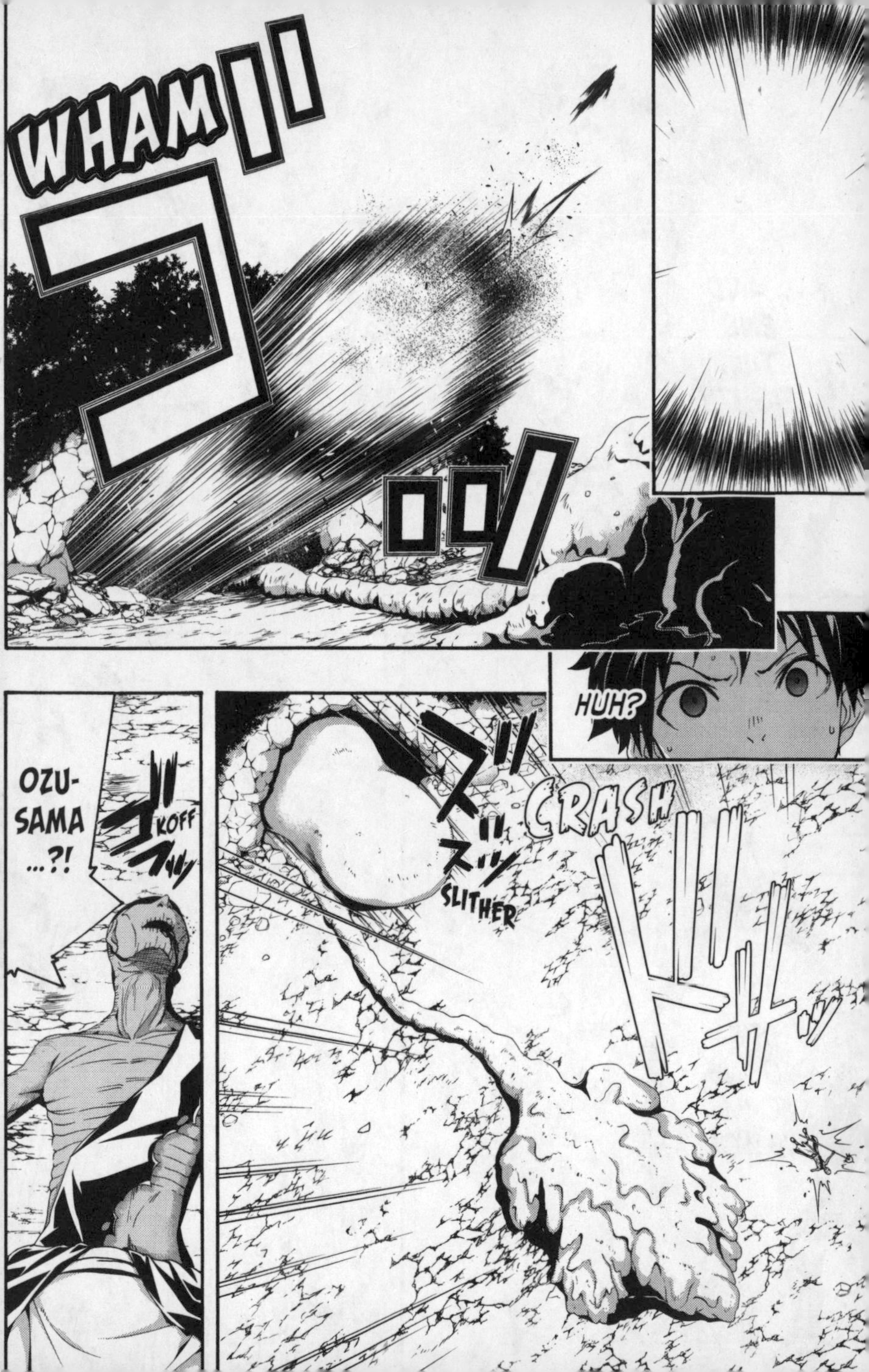
WHAM
HUH?
CRASH
SLITHER
OZU-SAMA ...?!
KOFF

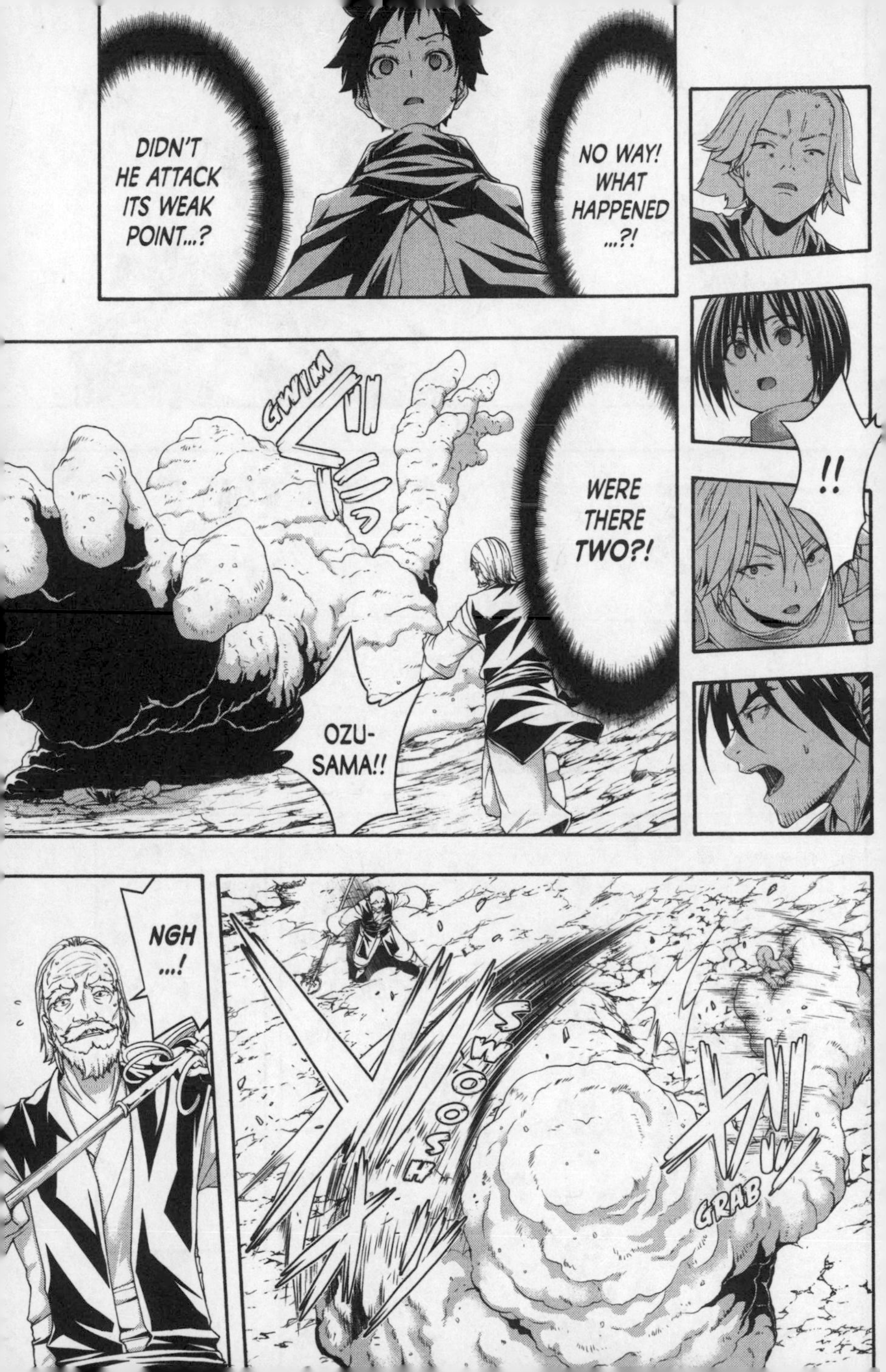
NO WAY! WHAT HAPPENED ...?!
DIDN'T HE ATTACK ITS WEAK POINT...?
!!
GWIIM
WERE THERE TWO?!
OZU-SAMA!!
GRAB
SWOOSH
NGH ...!

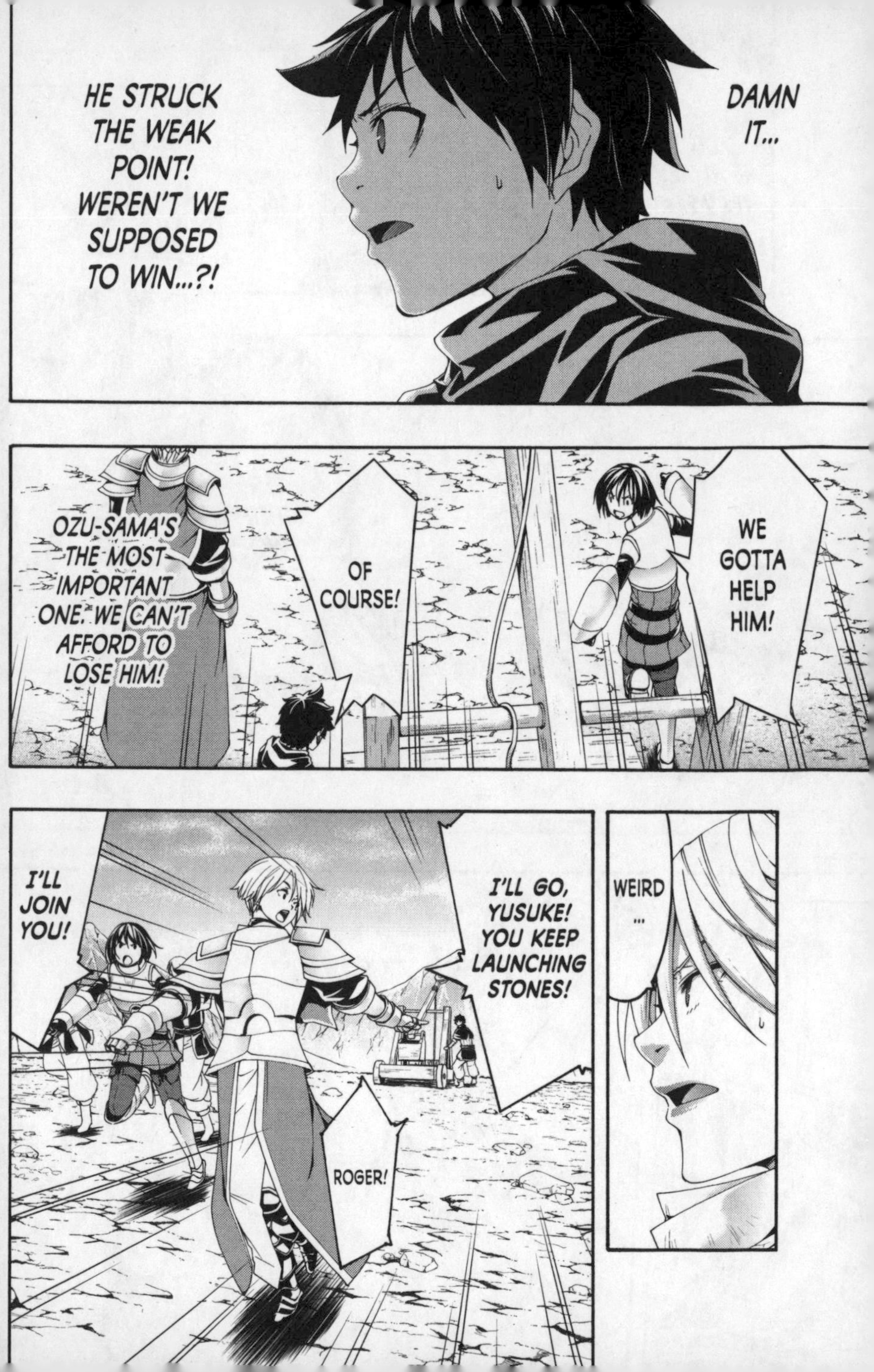
DAMN IT...
HE STRUCK THE WEAK POINT! WEREN'T WE SUPPOSED TO WIN...?!
WE GOTTA HELP HIM!
OF COURSE!
OZU-SAMA'S THE MOST IMPORTANT ONE. WE CAN'T AFFORD TO LOSE HIM!
WEIRD ...
I'LL GO, YUSUKE! YOU KEEP LAUNCHING STONES!
ROGER!
I'LL JOIN YOU!

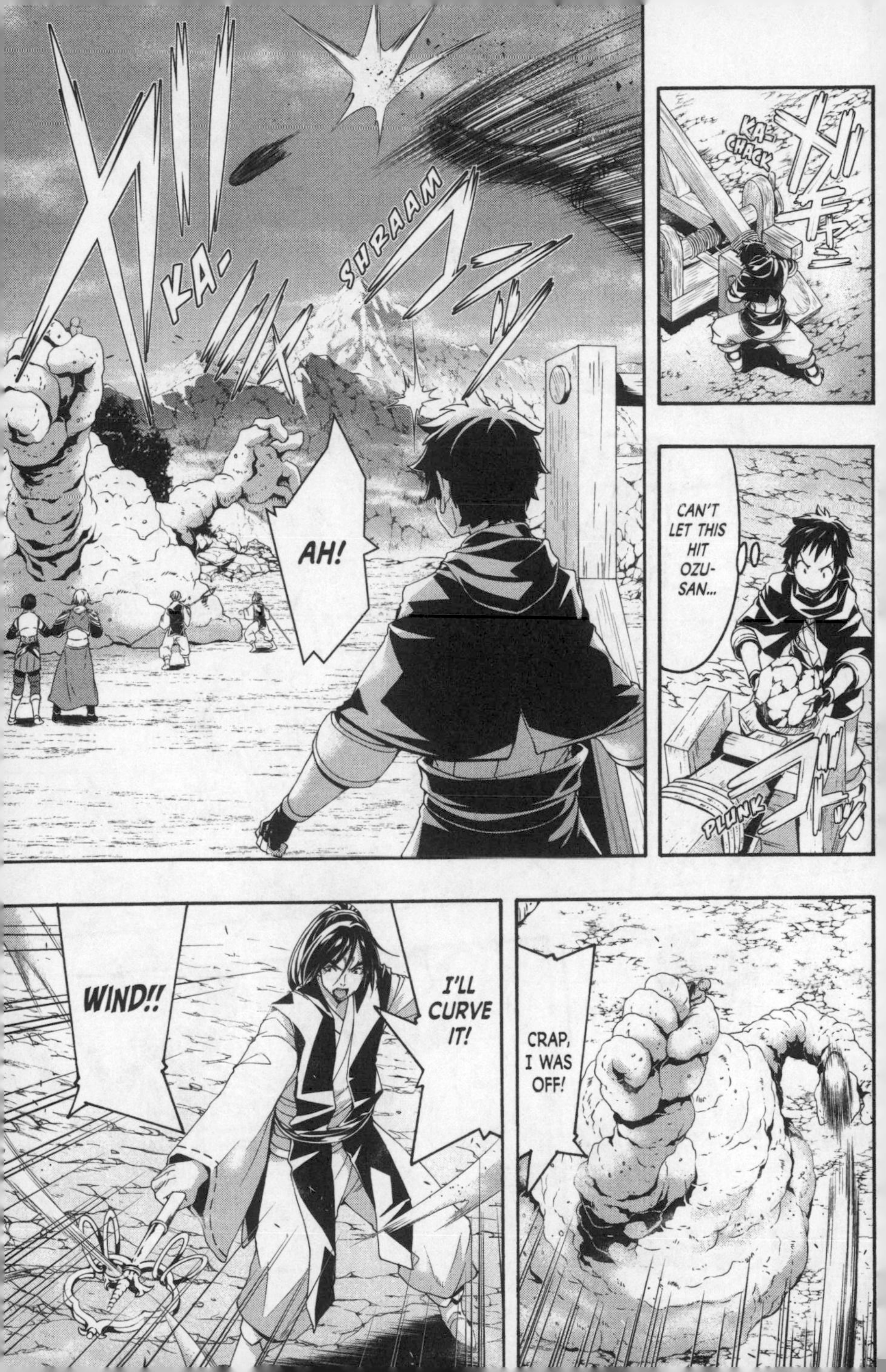
KA-CHACK
CAN'T LET THIS HIT OZU-SAN...
PLUNK
AH!
KA-
SHRAAAM
CRAP, I WAS OFF!
I'LL CURVE IT!
WIND!!

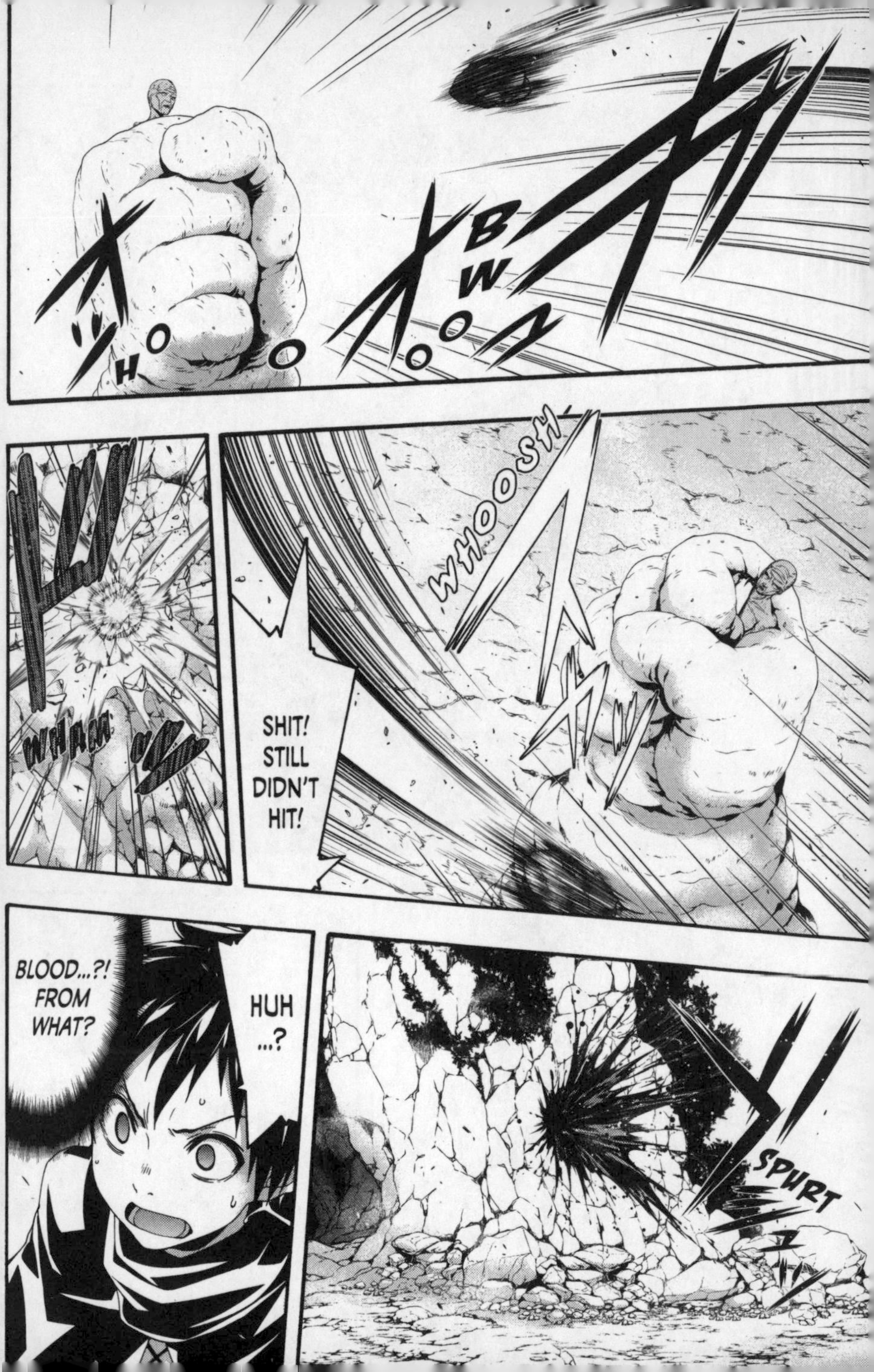
WHOOSH
SHIT! STILL DIDN'T HIT!
WHAM
SPURT
HUH ...?
BLOOD...?! FROM WHAT?

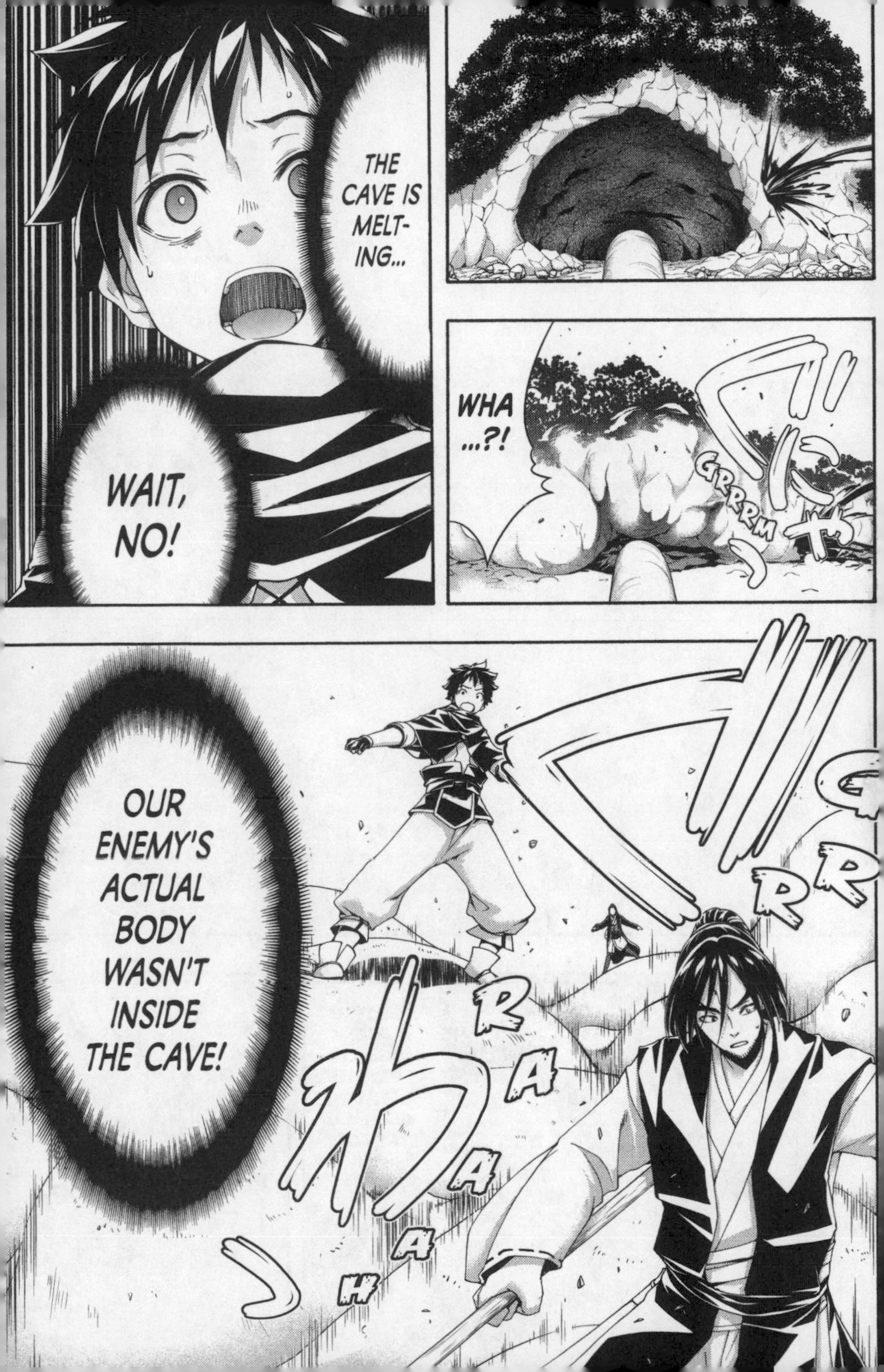
WHA ...?!
GRRRM
THE CAVE IS MELTING...
WAIT, NO!
GRRR
OUR ENEMY'S ACTUAL BODY WASN'T INSIDE THE CAVE!
RAAAH

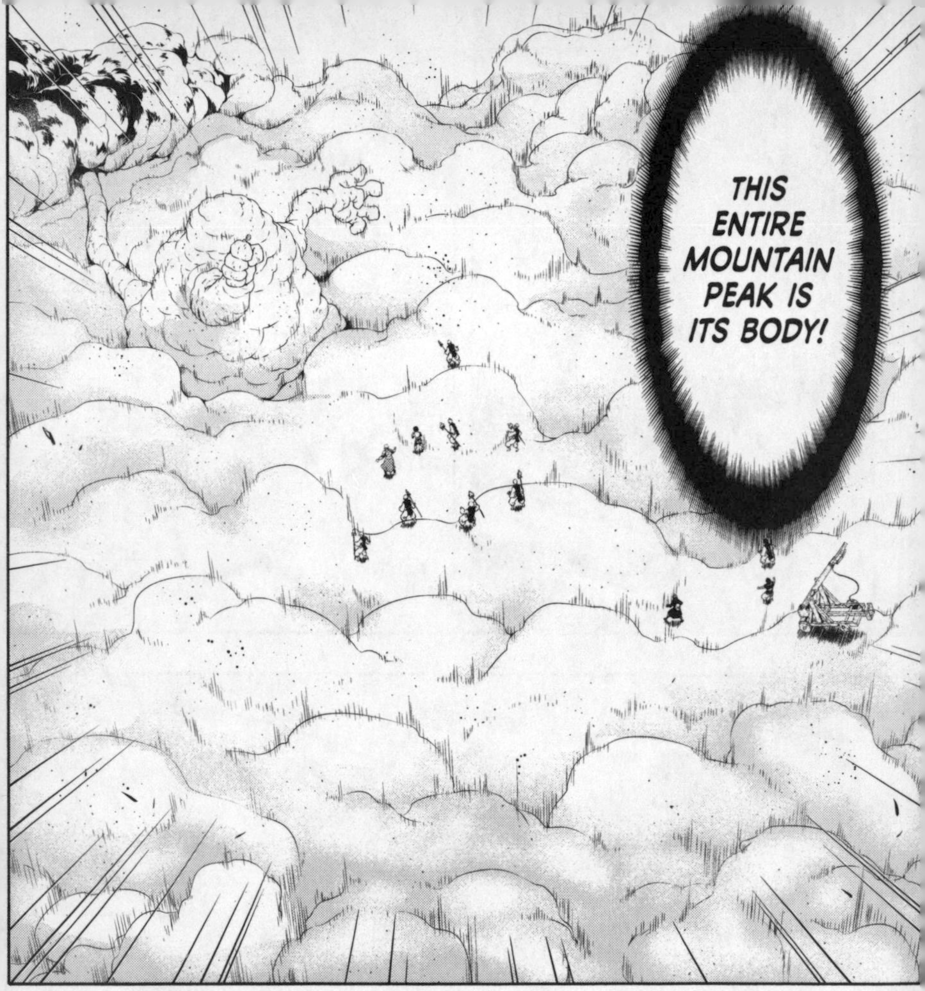
THIS ENTIRE MOUNTAIN PEAK IS ITS BODY!

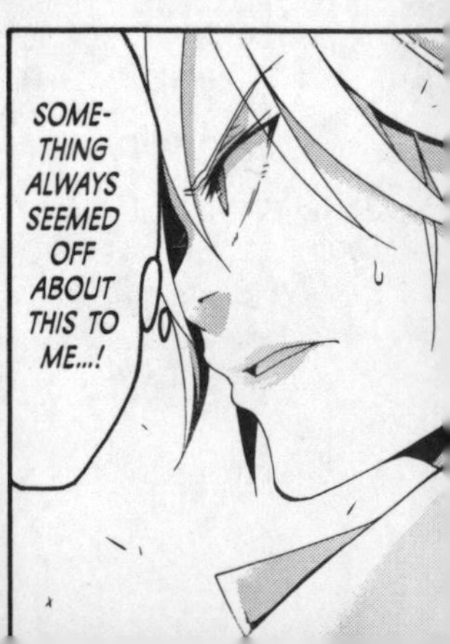
SOME-THING ALWAYS SEEMED OFF ABOUT THIS TO ME...!

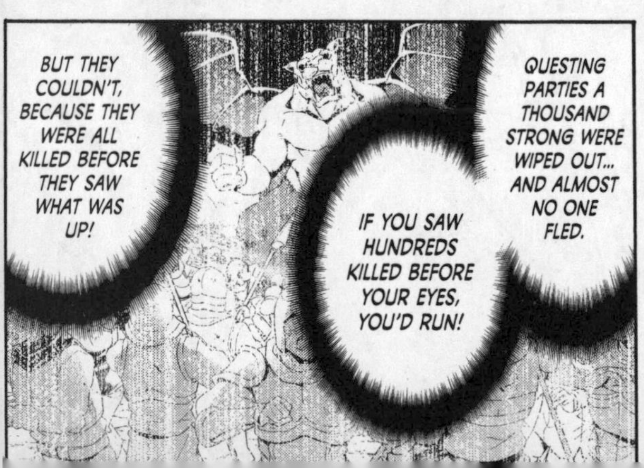
QUESTING PARTIES A THOUSAND STRONG WERE WIPED OUT... AND ALMOST NO ONE FLED.
IF YOU SAW HUNDREDS KILLED BEFORE YOUR EYES, YOU'D RUN!
BUT THEY COULDN'T, BECAUSE THEY WERE ALL KILLED BEFORE THEY SAW WHAT WAS UP!

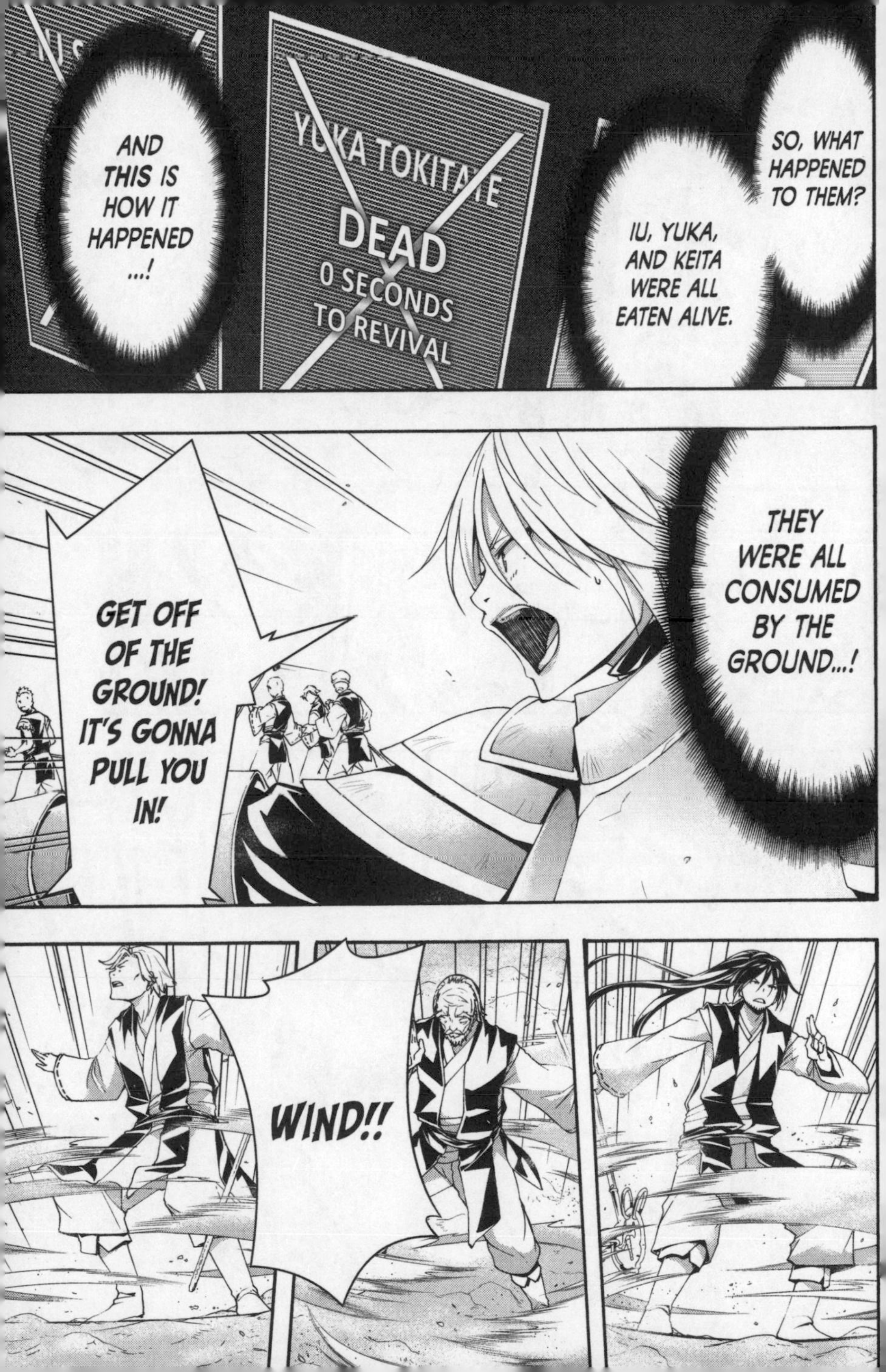
SO, WHAT HAPPENED TO THEM?
IU, YUKA, AND KEITA WERE ALL EATEN ALIVE.
YUKA TOKITATE
DEAD
0 SECONDS TO REVIVAL
AND THIS IS HOW IT HAPPENED ...!
THEY WERE ALL CONSUMED BY THE GROUND...!
GET OFF OF THE GROUND! IT'S GONNA PULL YOU IN!
WIND!!

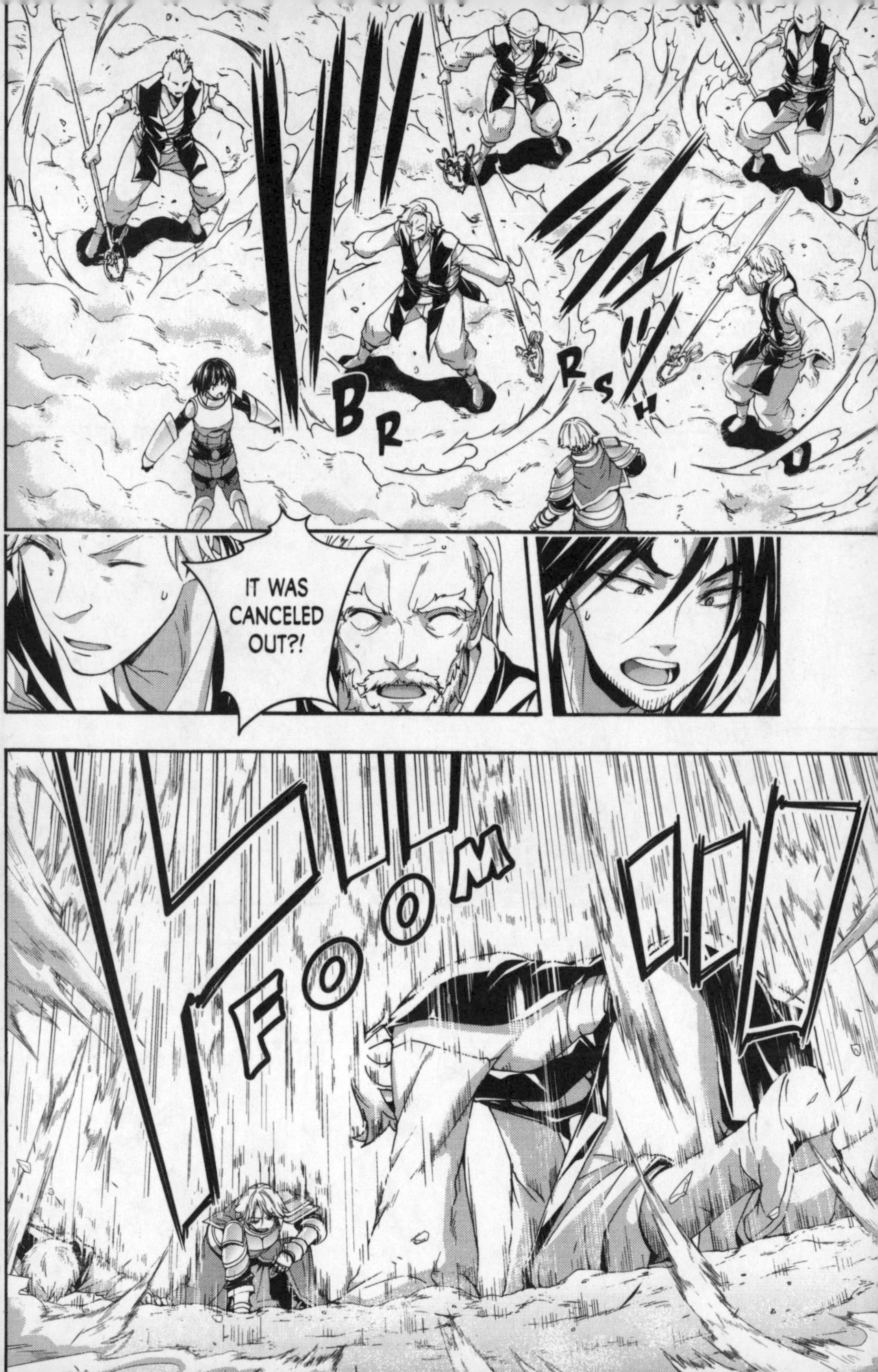
BRRSH
IT WAS CANCELED OUT?!
FOOM

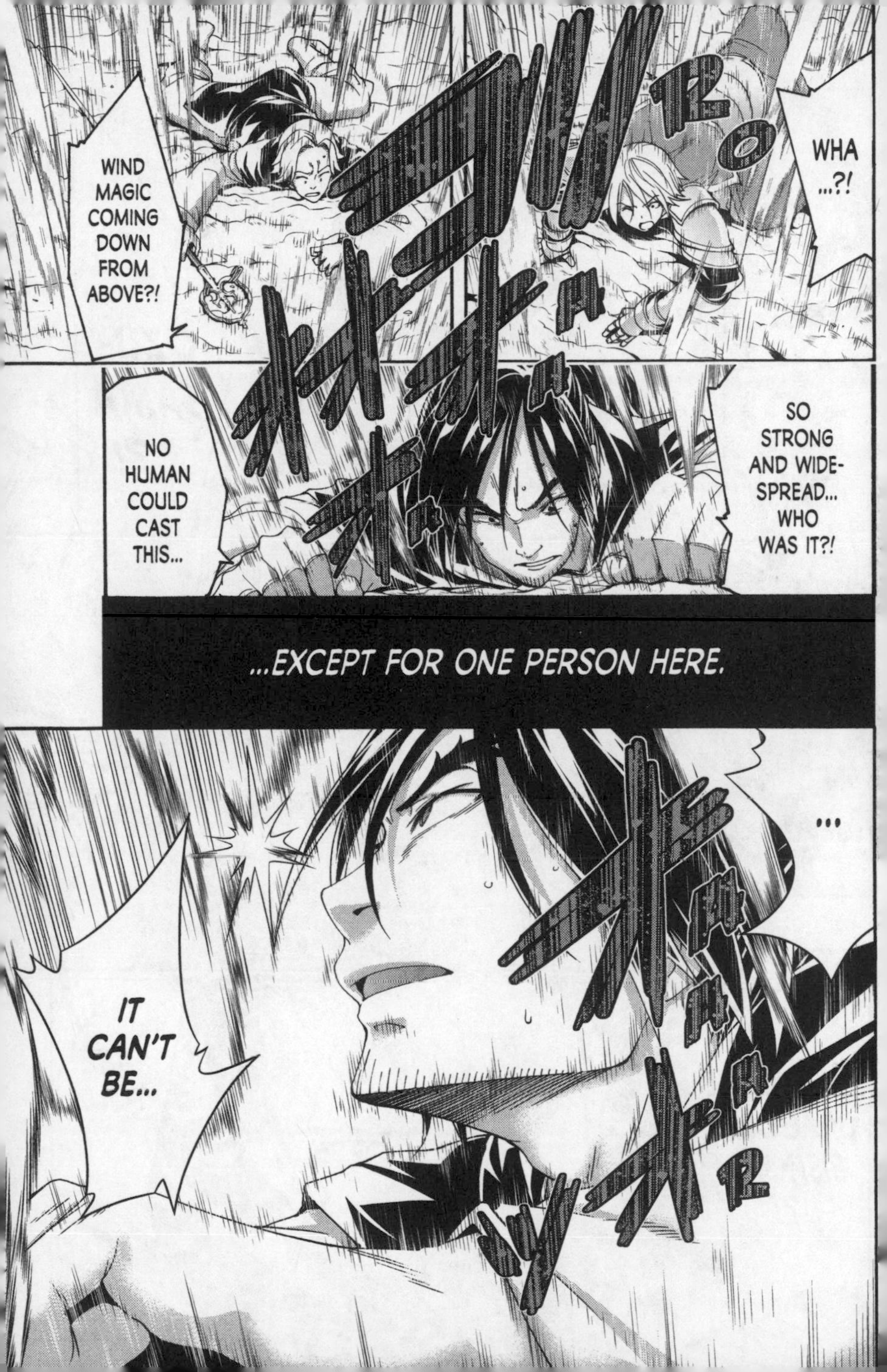
WHA ...?!
WIND MAGIC COMING DOWN FROM ABOVE?!
SO STRONG AND WIDE-SPREAD... WHO WAS IT?!
NO HUMAN COULD CAST THIS...
...EXCEPT FOR ONE PERSON HERE.
...
IT CAN'T BE...

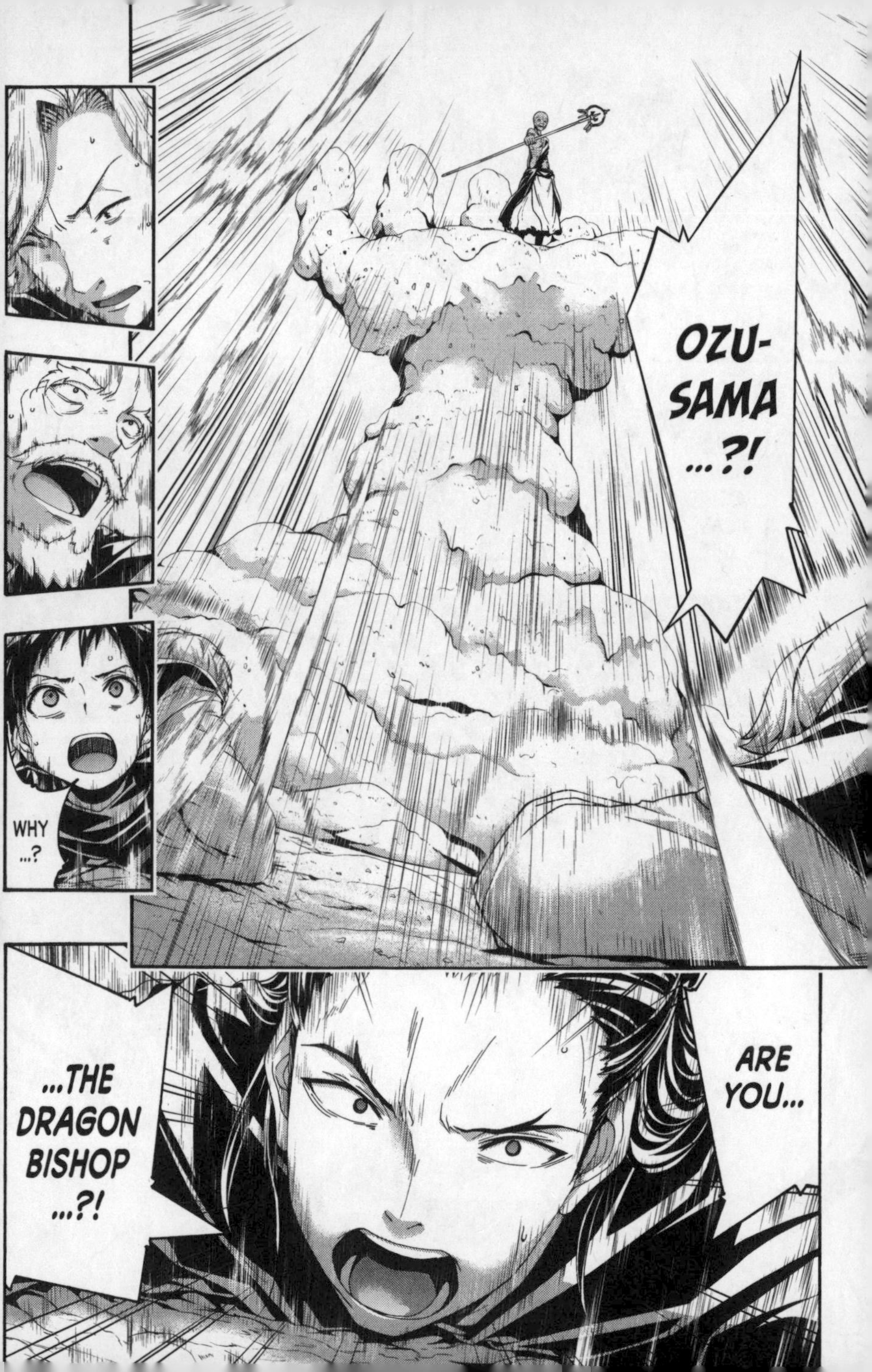
OZU-SAMA ...?!
WHY ...?
ARE YOU...
...THE DRAGON BISHOP ...?!

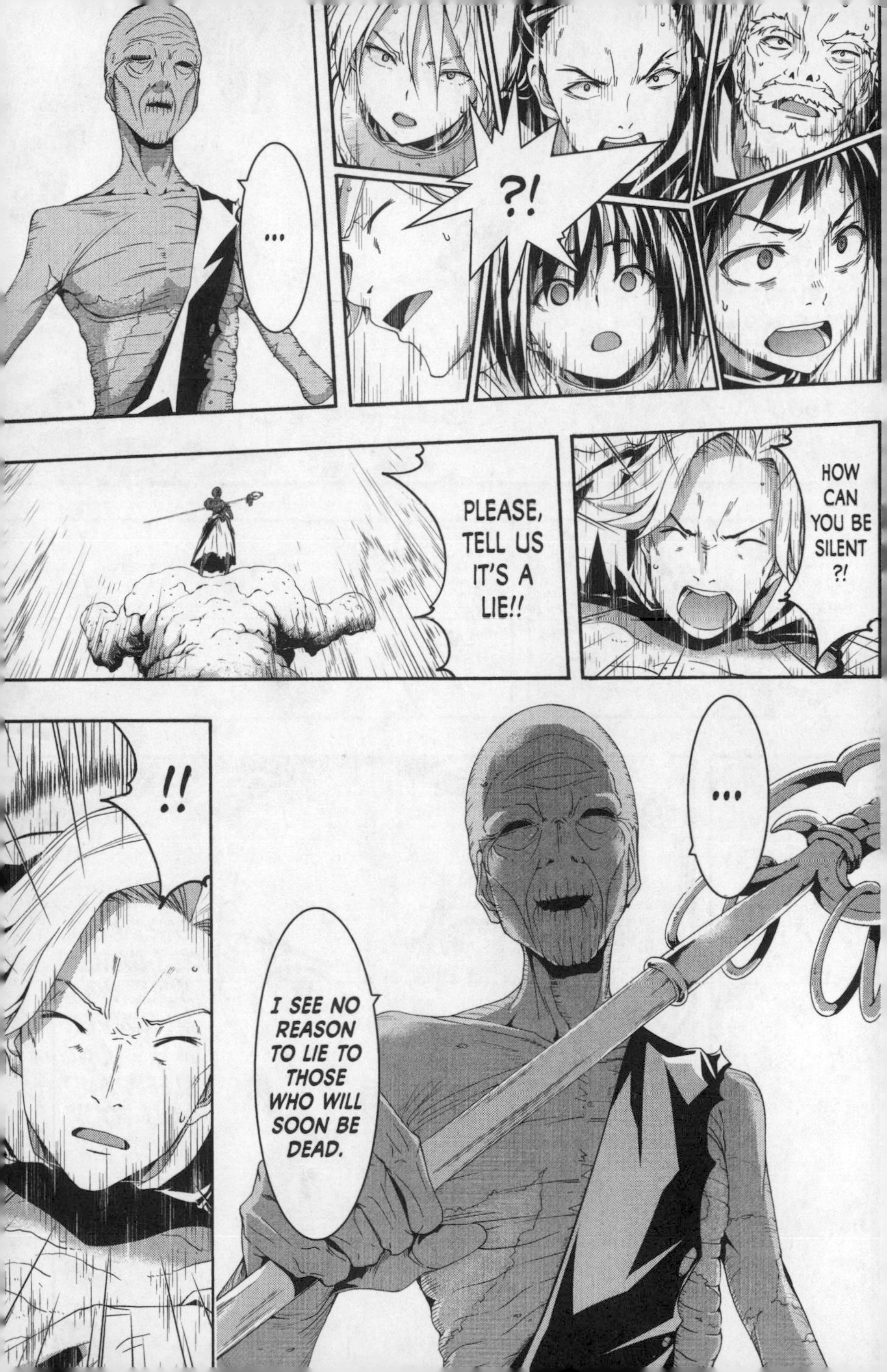
?!
...
HOW CAN YOU BE SILENT?!
PLEASE, TELL US IT'S A LIE!!
...
I SEE NO REASON TO LIE TO THOSE WHO WILL SOON BE DEAD.
!!

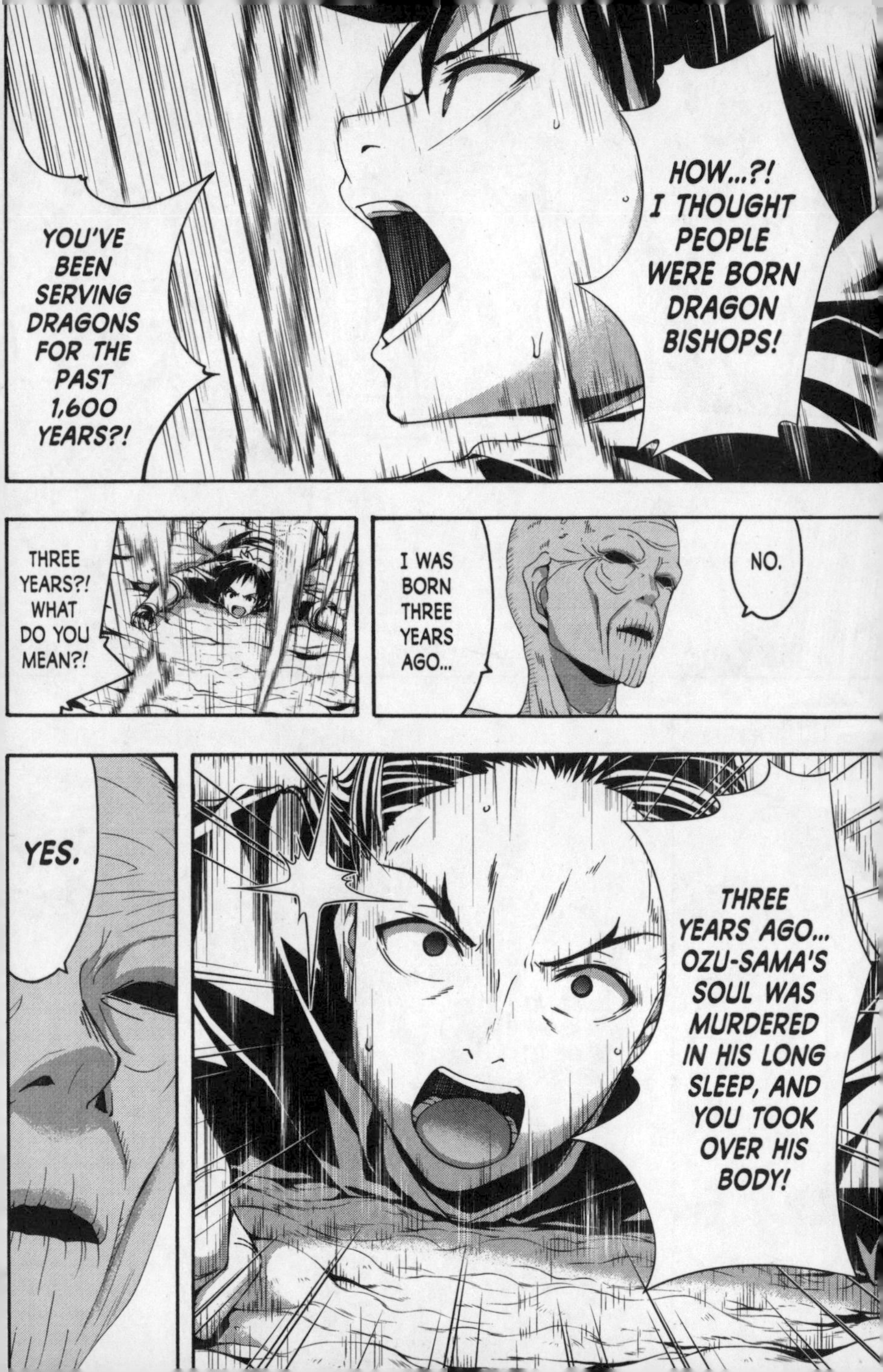
HOW...?! I THOUGHT PEOPLE WERE BORN DRAGON BISHOPS!
YOU'VE BEEN SERVING DRAGONS FOR THE PAST 1,600 YEARS?!
NO.
I WAS BORN THREE YEARS AGO...
THREE YEARS?! WHAT DO YOU MEAN?!
THREE YEARS AGO... OZU-SAMA'S SOUL WAS MURDERED IN HIS LONG SLEEP, AND YOU TOOK OVER HIS BODY!
YES.

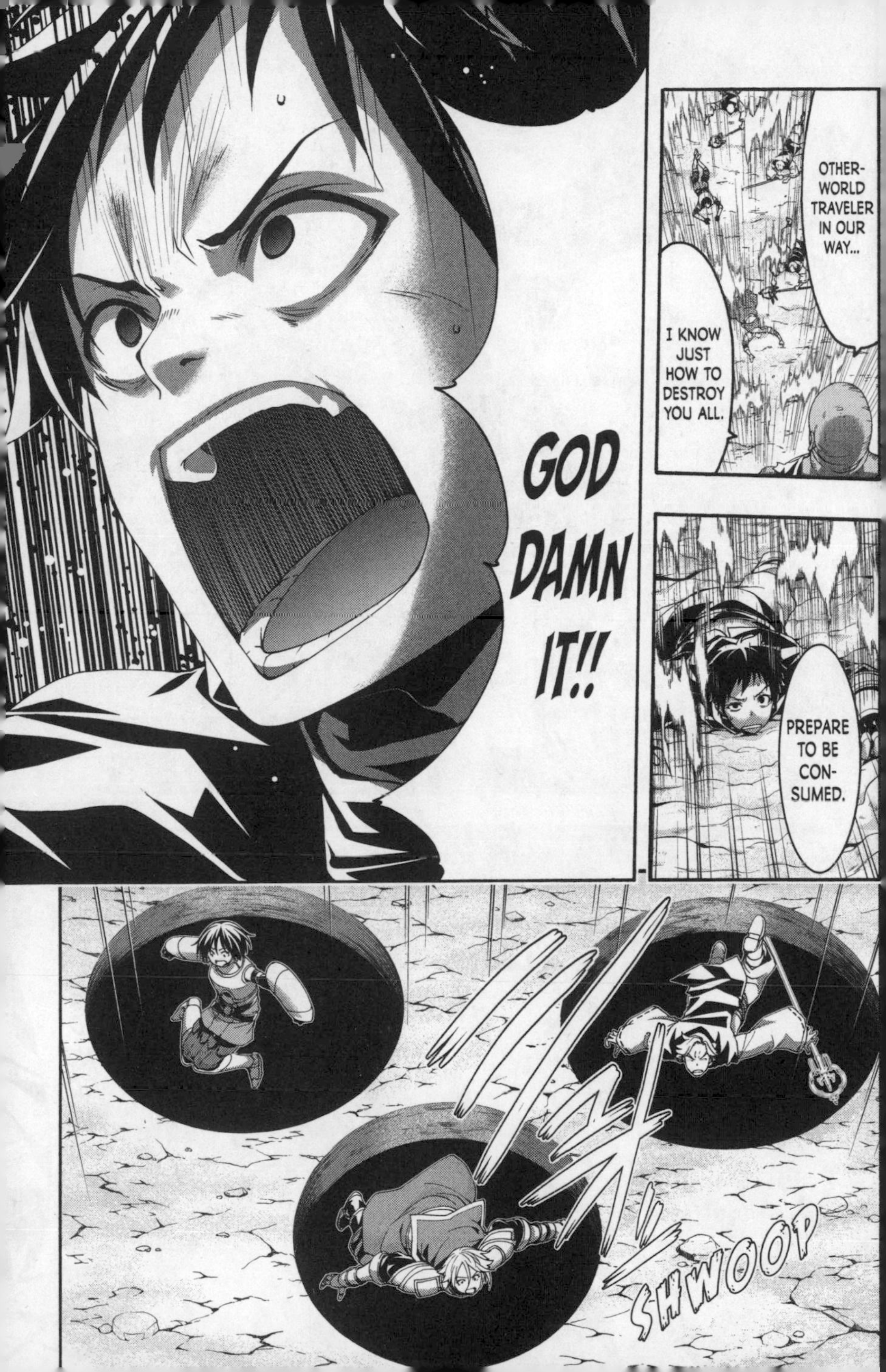
OTHER-WORLD TRAVELER IN OUR WAY...
I KNOW JUST HOW TO DESTROY YOU ALL.
PREPARE TO BE CON-SUMED.
GOD DAMN IT!!
SHWOOP

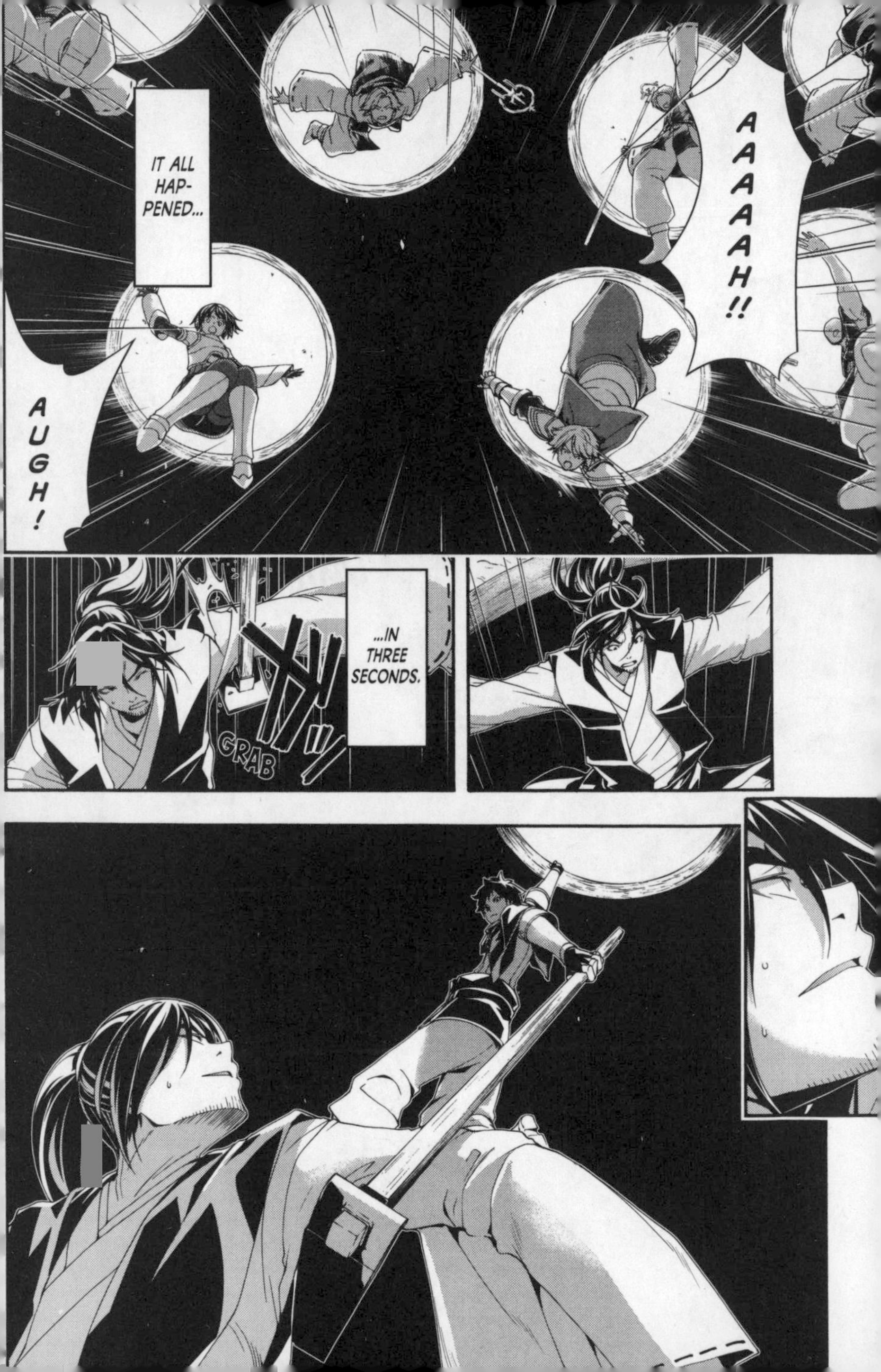
AAAAAH!!
IT ALL HAP-PENED...
AUGH!
...IN THREE SECONDS.
GRAB

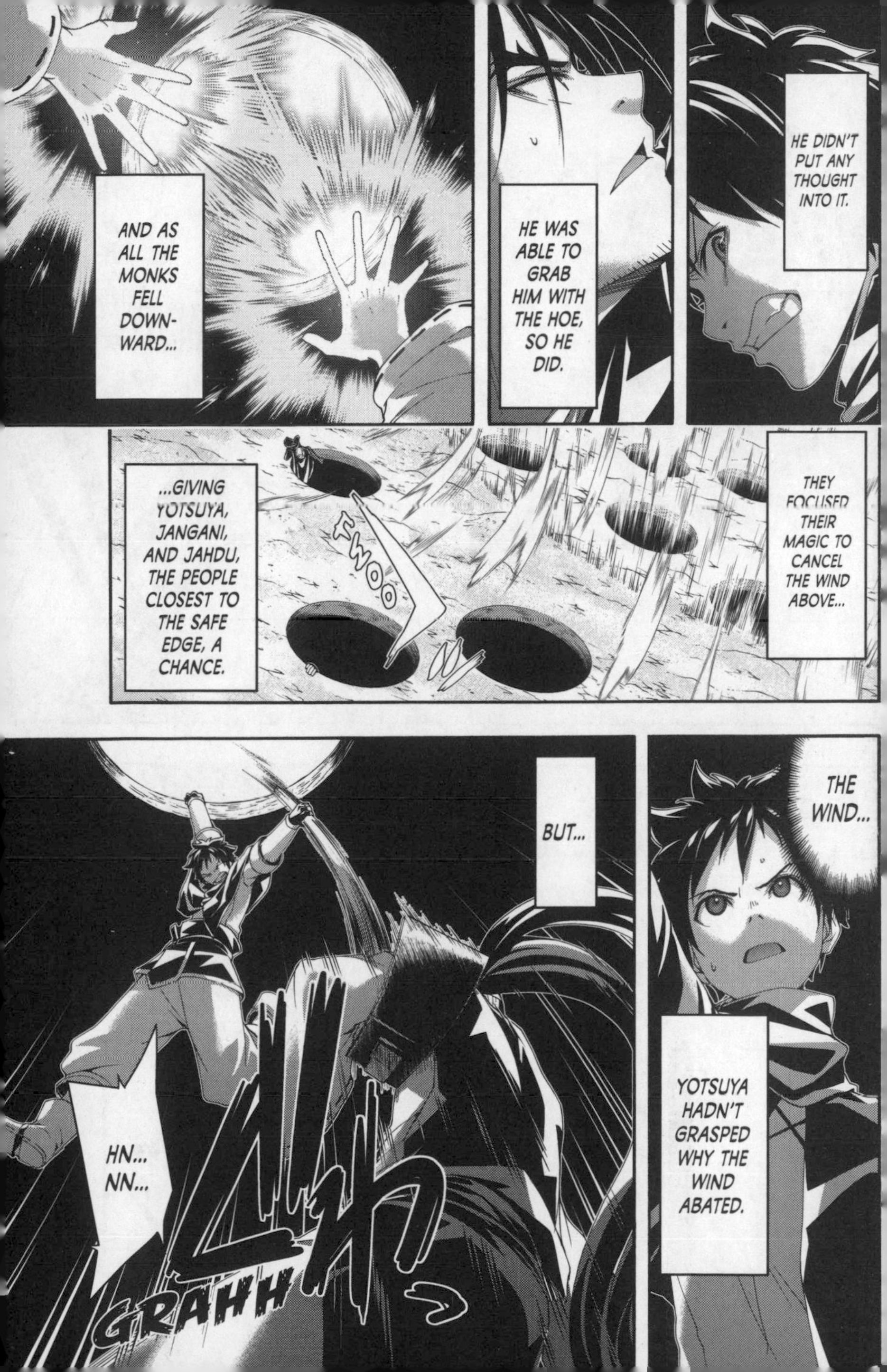
HE DIDN'T PUT ANY THOUGHT INTO IT.
HE WAS ABLE TO GRAB HIM WITH THE HOE, SO HE DID.
AND AS ALL THE MONKS FELL DOWNWARD...
THEY FOCUSED THEIR MAGIC TO CANCEL THE WIND ABOVE...
FWOO
...GIVING YOTSUYA, JANGANI, AND JAHDU, THE PEOPLE CLOSEST TO THE SAFE EDGE, A CHANCE.
THE WIND...
YOTSUYA HADN'T GRASPED WHY THE WIND ABATED.
BUT...
HN... NN...
GRAHH

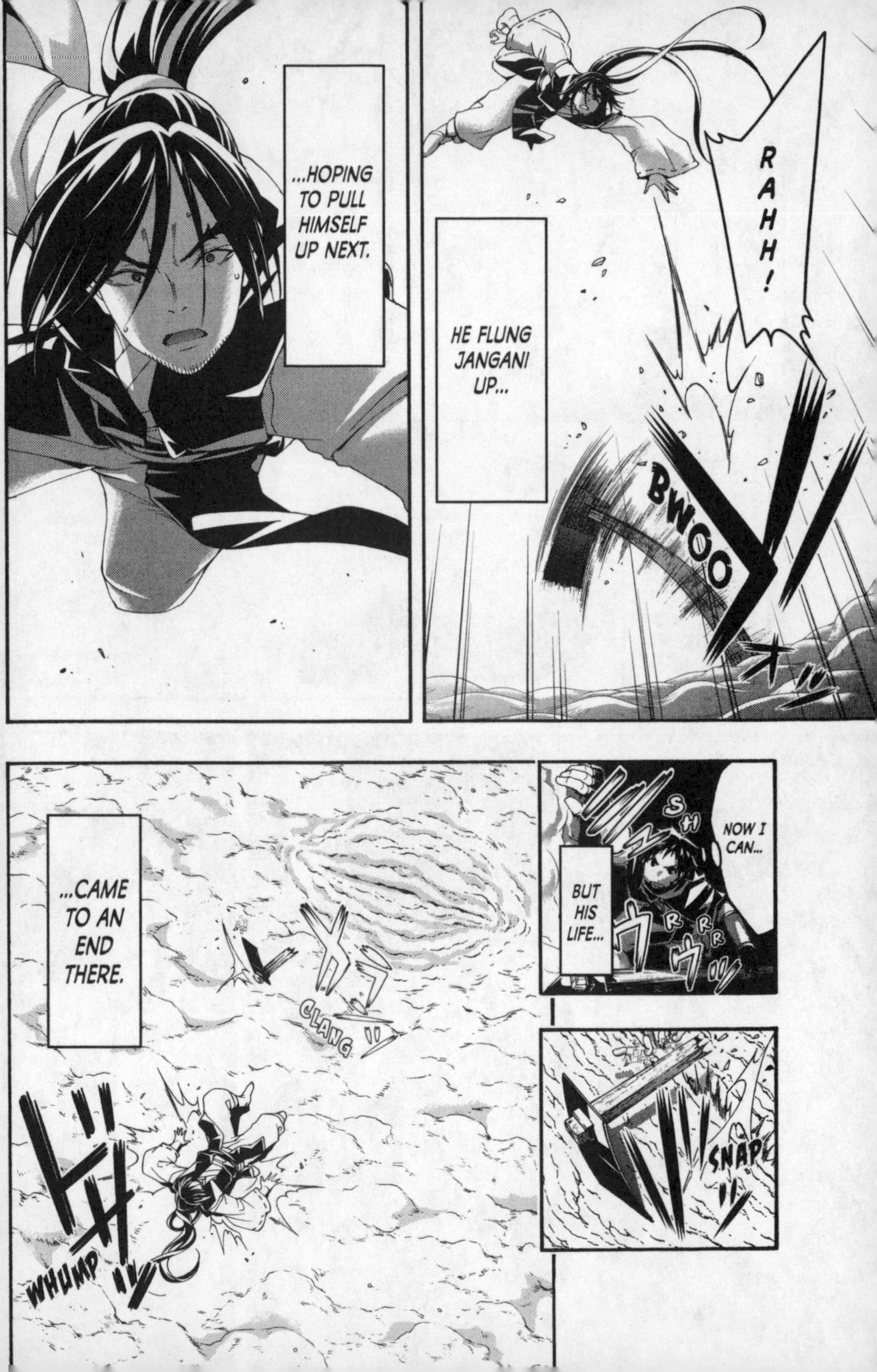
RAHH!
HE FLUNG JANGANI UP...
BWOO
...HOPING TO PULL HIMSELF UP NEXT.
NOW I CAN...
SH
BUT HIS LIFE...
RRR
SNAP
...CAME TO AN END THERE.
CLANG
WHUMP

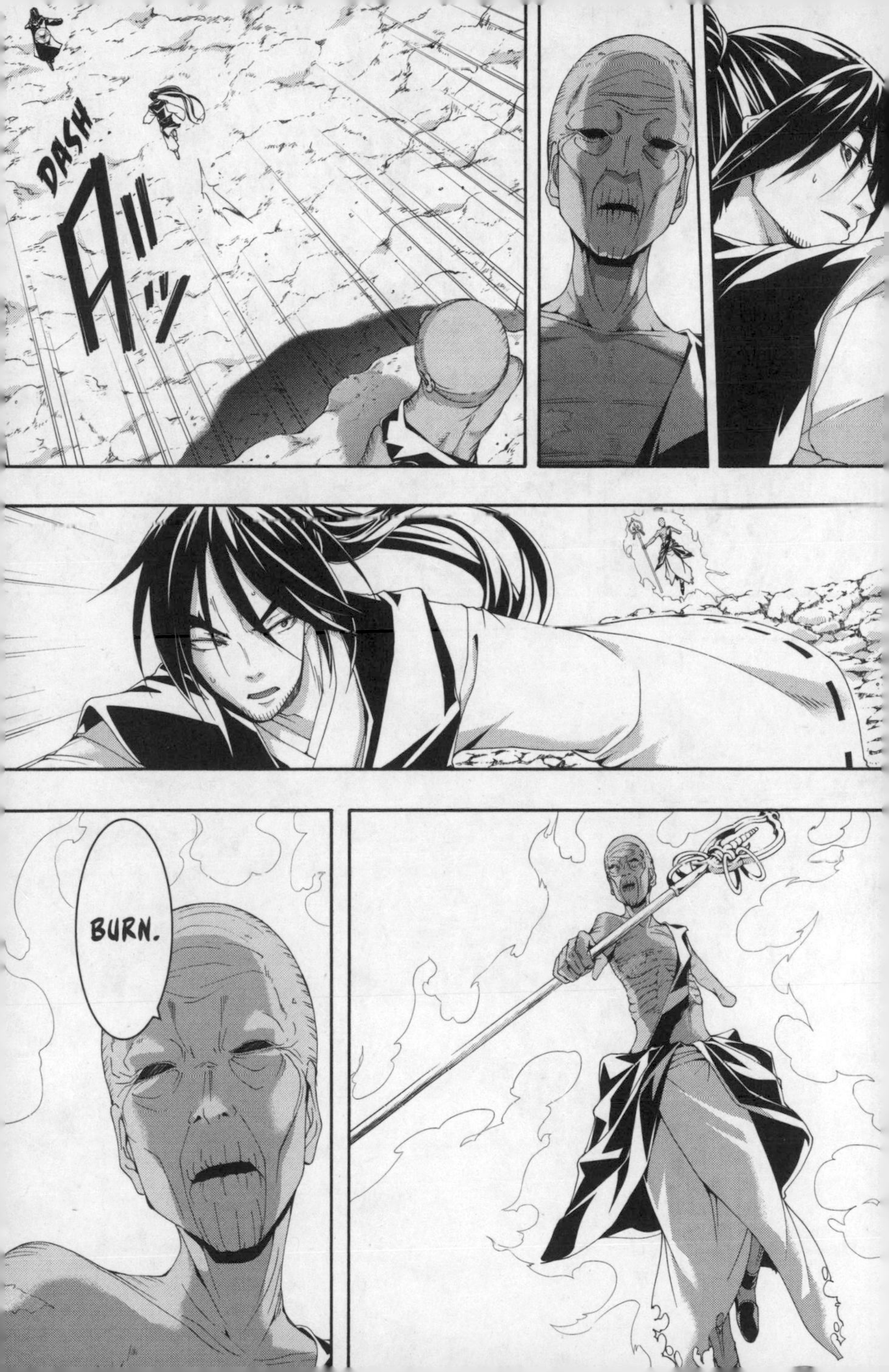
DASH
BURN.

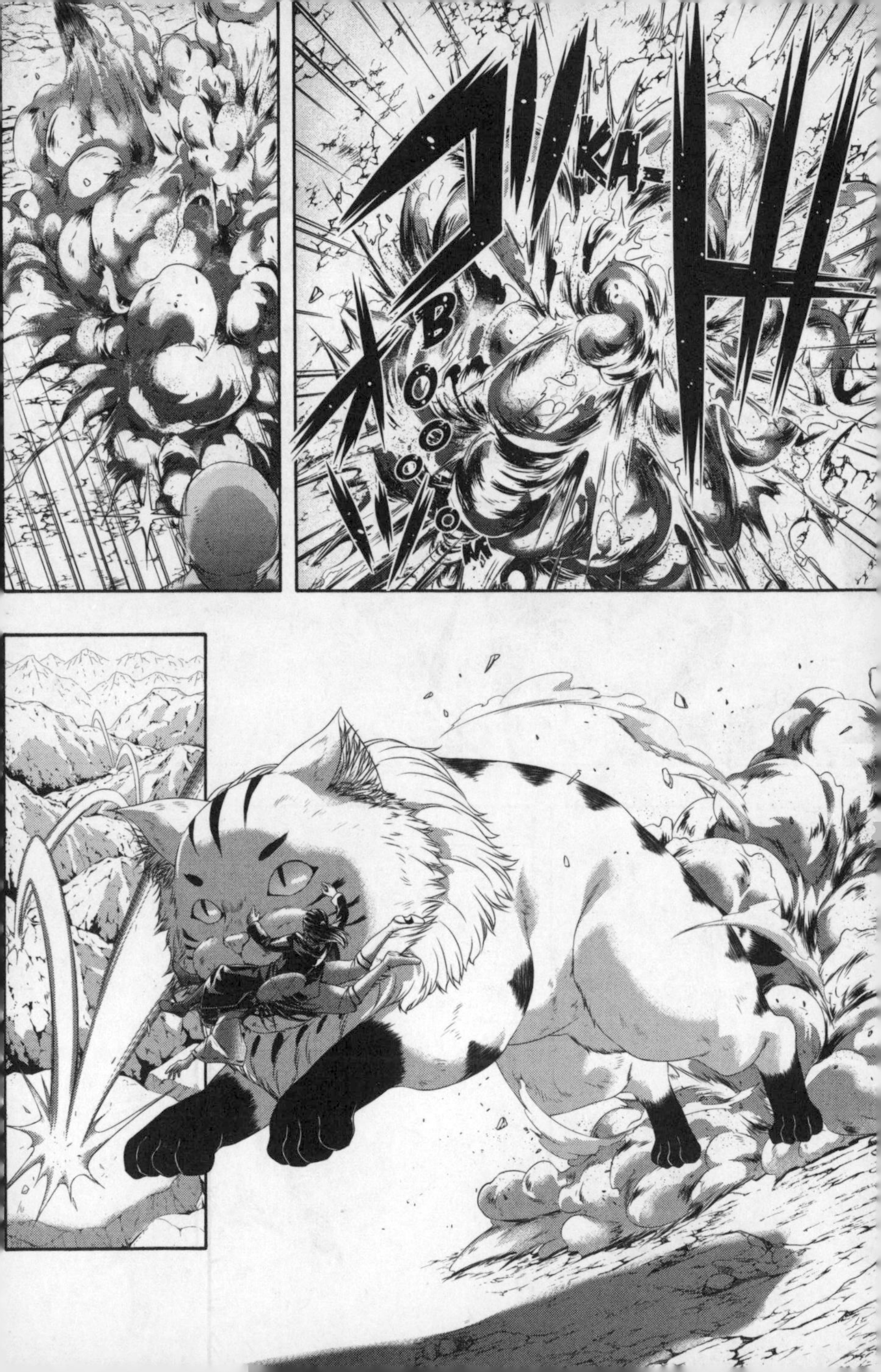
KA-
BOOOOOM

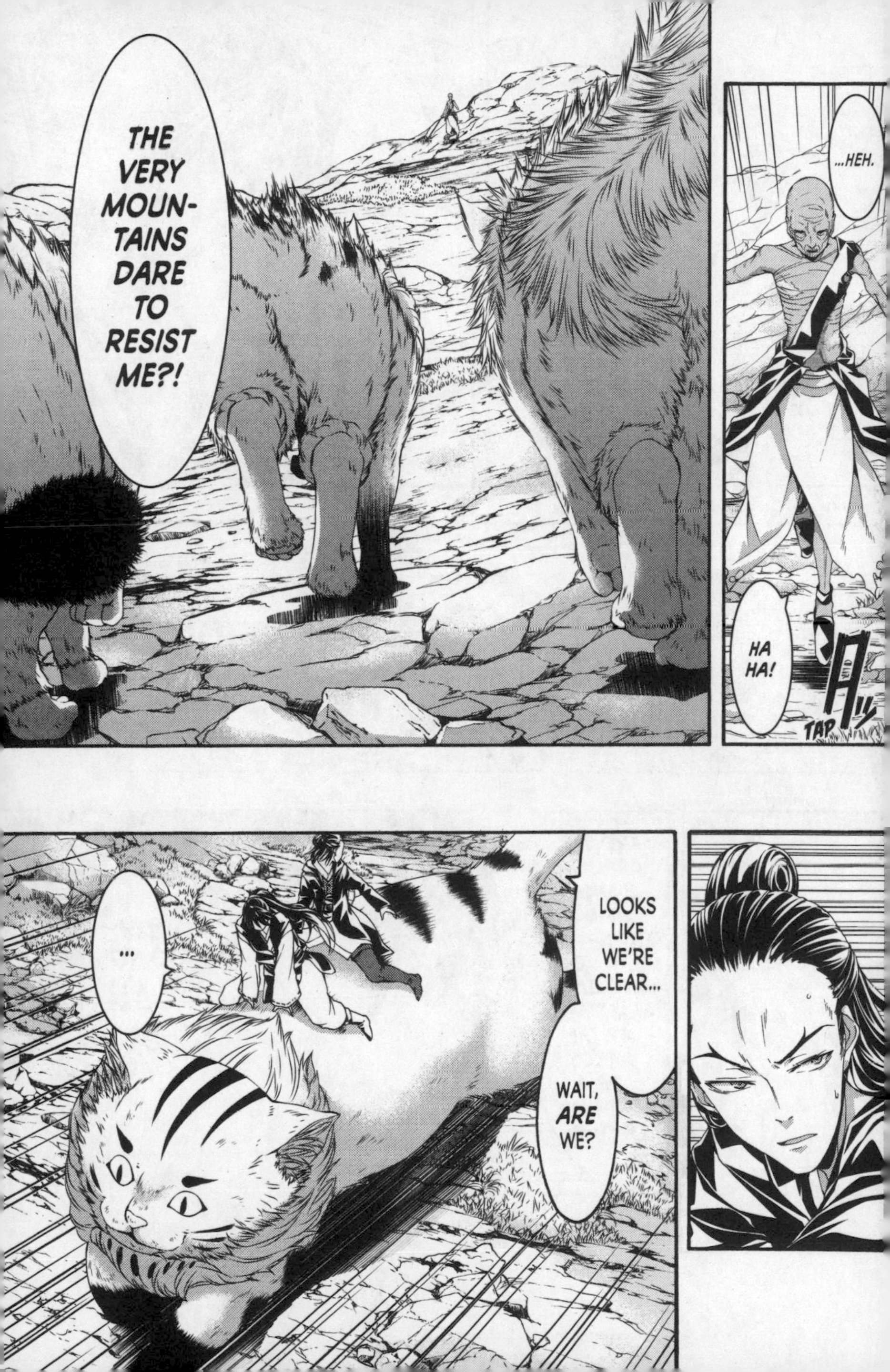
...HEH.
HA HA!
TAP
THE VERY MOUNTAINS DARE TO RESIST ME?!
LOOKS LIKE WE'RE CLEAR...
WAIT, ARE WE?
...

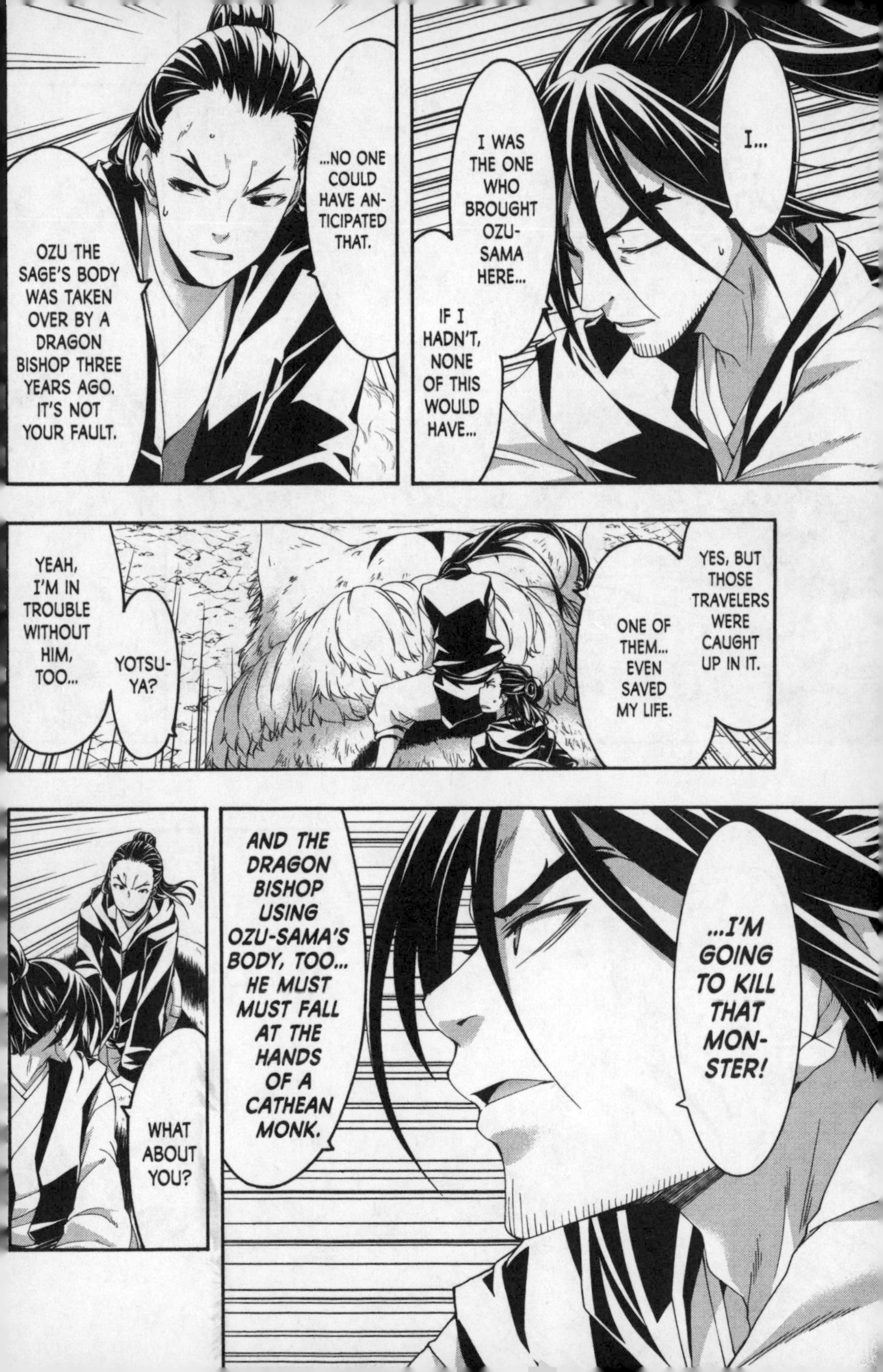
I...
I WAS THE ONE WHO BROUGHT OZU-SAMA HERE...
IF I HADN'T, NONE OF THIS WOULD HAVE...
...NO ONE COULD HAVE ANTICIPATED THAT.
OZU THE SAGE'S BODY WAS TAKEN OVER BY A DRAGON BISHOP THREE YEARS AGO. IT'S NOT YOUR FAULT.
YES, BUT THOSE TRAVELERS WERE CAUGHT UP IN IT.
ONE OF THEM... EVEN SAVED MY LIFE.
YEAH, I'M IN TROUBLE WITHOUT HIM, TOO...
YOTSUYA?
...I'M GOING TO KILL THAT MONSTER!
AND THE DRAGON BISHOP USING OZU-SAMA'S BODY, TOO... HE MUST MUST FALL AT THE HANDS OF A CATHEAN MONK.
WHAT ABOUT YOU?

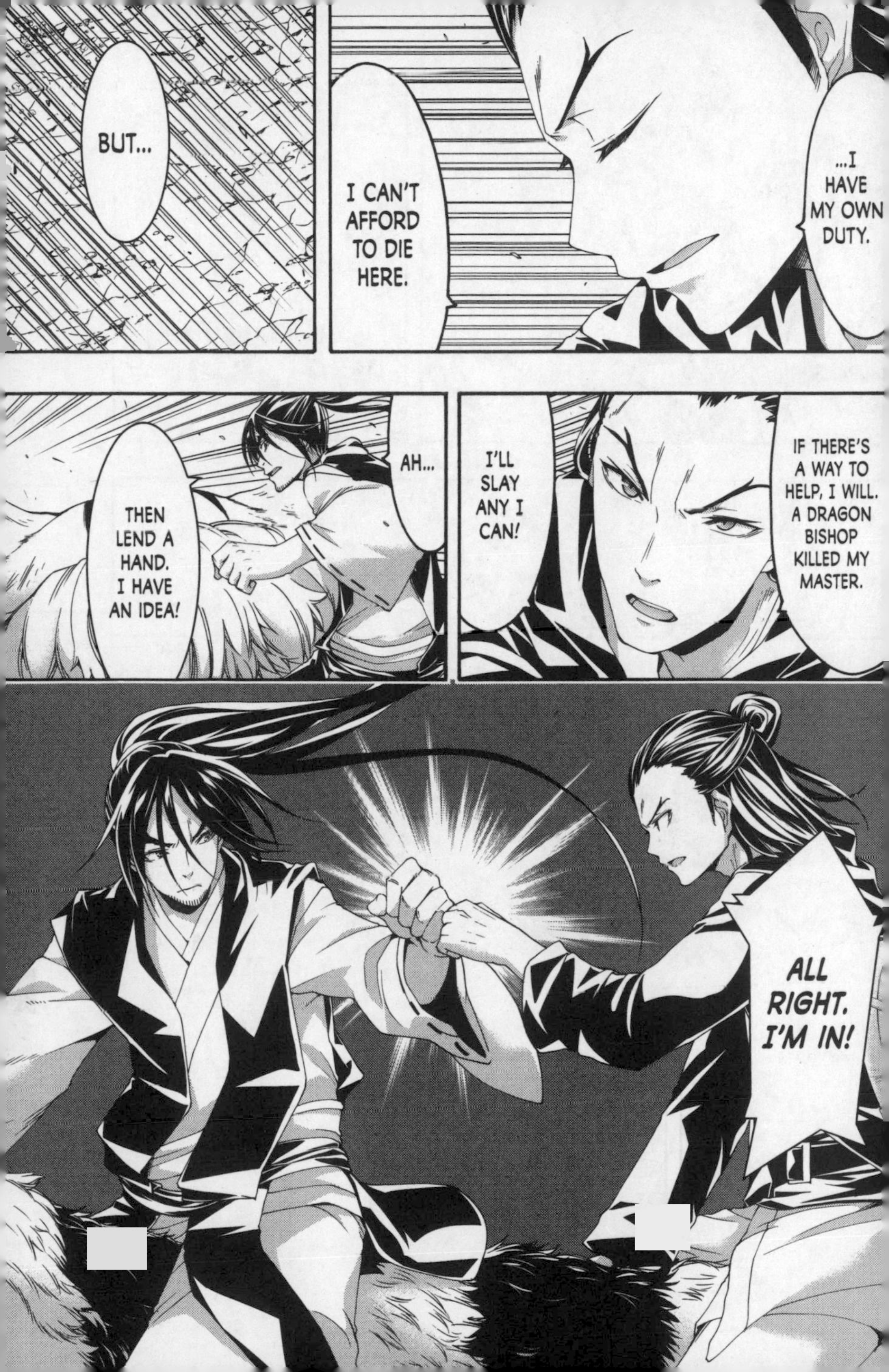
...I HAVE MY OWN DUTY.
I CAN'T AFFORD TO DIE HERE.
BUT...
IF THERE'S A WAY TO HELP, I WILL. A DRAGON BISHOP KILLED MY MASTER.
I'LL SLAY ANY I CAN!
AH...
THEN LEND A HAND. I HAVE AN IDEA!
ALL RIGHT. I'M IN!

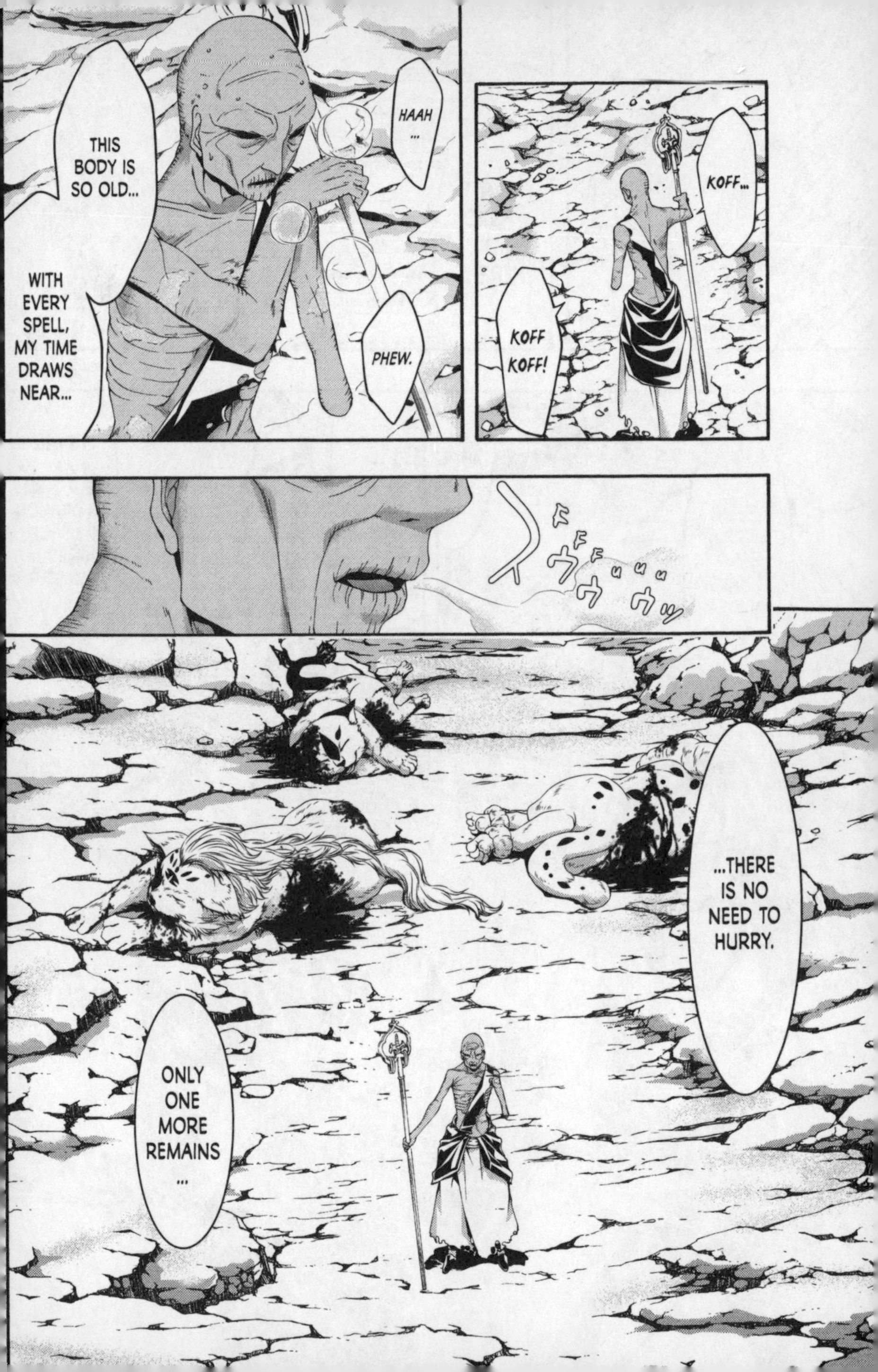
KOFF...
KOFF KOFF!
HAAH ...
THIS BODY IS SO OLD...
WITH EVERY SPELL, MY TIME DRAWS NEAR...
PHEW.
...THERE IS NO NEED TO HURRY.
ONLY ONE MORE REMAINS ...

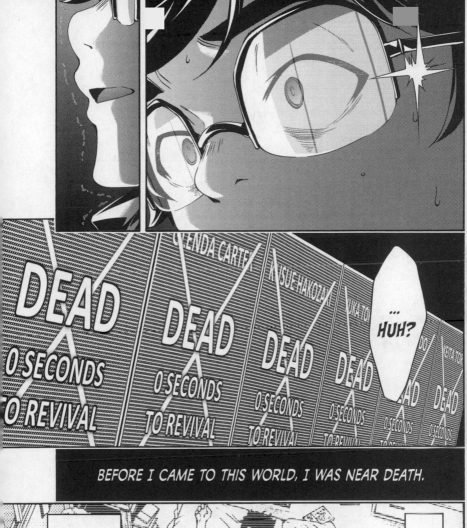

DEAD
0 SECONDS
TO REVIVAL

DEAD
0 SECONDS
TO REVIVAL

DEAD
0 SECONDS
TO REVIVAL

DEAD
0 SECONDS
TO REVIVAL

...HUH?

GLENDA CARTER

KISUE HAKOZAKI

BEFORE I CAME TO THIS WORLD, I WAS NEAR DEATH.

I FIGURED IT'D BE FINE TO DIE IN EITHER WORLD.

AT FIRST...

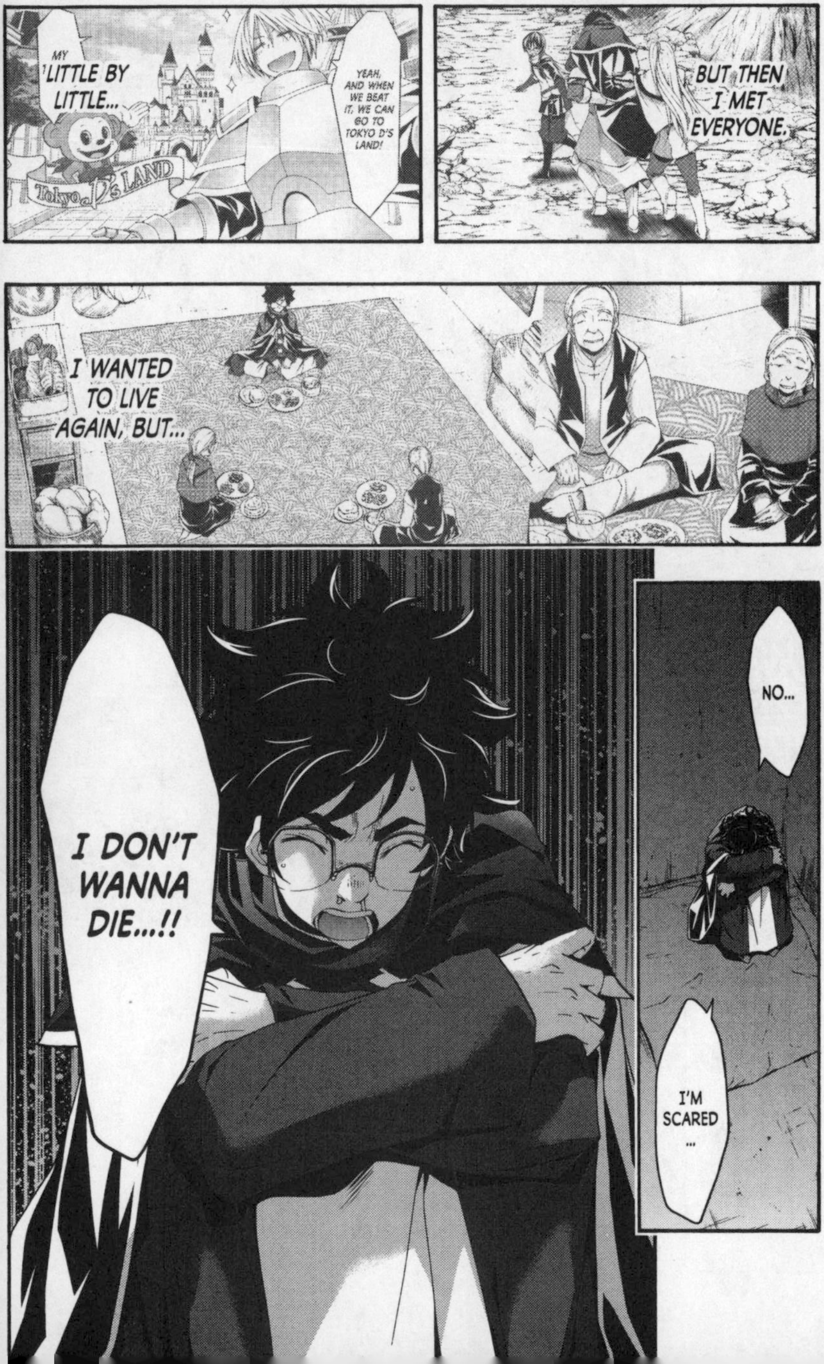
BUT THEN I MET EVERYONE.
YEAH, AND WHEN WE BEAT IT, WE CAN GO TO TOKYO D's LAND!
MY LITTLE BY LITTLE...
Tokyo D's LAND
I WANTED TO LIVE AGAIN, BUT...
NO...
I'M SCARED ...
I DON'T WANNA DIE...!!

I'M STANDING ON A MILLION LIVES

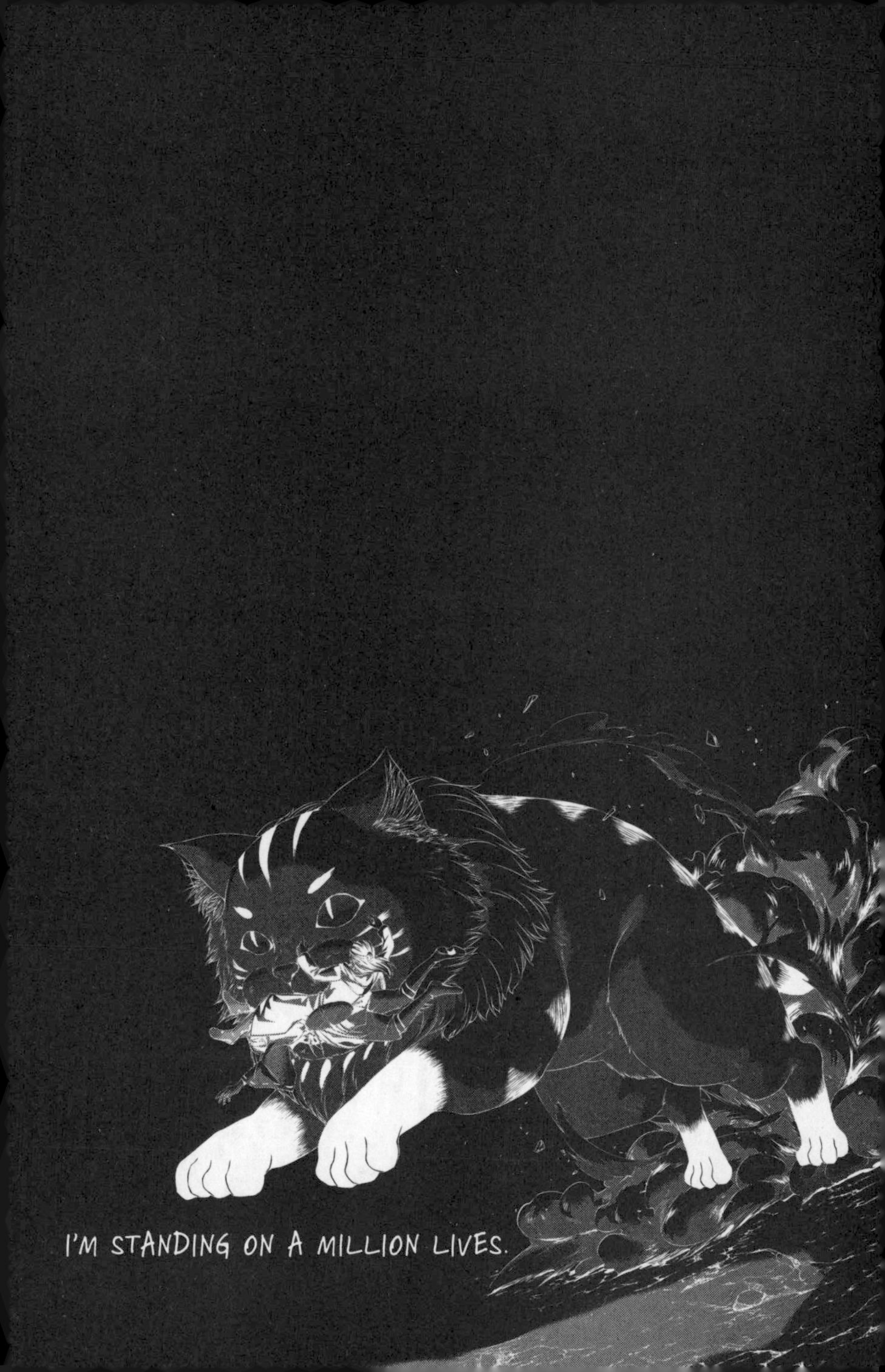
I'M STANDING ON A MILLION LIVES.

#57 Considering an Alternate Program

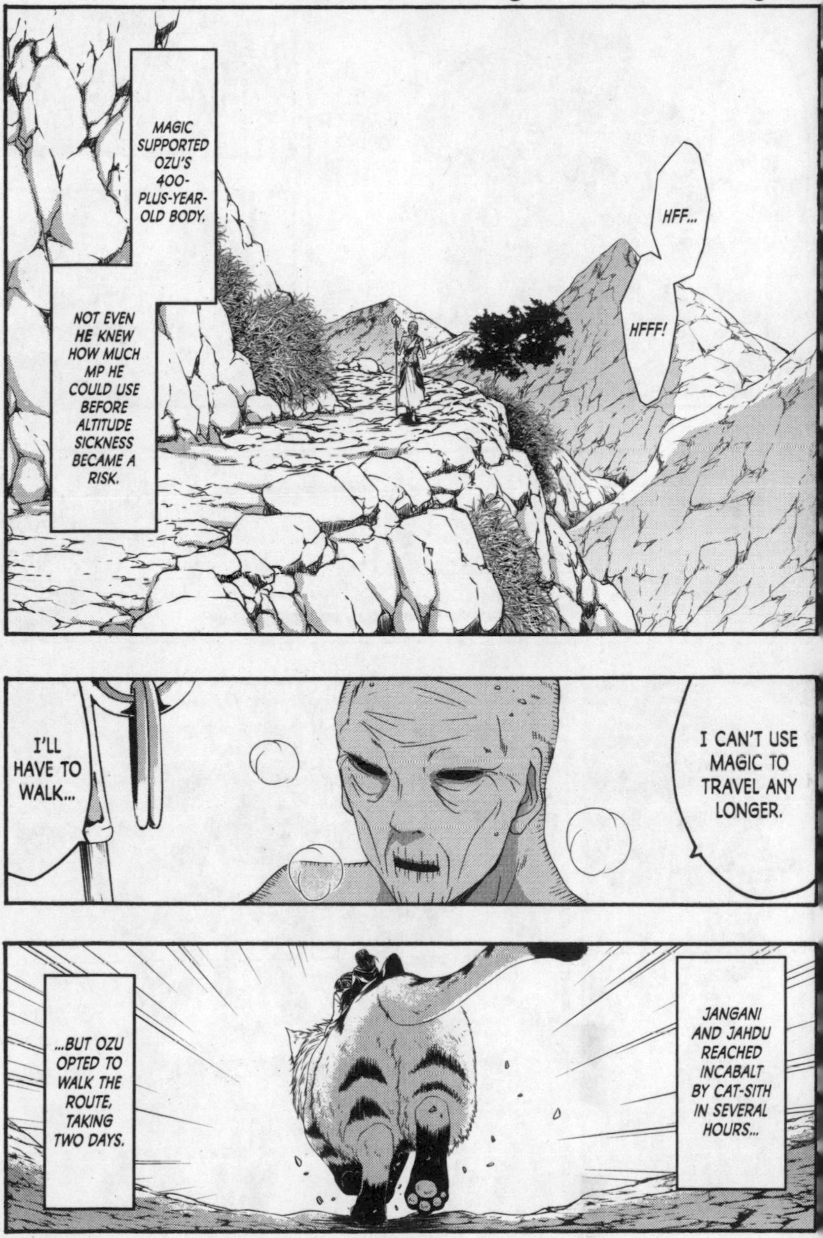
HFF...
HFFF!
MAGIC SUPPORTED OZU'S 400-PLUS-YEAR-OLD BODY.
NOT EVEN HE KNEW HOW MUCH MP HE COULD USE BEFORE ALTITUDE SICKNESS BECAME A RISK.
I CAN'T USE MAGIC TO TRAVEL ANY LONGER.
I'LL HAVE TO WALK...
JANGANI AND JAHDU REACHED INCABALT BY CAT-SITH IN SEVERAL HOURS...
...BUT OZU OPTED TO WALK THE ROUTE, TAKING TWO DAYS.

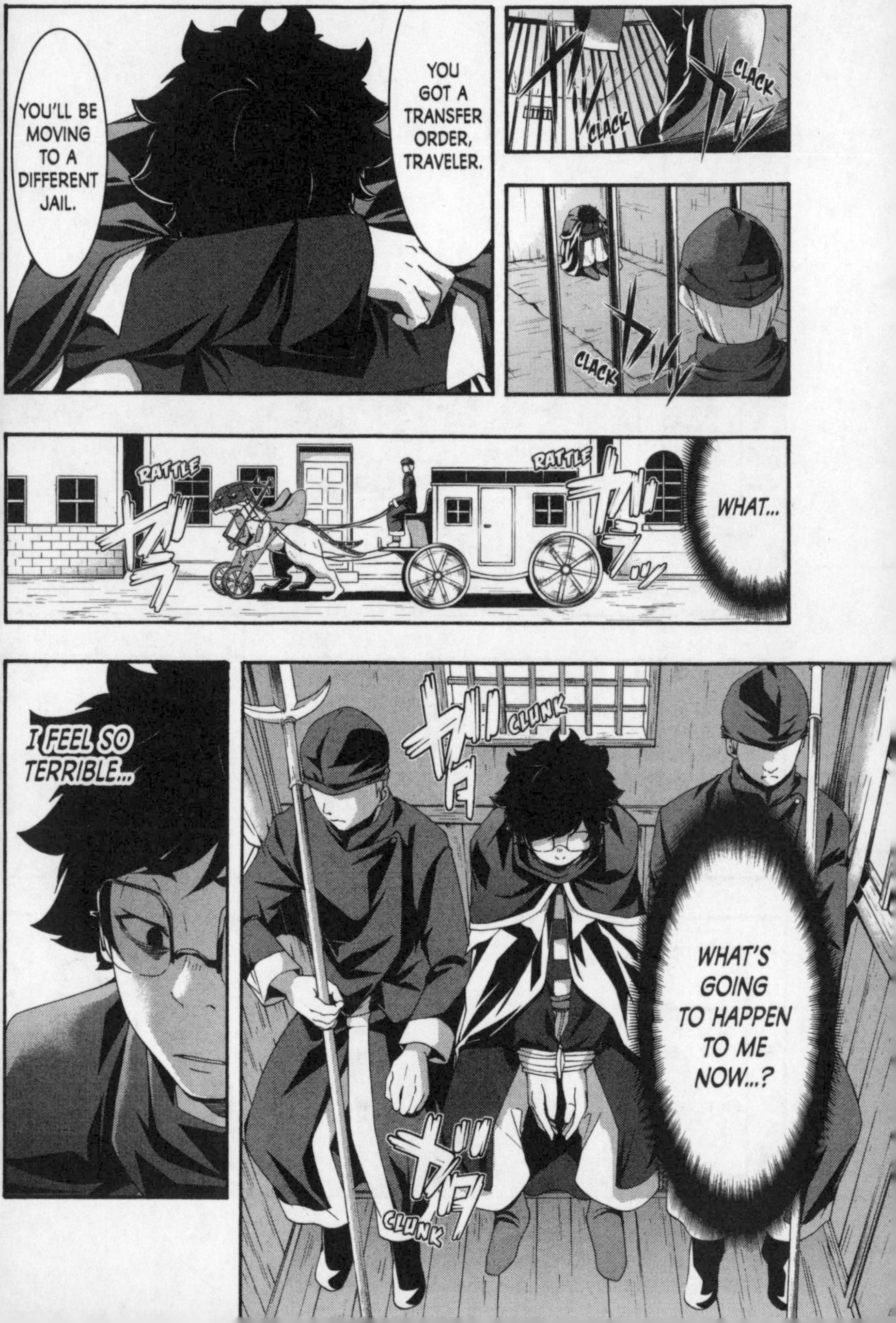
CLACK
CLACK
CLACK
YOU GOT A TRANSFER ORDER, TRAVELER.
YOU'LL BE MOVING TO A DIFFERENT JAIL.
WHAT...
RATTLE
RATTLE
CLUNK
WHAT'S GOING TO HAPPEN TO ME NOW...?
CLUNK
I FEEL SO TERRIBLE...

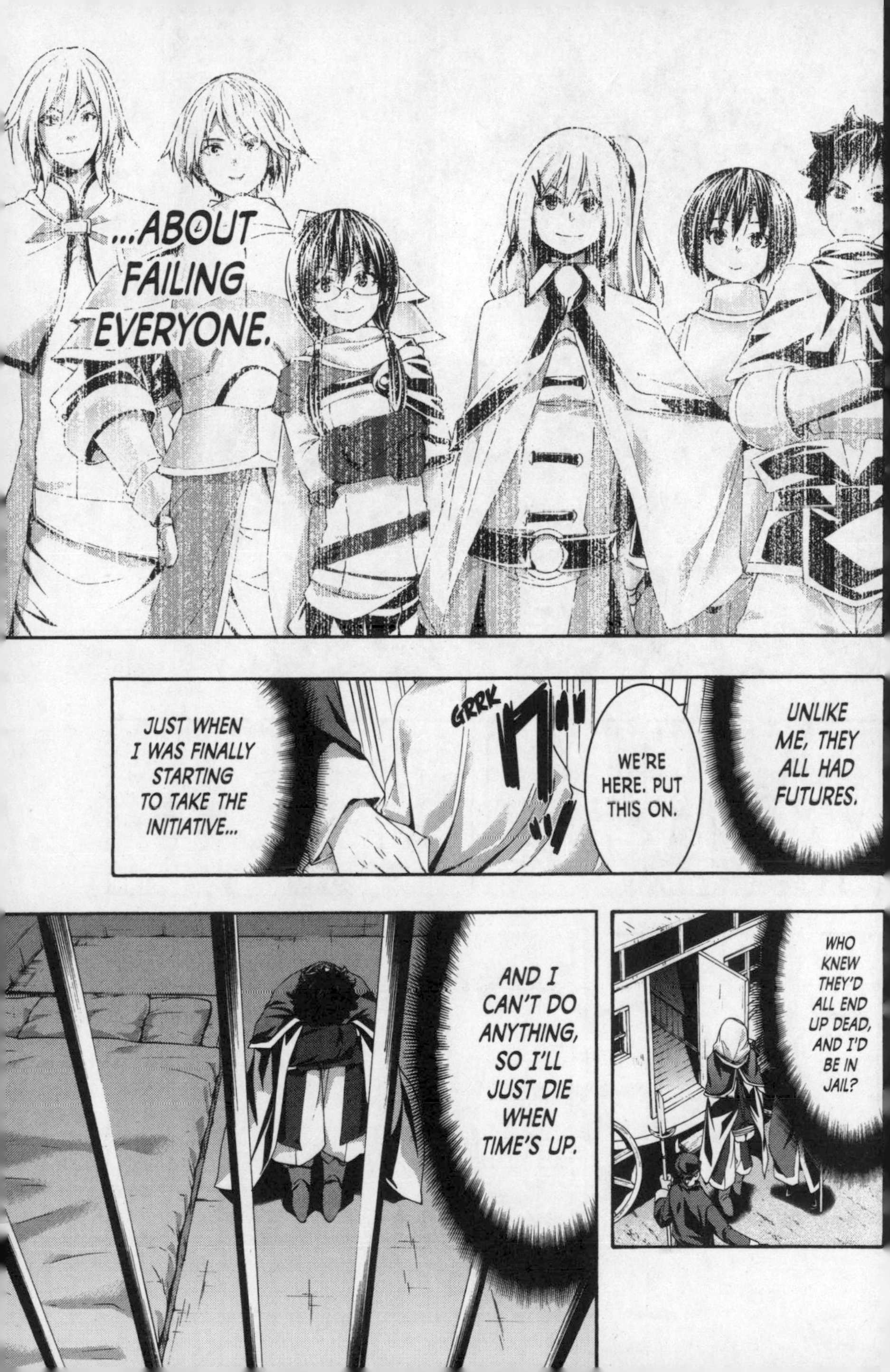
...ABOUT FAILING EVERYONE.
UNLIKE ME, THEY ALL HAD FUTURES.
WE'RE HERE. PUT THIS ON.
GRRK
JUST WHEN I WAS FINALLY STARTING TO TAKE THE INITIATIVE...
WHO KNEW THEY'D ALL END UP DEAD, AND I'D BE IN JAIL?
AND I CAN'T DO ANYTHING, SO I'LL JUST DIE WHEN TIME'S UP.

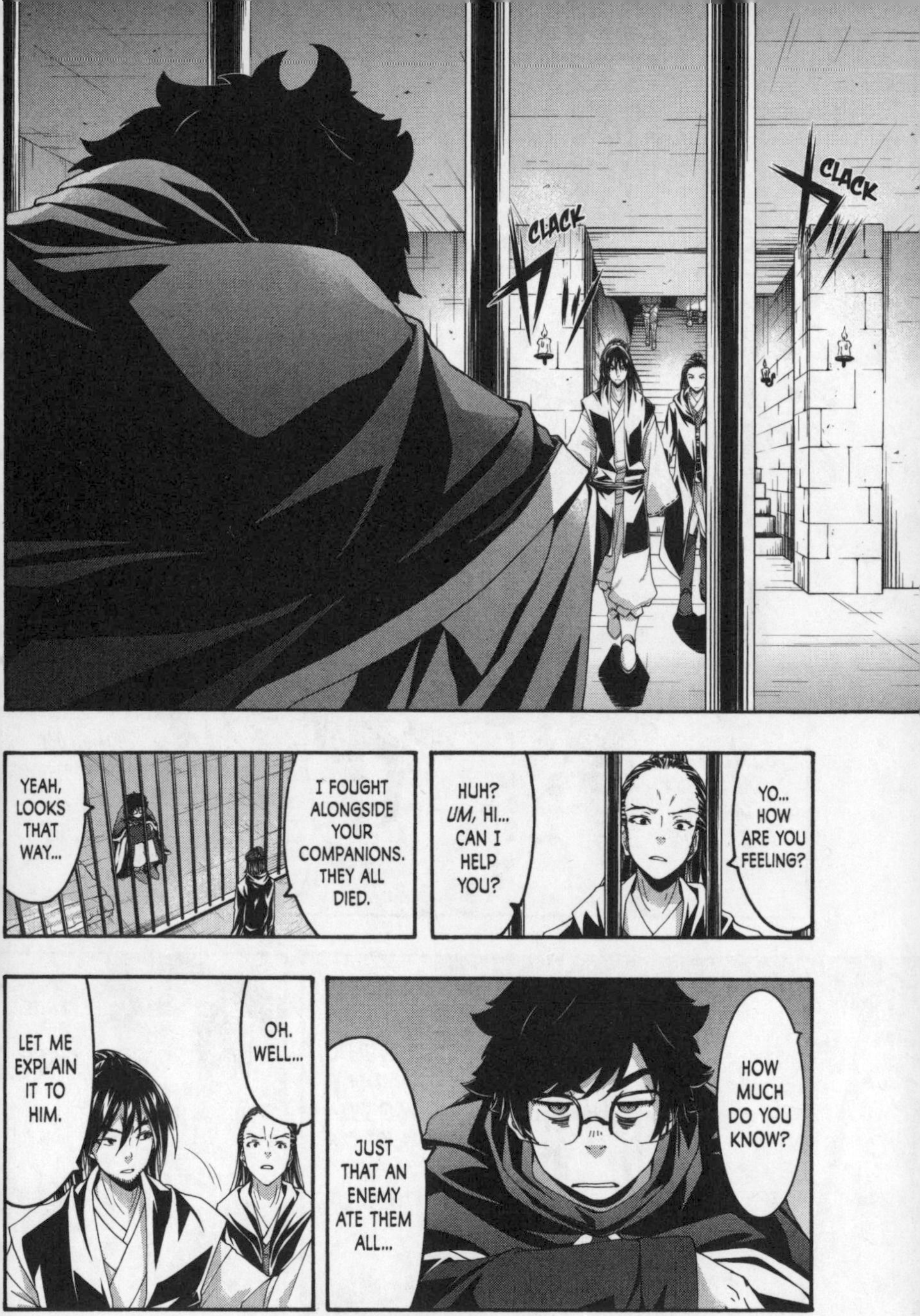
CLACK
CLACK
YO... HOW ARE YOU FEELING?
HUH? *UM,* HI... CAN I HELP YOU?
I FOUGHT ALONGSIDE YOUR COMPANIONS. THEY ALL DIED.
YEAH, LOOKS THAT WAY...
HOW MUCH DO YOU KNOW?
JUST THAT AN ENEMY ATE THEM ALL...
OH. WELL...
LET ME EXPLAIN IT TO HIM.

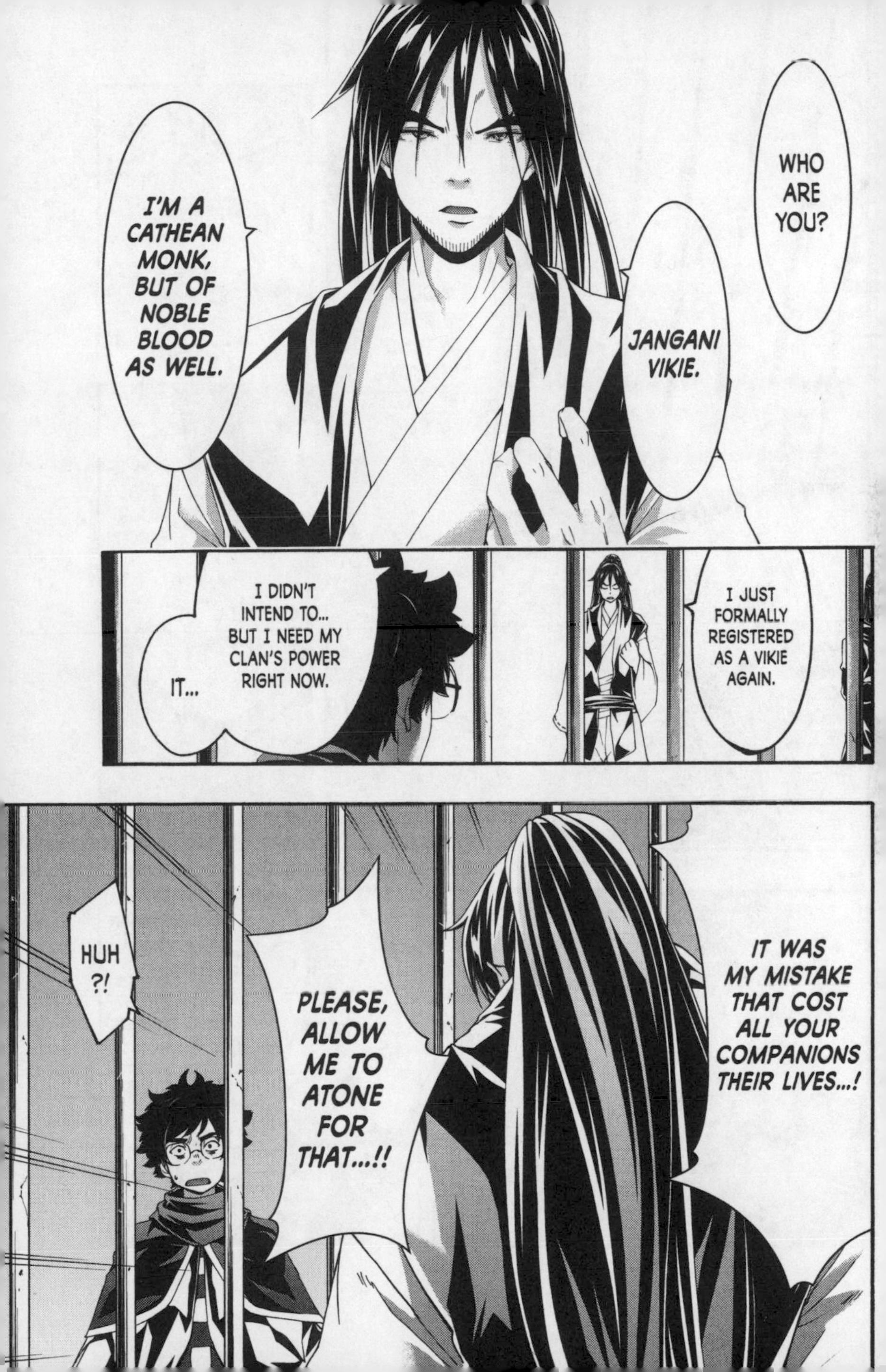
WHO ARE YOU?
JANGANI VIKIE.
I'M A CATHEAN MONK, BUT OF NOBLE BLOOD AS WELL.
I JUST FORMALLY REGISTERED AS A VIKIE AGAIN.
I DIDN'T INTEND TO... BUT I NEED MY CLAN'S POWER RIGHT NOW.
IT...
IT WAS MY MISTAKE THAT COST ALL YOUR COMPANIONS THEIR LIVES...!
PLEASE, ALLOW ME TO ATONE FOR THAT...!!
HUH?!

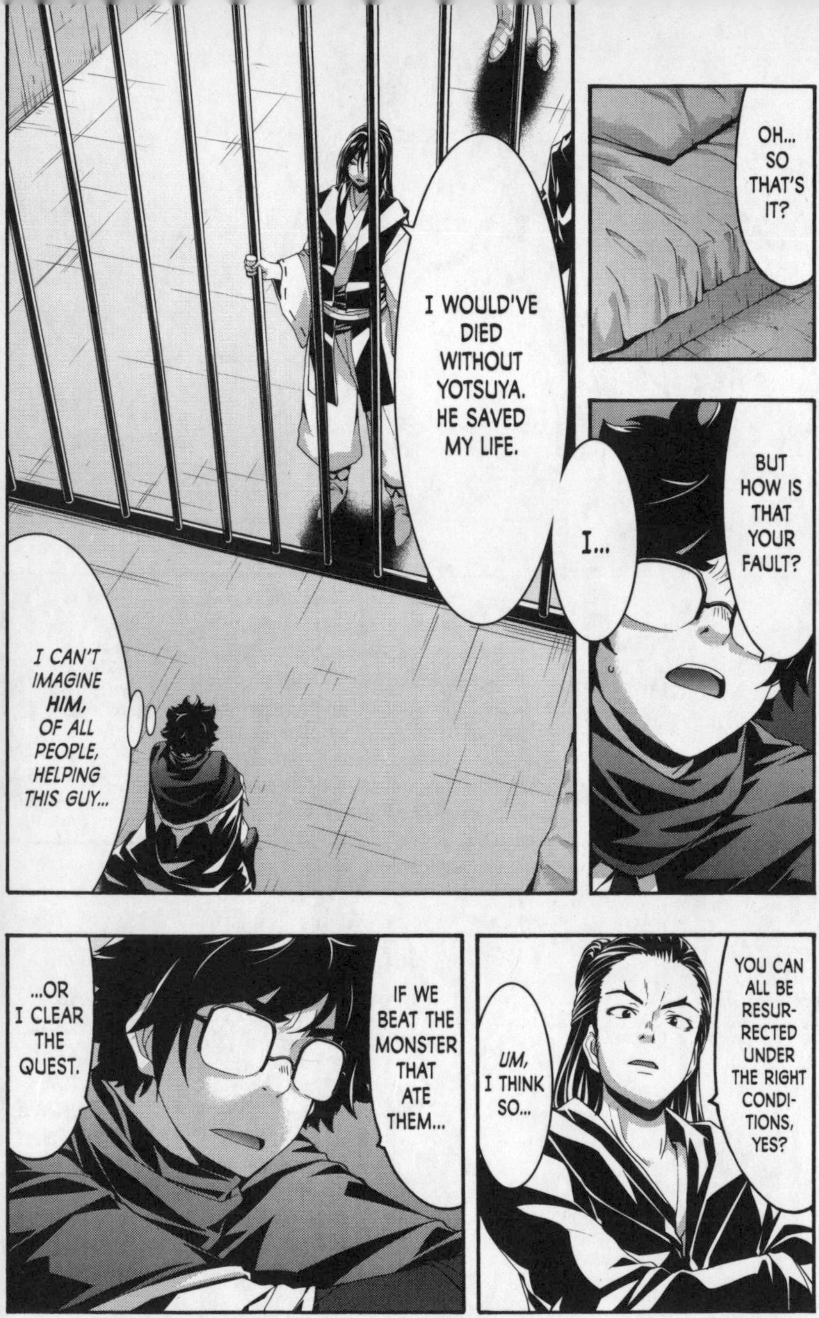
OH... SO THAT'S IT?
BUT HOW IS THAT YOUR FAULT?
I...
I WOULD'VE DIED WITHOUT YOTSUYA. HE SAVED MY LIFE.
*I CAN'T IMAGINE **HIM**, OF ALL PEOPLE, HELPING THIS GUY...*
YOU CAN ALL BE RESUR-RECTED UNDER THE RIGHT CONDI-TIONS, YES?
UM, I THINK SO...
IF WE BEAT THE MONSTER THAT ATE THEM...
...OR I CLEAR THE QUEST.

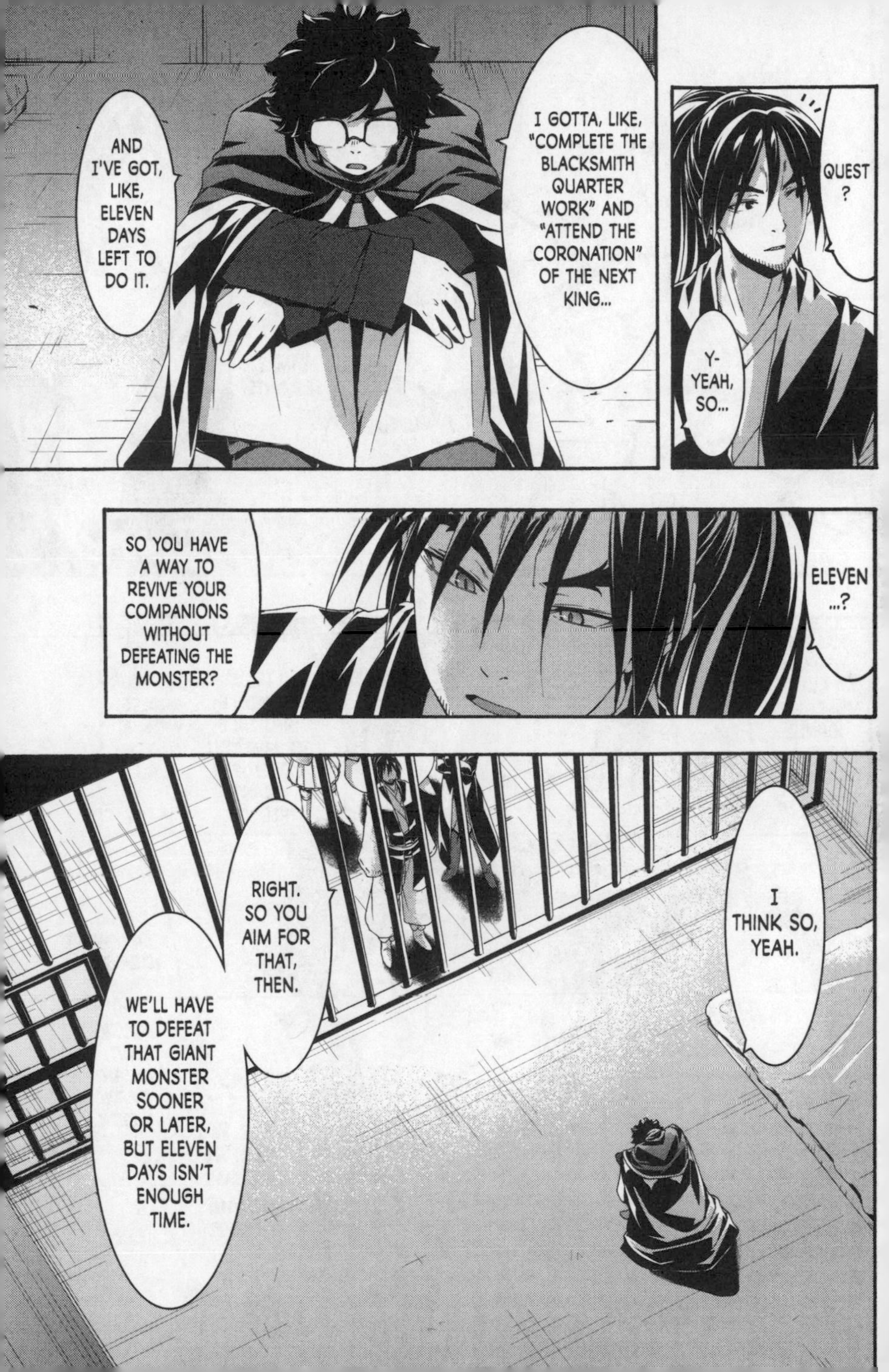
QUEST?
Y-YEAH, SO...
I GOTTA, LIKE, "COMPLETE THE BLACKSMITH QUARTER WORK" AND "ATTEND THE CORONATION" OF THE NEXT KING...
AND I'VE GOT, LIKE, ELEVEN DAYS LEFT TO DO IT.
ELEVEN...?
SO YOU HAVE A WAY TO REVIVE YOUR COMPANIONS WITHOUT DEFEATING THE MONSTER?
I THINK SO, YEAH.
RIGHT. SO YOU AIM FOR THAT, THEN.
WE'LL HAVE TO DEFEAT THAT GIANT MONSTER SOONER OR LATER, BUT ELEVEN DAYS ISN'T ENOUGH TIME.

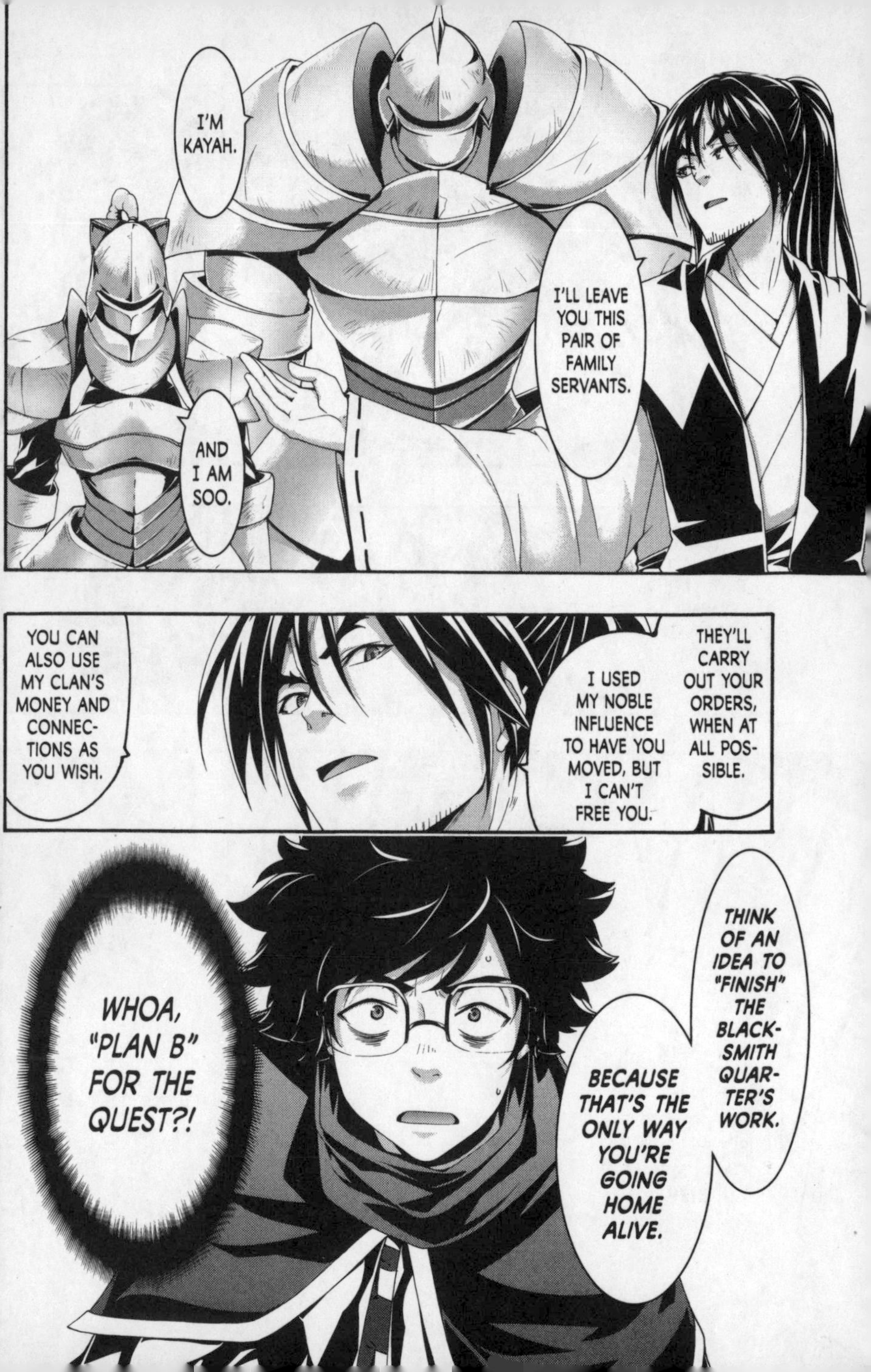
I'LL LEAVE YOU THIS PAIR OF FAMILY SERVANTS.
I'M KAYAH.
AND I AM SOO.
THEY'LL CARRY OUT YOUR ORDERS, WHEN AT ALL POS-SIBLE.
I USED MY NOBLE INFLUENCE TO HAVE YOU MOVED, BUT I CAN'T FREE YOU.
YOU CAN ALSO USE MY CLAN'S MONEY AND CONNEC-TIONS AS YOU WISH.
THINK OF AN IDEA TO "FINISH" THE BLACK-SMITH QUAR-TER'S WORK.
BECAUSE THAT'S THE ONLY WAY YOU'RE GOING HOME ALIVE.
WHOA, "PLAN B" FOR THE QUEST?!

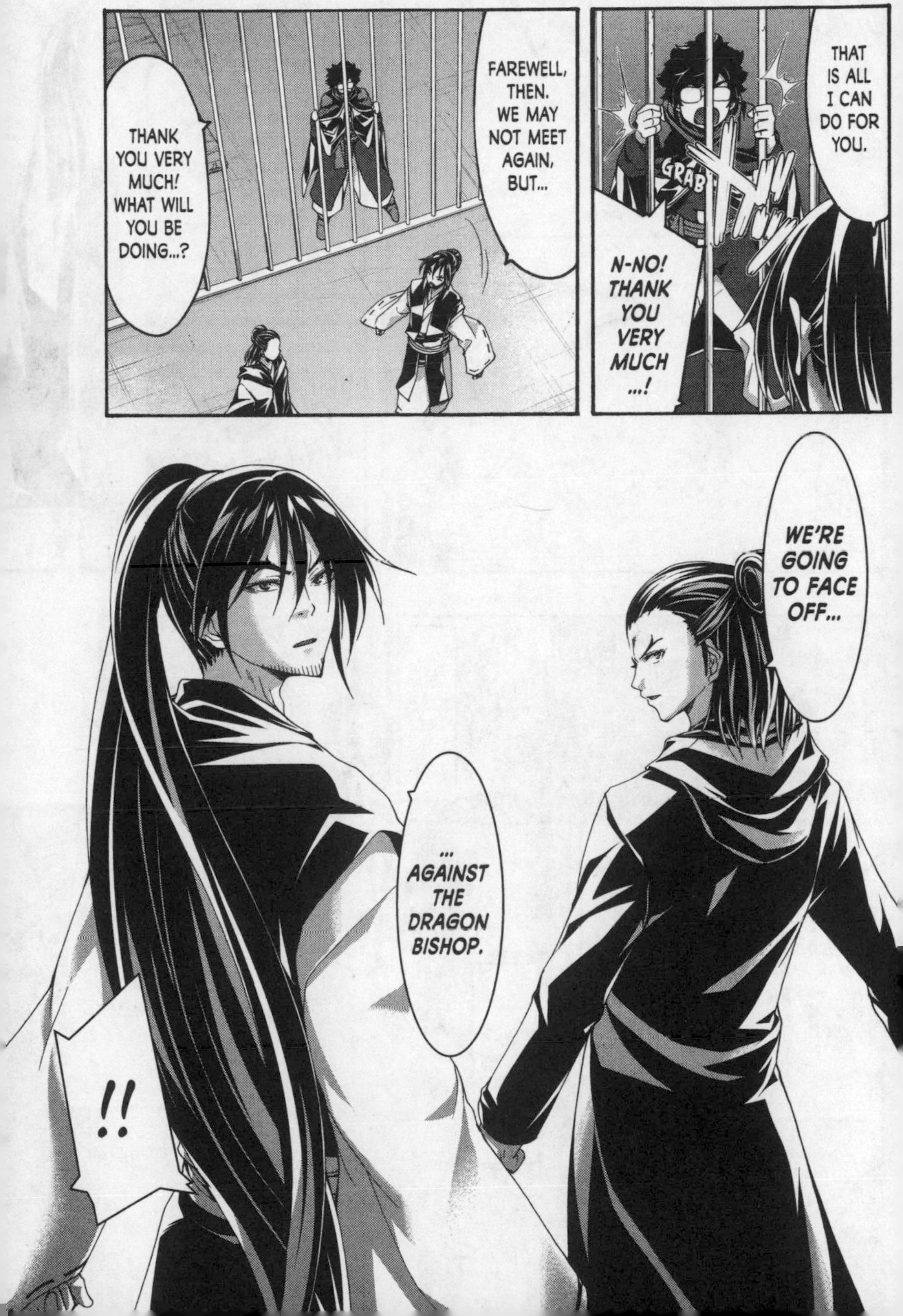
THAT IS ALL I CAN DO FOR YOU.
GRAB
N-NO! THANK YOU VERY MUCH ...!
FAREWELL, THEN. WE MAY NOT MEET AGAIN, BUT...
THANK YOU VERY MUCH! WHAT WILL YOU BE DOING...?
WE'RE GOING TO FACE OFF...
... AGAINST THE DRAGON BISHOP.
!!

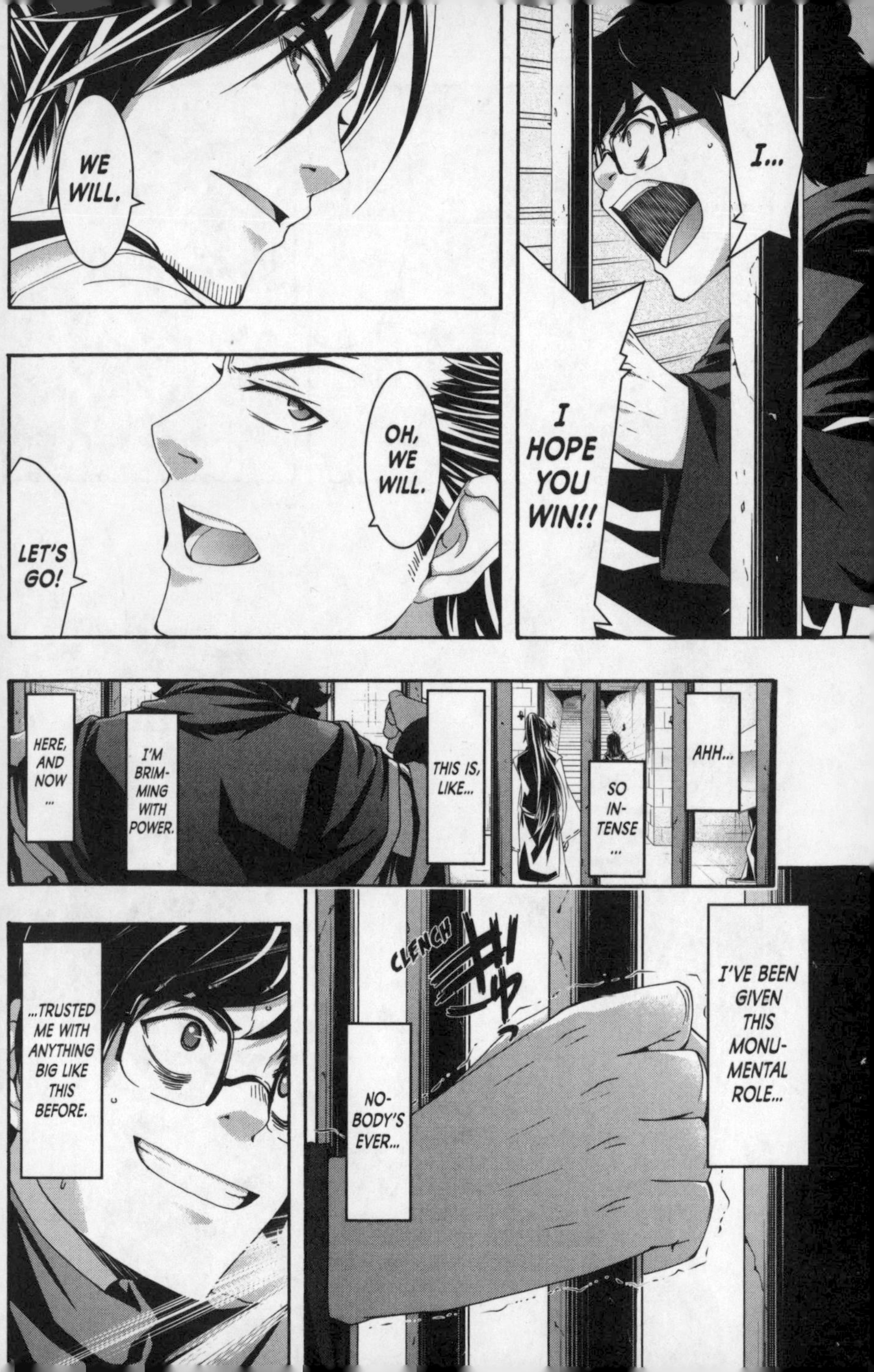
I...
I HOPE YOU WIN!!
WE WILL.
OH, WE WILL.
LET'S GO!
AHH...
SO INTENSE...
THIS IS, LIKE...
I'M BRIMMING WITH POWER.
HERE, AND NOW...
I'VE BEEN GIVEN THIS MONUMENTAL ROLE...
CLENCH
NOBODY'S EVER...
...TRUSTED ME WITH ANYTHING BIG LIKE THIS BEFORE.

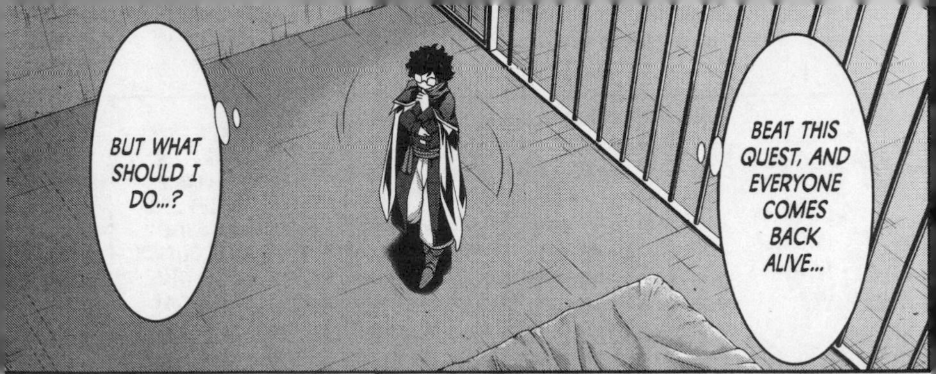
BEAT THIS QUEST, AND EVERYONE COMES BACK ALIVE...
BUT WHAT SHOULD I DO...?

PROGRAMMERS HAVE DIFFERENT SKILL LEVELS.

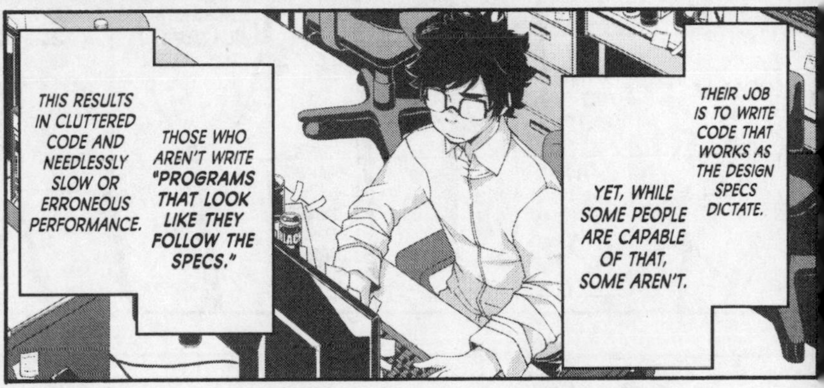
THEIR JOB IS TO WRITE CODE THAT WORKS AS THE DESIGN SPECS DICTATE.
YET, WHILE SOME PEOPLE ARE CAPABLE OF THAT, SOME AREN'T.
THOSE WHO AREN'T WRITE "PROGRAMS THAT LOOK LIKE THEY FOLLOW THE SPECS."
THIS RESULTS IN CLUTTERED CODE AND NEEDLESSLY SLOW OR ERRONEOUS PERFORMANCE.

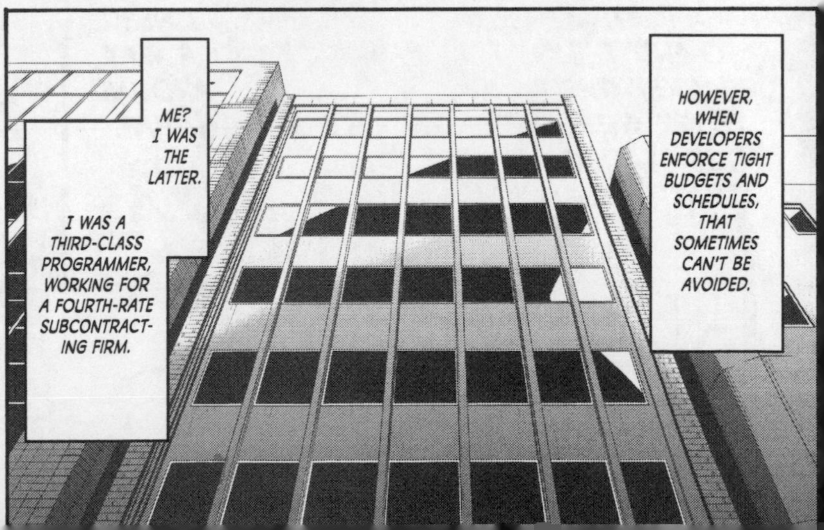
HOWEVER, WHEN DEVELOPERS ENFORCE TIGHT BUDGETS AND SCHEDULES, THAT SOMETIMES CAN'T BE AVOIDED.
ME? I WAS THE LATTER.
I WAS A THIRD-CLASS PROGRAMMER, WORKING FOR A FOURTH-RATE SUBCONTRACTING FIRM.

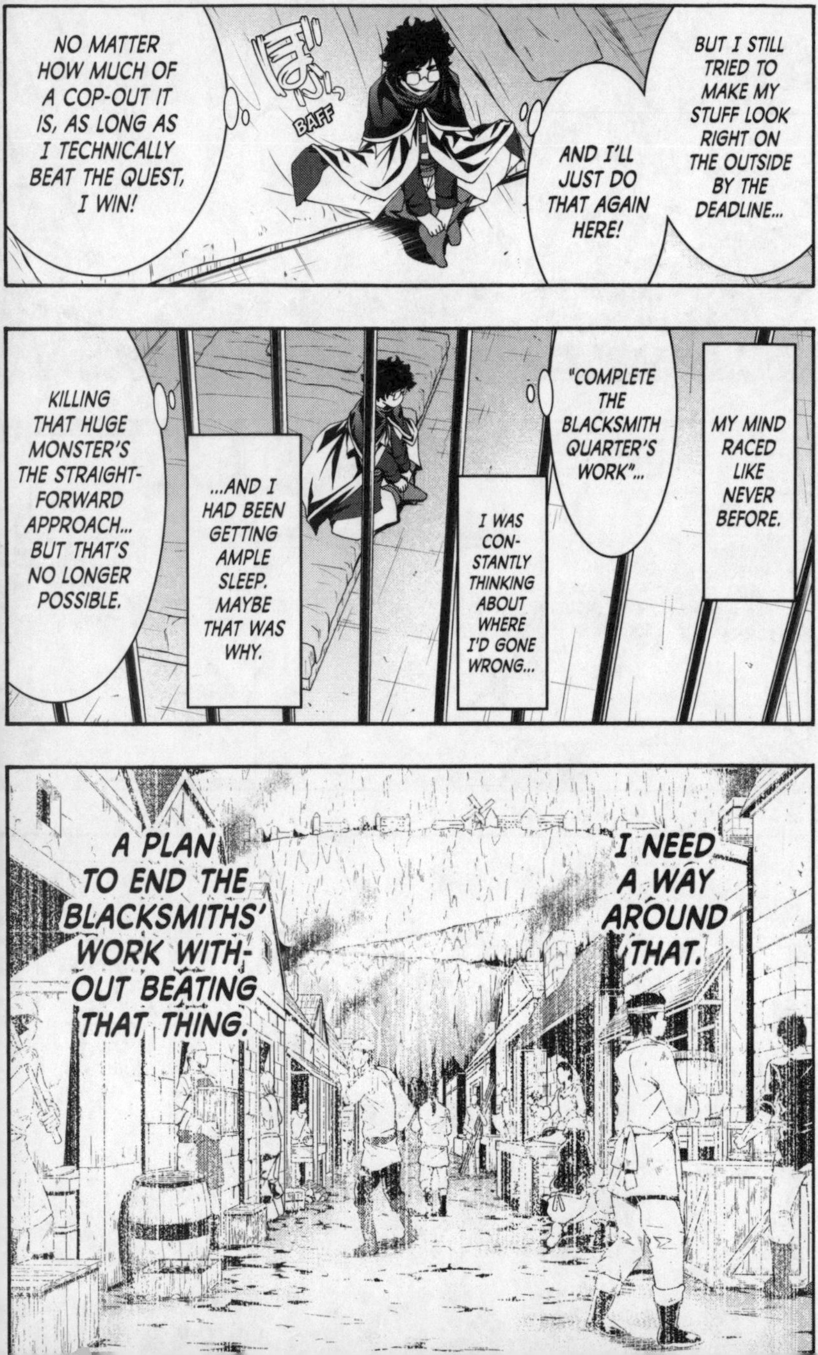
BUT I STILL TRIED TO MAKE MY STUFF LOOK RIGHT ON THE OUTSIDE BY THE DEADLINE...
AND I'LL JUST DO THAT AGAIN HERE!
BAFF
NO MATTER HOW MUCH OF A COP-OUT IT IS, AS LONG AS I TECHNICALLY BEAT THE QUEST, I WIN!
MY MIND RACED LIKE NEVER BEFORE.
"COMPLETE THE BLACKSMITH QUARTER'S WORK"...
I WAS CON-STANTLY THINKING ABOUT WHERE I'D GONE WRONG...
...AND I HAD BEEN GETTING AMPLE SLEEP. MAYBE THAT WAS WHY.
KILLING THAT HUGE MONSTER'S THE STRAIGHT-FORWARD APPROACH... BUT THAT'S NO LONGER POSSIBLE.
I NEED A WAY AROUND THAT.
A PLAN TO END THE BLACKSMITHS' WORK WITH-OUT BEATING THAT THING.

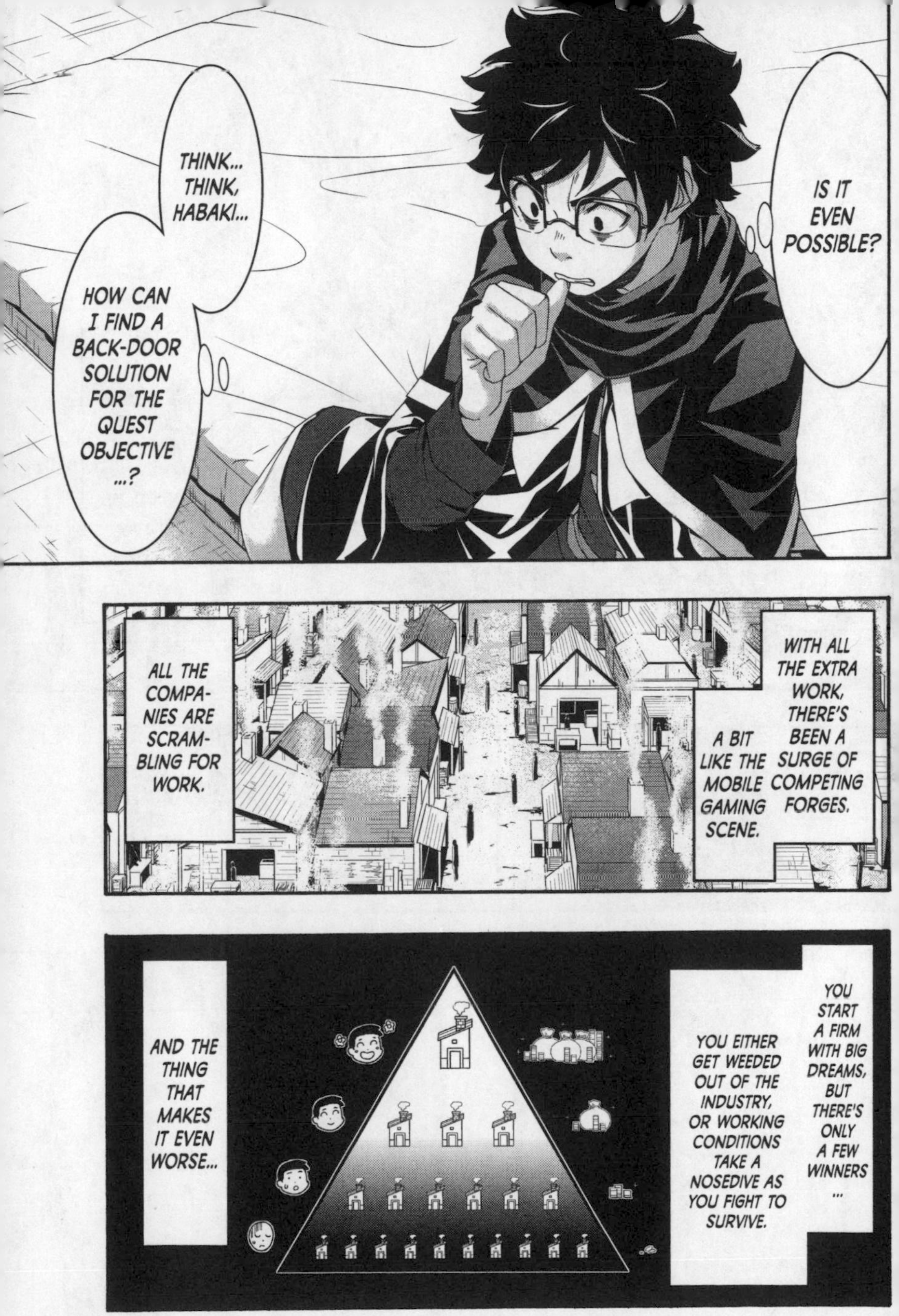
IS IT EVEN POSSIBLE?
THINK... THINK, HABAKI...
HOW CAN I FIND A BACK-DOOR SOLUTION FOR THE QUEST OBJECTIVE ...?
WITH ALL THE EXTRA WORK, THERE'S BEEN A SURGE OF COMPETING FORGES.
A BIT LIKE THE MOBILE GAMING SCENE.
ALL THE COMPANIES ARE SCRAMBLING FOR WORK.
YOU START A FIRM WITH BIG DREAMS, BUT THERE'S ONLY A FEW WINNERS ...
YOU EITHER GET WEEDED OUT OF THE INDUSTRY, OR WORKING CONDITIONS TAKE A NOSEDIVE AS YOU FIGHT TO SURVIVE.
AND THE THING THAT MAKES IT EVEN WORSE...

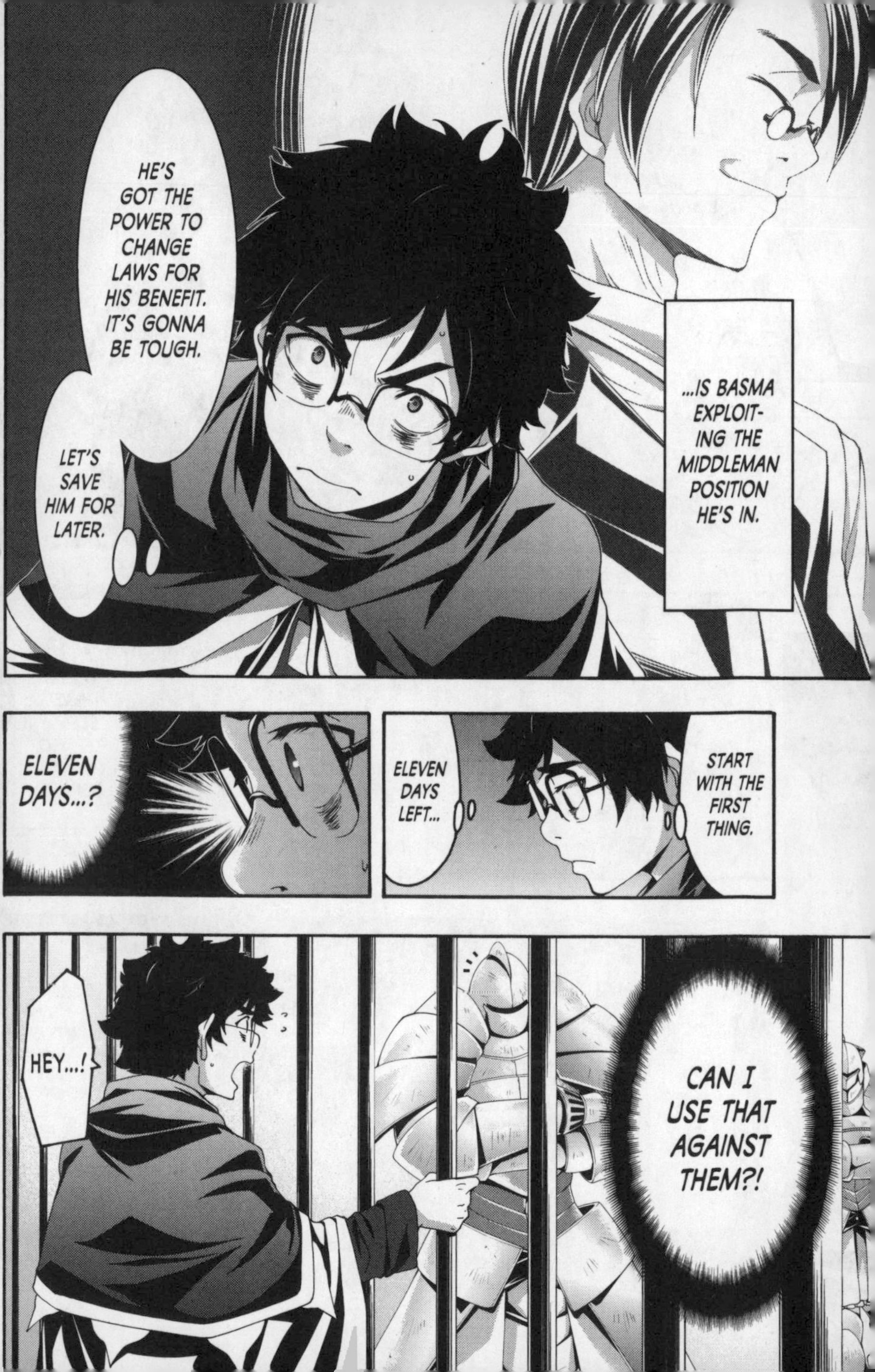
...IS BASMA EXPLOIT-ING THE MIDDLEMAN POSITION HE'S IN.
HE'S GOT THE POWER TO CHANGE LAWS FOR HIS BENEFIT. IT'S GONNA BE TOUGH.
LET'S SAVE HIM FOR LATER.
START WITH THE FIRST THING.
ELEVEN DAYS LEFT...
ELEVEN DAYS...?
CAN I USE THAT AGAINST THEM?!
HEY...!

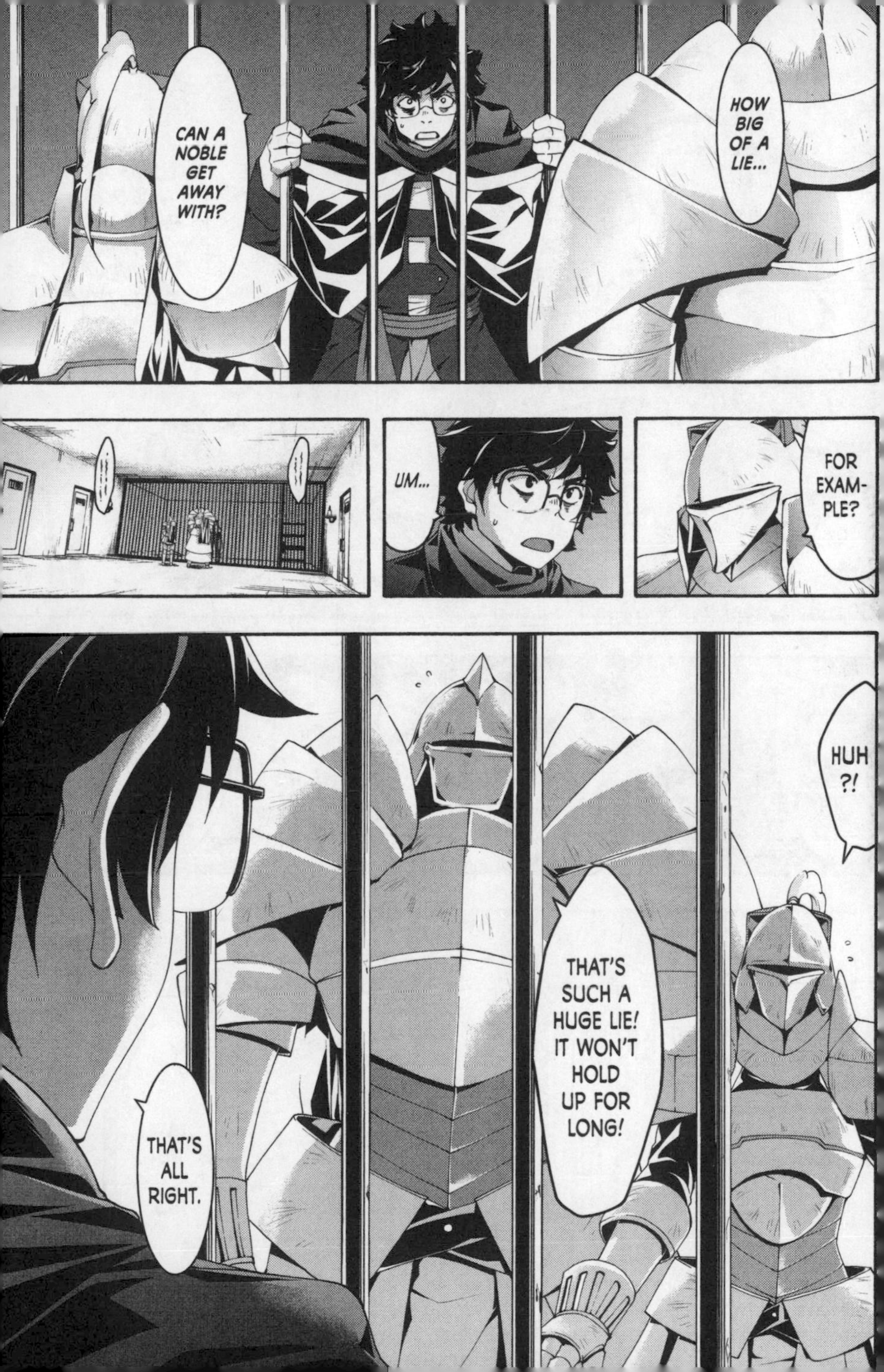
HOW BIG OF A LIE...
CAN A NOBLE GET AWAY WITH?
FOR EXAMPLE?
UM...
HUH?!
THAT'S SUCH A HUGE LIE! IT WON'T HOLD UP FOR LONG!
THAT'S ALL RIGHT.

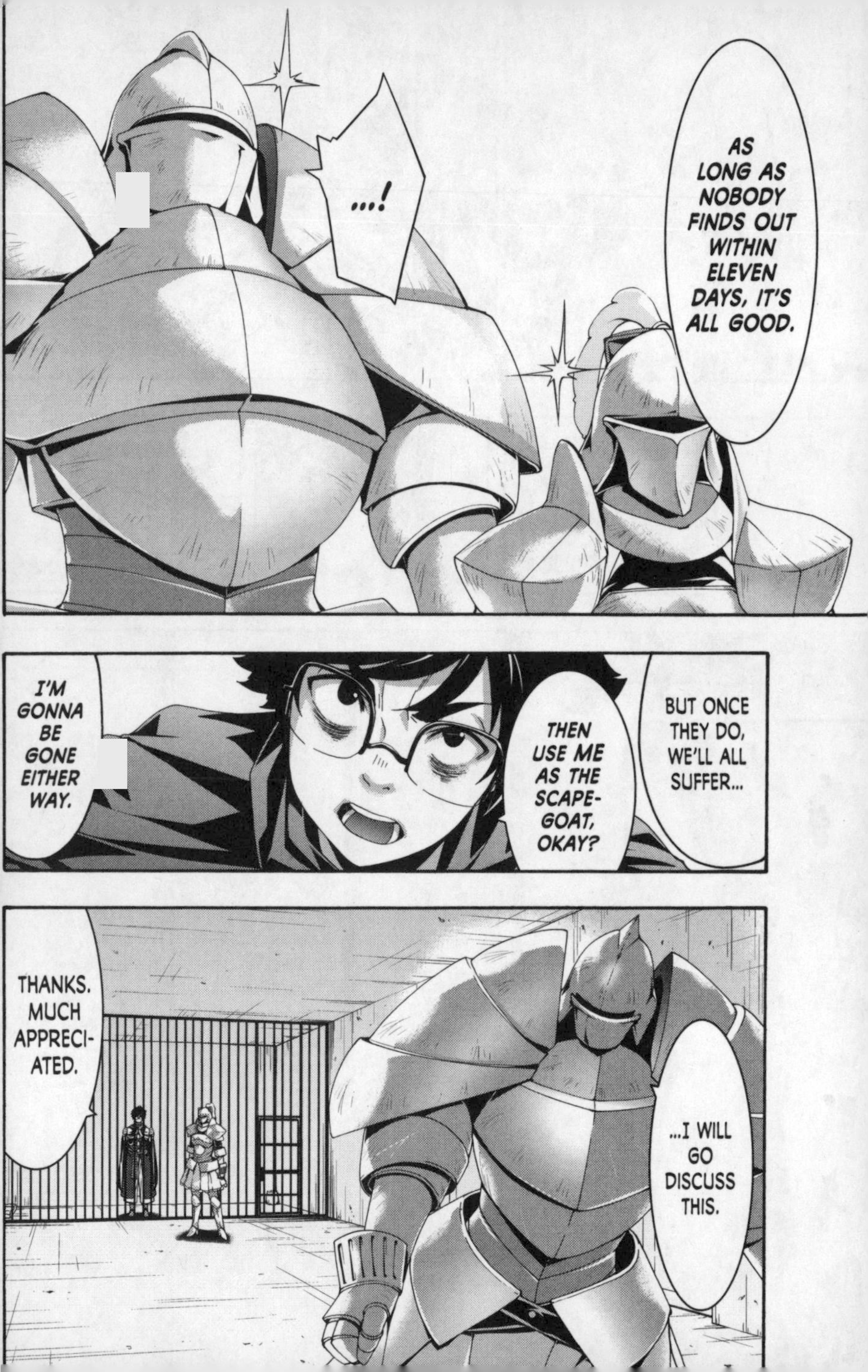
AS LONG AS NOBODY FINDS OUT WITHIN ELEVEN DAYS, IT'S ALL GOOD.
...!
BUT ONCE THEY DO, WE'LL ALL SUFFER...
THEN USE ME AS THE SCAPE-GOAT, OKAY?
I'M GONNA BE GONE EITHER WAY.
...I WILL GO DISCUSS THIS.
THANKS. MUCH APPRECI-ATED.

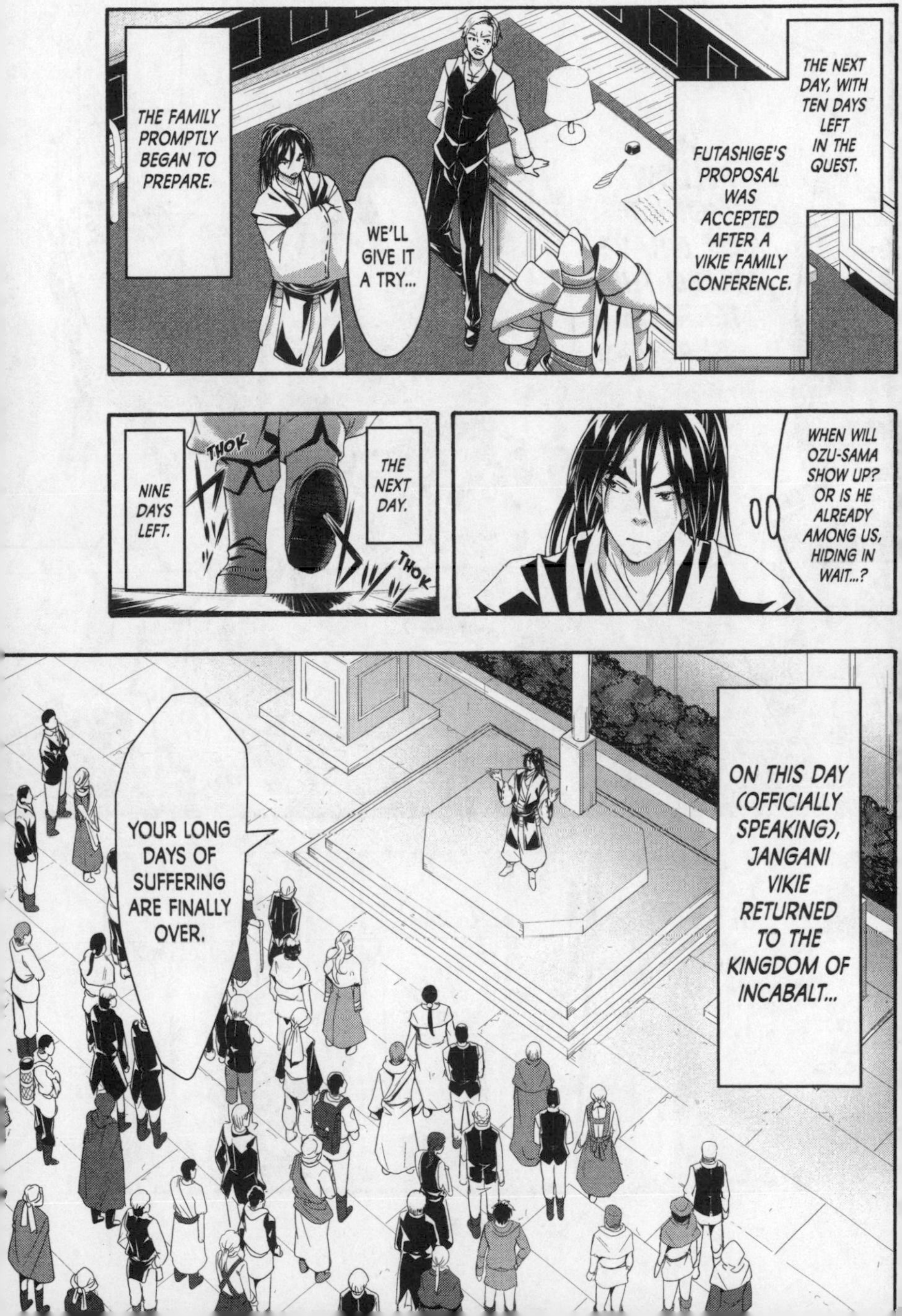
THE NEXT DAY, WITH TEN DAYS LEFT IN THE QUEST.
FUTASHIGE'S PROPOSAL WAS ACCEPTED AFTER A VIKIE FAMILY CONFERENCE.
WE'LL GIVE IT A TRY...
THE FAMILY PROMPTLY BEGAN TO PREPARE.
WHEN WILL OZU-SAMA SHOW UP? OR IS HE ALREADY AMONG US, HIDING IN WAIT...?
THE NEXT DAY.
THOK
NINE DAYS LEFT.
THOK
ON THIS DAY (OFFICIALLY SPEAKING), JANGANI VIKIE RETURNED TO THE KINGDOM OF INCABALT...
YOUR LONG DAYS OF SUFFERING ARE FINALLY OVER.

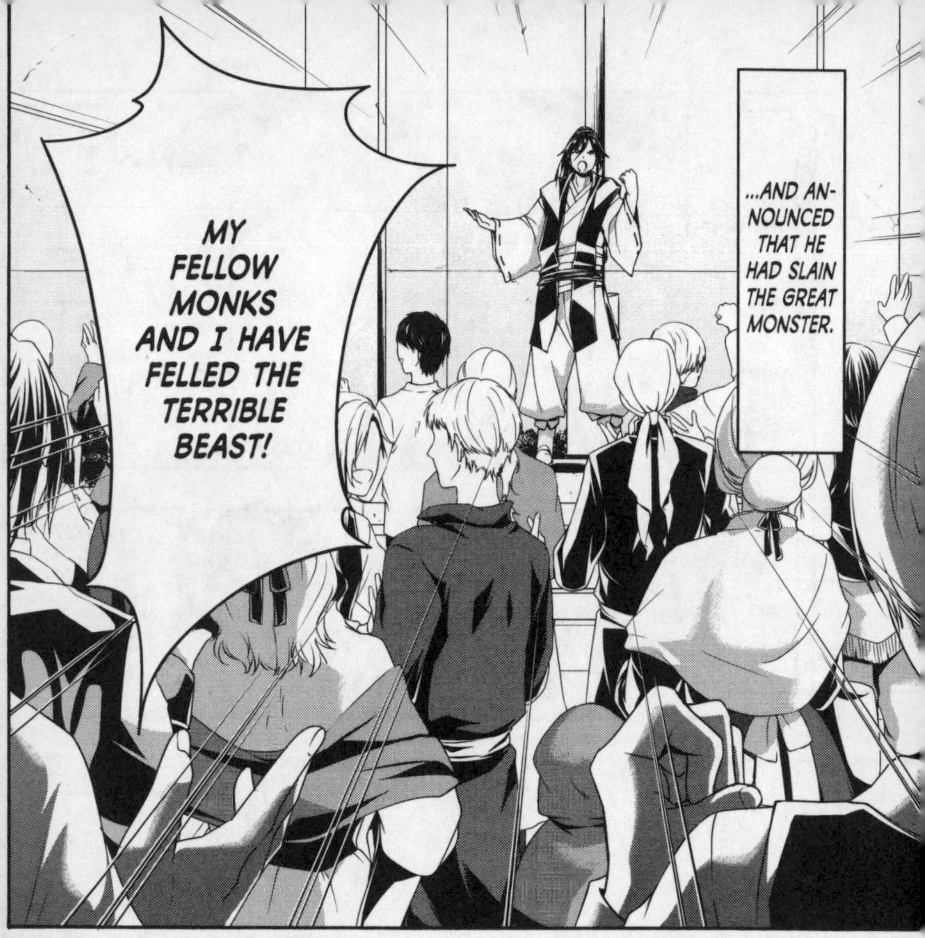
...AND AN-NOUNCED THAT HE HAD SLAIN THE GREAT MONSTER.
MY FELLOW MONKS AND I HAVE FELLED THE TERRIBLE BEAST!

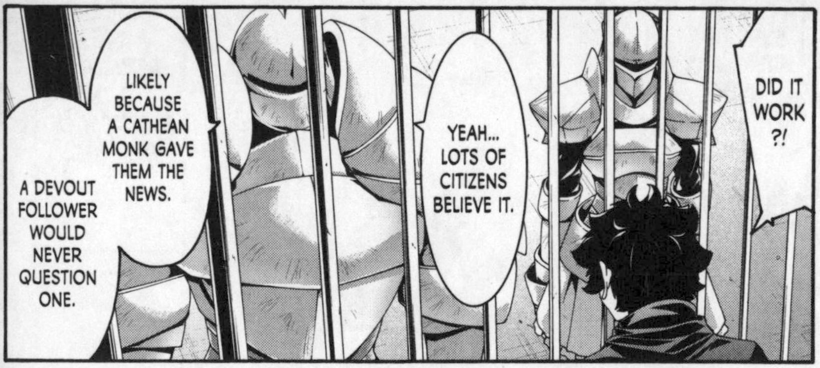
DID IT WORK?!
YEAH... LOTS OF CITIZENS BELIEVE IT.
LIKELY BECAUSE A CATHEAN MONK GAVE THEM THE NEWS.
A DEVOUT FOLLOWER WOULD NEVER QUESTION ONE.

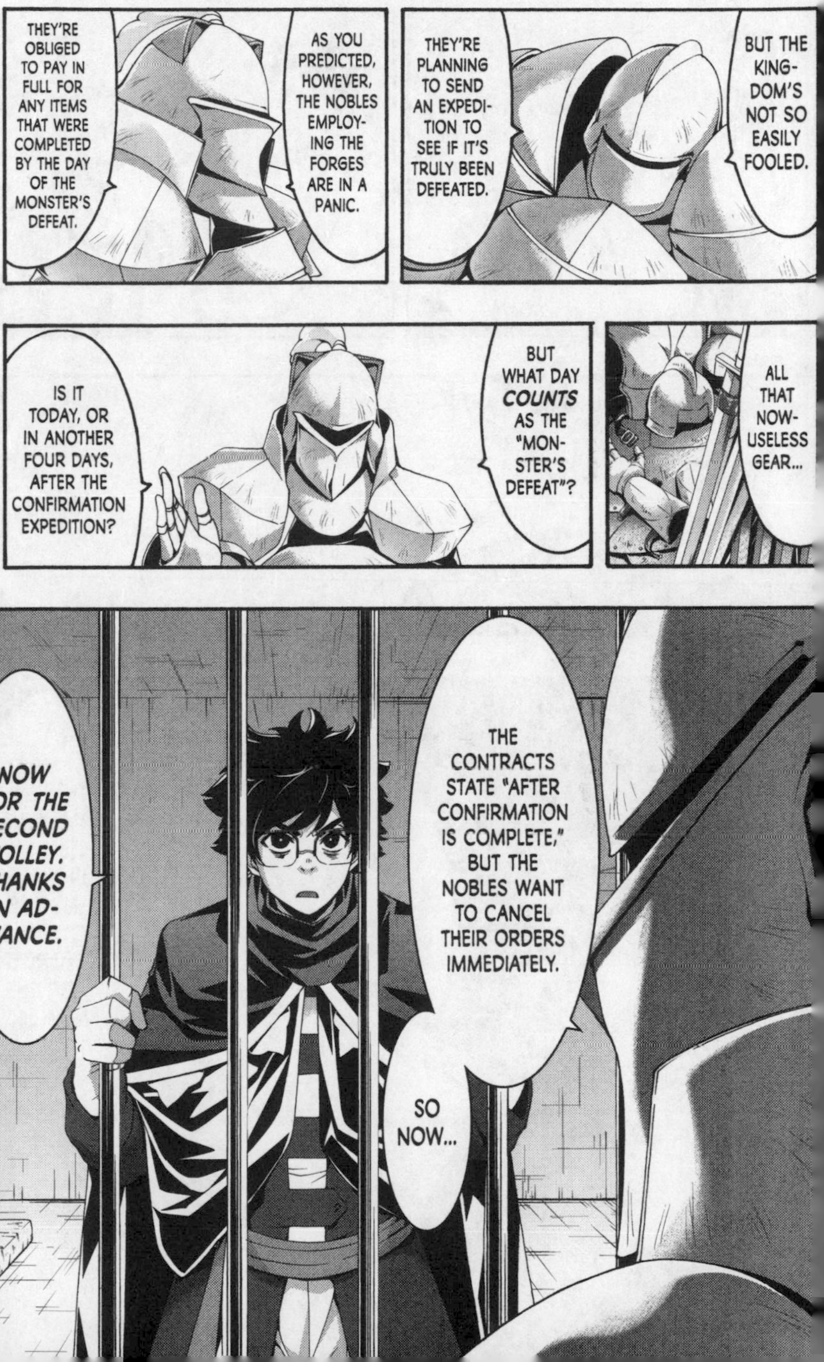
BUT THE KINGDOM'S NOT SO EASILY FOOLED.
THEY'RE PLANNING TO SEND AN EXPEDITION TO SEE IF IT'S TRULY BEEN DEFEATED.
AS YOU PREDICTED, HOWEVER, THE NOBLES EMPLOYING THE FORGES ARE IN A PANIC.
THEY'RE OBLIGED TO PAY IN FULL FOR ANY ITEMS THAT WERE COMPLETED BY THE DAY OF THE MONSTER'S DEFEAT.
ALL THAT NOW-USELESS GEAR...
BUT WHAT DAY *COUNTS* AS THE "MONSTER'S DEFEAT"?
IS IT TODAY, OR IN ANOTHER FOUR DAYS, AFTER THE CONFIRMATION EXPEDITION?
THE CONTRACTS STATE "AFTER CONFIRMATION IS COMPLETE," BUT THE NOBLES WANT TO CANCEL THEIR ORDERS IMMEDIATELY.
SO NOW...
NOW FOR THE SECOND VOLLEY. THANKS IN ADVANCE.

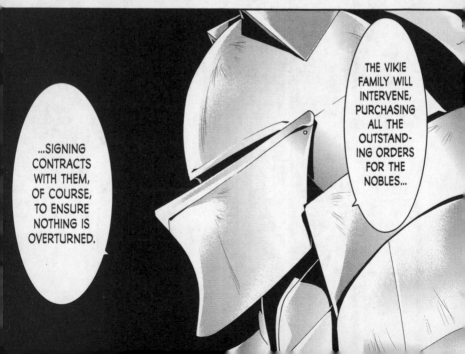

THE VIKIE FAMILY WILL INTERVENE, PURCHASING ALL THE OUTSTAND-ING ORDERS FOR THE NOBLES...

...SIGNING CONTRACTS WITH THEM, OF COURSE, TO ENSURE NOTHING IS OVERTURNED.

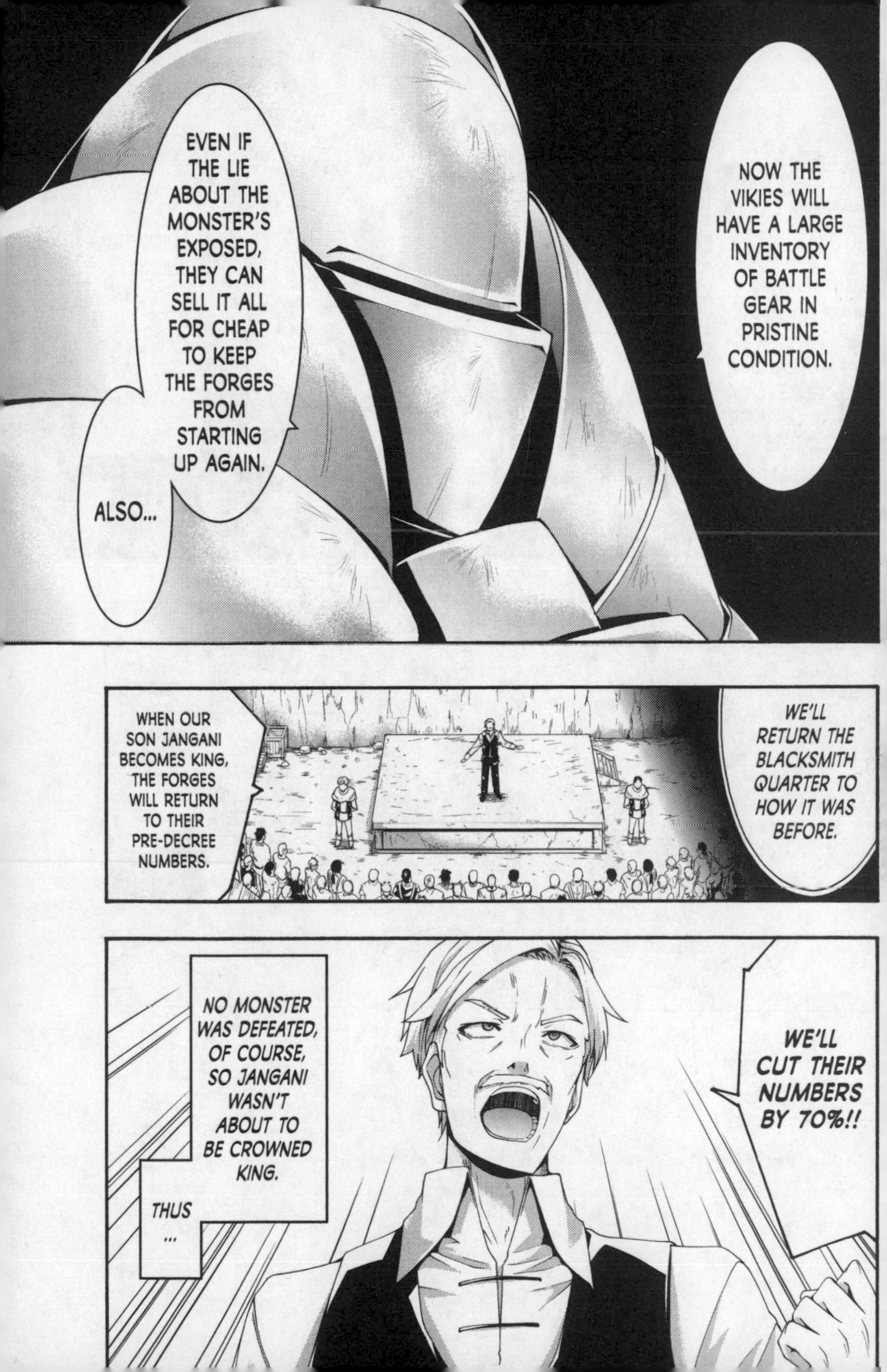
NOW THE VIKIES WILL HAVE A LARGE INVENTORY OF BATTLE GEAR IN PRISTINE CONDITION.
EVEN IF THE LIE ABOUT THE MONSTER'S EXPOSED, THEY CAN SELL IT ALL FOR CHEAP TO KEEP THE FORGES FROM STARTING UP AGAIN.
ALSO...
WE'LL RETURN THE BLACKSMITH QUARTER TO HOW IT WAS BEFORE.
WHEN OUR SON JANGANI BECOMES KING, THE FORGES WILL RETURN TO THEIR PRE-DECREE NUMBERS.
WE'LL CUT THEIR NUMBERS BY 70%!!
NO MONSTER WAS DEFEATED, OF COURSE, SO JANGANI WASN'T ABOUT TO BE CROWNED KING.
THUS ...

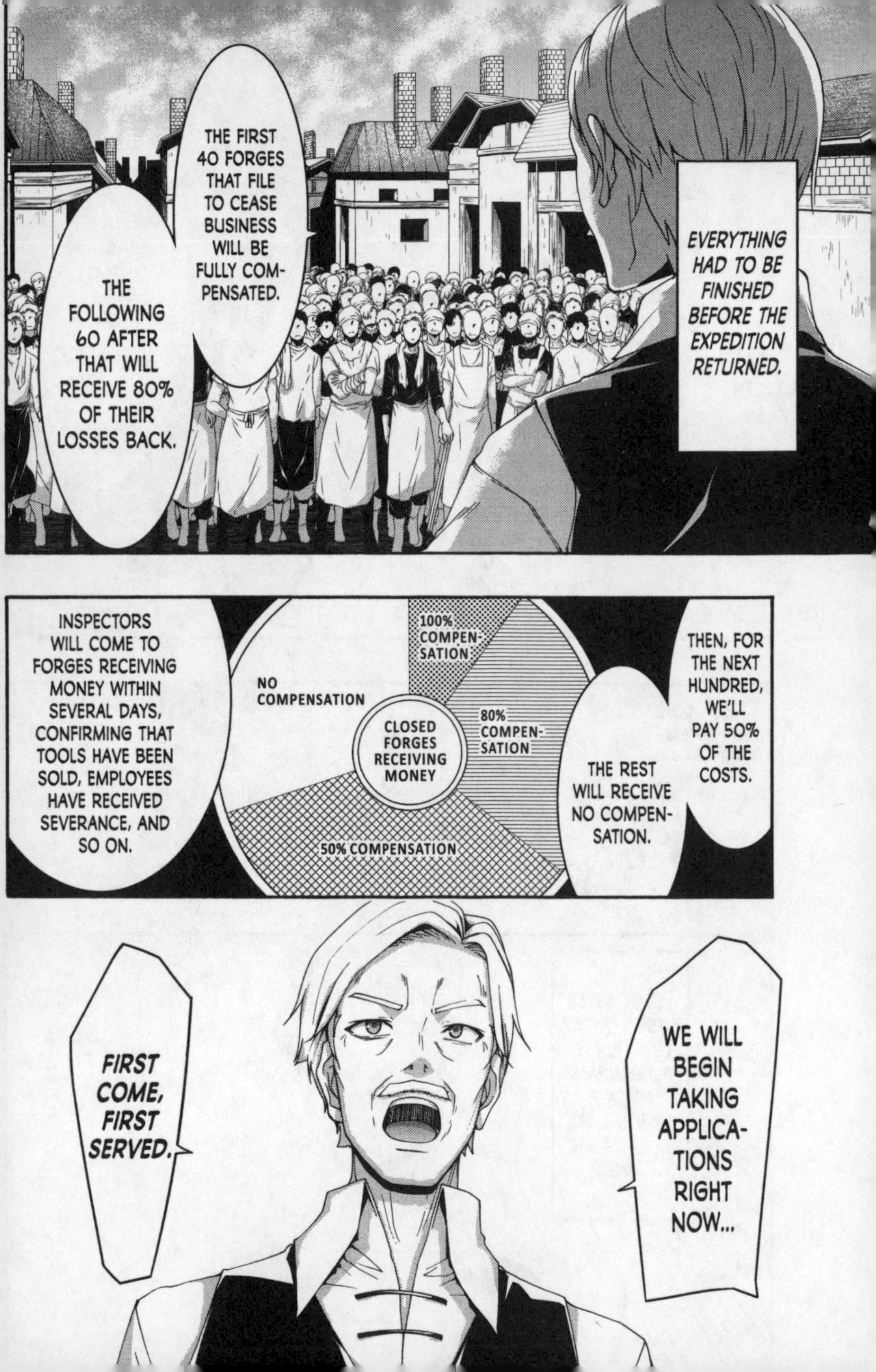
EVERYTHING HAD TO BE FINISHED BEFORE THE EXPEDITION RETURNED.
THE FIRST 40 FORGES THAT FILE TO CEASE BUSINESS WILL BE FULLY COMPENSATED.
THE FOLLOWING 60 AFTER THAT WILL RECEIVE 80% OF THEIR LOSSES BACK.
THEN, FOR THE NEXT HUNDRED, WE'LL PAY 50% OF THE COSTS.
THE REST WILL RECEIVE NO COMPENSATION.
100% COMPENSATION
80% COMPENSATION
50% COMPENSATION
NO COMPENSATION
CLOSED FORGES RECEIVING MONEY
INSPECTORS WILL COME TO FORGES RECEIVING MONEY WITHIN SEVERAL DAYS, CONFIRMING THAT TOOLS HAVE BEEN SOLD, EMPLOYEES HAVE RECEIVED SEVERANCE, AND SO ON.
WE WILL BEGIN TAKING APPLICATIONS RIGHT NOW...
FIRST COME, FIRST SERVED.

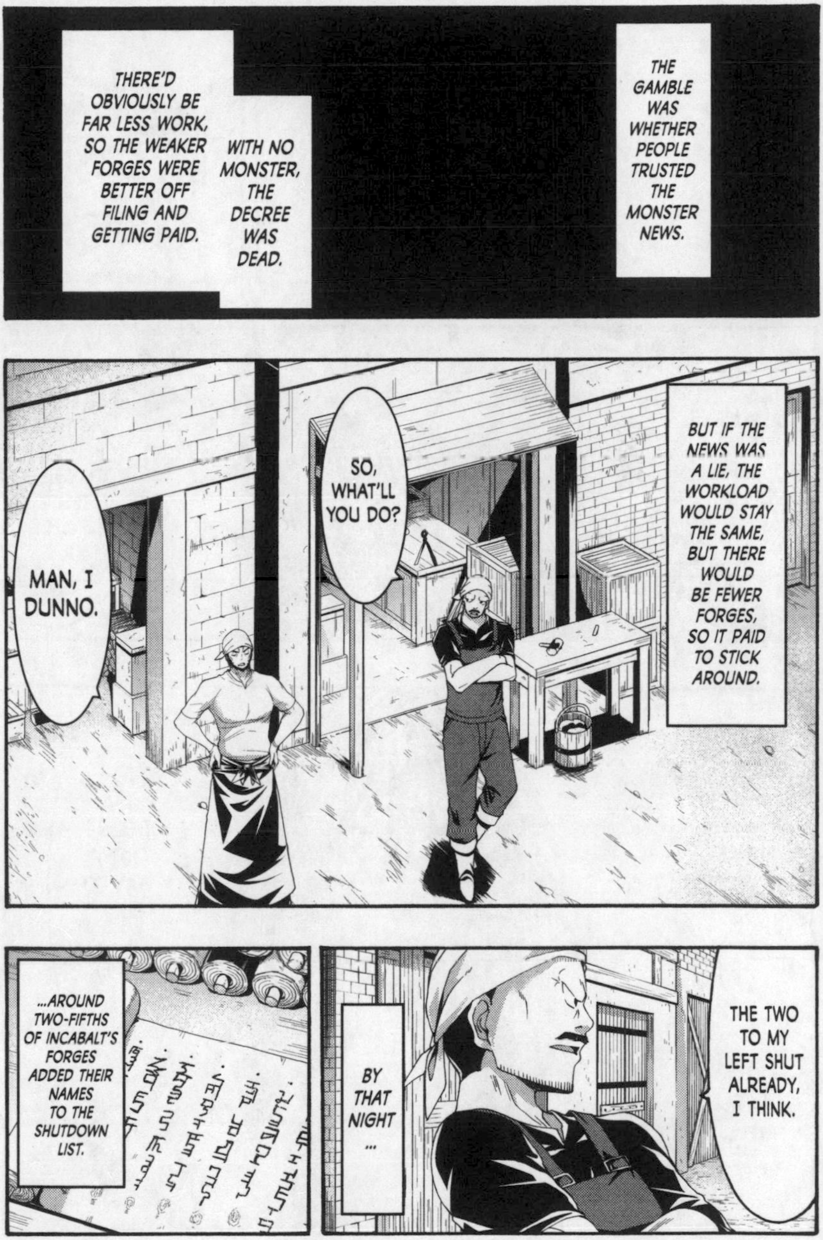
THE GAMBLE WAS WHETHER PEOPLE TRUSTED THE MONSTER NEWS.
WITH NO MONSTER, THE DECREE WAS DEAD.
THERE'D OBVIOUSLY BE FAR LESS WORK, SO THE WEAKER FORGES WERE BETTER OFF FILING AND GETTING PAID.
BUT IF THE NEWS WAS A LIE, THE WORKLOAD WOULD STAY THE SAME, BUT THERE WOULD BE FEWER FORGES, SO IT PAID TO STICK AROUND.
SO, WHAT'LL YOU DO?
MAN, I DUNNO.
THE TWO TO MY LEFT SHUT ALREADY, I THINK.
BY THAT NIGHT ...
...AROUND TWO-FIFTHS OF INCABALT'S FORGES ADDED THEIR NAMES TO THE SHUTDOWN LIST.

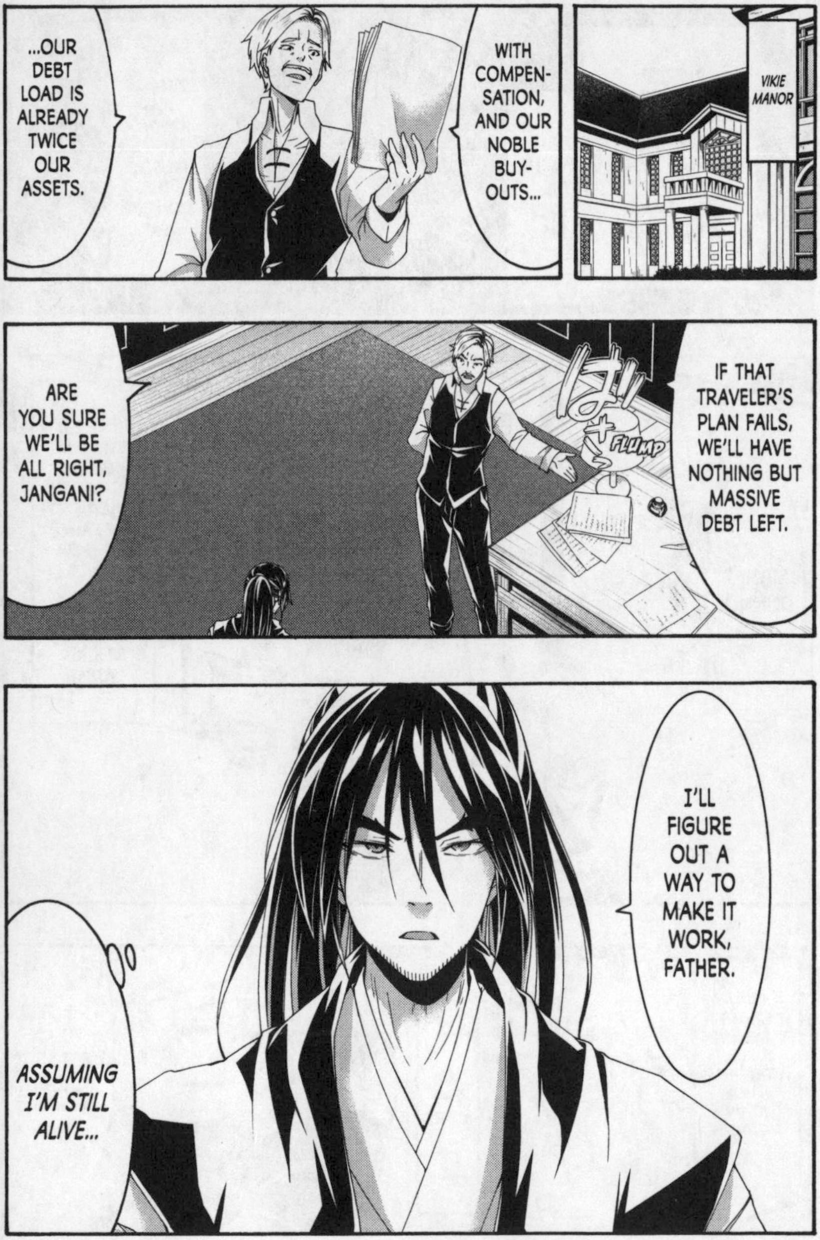
VIKIE MANOR
WITH COMPENSATION, AND OUR NOBLE BUY-OUTS...
...OUR DEBT LOAD IS ALREADY TWICE OUR ASSETS.
IF THAT TRAVELER'S PLAN FAILS, WE'LL HAVE NOTHING BUT MASSIVE DEBT LEFT.
FLUMP
ARE YOU SURE WE'LL BE ALL RIGHT, JANGANI?
I'LL FIGURE OUT A WAY TO MAKE IT WORK, FATHER.
ASSUMING I'M STILL ALIVE...

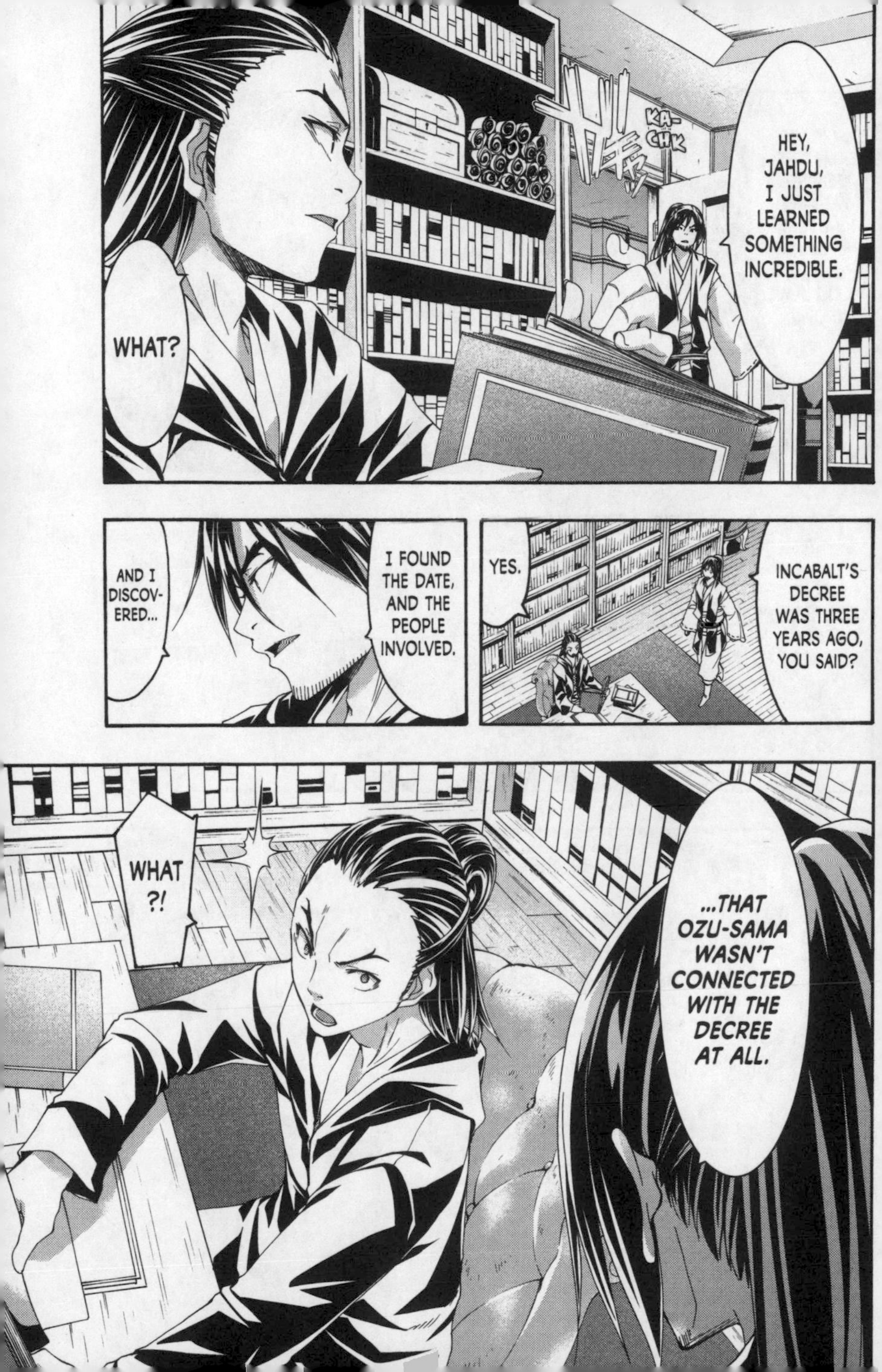
KA-CHK
HEY, JAHDU, I JUST LEARNED SOMETHING INCREDIBLE.
WHAT?
INCABALT'S DECREE WAS THREE YEARS AGO, YOU SAID?
YES.
I FOUND THE DATE, AND THE PEOPLE INVOLVED.
AND I DISCOVERED...
...THAT OZU-SAMA WASN'T CONNECTED WITH THE DECREE AT ALL.
WHAT ?!

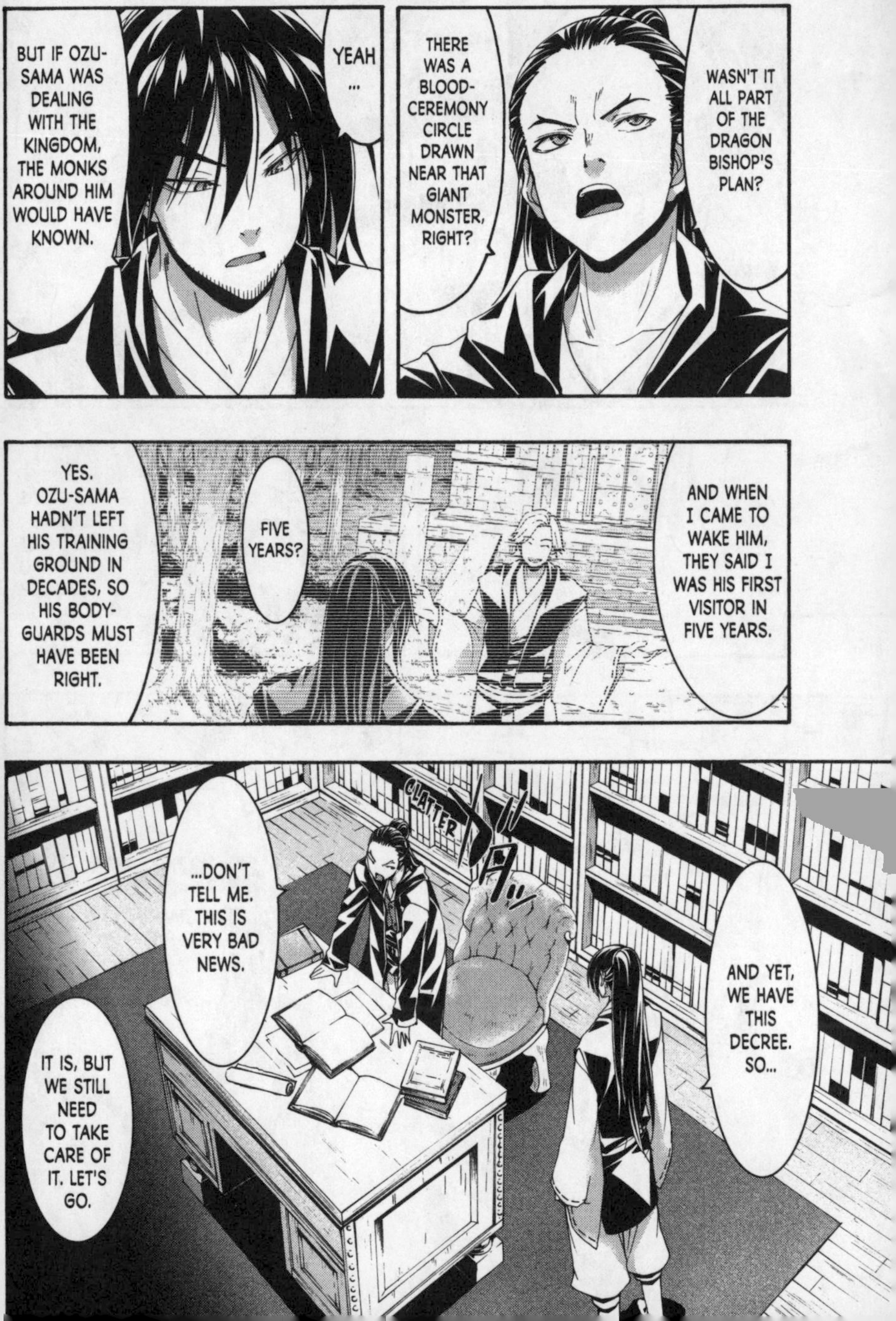
WASN'T IT ALL PART OF THE DRAGON BISHOP'S PLAN?
THERE WAS A BLOOD-CEREMONY CIRCLE DRAWN NEAR THAT GIANT MONSTER, RIGHT?
YEAH ...
BUT IF OZU-SAMA WAS DEALING WITH THE KINGDOM, THE MONKS AROUND HIM WOULD HAVE KNOWN.
AND WHEN I CAME TO WAKE HIM, THEY SAID I WAS HIS FIRST VISITOR IN FIVE YEARS.
FIVE YEARS?
YES. OZU-SAMA HADN'T LEFT HIS TRAINING GROUND IN DECADES, SO HIS BODY-GUARDS MUST HAVE BEEN RIGHT.
AND YET, WE HAVE THIS DECREE. SO...
CLATTER
...DON'T TELL ME. THIS IS VERY BAD NEWS.
IT IS, BUT WE STILL NEED TO TAKE CARE OF IT. LET'S GO.

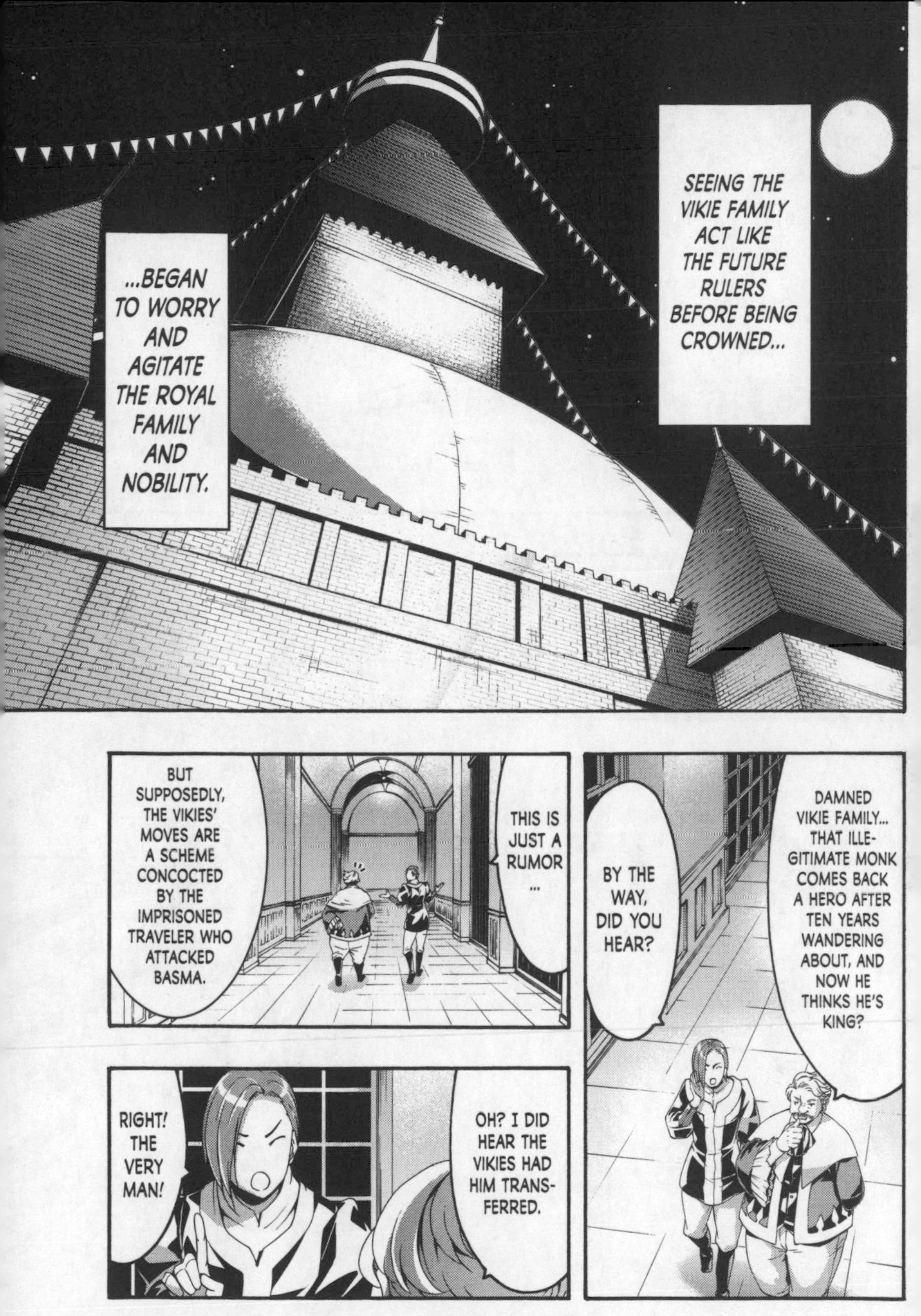
SEEING THE VIKIE FAMILY ACT LIKE THE FUTURE RULERS BEFORE BEING CROWNED...
...BEGAN TO WORRY AND AGITATE THE ROYAL FAMILY AND NOBILITY.
DAMNED VIKIE FAMILY... THAT ILLE-GITIMATE MONK COMES BACK A HERO AFTER TEN YEARS WANDERING ABOUT, AND NOW HE THINKS HE'S KING?
BY THE WAY, DID YOU HEAR?
THIS IS JUST A RUMOR ...
BUT SUPPOSEDLY, THE VIKIES' MOVES ARE A SCHEME CONCOCTED BY THE IMPRISONED TRAVELER WHO ATTACKED BASMA.
OH? I DID HEAR THE VIKIES HAD HIM TRANS-FERRED.
RIGHT! THE VERY MAN!

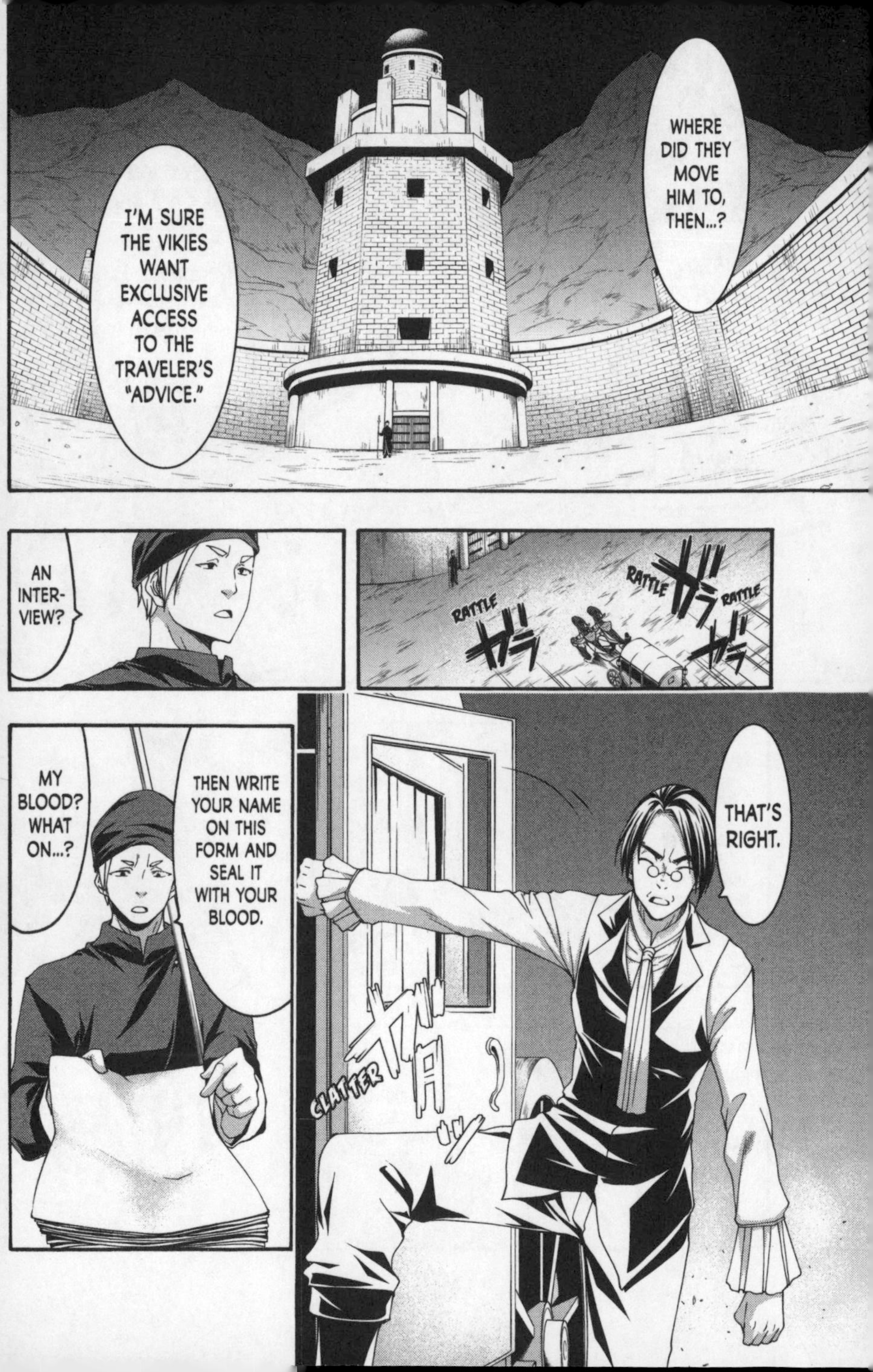
WHERE DID THEY MOVE HIM TO, THEN...?
I'M SURE THE VIKIES WANT EXCLUSIVE ACCESS TO THE TRAVELER'S "ADVICE."
RATTLE
RATTLE
RATTLE
AN INTER-VIEW?
THAT'S RIGHT.
CLATTER
THEN WRITE YOUR NAME ON THIS FORM AND SEAL IT WITH YOUR BLOOD.
MY BLOOD? WHAT ON...?

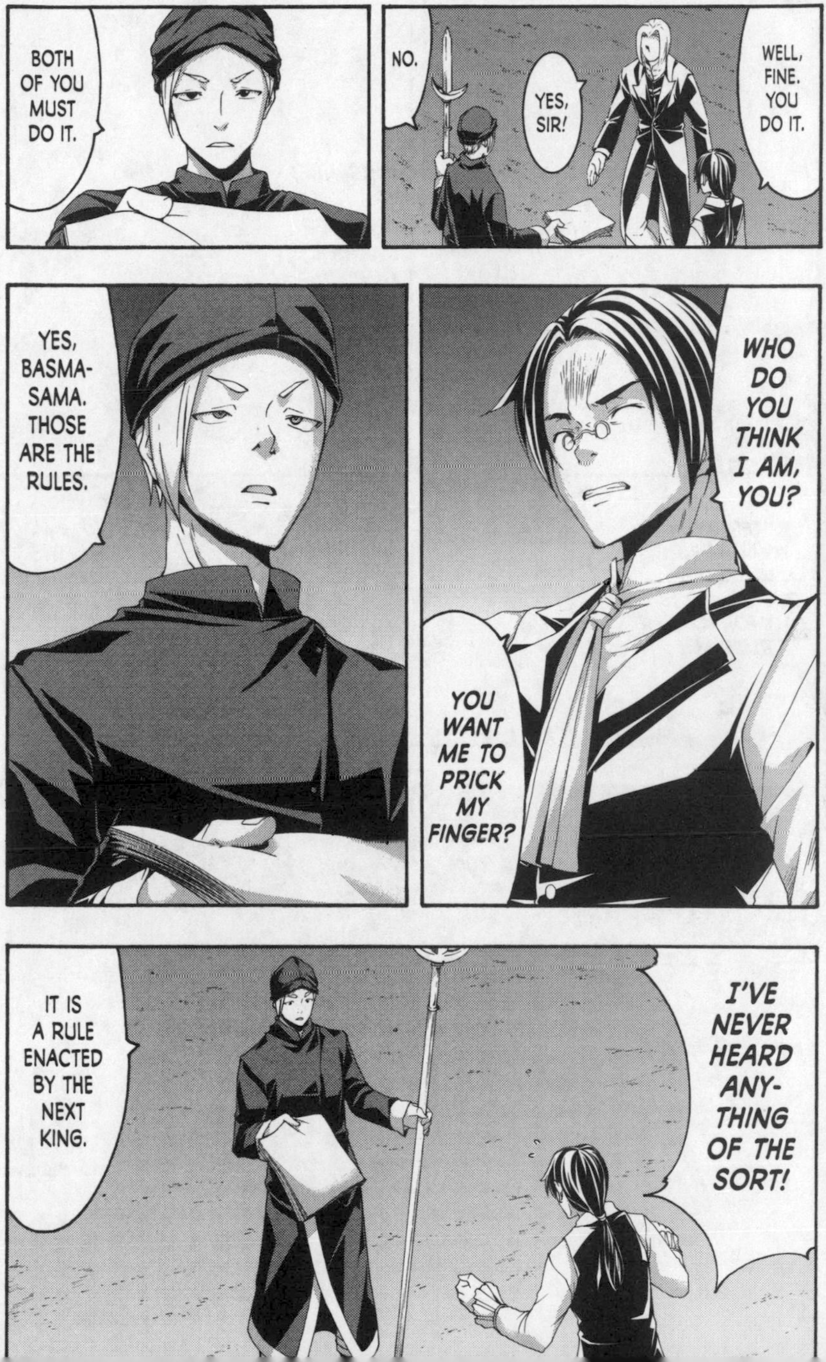
WELL, FINE. YOU DO IT.
YES, SIR!
NO.
BOTH OF YOU MUST DO IT.
WHO DO YOU THINK I AM, YOU?
YOU WANT ME TO PRICK MY FINGER?
YES, BASMA-SAMA. THOSE ARE THE RULES.
I'VE NEVER HEARD ANY-THING OF THE SORT!
IT IS A RULE ENACTED BY THE NEXT KING.

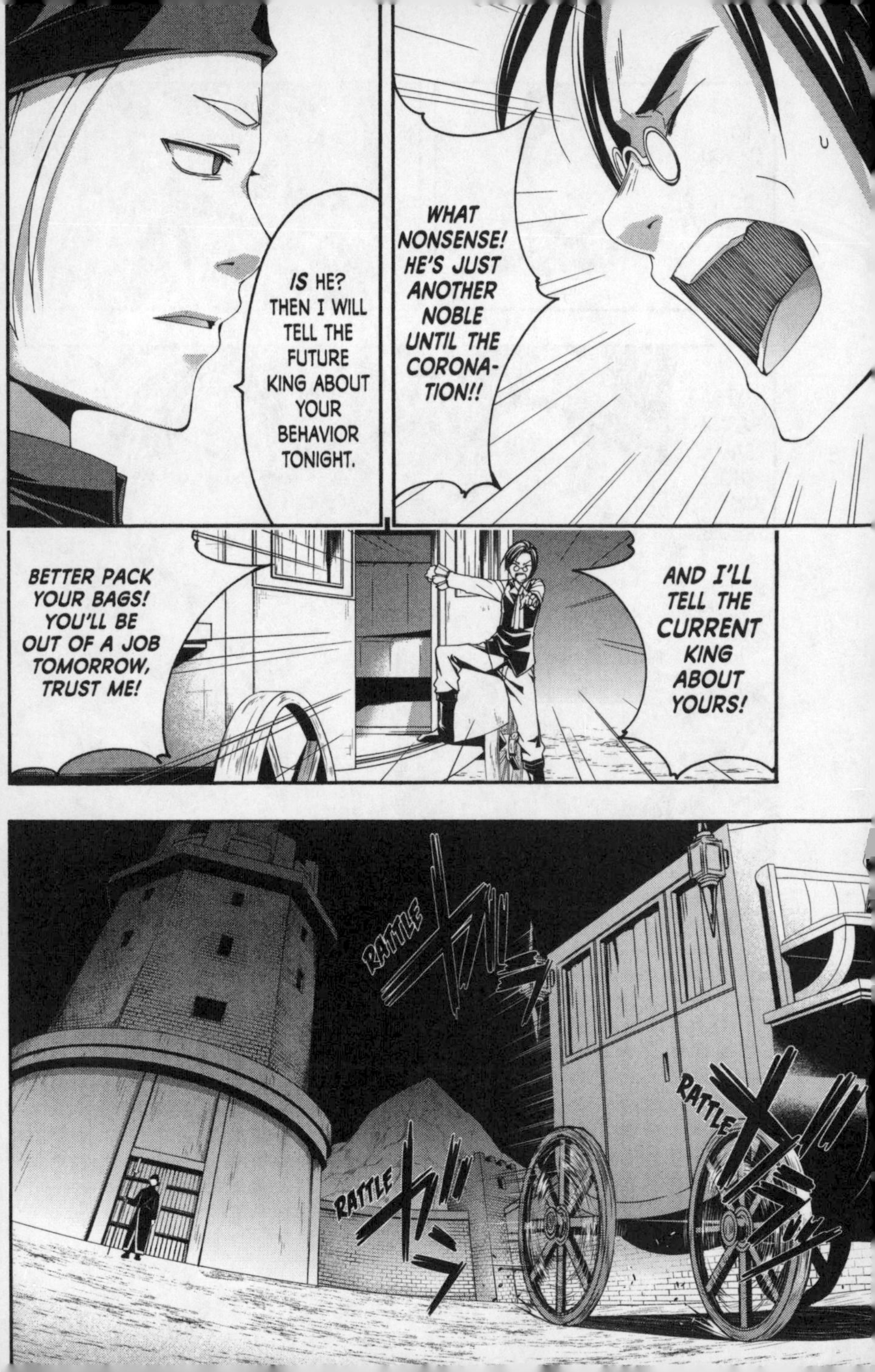
WHAT NONSENSE! HE'S JUST ANOTHER NOBLE UNTIL THE CORONA-TION!!
IS HE? THEN I WILL TELL THE FUTURE KING ABOUT YOUR BEHAVIOR TONIGHT.
AND I'LL TELL THE CURRENT KING ABOUT YOURS!
BETTER PACK YOUR BAGS! YOU'LL BE OUT OF A JOB TOMORROW, TRUST ME!
RATTLE
RATTLE
RATTLE

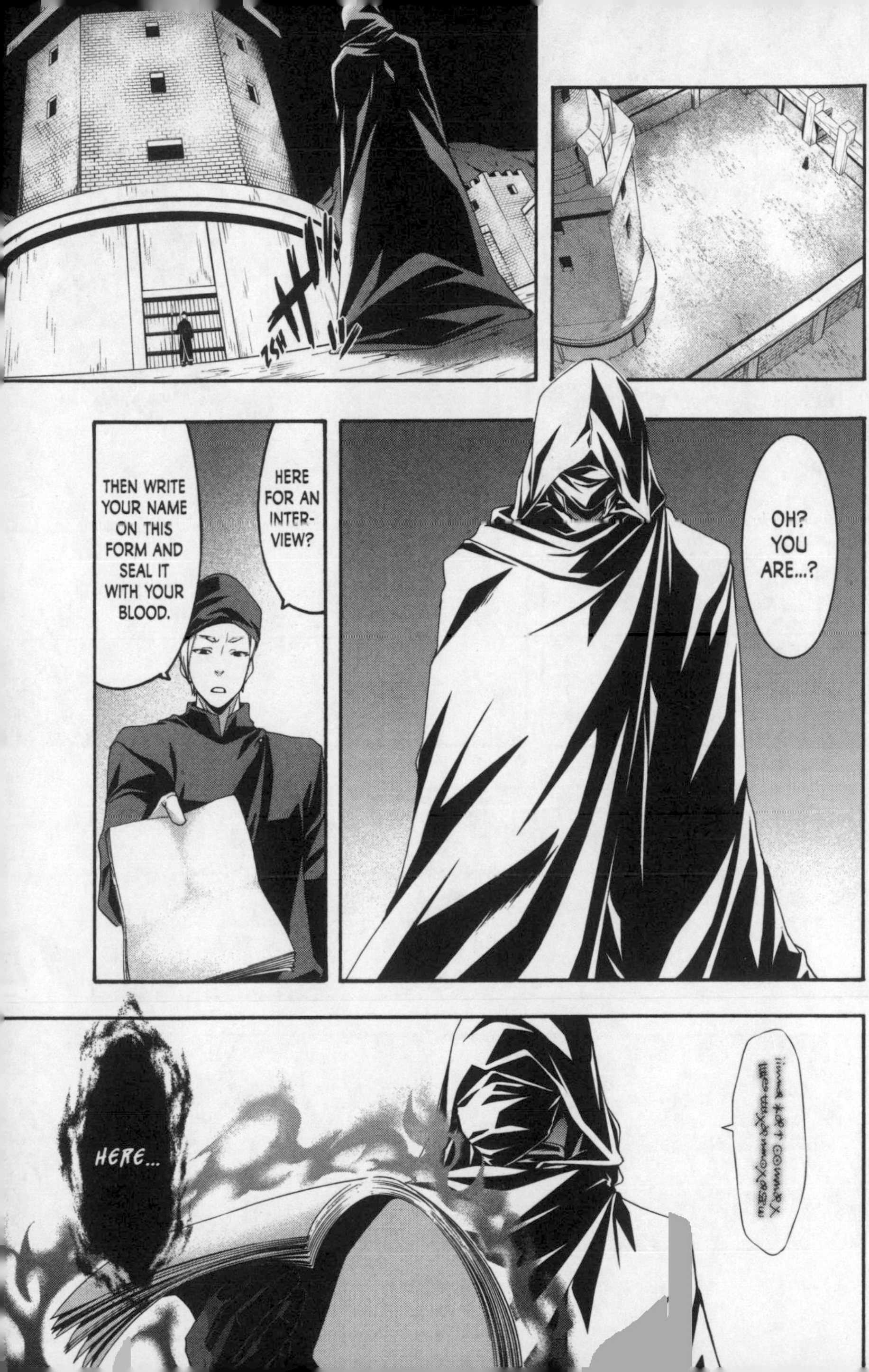
ZSH
OH? YOU ARE...?
HERE FOR AN INTER-VIEW?
THEN WRITE YOUR NAME ON THIS FORM AND SEAL IT WITH YOUR BLOOD.
HERE...

...THAT YOU HAVE.

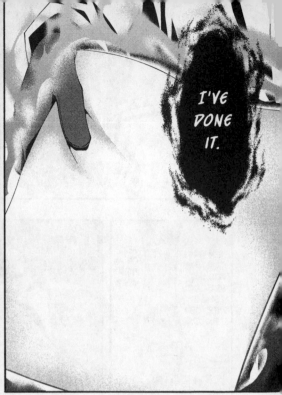

I'VE DONE IT.

YOU MAY PASS.

CREAK

TAP

TAP

TAP

108

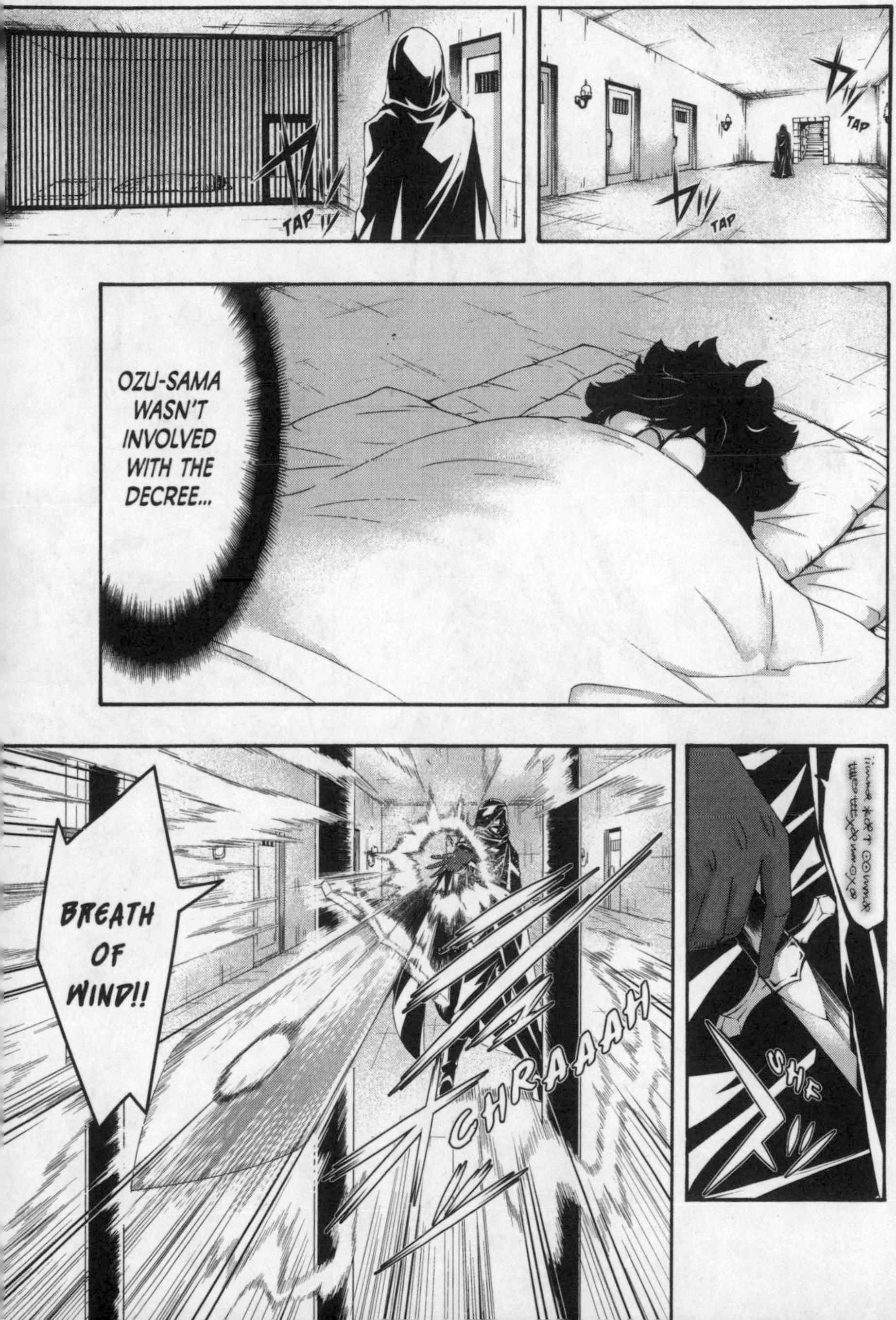
TAP
TAP
TAP
OZU-SAMA WASN'T INVOLVED WITH THE DECREE...
SHF
BREATH OF WIND!!
CHRAAAAH

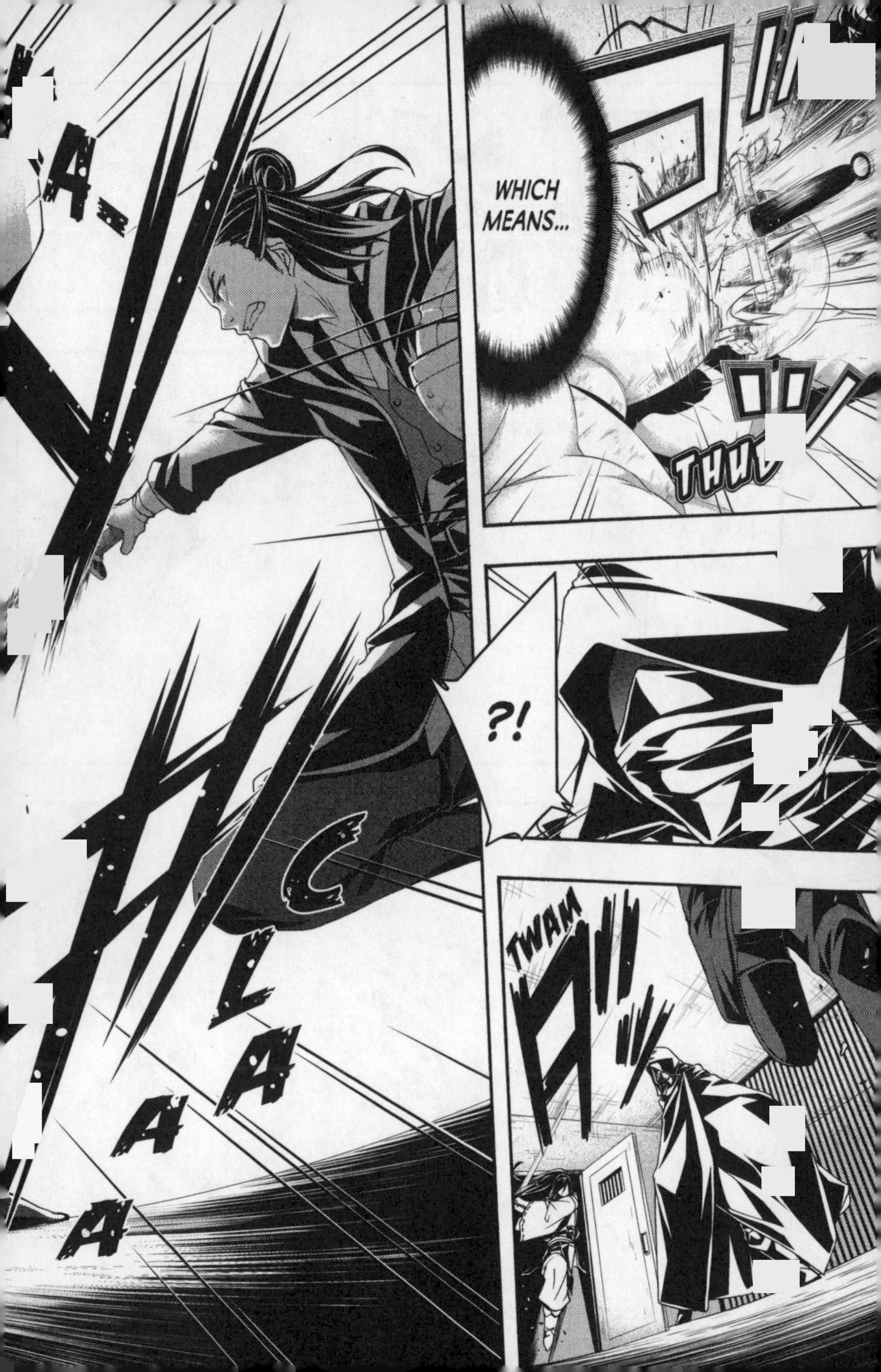
WHICH MEANS...
THU
?!
TWAM
A-A-
AAAA

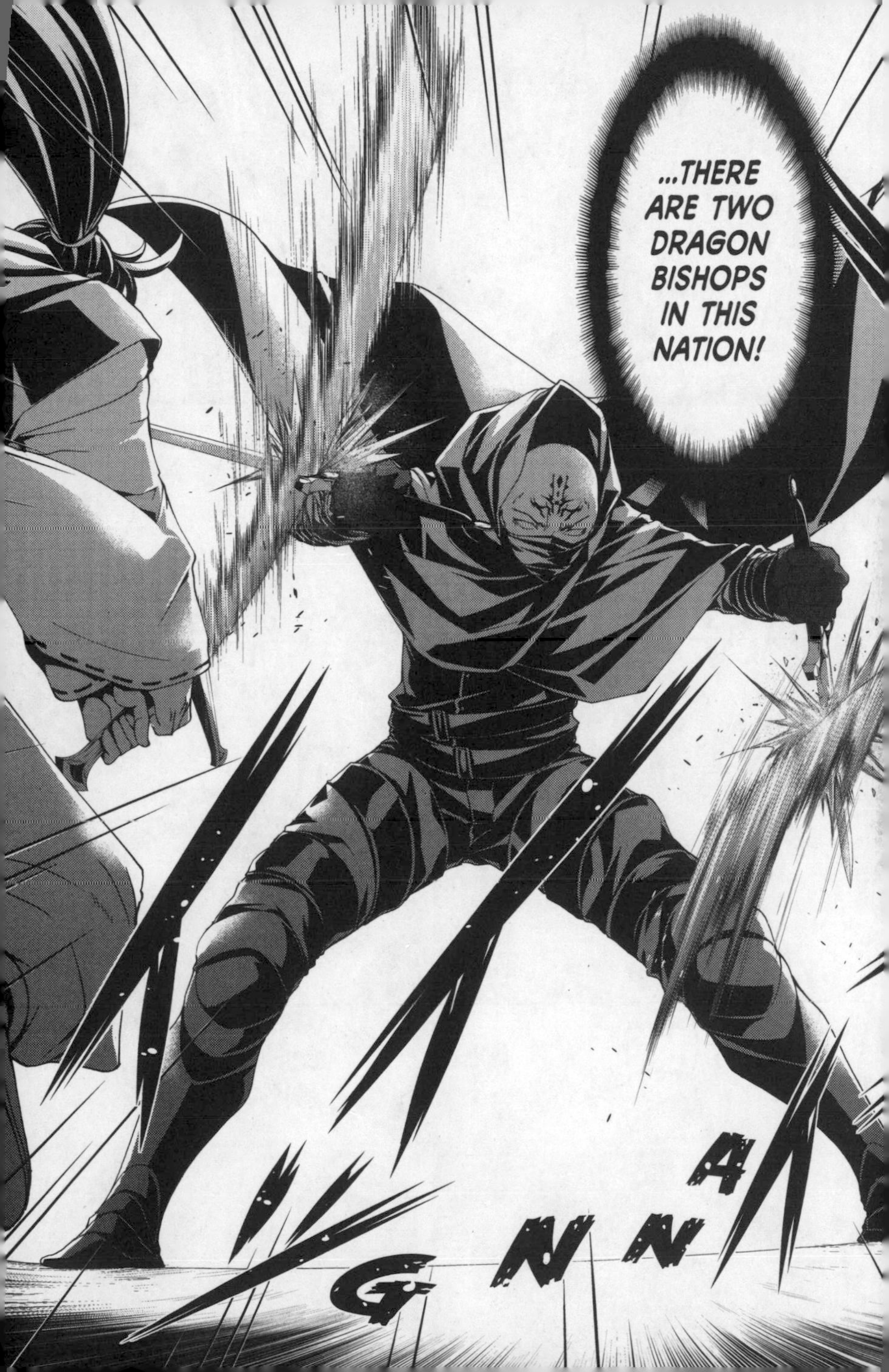
...THERE ARE TWO DRAGON BISHOPS IN THIS NATION!
GNNNA

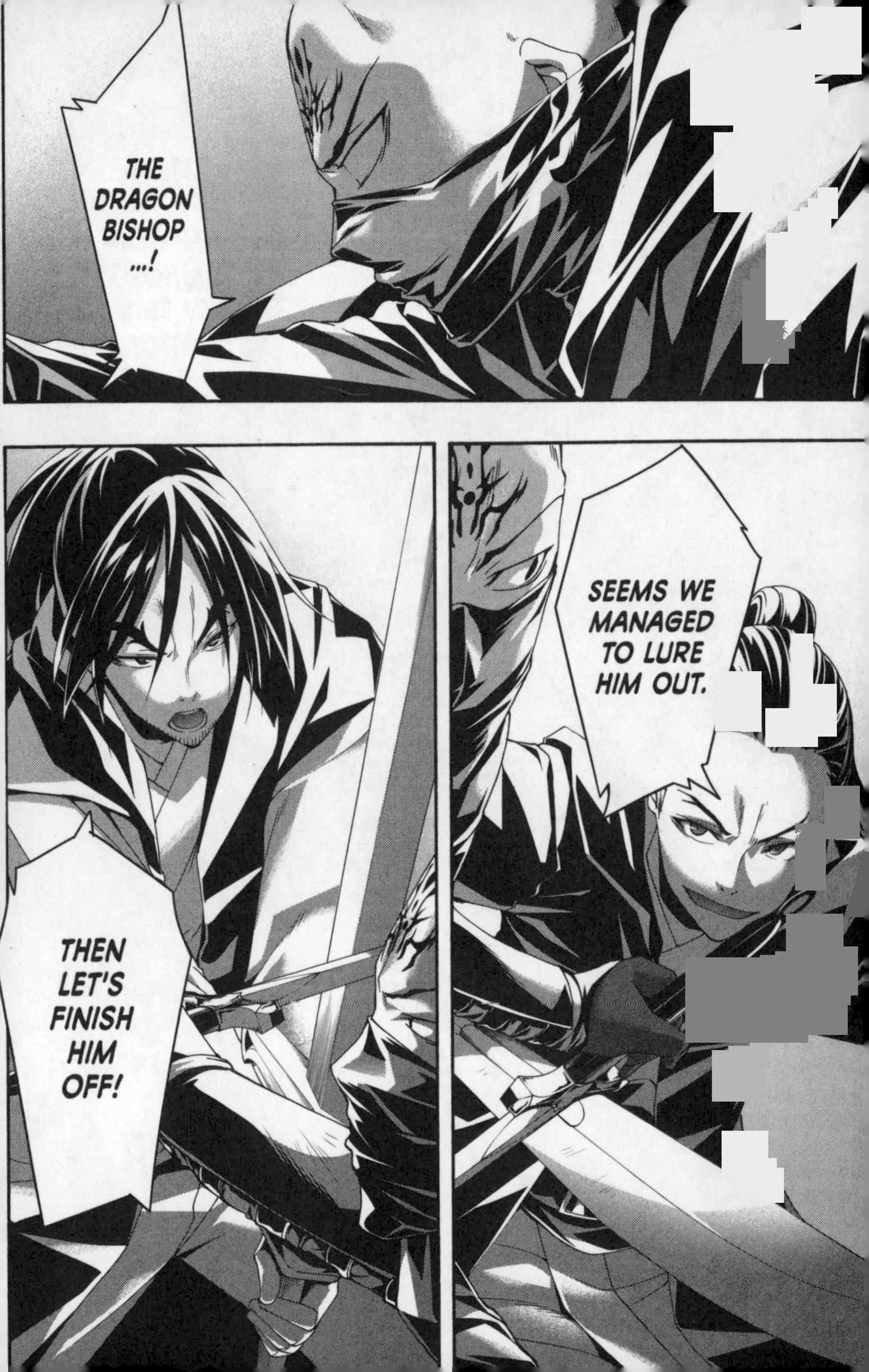
THE DRAGON BISHOP ...!
SEEMS WE MANAGED TO LURE HIM OUT.
THEN LET'S FINISH HIM OFF!

I'M STANDING ON A MILLION LIVES

I'M STANDING ON A MILLION LIVES.

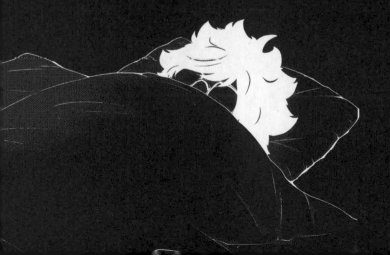

#58 My Magic

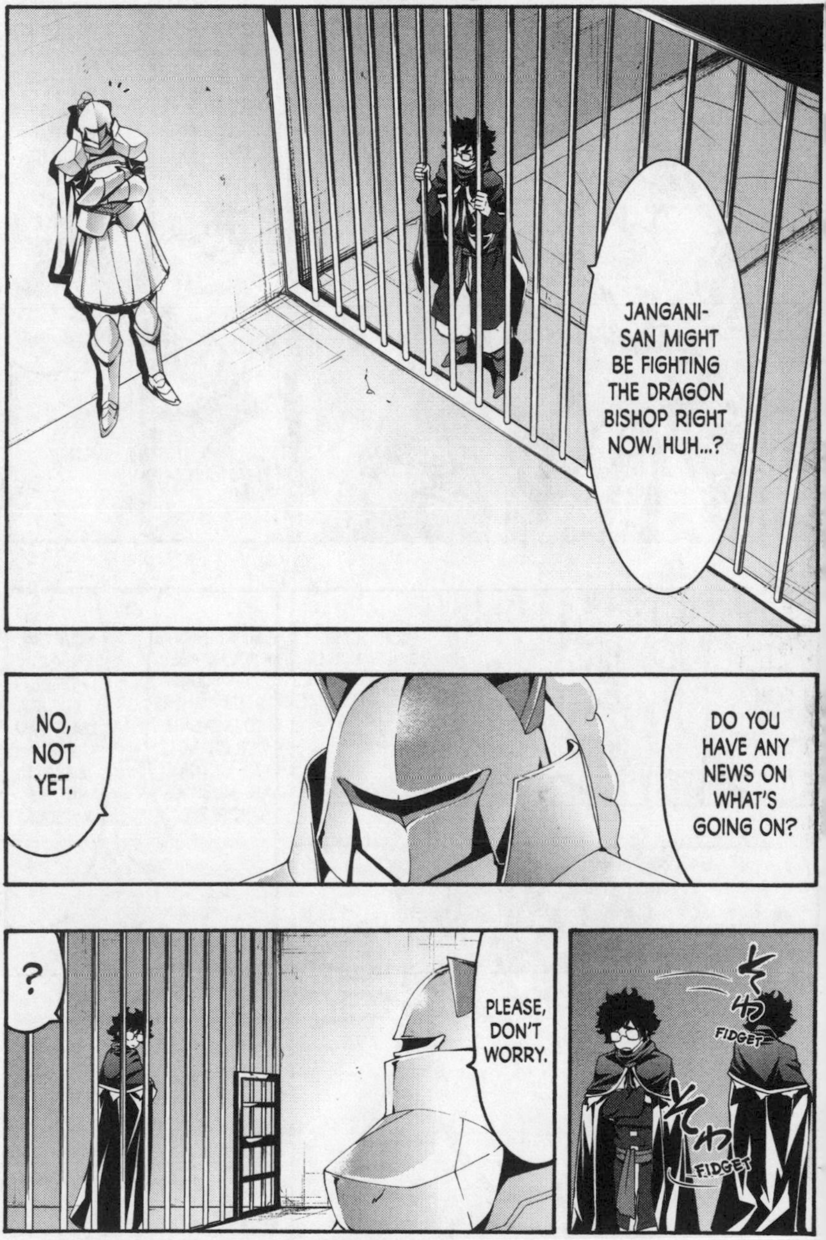
JANGANI-SAN MIGHT BE FIGHTING THE DRAGON BISHOP RIGHT NOW, HUH...?
DO YOU HAVE ANY NEWS ON WHAT'S GOING ON?
NO, NOT YET.
そわ
FIDGET
そわ
FIDGET
PLEASE, DON'T WORRY.
?

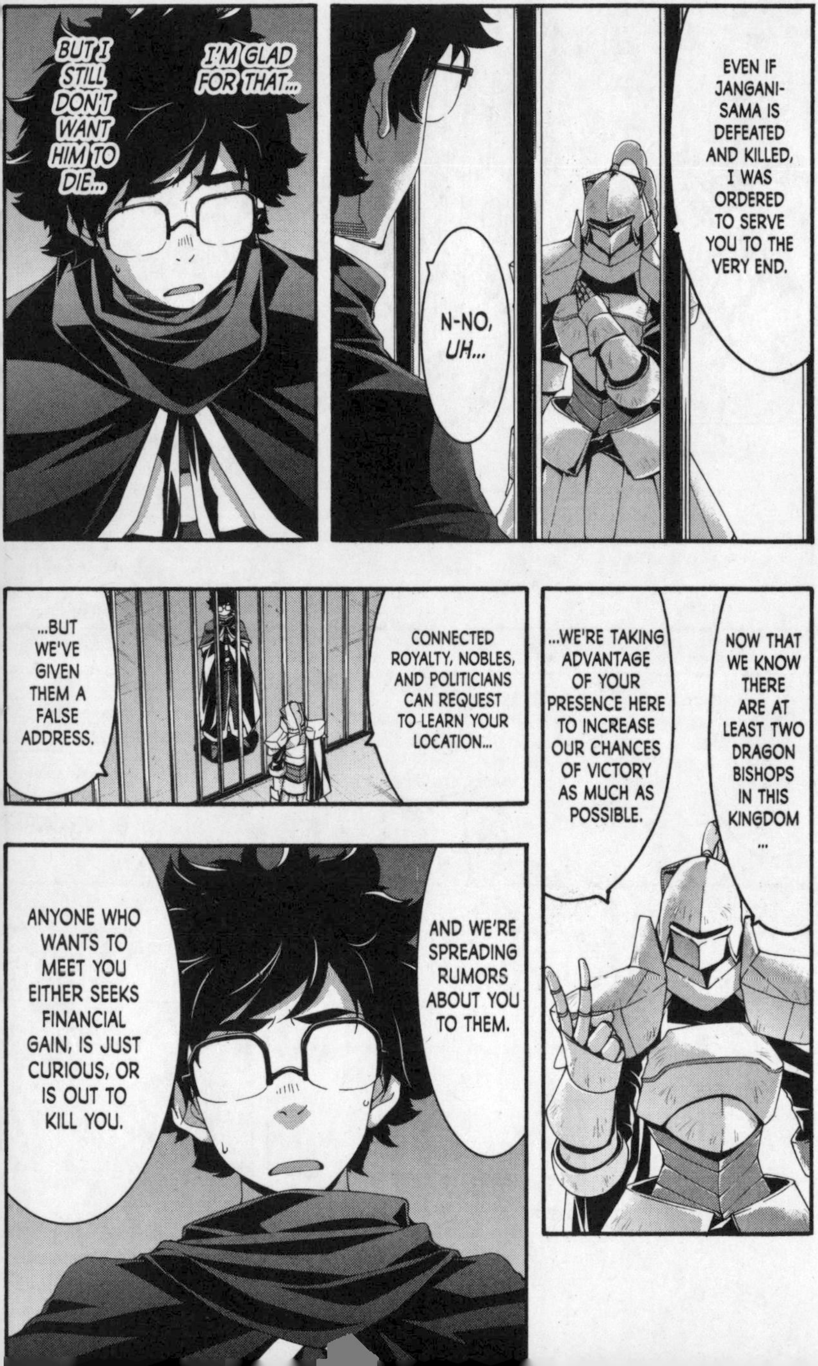
EVEN IF JANGANI-SAMA IS DEFEATED AND KILLED, I WAS ORDERED TO SERVE YOU TO THE VERY END.
N-NO, *UH...*
I'M GLAD FOR THAT...
BUT I STILL DON'T WANT HIM TO DIE...
NOW THAT WE KNOW THERE ARE AT LEAST TWO DRAGON BISHOPS IN THIS KINGDOM...
...WE'RE TAKING ADVANTAGE OF YOUR PRESENCE HERE TO INCREASE OUR CHANCES OF VICTORY AS MUCH AS POSSIBLE.
CONNECTED ROYALTY, NOBLES, AND POLITICIANS CAN REQUEST TO LEARN YOUR LOCATION...
...BUT WE'VE GIVEN THEM A FALSE ADDRESS.
AND WE'RE SPREADING RUMORS ABOUT YOU TO THEM.
ANYONE WHO WANTS TO MEET YOU EITHER SEEKS FINANCIAL GAIN, IS JUST CURIOUS, OR IS OUT TO KILL YOU.

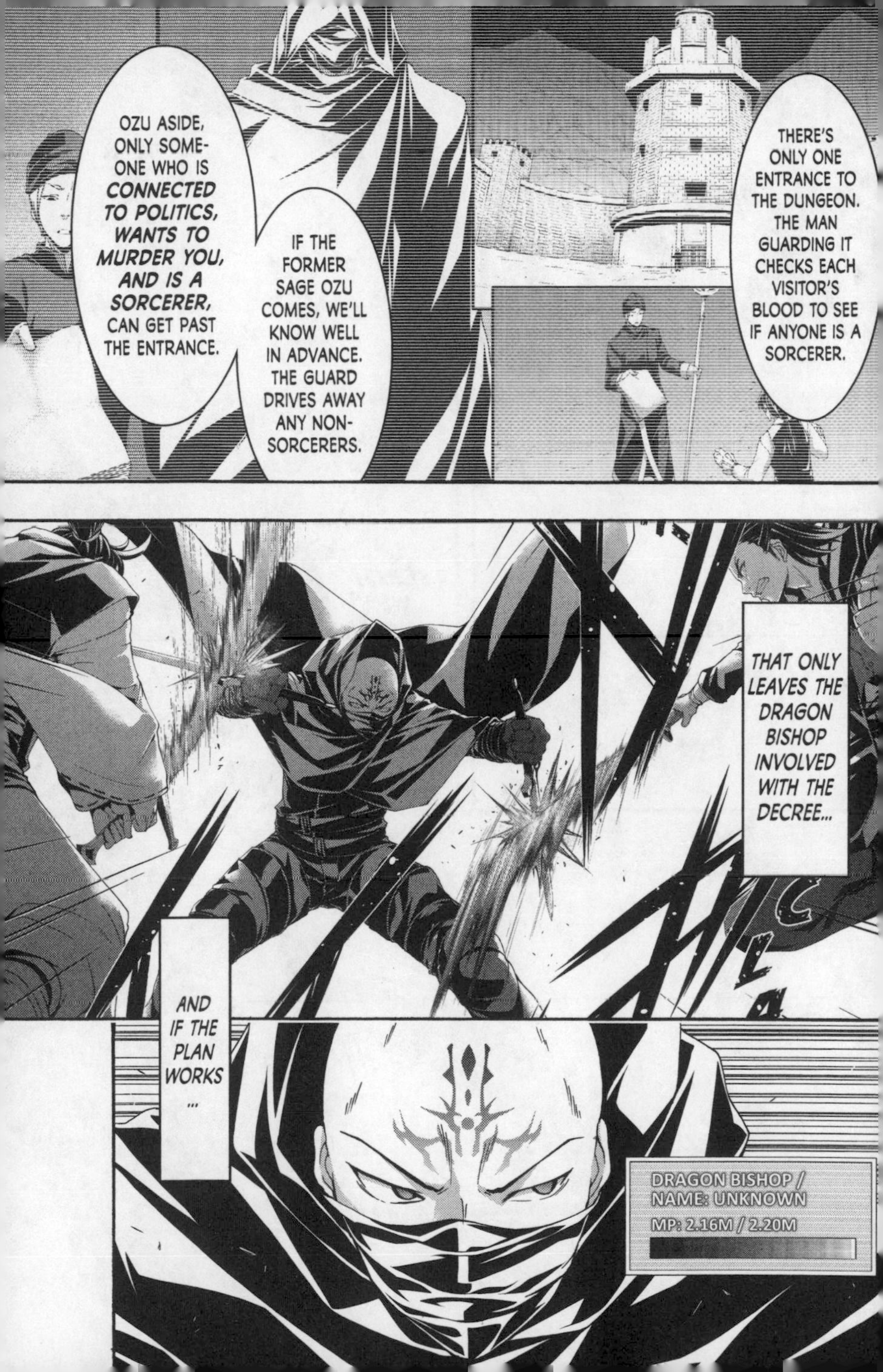
THERE'S ONLY ONE ENTRANCE TO THE DUNGEON. THE MAN GUARDING IT CHECKS EACH VISITOR'S BLOOD TO SEE IF ANYONE IS A SORCERER.
IF THE FORMER SAGE OZU COMES, WE'LL KNOW WELL IN ADVANCE. THE GUARD DRIVES AWAY ANY NON-SORCERERS.
OZU ASIDE, ONLY SOMEONE WHO IS *CONNECTED TO POLITICS, WANTS TO MURDER YOU, AND IS A SORCERER,* CAN GET PAST THE ENTRANCE.
THAT ONLY LEAVES THE DRAGON BISHOP INVOLVED WITH THE DECREE...
AND IF THE PLAN WORKS...
DRAGON BISHOP / NAME: UNKNOWN
MP: 2.16M / 2.20M

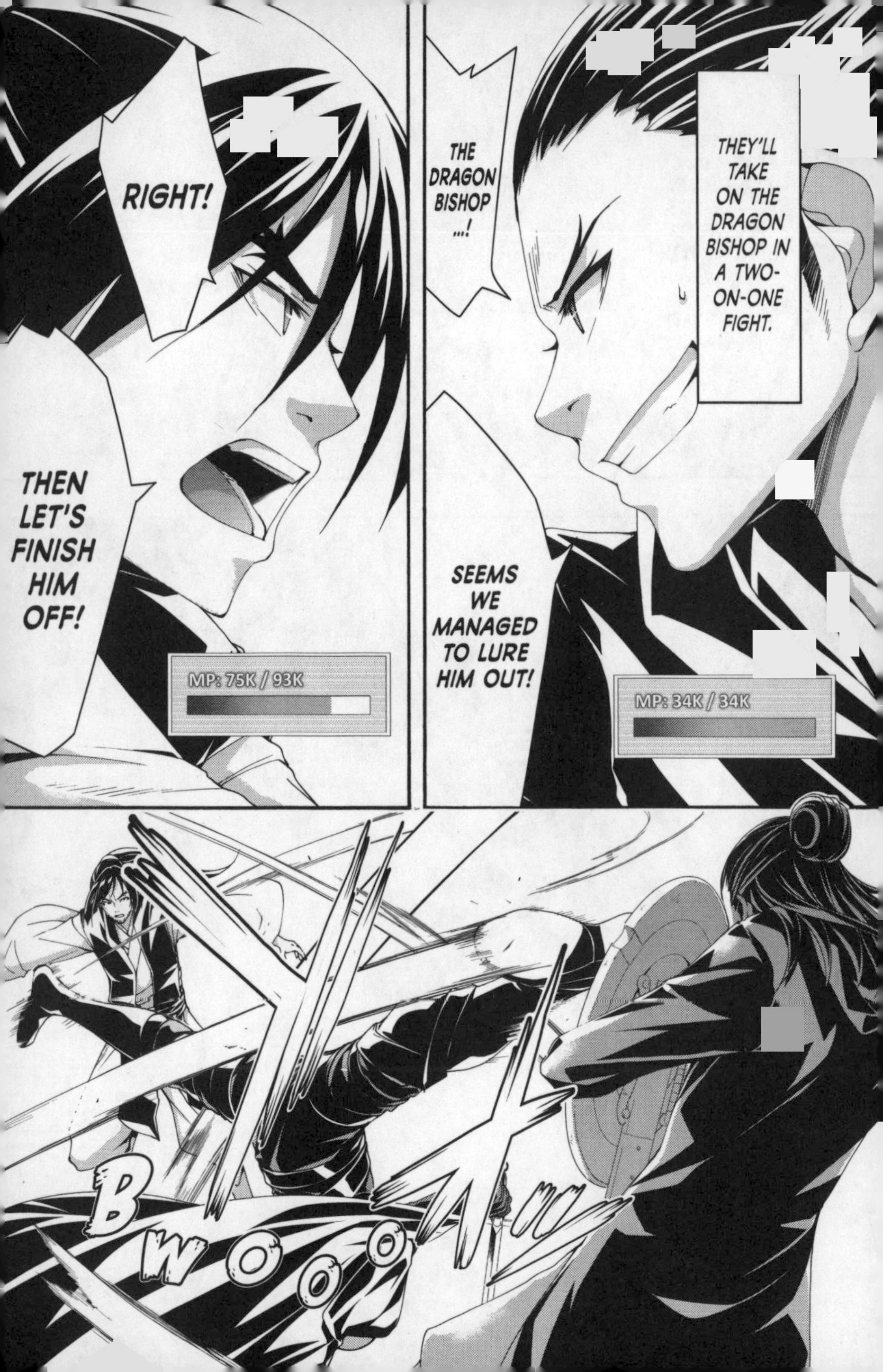
THEY'LL TAKE ON THE DRAGON BISHOP IN A TWO-ON-ONE FIGHT.
THE DRAGON BISHOP ...!
SEEMS WE MANAGED TO LURE HIM OUT!
MP: 34K / 34K
RIGHT!
THEN LET'S FINISH HIM OFF!
MP: 75K / 93K
BWOOOO

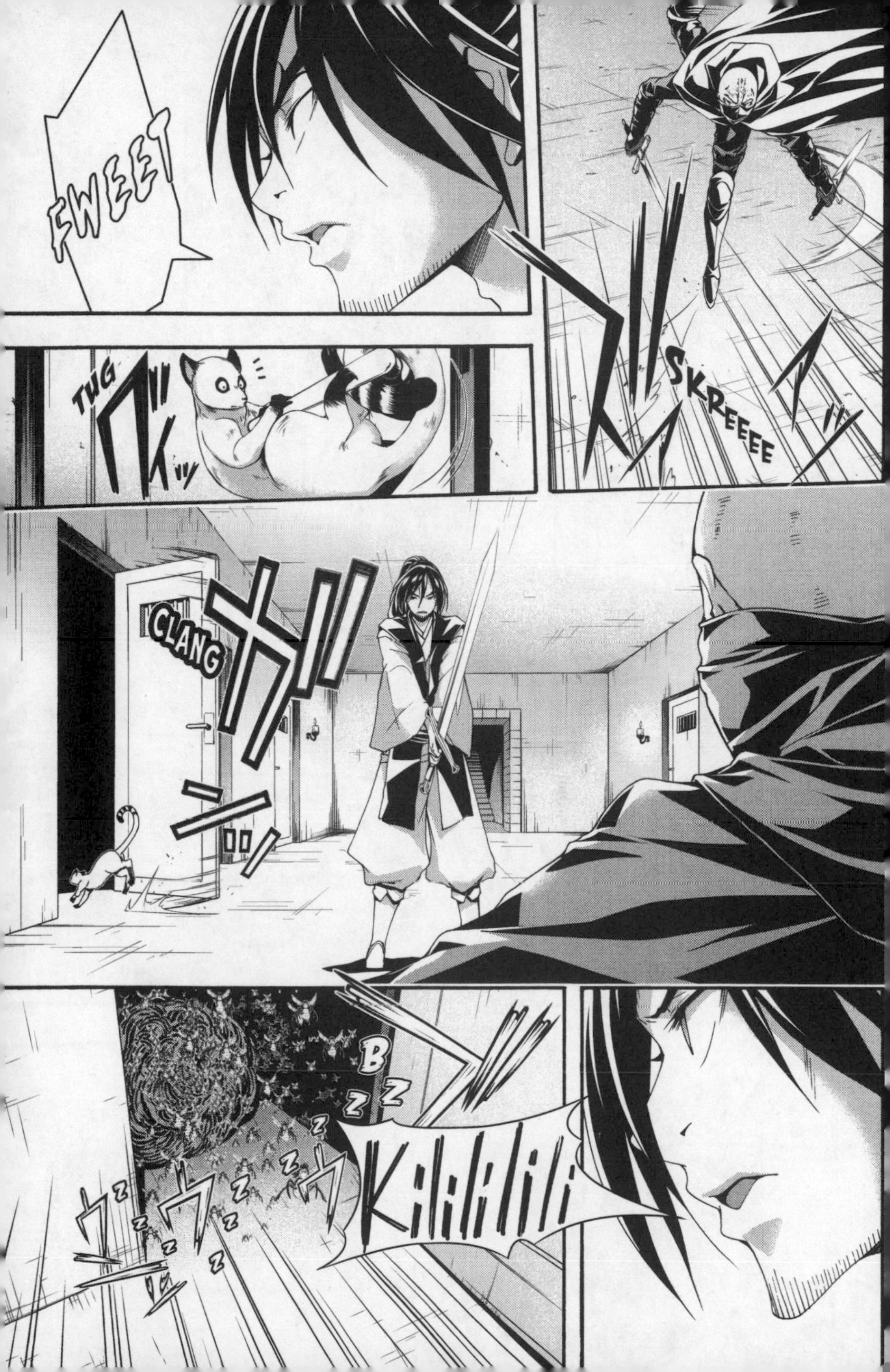
SKREEEEE
FWEET
TUG
CLANG
Kilililili
BZZ

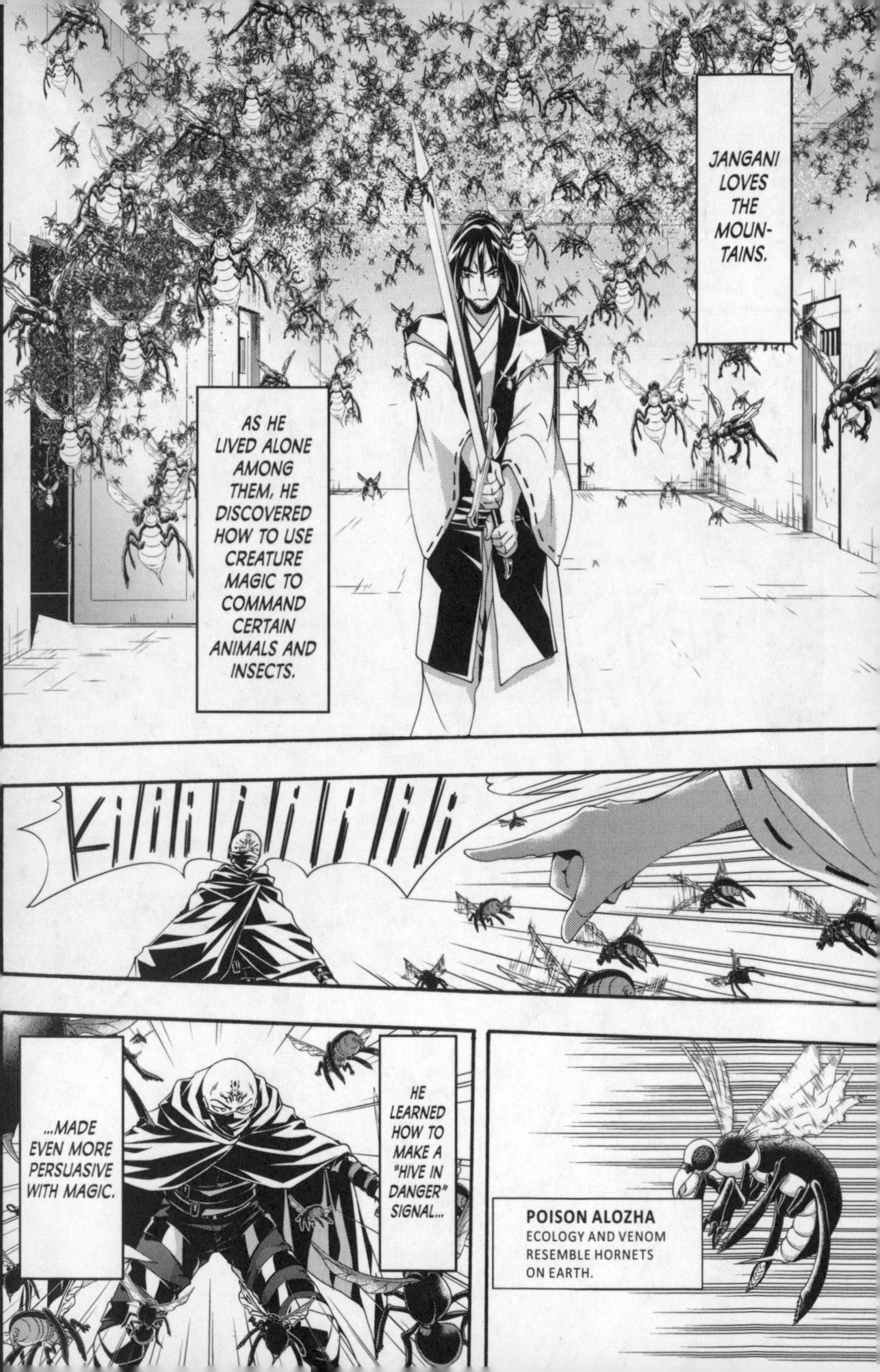
JANGANI LOVES THE MOUNTAINS.
AS HE LIVED ALONE AMONG THEM, HE DISCOVERED HOW TO USE CREATURE MAGIC TO COMMAND CERTAIN ANIMALS AND INSECTS.
POISON ALOZHA
ECOLOGY AND VENOM RESEMBLE HORNETS ON EARTH.
HE LEARNED HOW TO MAKE A "HIVE IN DANGER" SIGNAL...
...MADE EVEN MORE PERSUASIVE WITH MAGIC.

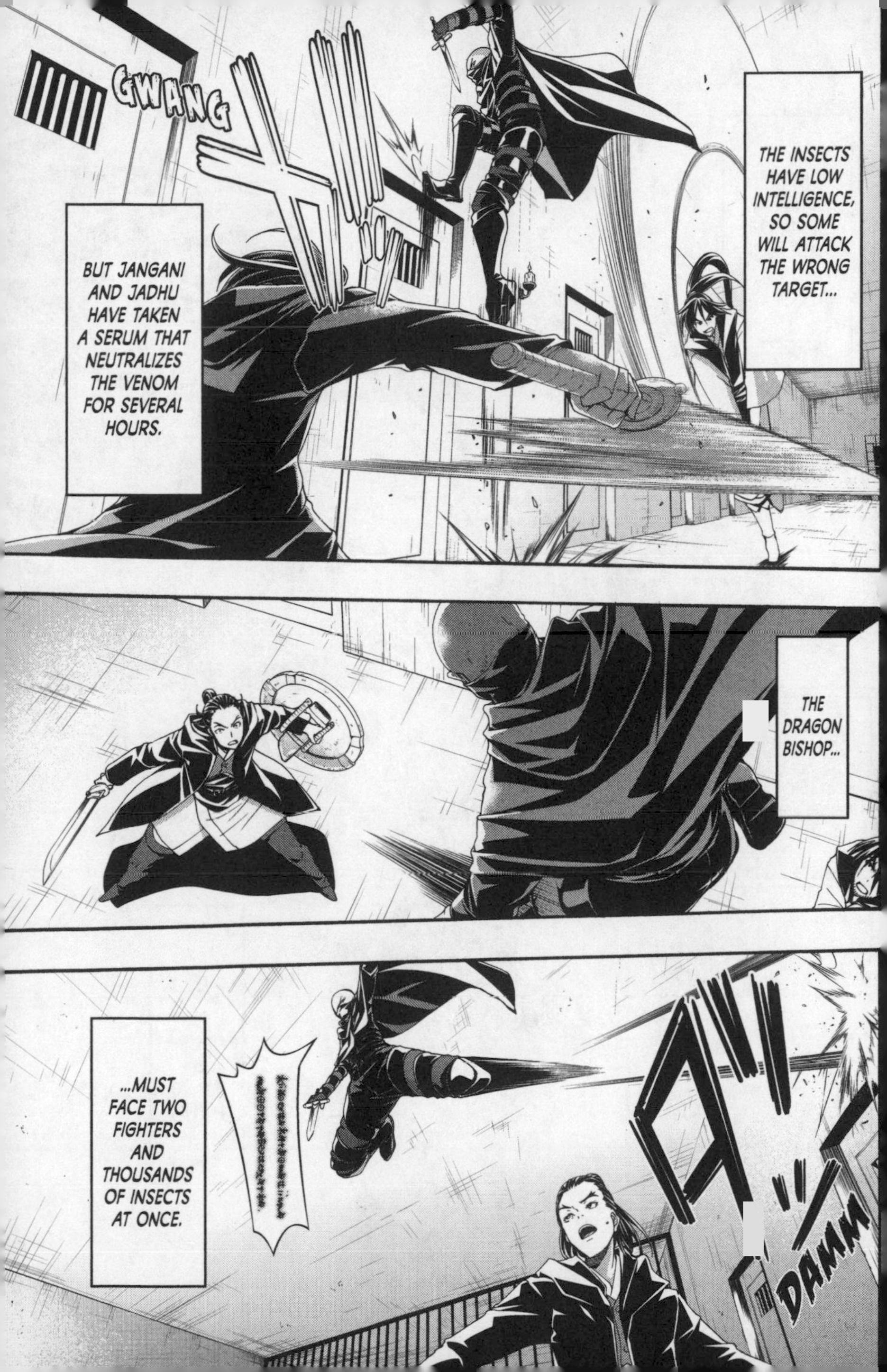
THE INSECTS HAVE LOW INTELLIGENCE, SO SOME WILL ATTACK THE WRONG TARGET...
GWANG
BUT JANGANI AND JADHU HAVE TAKEN A SERUM THAT NEUTRALIZES THE VENOM FOR SEVERAL HOURS.
THE DRAGON BISHOP...
...MUST FACE TWO FIGHTERS AND THOUSANDS OF INSECTS AT ONCE.
DAMM

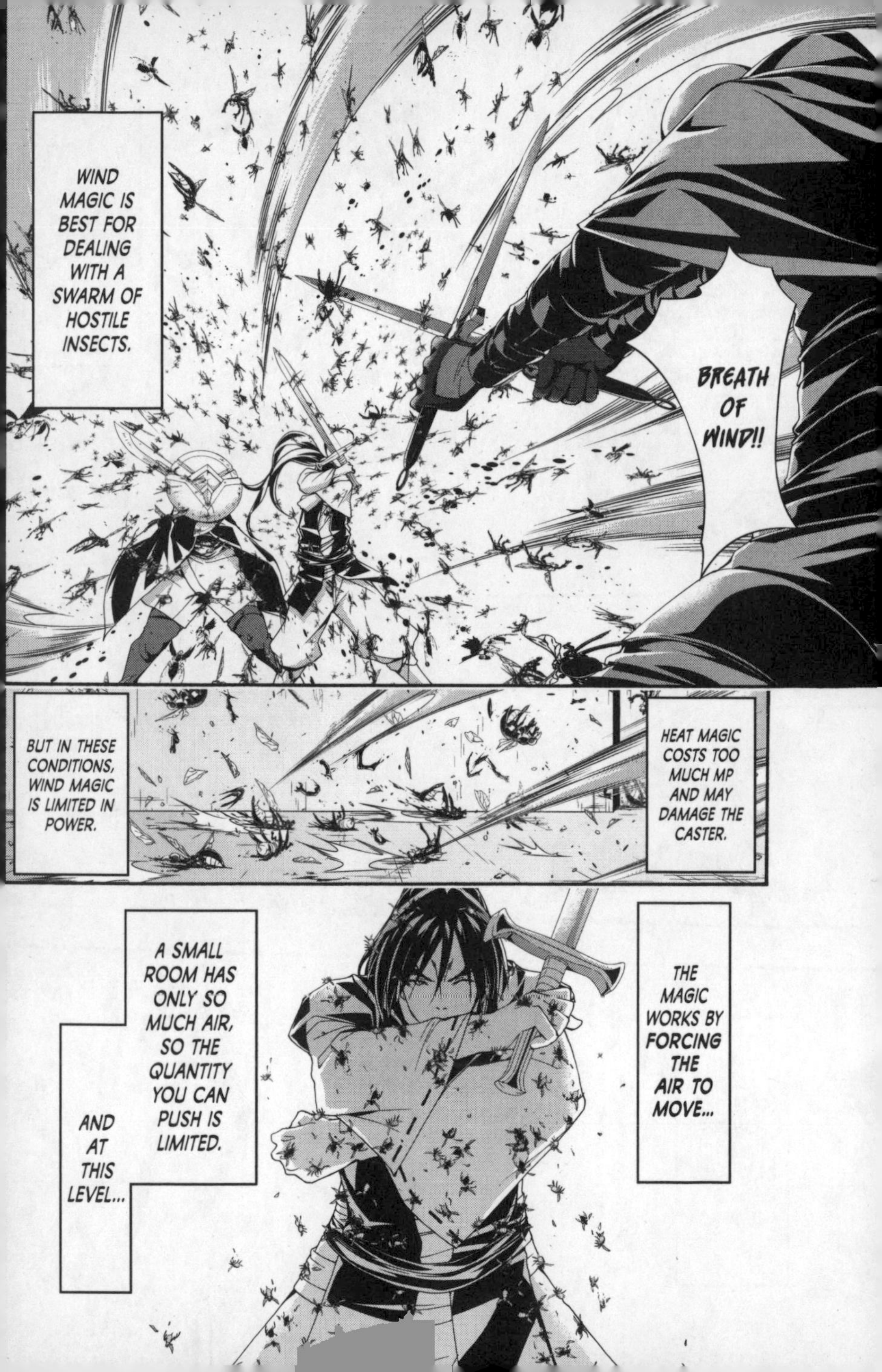
BREATH OF WIND!!
WIND MAGIC IS BEST FOR DEALING WITH A SWARM OF HOSTILE INSECTS.
HEAT MAGIC COSTS TOO MUCH MP AND MAY DAMAGE THE CASTER.
BUT IN THESE CONDITIONS, WIND MAGIC IS LIMITED IN POWER.
THE MAGIC WORKS BY FORCING THE AIR TO MOVE...
A SMALL ROOM HAS ONLY SO MUCH AIR, SO THE QUANTITY YOU CAN PUSH IS LIMITED.
AND AT THIS LEVEL...

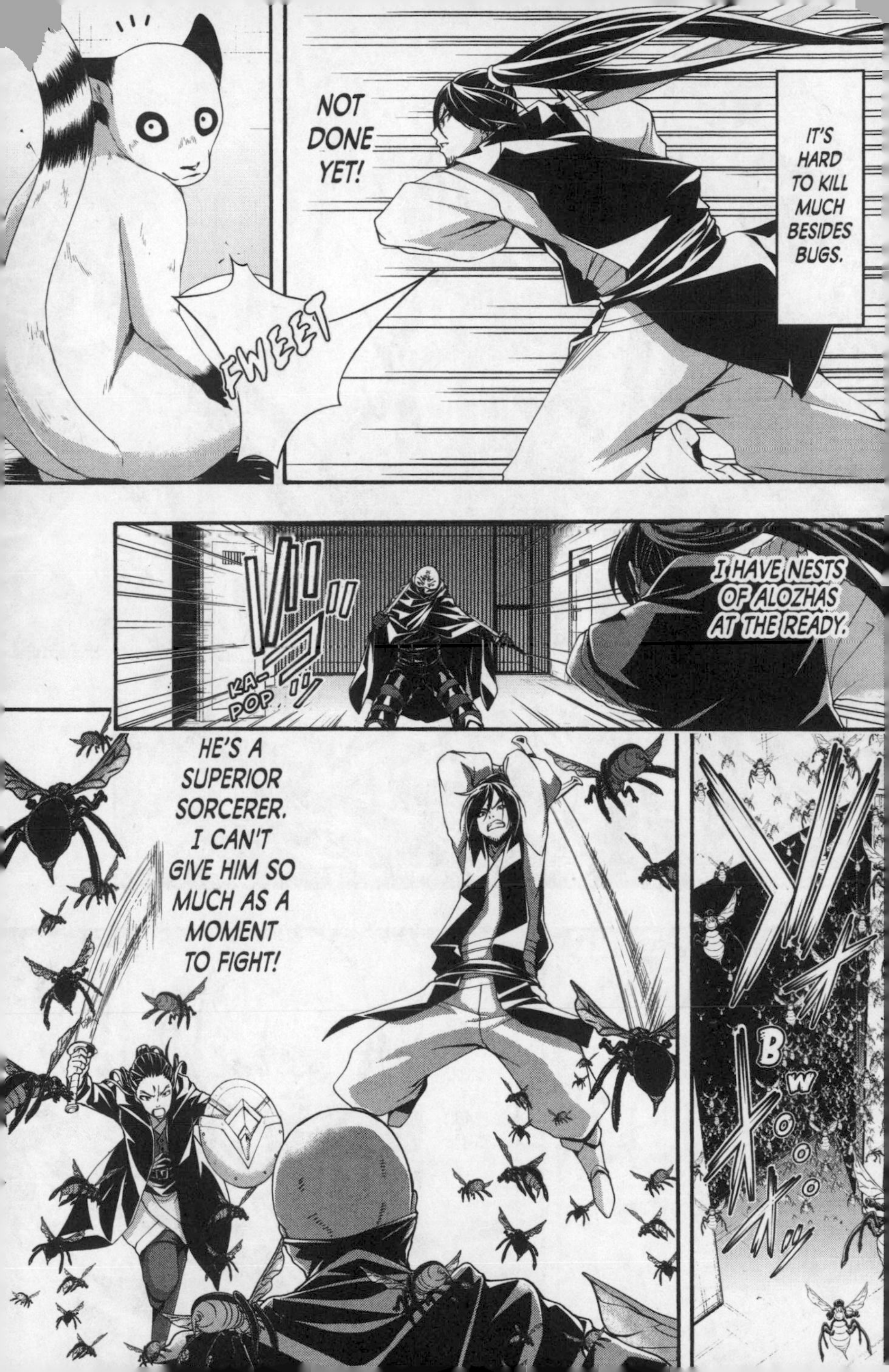
IT'S HARD TO KILL MUCH BESIDES BUGS.
NOT DONE YET!
FWEET
I HAVE NESTS OF ALOZHAS AT THE READY.
KA-POP
HE'S A SUPERIOR SORCERER. I CAN'T GIVE HIM SO MUCH AS A MOMENT TO FIGHT!

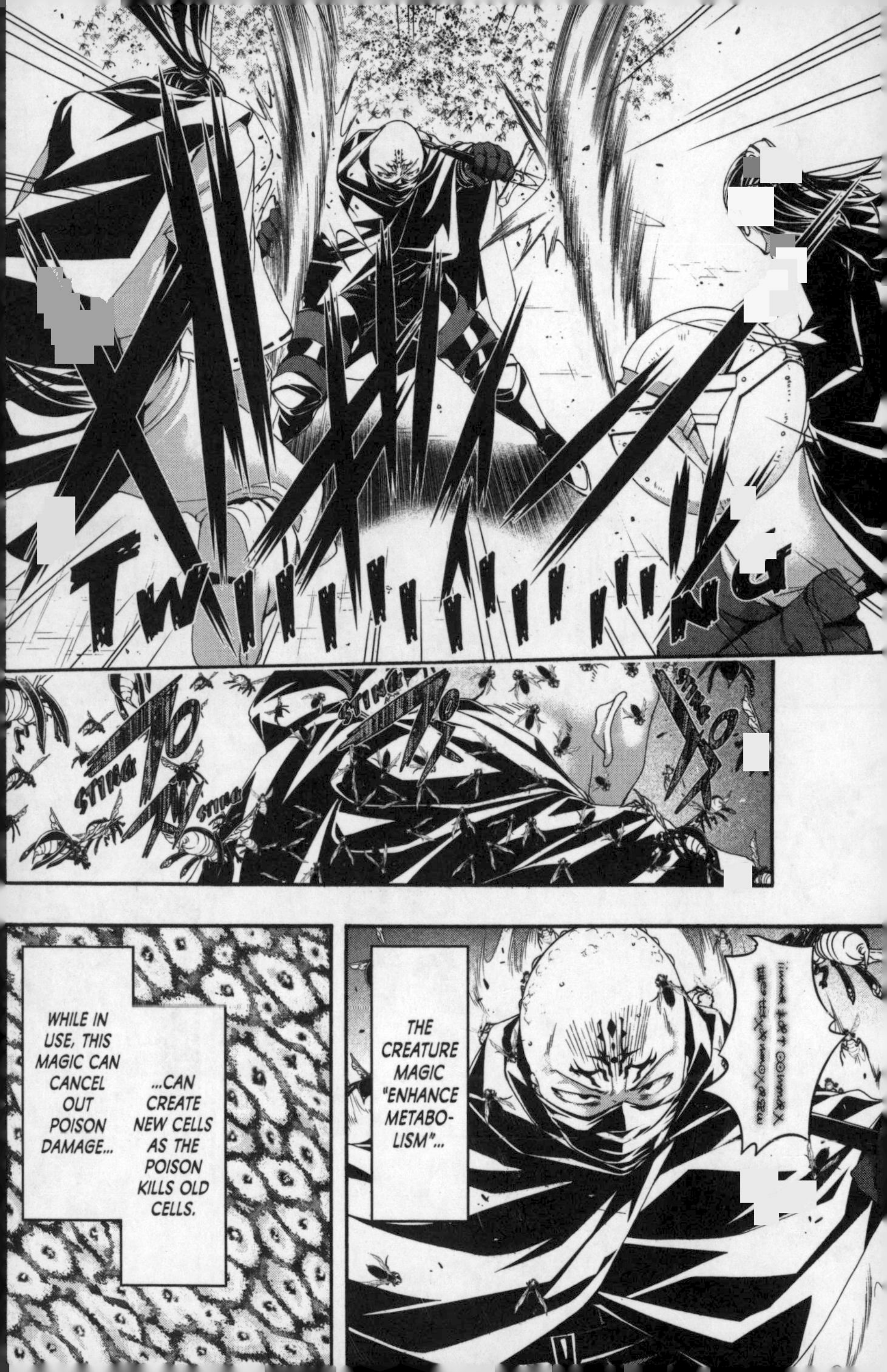
TWIIIIIIIIIIIING
STING
STING
STING
STING
THE CREATURE MAGIC "ENHANCE METABO-LISM"...
WHILE IN USE, THIS MAGIC CAN CANCEL OUT POISON DAMAGE...
...CAN CREATE NEW CELLS AS THE POISON KILLS OLD CELLS.

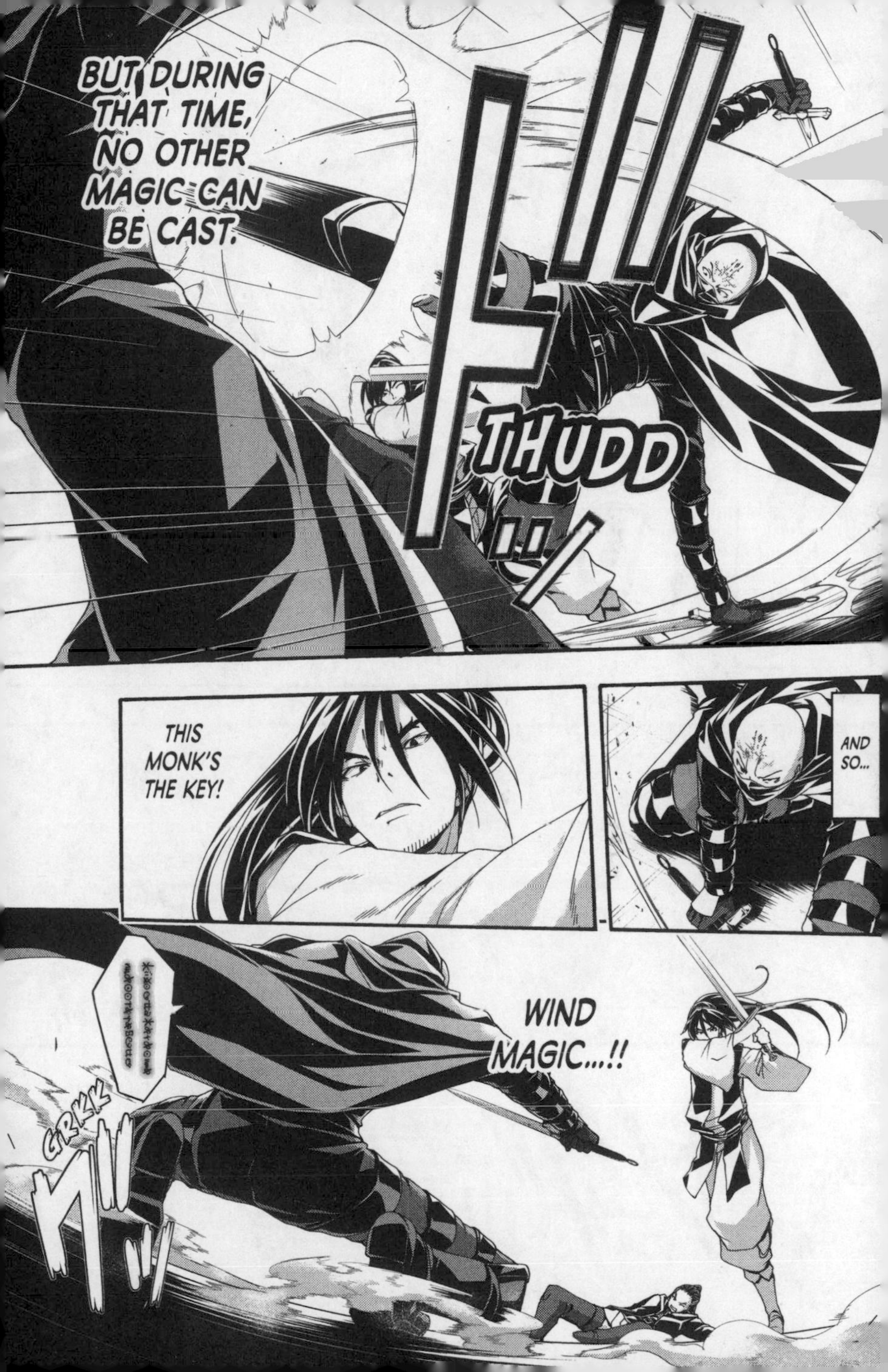
BUT DURING THAT TIME, NO OTHER MAGIC CAN BE CAST.
THUDD
AND SO...
THIS MONK'S THE KEY!
WIND MAGIC...!!
GRKK

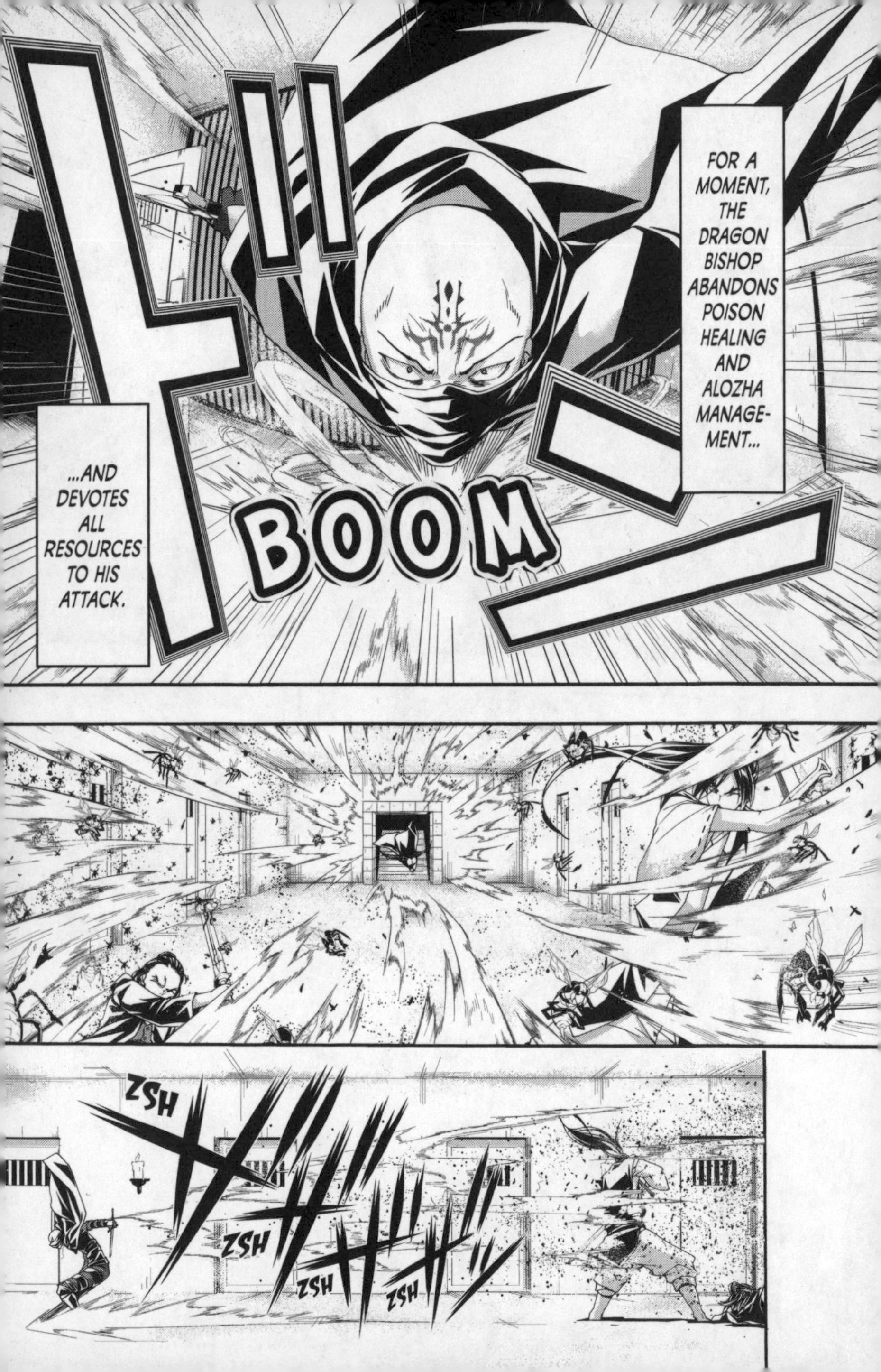
FOR A MOMENT, THE DRAGON BISHOP ABANDONS POISON HEALING AND ALOZHA MANAGEMENT...
...AND DEVOTES ALL RESOURCES TO HIS ATTACK.
BOOM
ZSH
ZSH
ZSH
ZSH

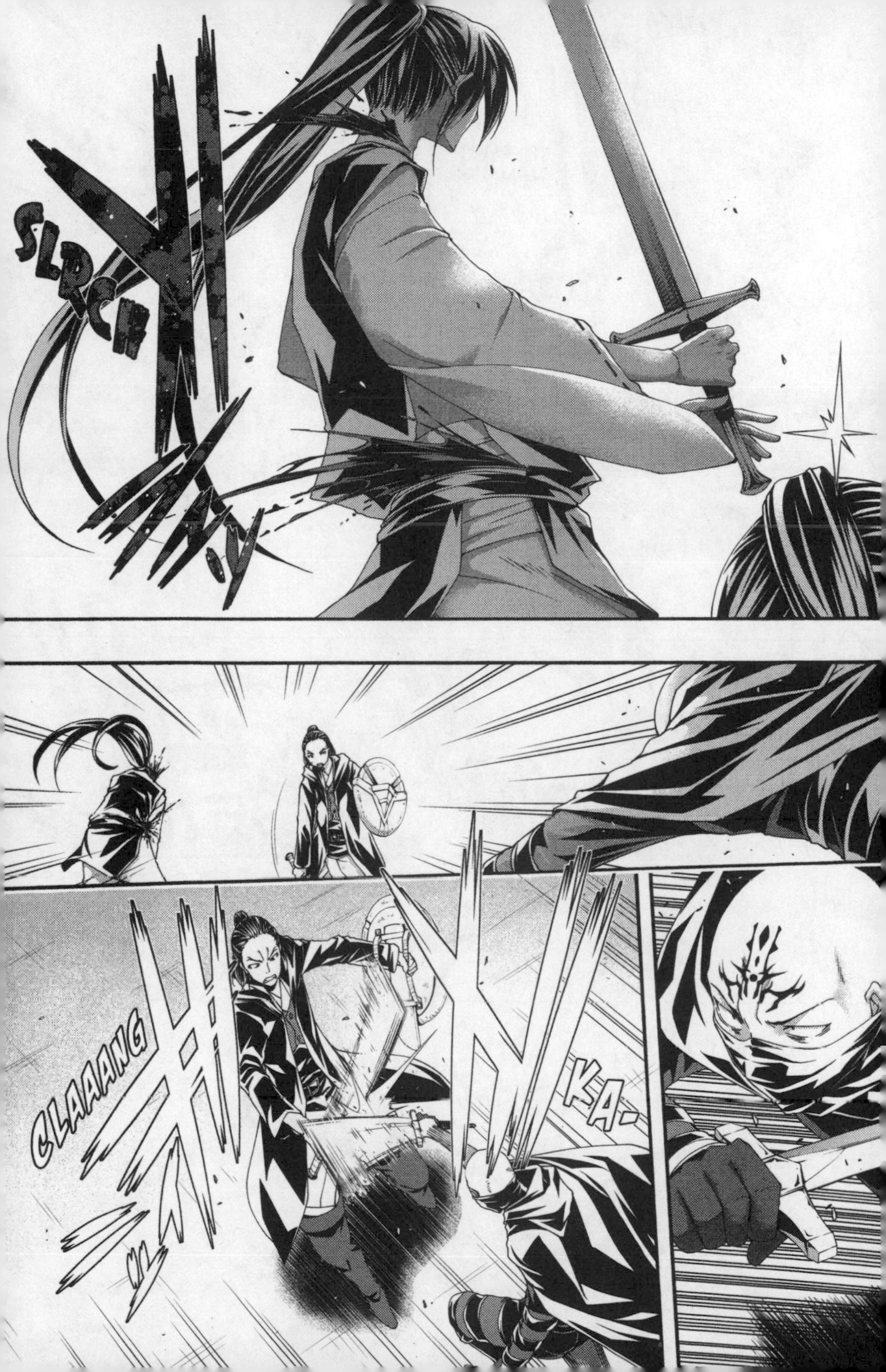
SLRCH
KA-
CLAAANG

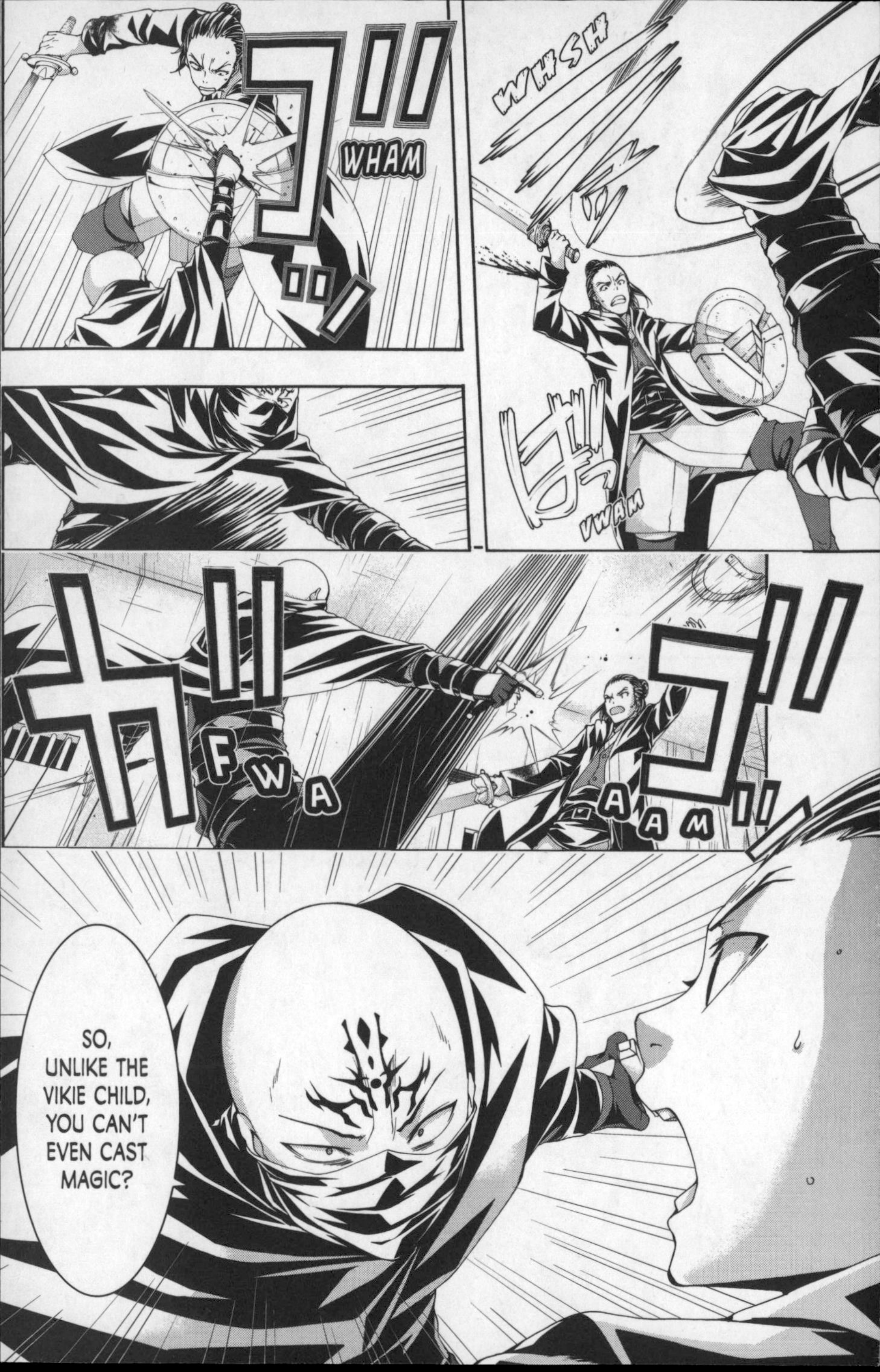
WHSH
VWAM
WHAM
AAM
FWA
SO, UNLIKE THE VIKIE CHILD, YOU CAN'T EVEN CAST MAGIC?

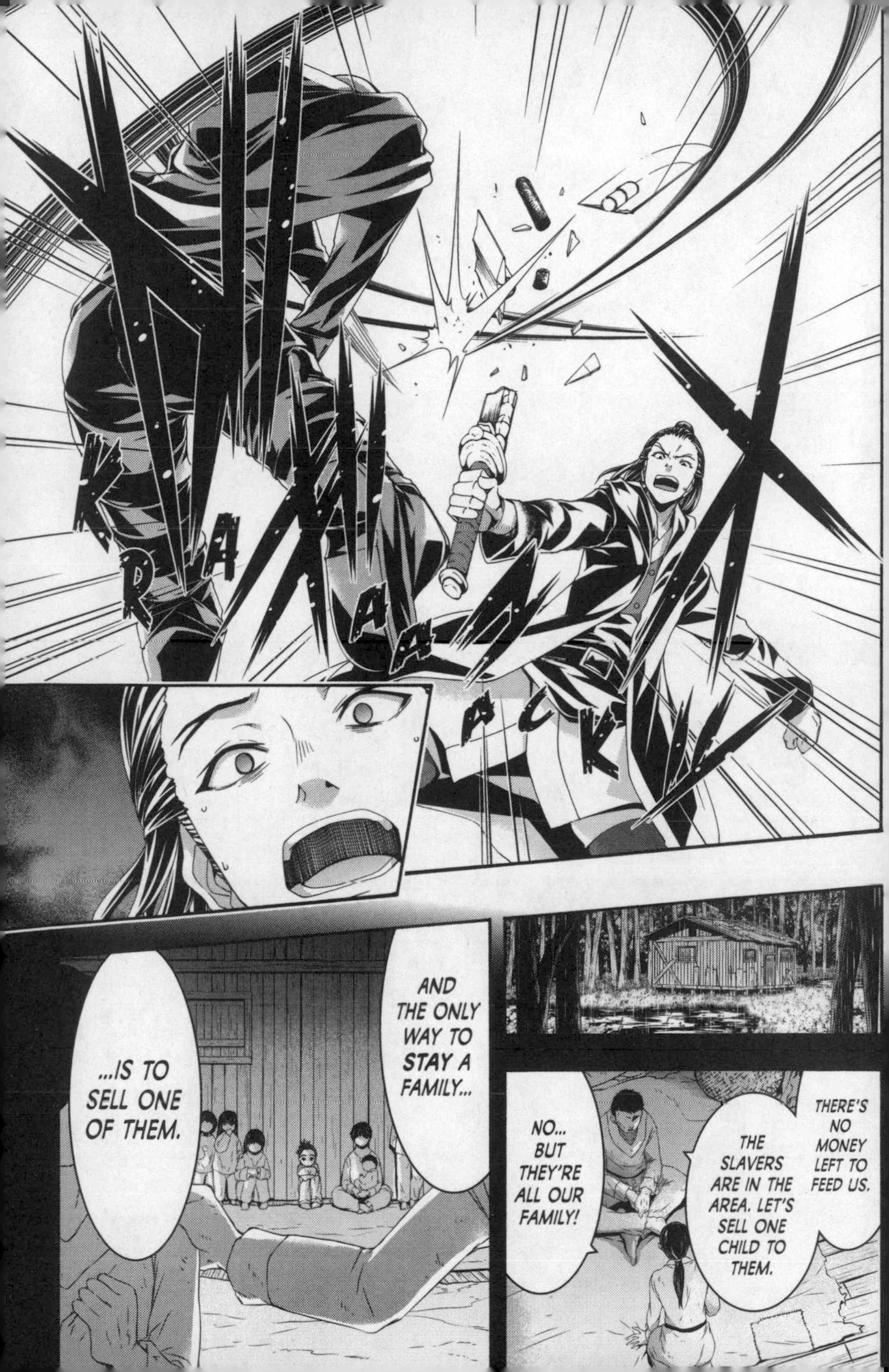
KRAAAACK
THERE'S NO MONEY LEFT TO FEED US.
THE SLAVERS ARE IN THE AREA. LET'S SELL ONE CHILD TO THEM.
NO... BUT THEY'RE ALL OUR FAMILY!
AND THE ONLY WAY TO STAY A FAMILY...
...IS TO SELL ONE OF THEM.

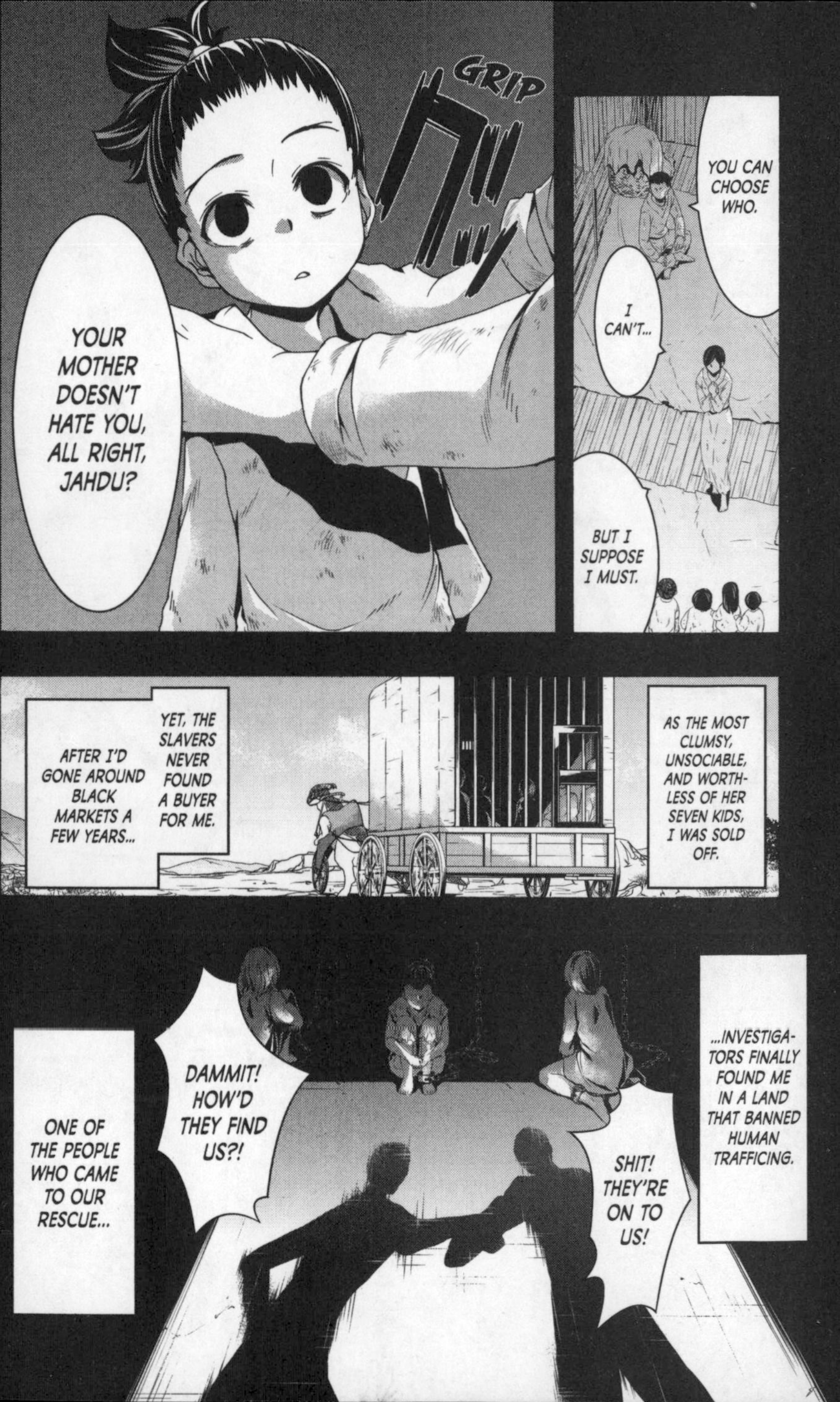
YOU CAN CHOOSE WHO.
I CAN'T...
BUT I SUPPOSE I MUST.
GRIP
YOUR MOTHER DOESN'T HATE YOU, ALL RIGHT, JAHDU?
AS THE MOST CLUMSY, UNSOCIABLE, AND WORTHLESS OF HER SEVEN KIDS, I WAS SOLD OFF.
YET, THE SLAVERS NEVER FOUND A BUYER FOR ME.
AFTER I'D GONE AROUND BLACK MARKETS A FEW YEARS...
...INVESTIGATORS FINALLY FOUND ME IN A LAND THAT BANNED HUMAN TRAFFICING.
SHIT! THEY'RE ON TO US!
DAMMIT! HOW'D THEY FIND US?!
ONE OF THE PEOPLE WHO CAME TO OUR RESCUE...

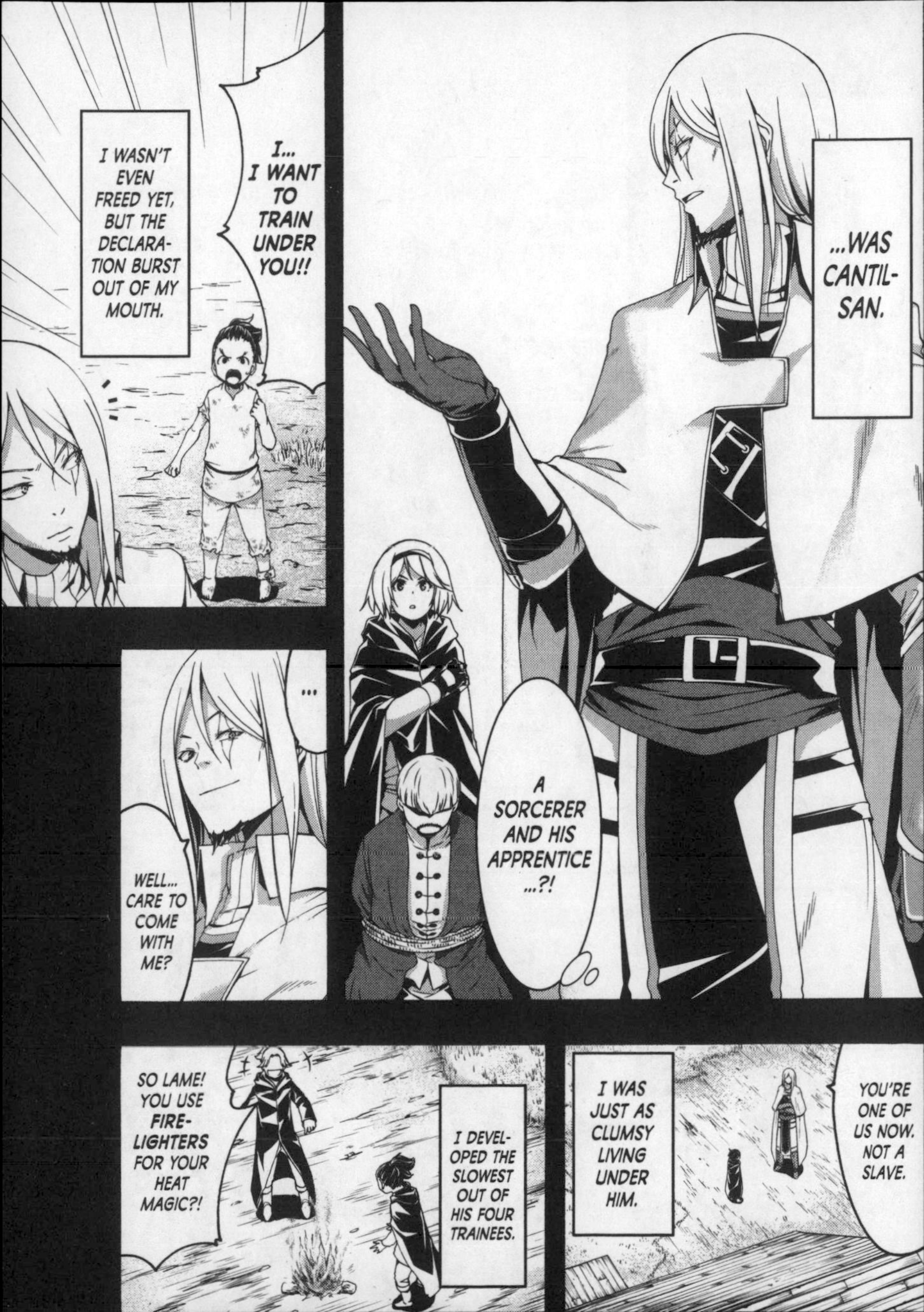

...WAS CANTIL-SAN.
A SORCERER AND HIS APPRENTICE ...?!
I... I WANT TO TRAIN UNDER YOU!!
I WASN'T EVEN FREED YET, BUT THE DECLARATION BURST OUT OF MY MOUTH.
...
WELL... CARE TO COME WITH ME?
YOU'RE ONE OF US NOW. NOT A SLAVE.
I WAS JUST AS CLUMSY LIVING UNDER HIM.
I DEVELOPED THE SLOWEST OUT OF HIS FOUR TRAINEES.
SO LAME! YOU USE FIRE-LIGHTERS FOR YOUR HEAT MAGIC?!

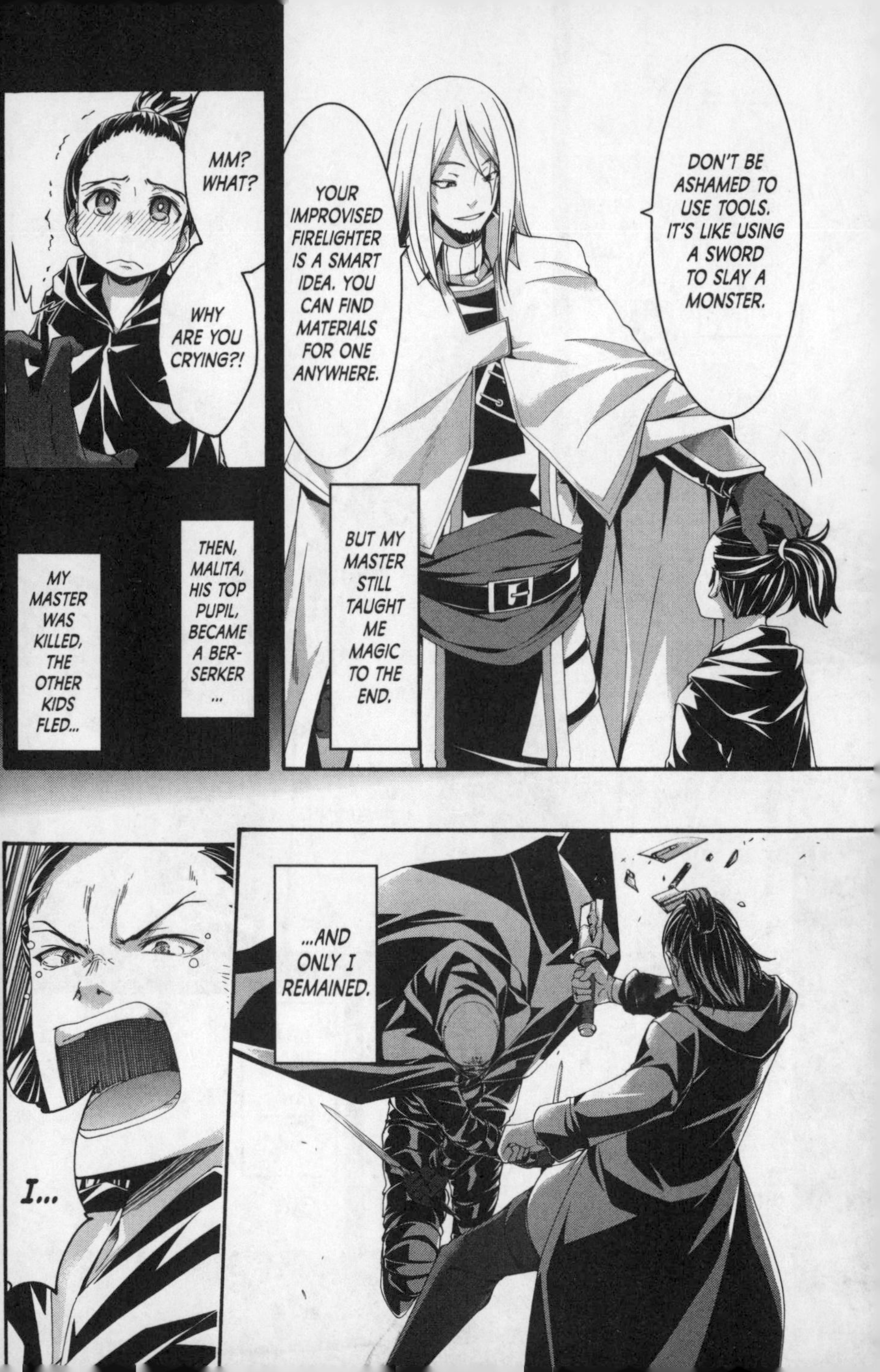
DON'T BE ASHAMED TO USE TOOLS. IT'S LIKE USING A SWORD TO SLAY A MONSTER.
YOUR IMPROVISED FIRELIGHTER IS A SMART IDEA. YOU CAN FIND MATERIALS FOR ONE ANYWHERE.
BUT MY MASTER STILL TAUGHT ME MAGIC TO THE END.
MM? WHAT?
WHY ARE YOU CRYING?!
THEN, MALITA, HIS TOP PUPIL, BECAME A BER-SERKER ...
MY MASTER WAS KILLED, THE OTHER KIDS FLED...
...AND ONLY I REMAINED.
I...

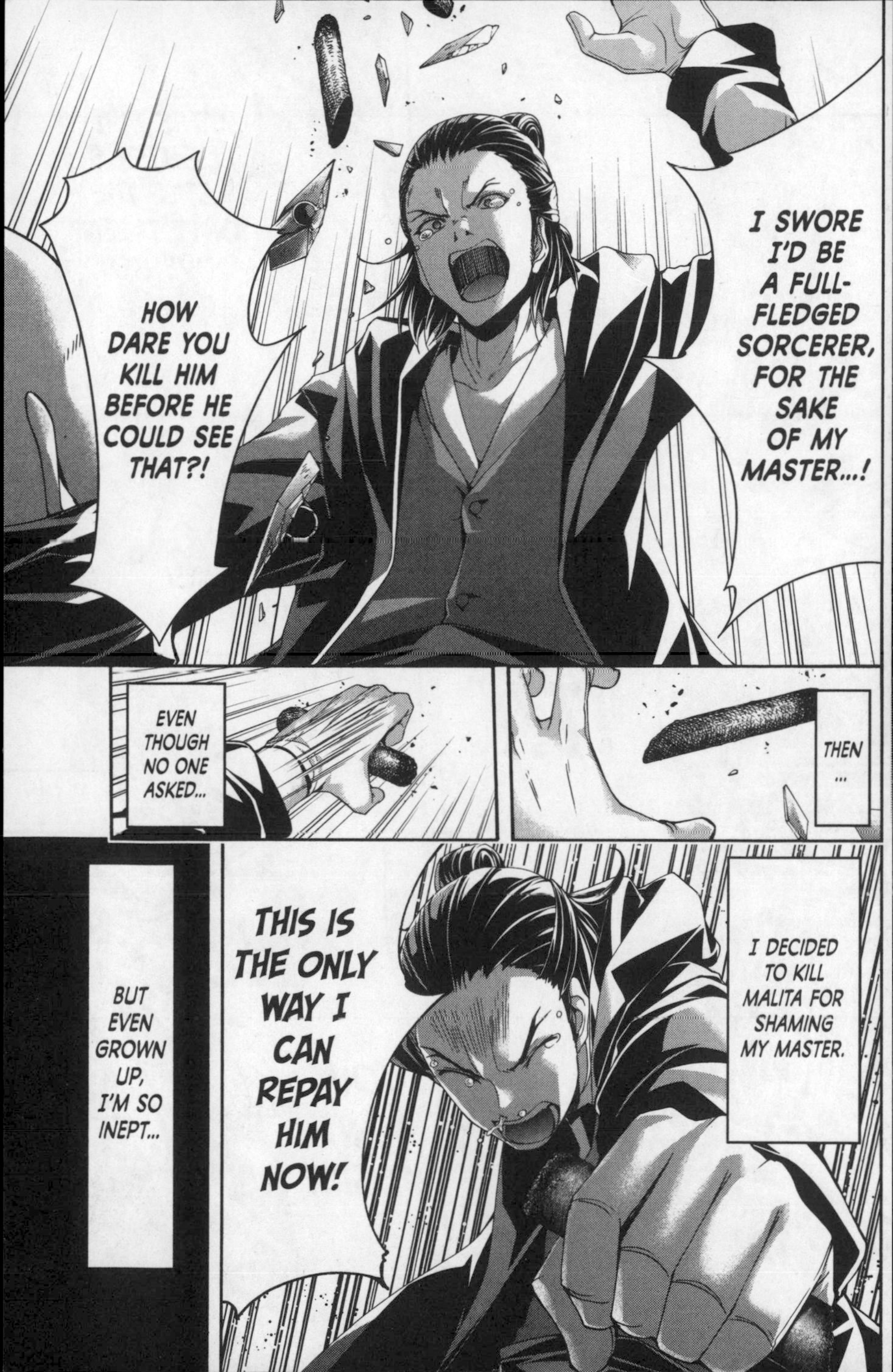
I SWORE I'D BE A FULL-FLEDGED SORCERER, FOR THE SAKE OF MY MASTER...!
HOW DARE YOU KILL HIM BEFORE HE COULD SEE THAT?!
THEN ...
EVEN THOUGH NO ONE ASKED...
I DECIDED TO KILL MALITA FOR SHAMING MY MASTER.
THIS IS THE ONLY WAY I CAN REPAY HIM NOW!
BUT EVEN GROWN UP, I'M SO INEPT...

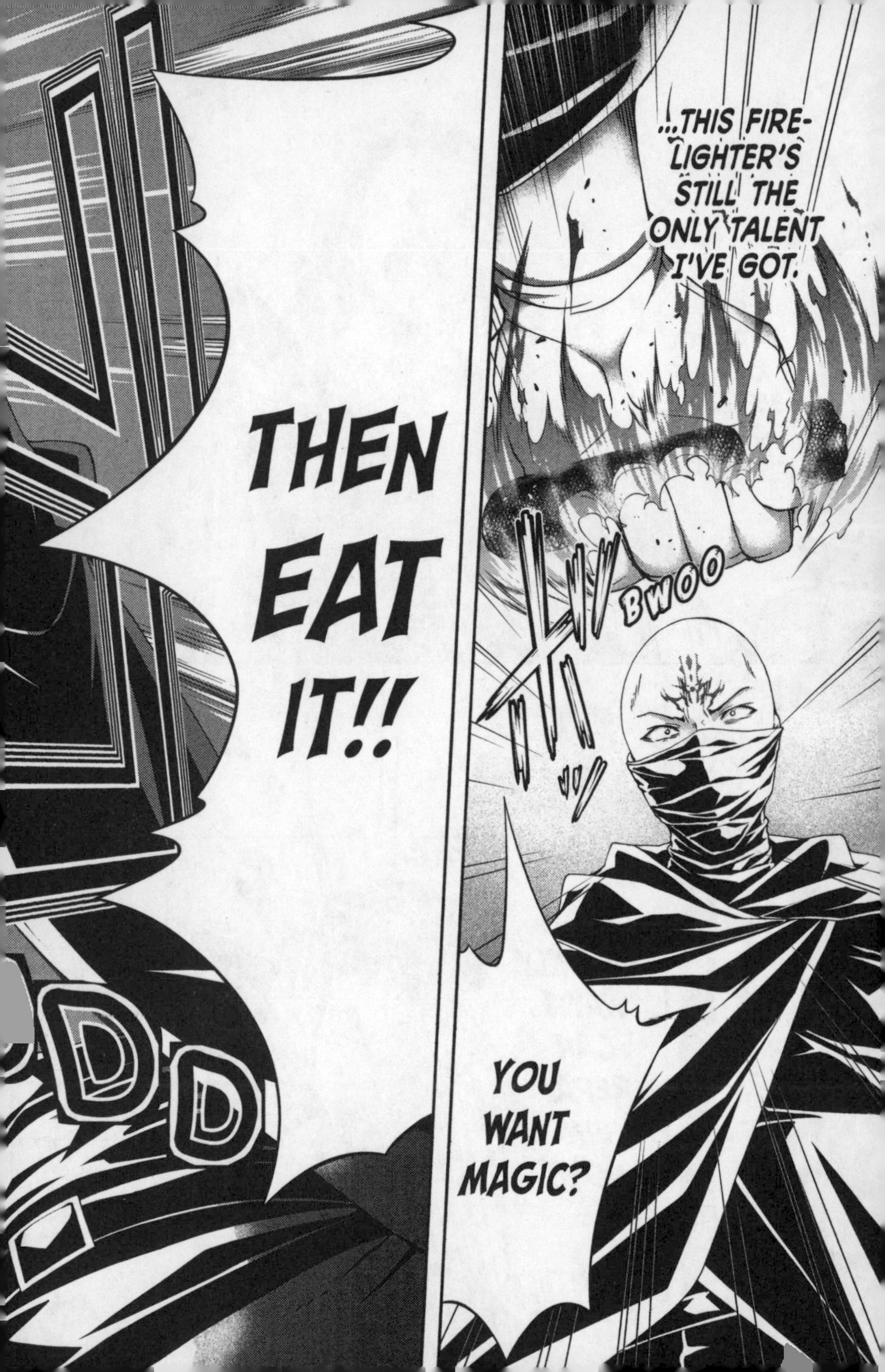
...THIS FIRE-LIGHTER'S STILL THE ONLY TALENT I'VE GOT.
BWOO
YOU WANT MAGIC?
THEN EAT IT!!

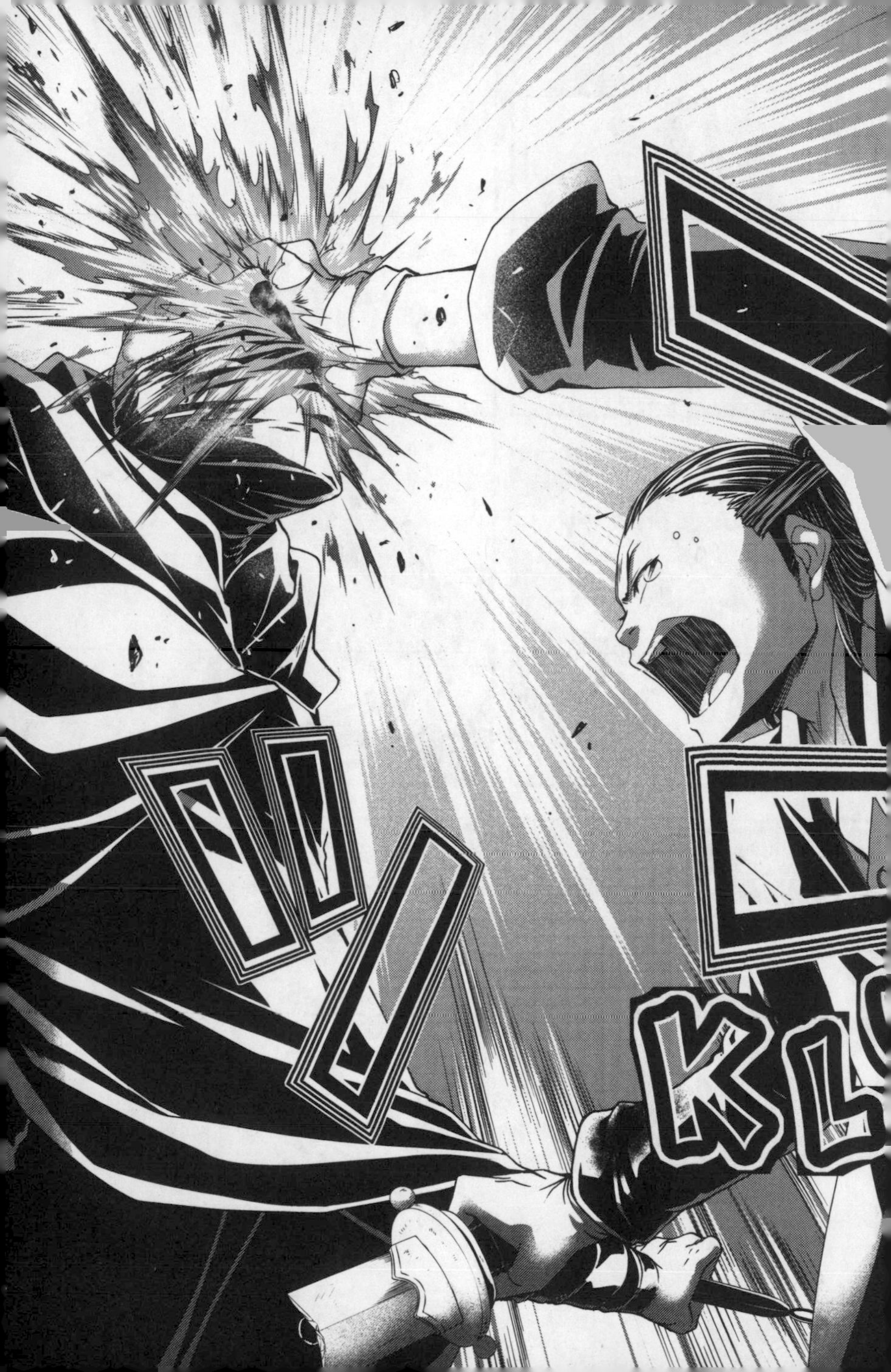

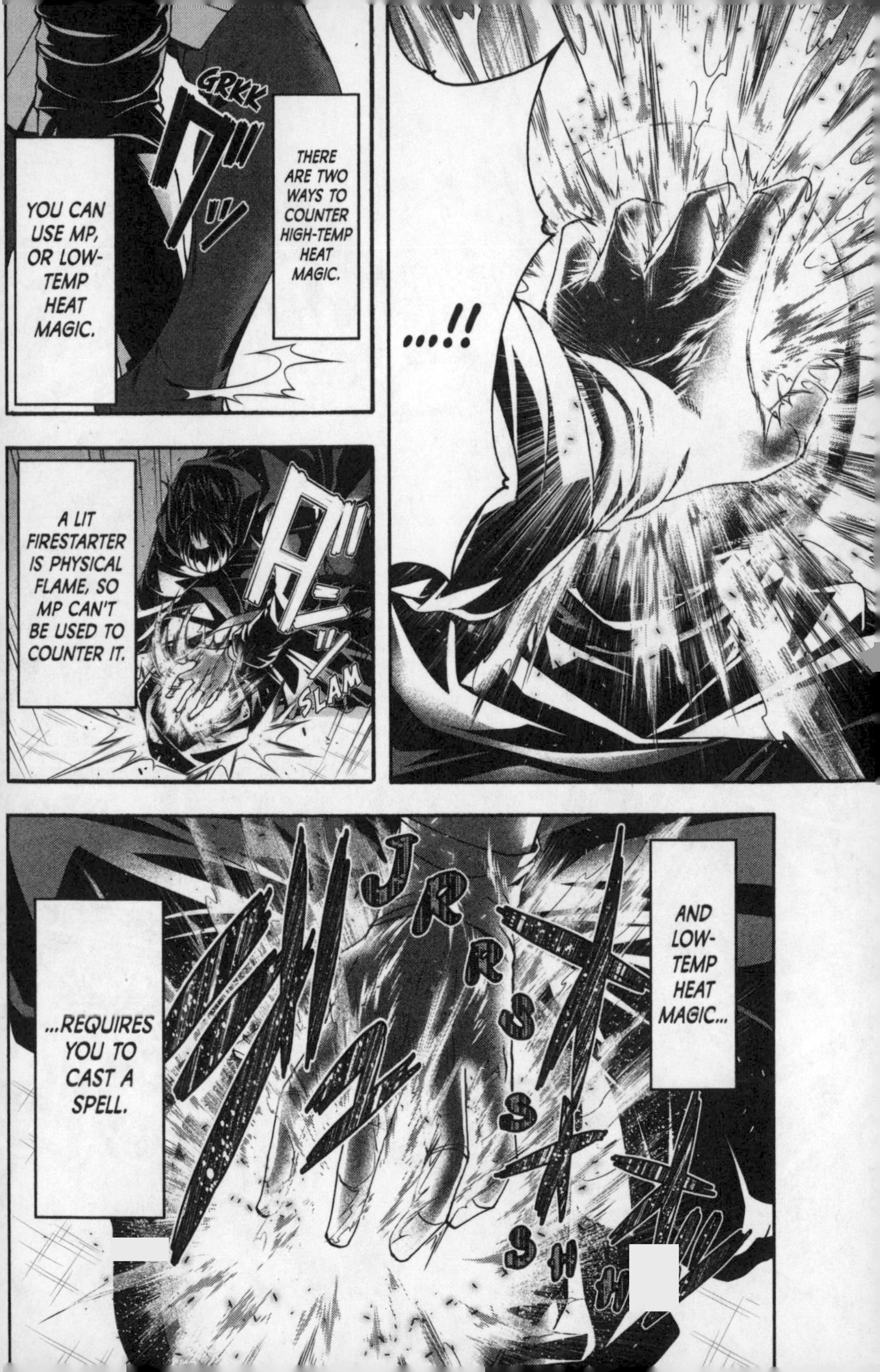
...!!
GRKK
THERE ARE TWO WAYS TO COUNTER HIGH-TEMP HEAT MAGIC.
YOU CAN USE MP, OR LOW-TEMP HEAT MAGIC.
A LIT FIRESTARTER IS PHYSICAL FLAME, SO MP CAN'T BE USED TO COUNTER IT.
SLAM
AND LOW-TEMP HEAT MAGIC...
JRRSSSHH
...REQUIRES YOU TO CAST A SPELL.

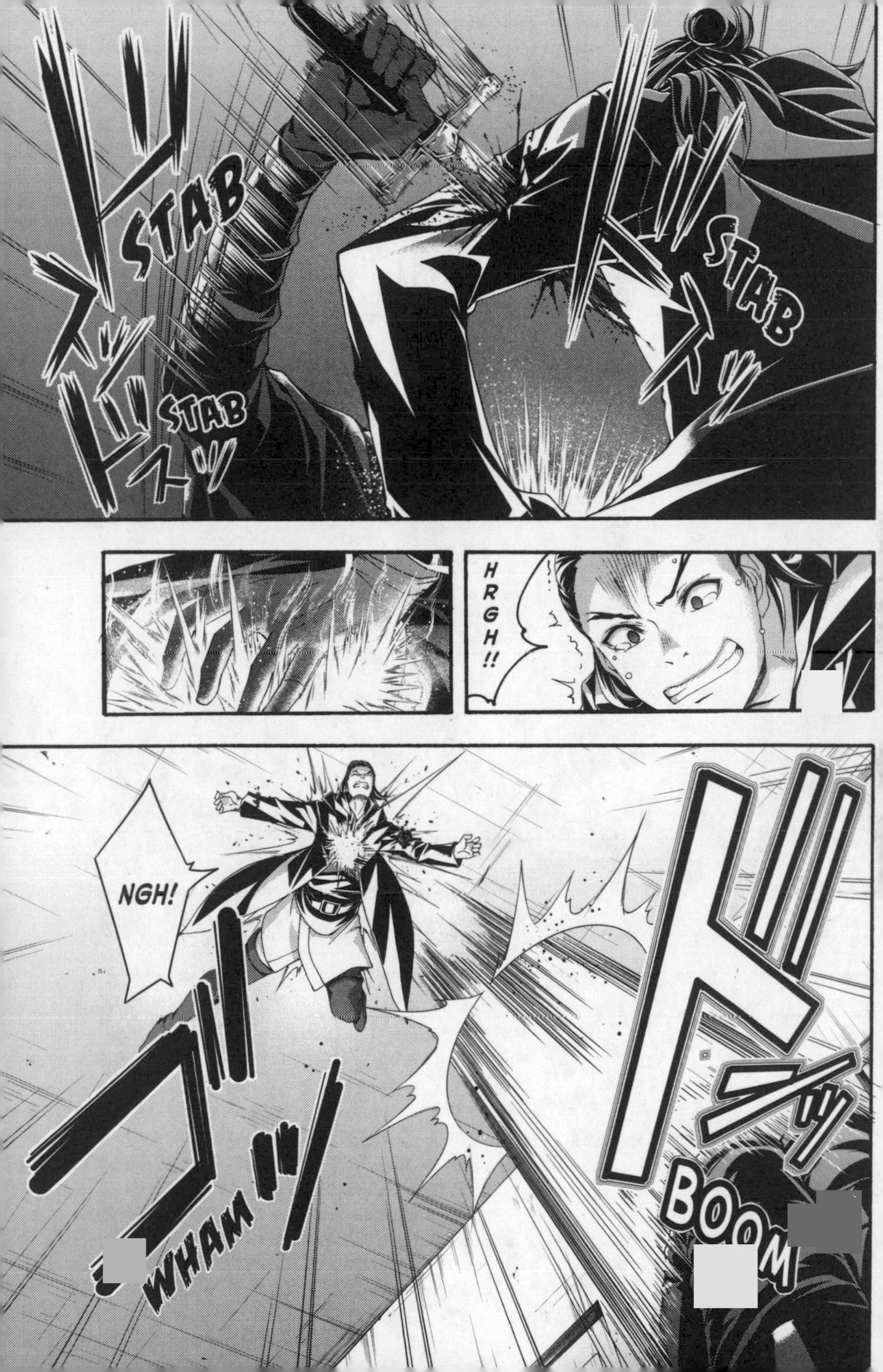

STAB
STAB
STAB
HRGH!!
BOOM
NGH!
WHAM

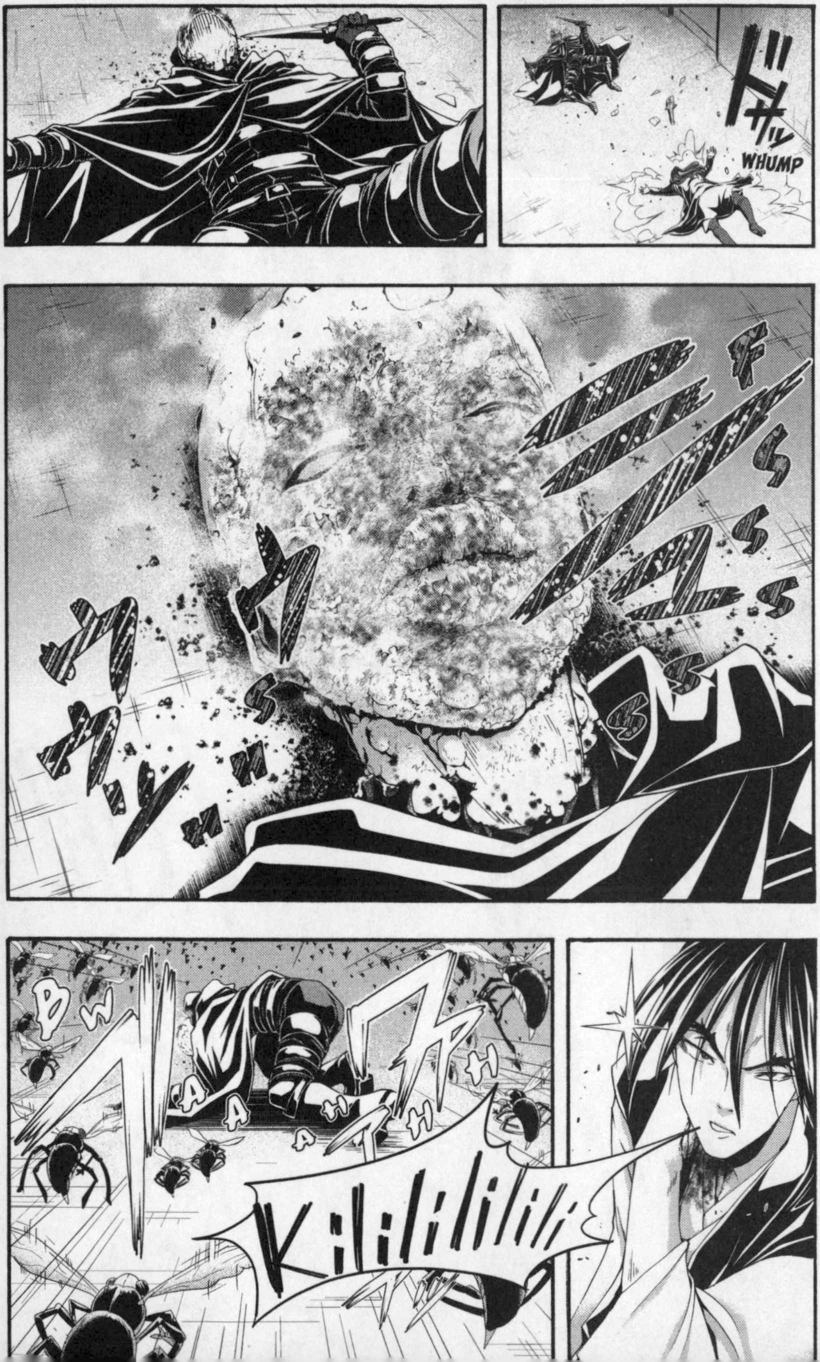
ドサッ
WHUMP
FSSSSSS
BWAAAAHHHH
KILILILILI

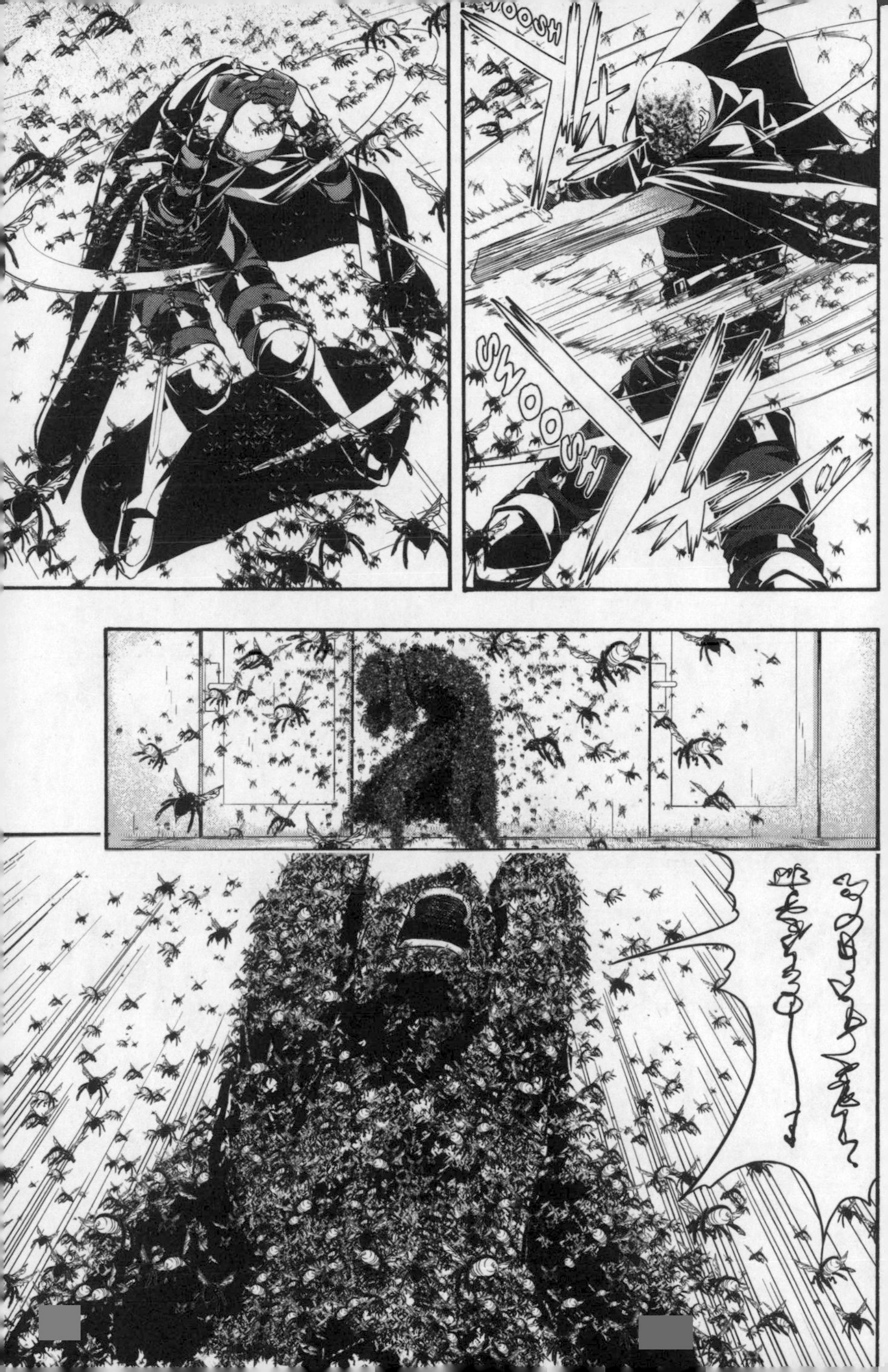
SWOOSH
SWOOSH

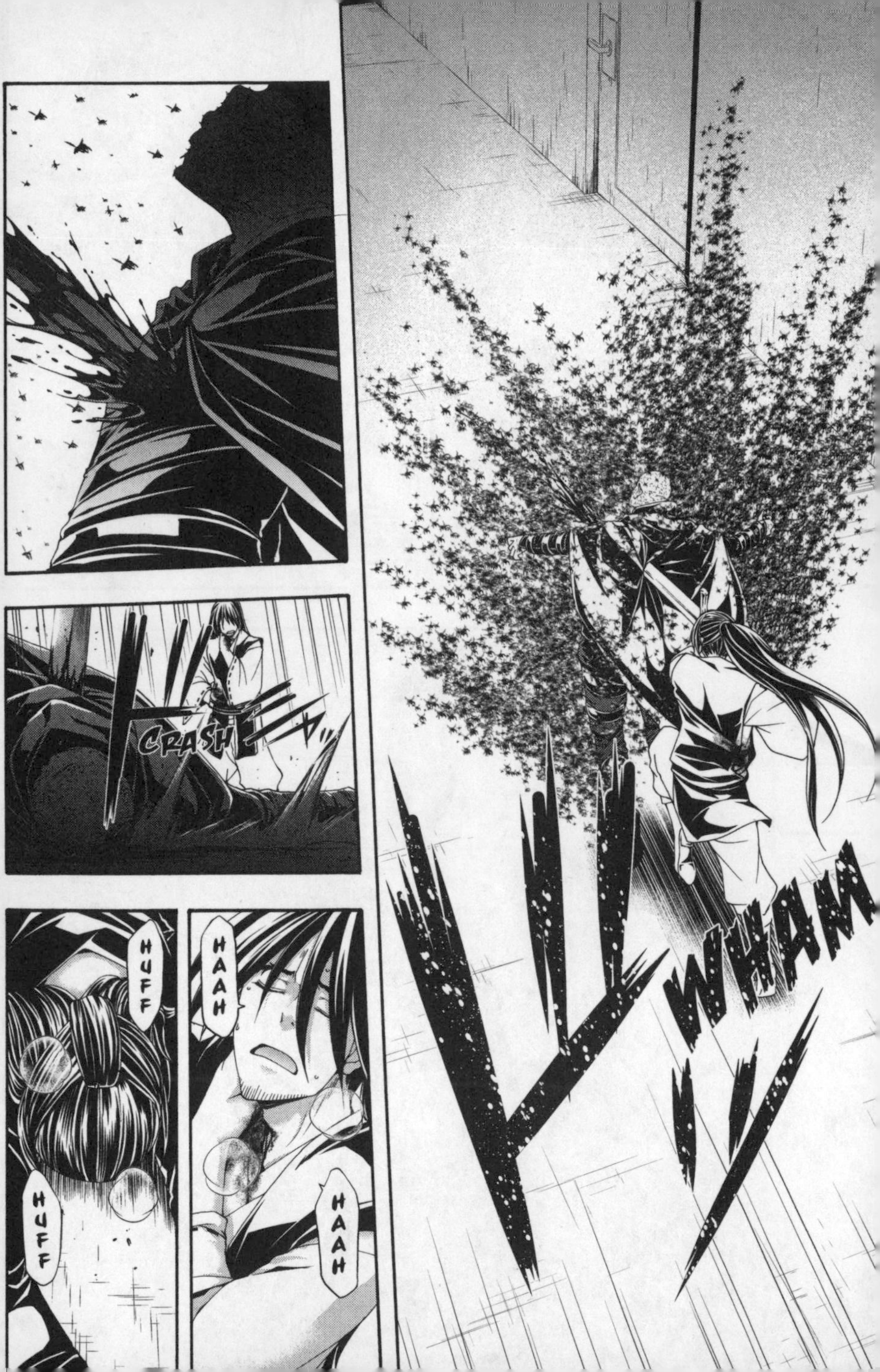
WHAM
CRASH
HAAH
HAAH
HUFF
HUFF

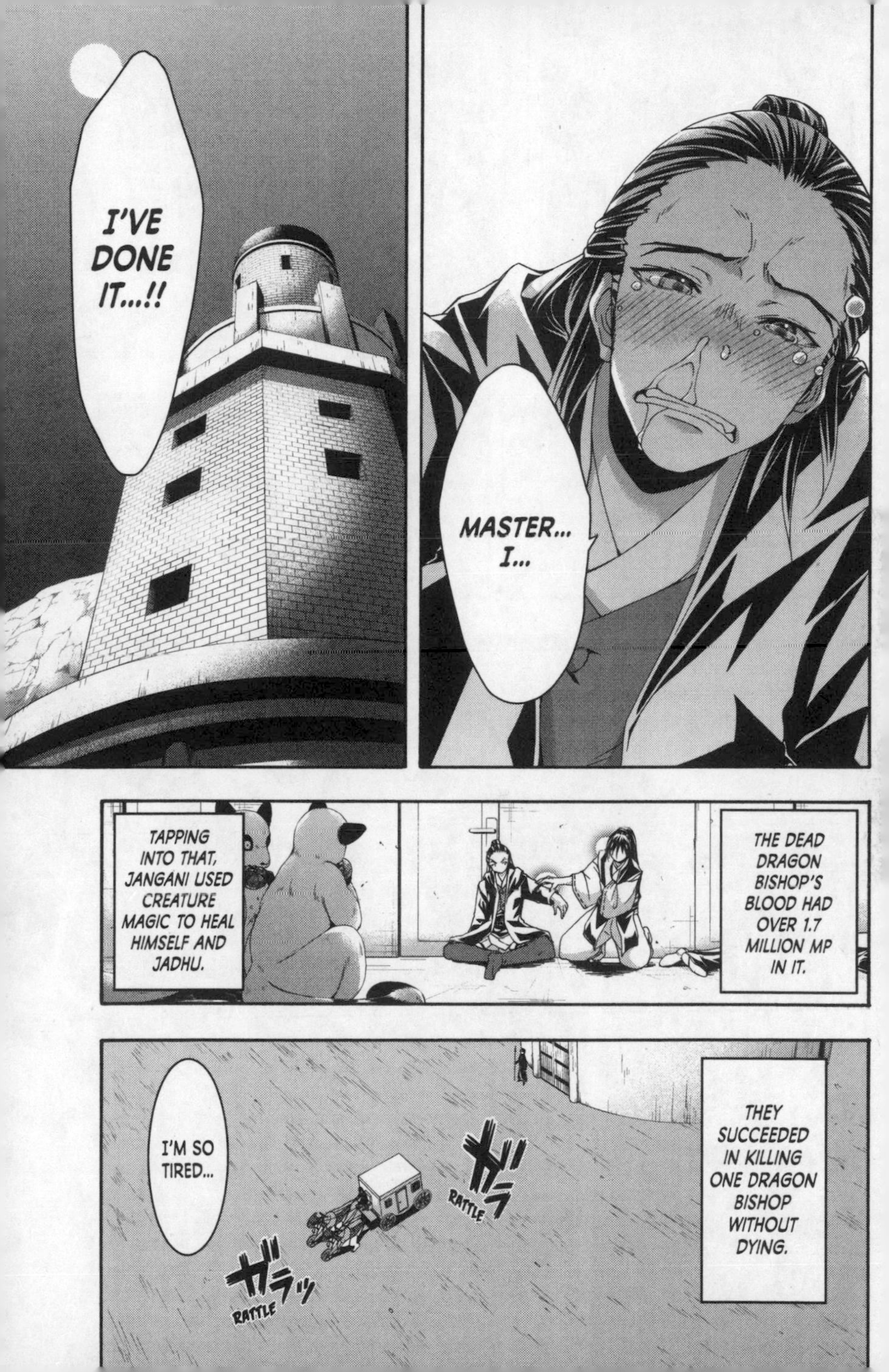
MASTER... I...
I'VE DONE IT...!!
THE DEAD DRAGON BISHOP'S BLOOD HAD OVER 1.7 MILLION MP IN IT.
TAPPING INTO THAT, JANGANI USED CREATURE MAGIC TO HEAL HIMSELF AND JADHU.
THEY SUCCEEDED IN KILLING ONE DRAGON BISHOP WITHOUT DYING.
I'M SO TIRED...
ガラ
RATTLE
ガラッ
RATTLE

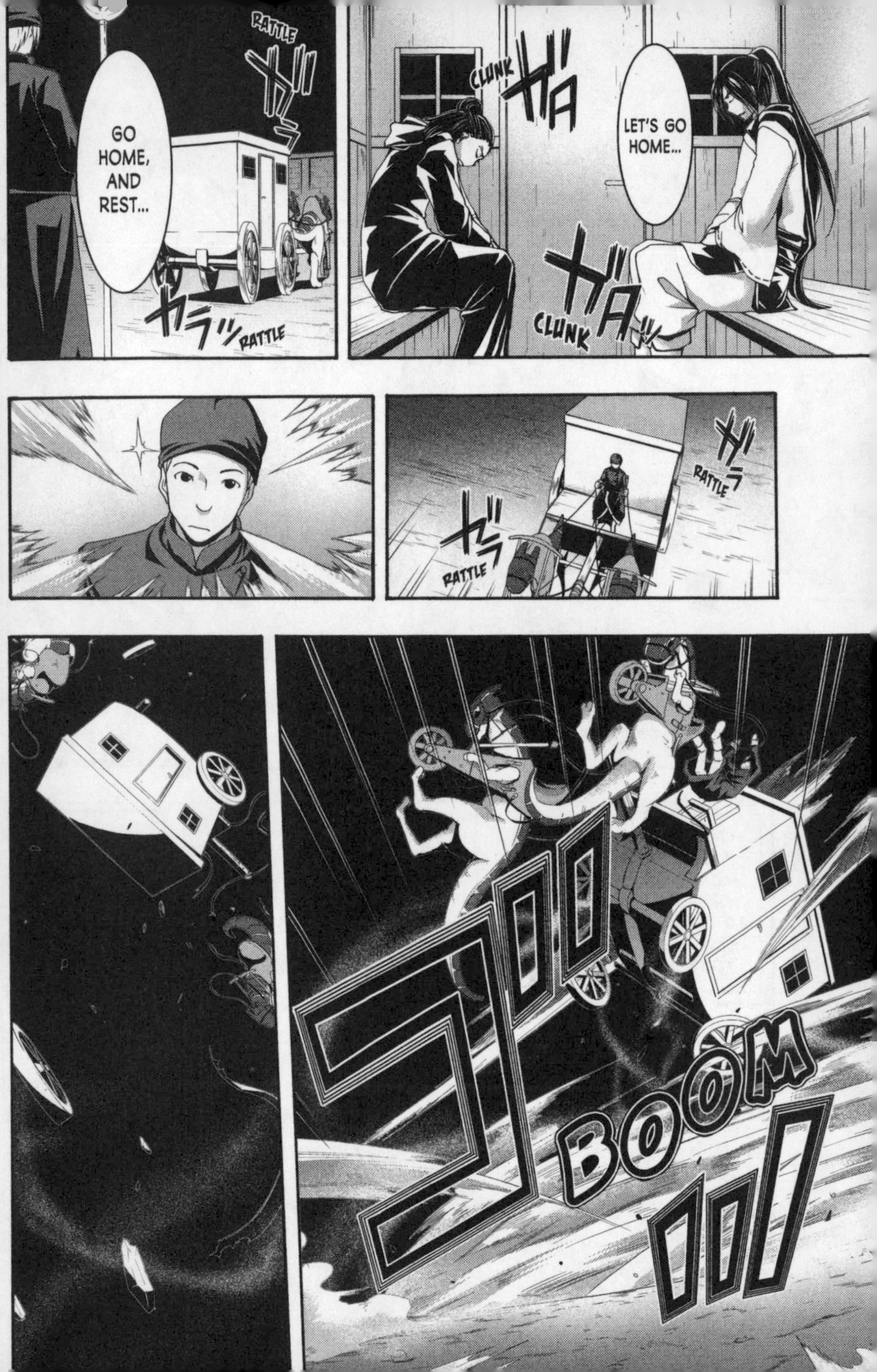
CLUNK
LET'S GO HOME...
CLUNK
RATTLE
GO HOME, AND REST...
RATTLE
RATTLE
RATTLE
BOOM

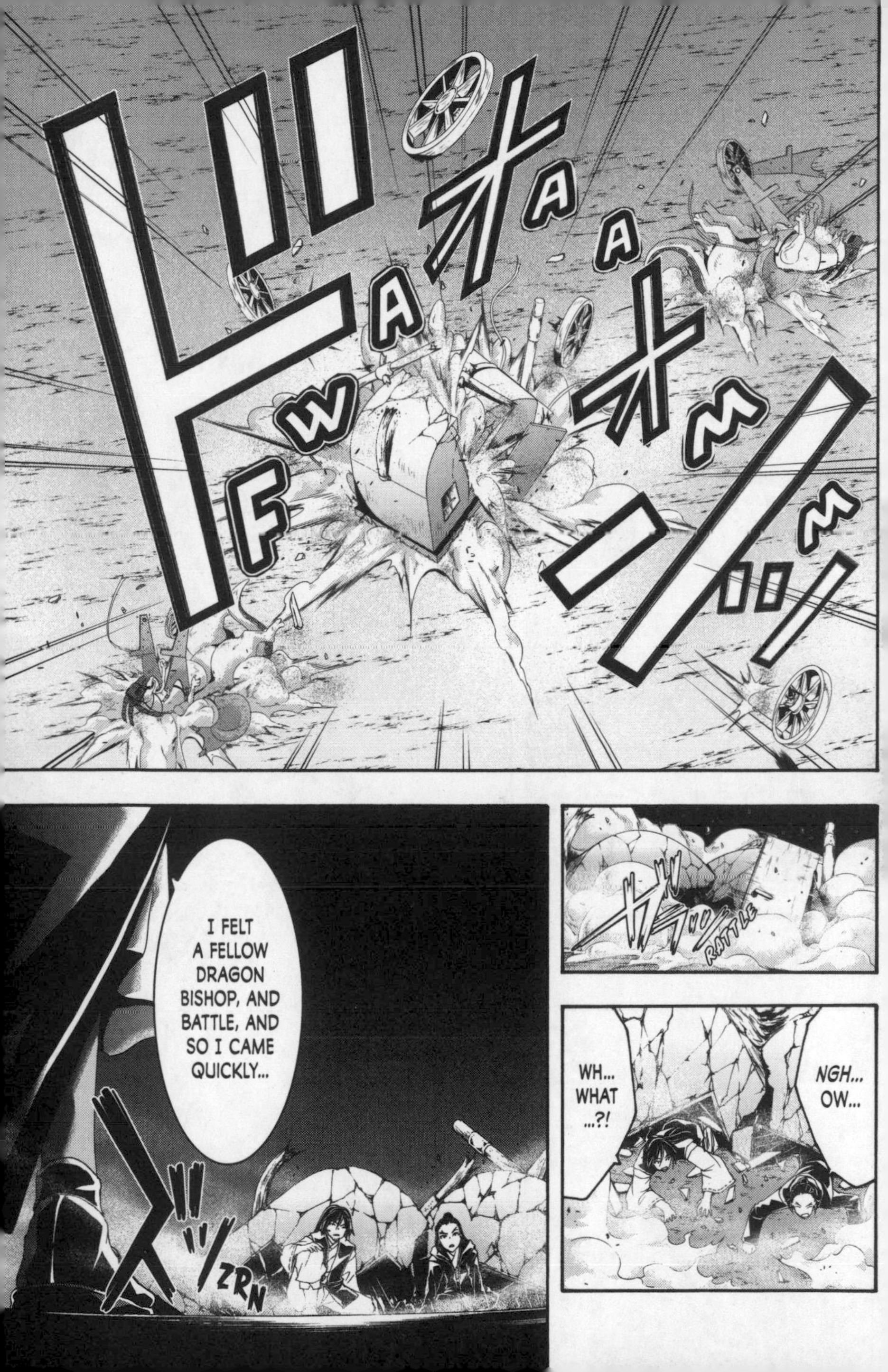
FWAAAMM
RATTLE
NGH... OW...
WH... WHAT ...?!
I FELT A FELLOW DRAGON BISHOP, AND BATTLE, AND SO I CAME QUICKLY...
ZRN

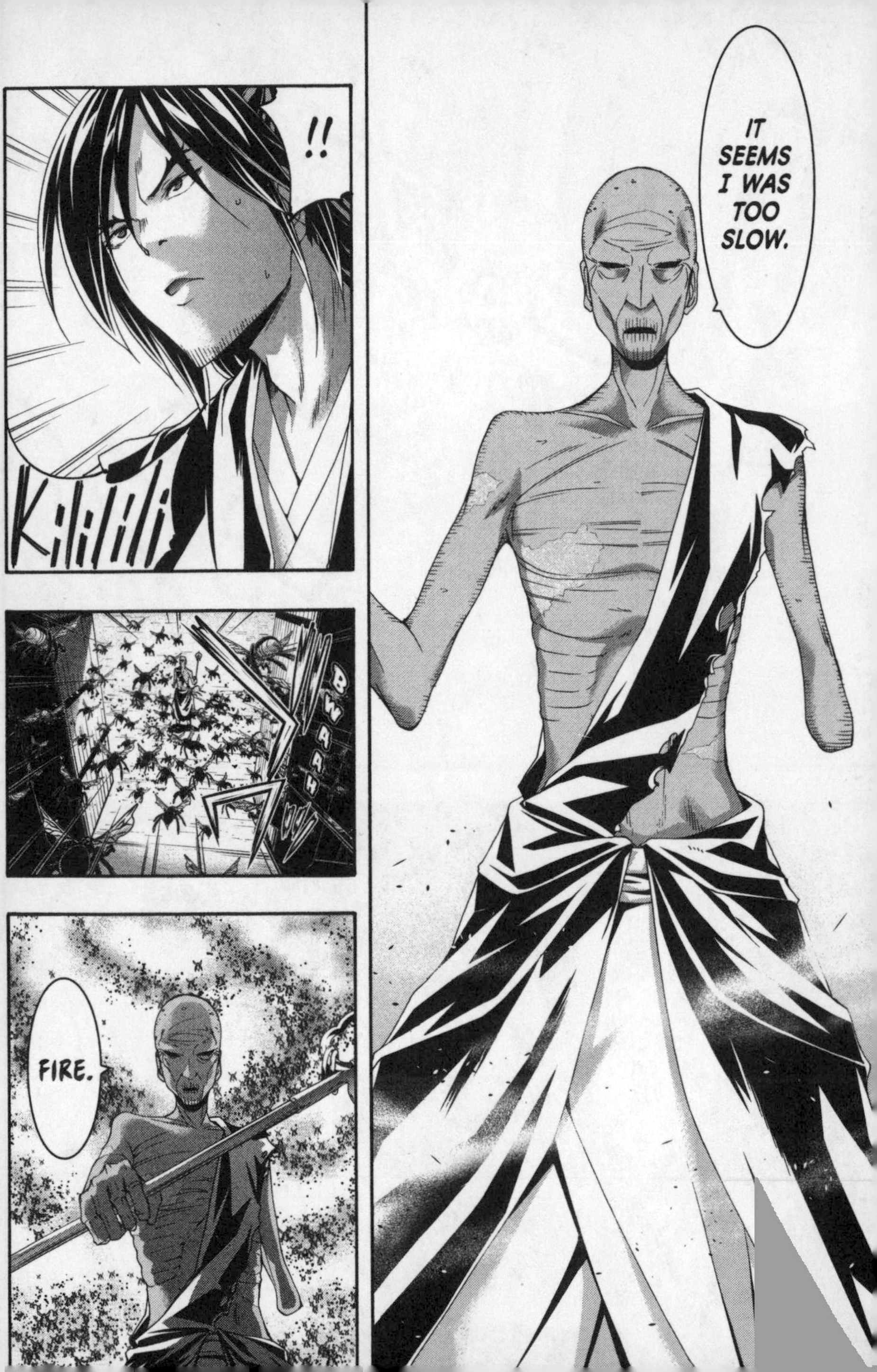
IT SEEMS I WAS TOO SLOW.
!!
Kililili
BWAAAH
FIRE.

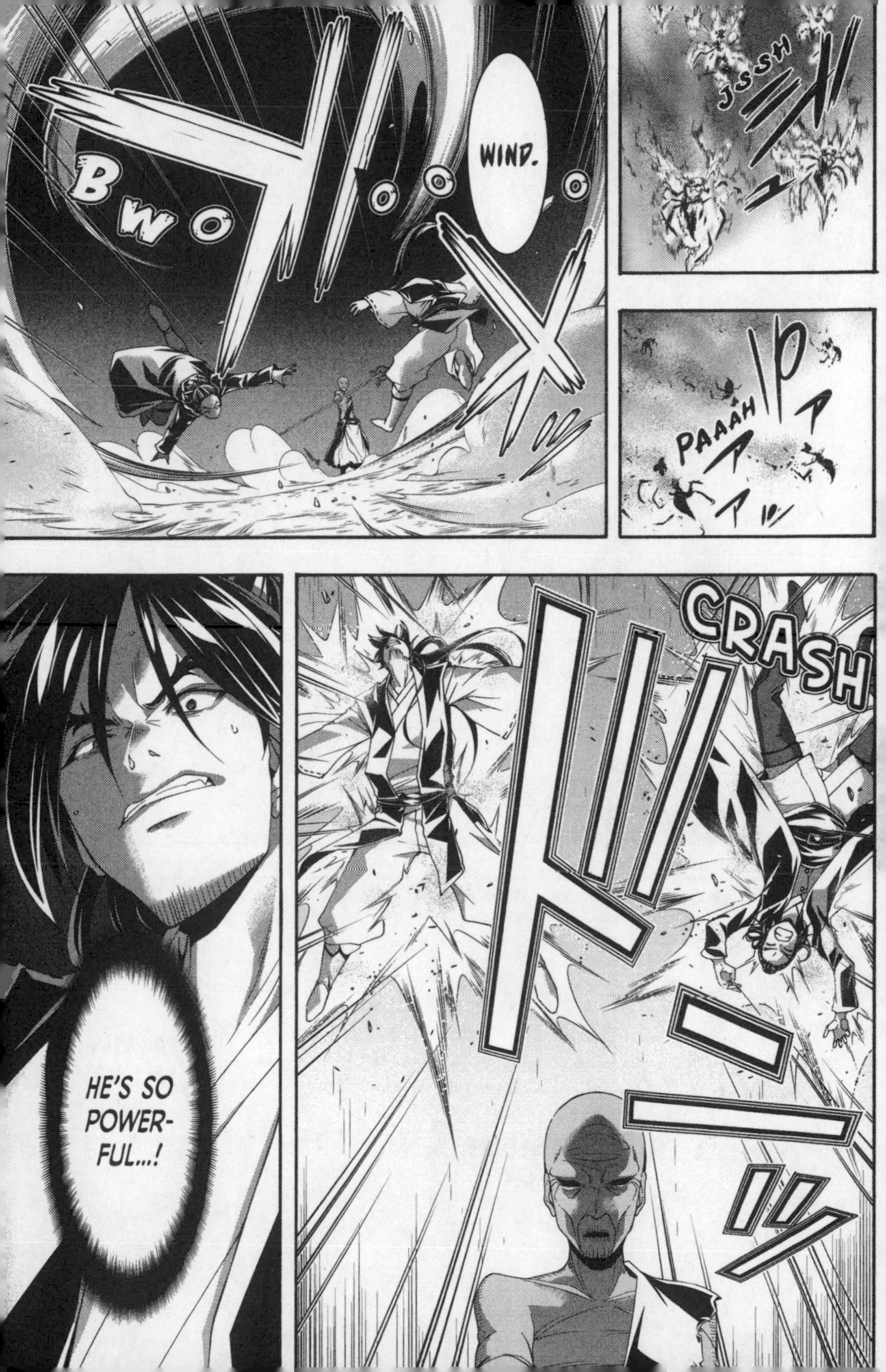
JSSH
PAAAH
BWOOOO
WIND.
CRASH
HE'S SO POWER-FUL...!

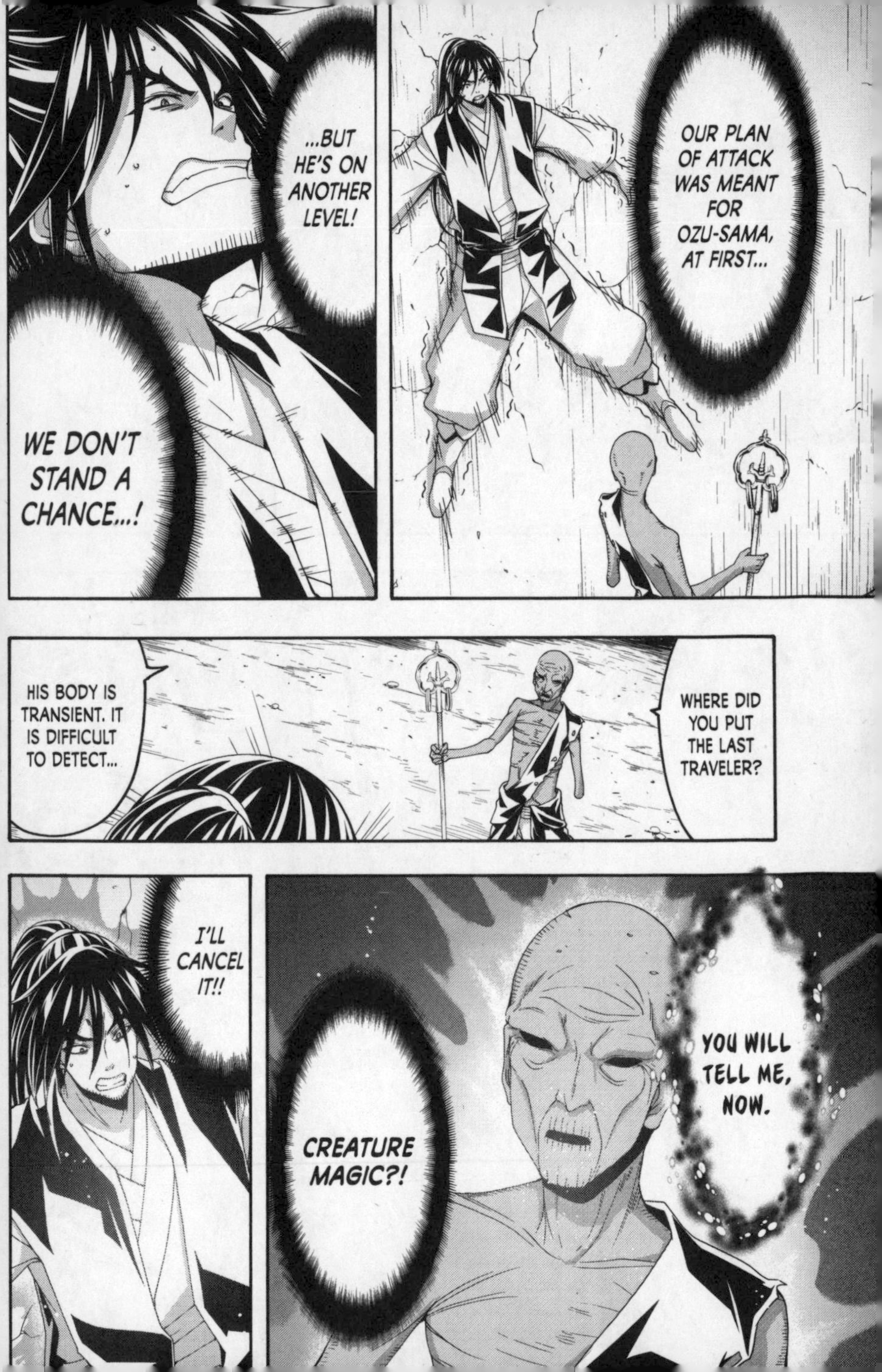
OUR PLAN OF ATTACK WAS MEANT FOR OZU-SAMA, AT FIRST...
...BUT HE'S ON ANOTHER LEVEL!
WE DON'T STAND A CHANCE...!
WHERE DID YOU PUT THE LAST TRAVELER?
HIS BODY IS TRANSIENT. IT IS DIFFICULT TO DETECT...
YOU WILL TELL ME, NOW.
CREATURE MAGIC?!
I'LL CANCEL IT!!

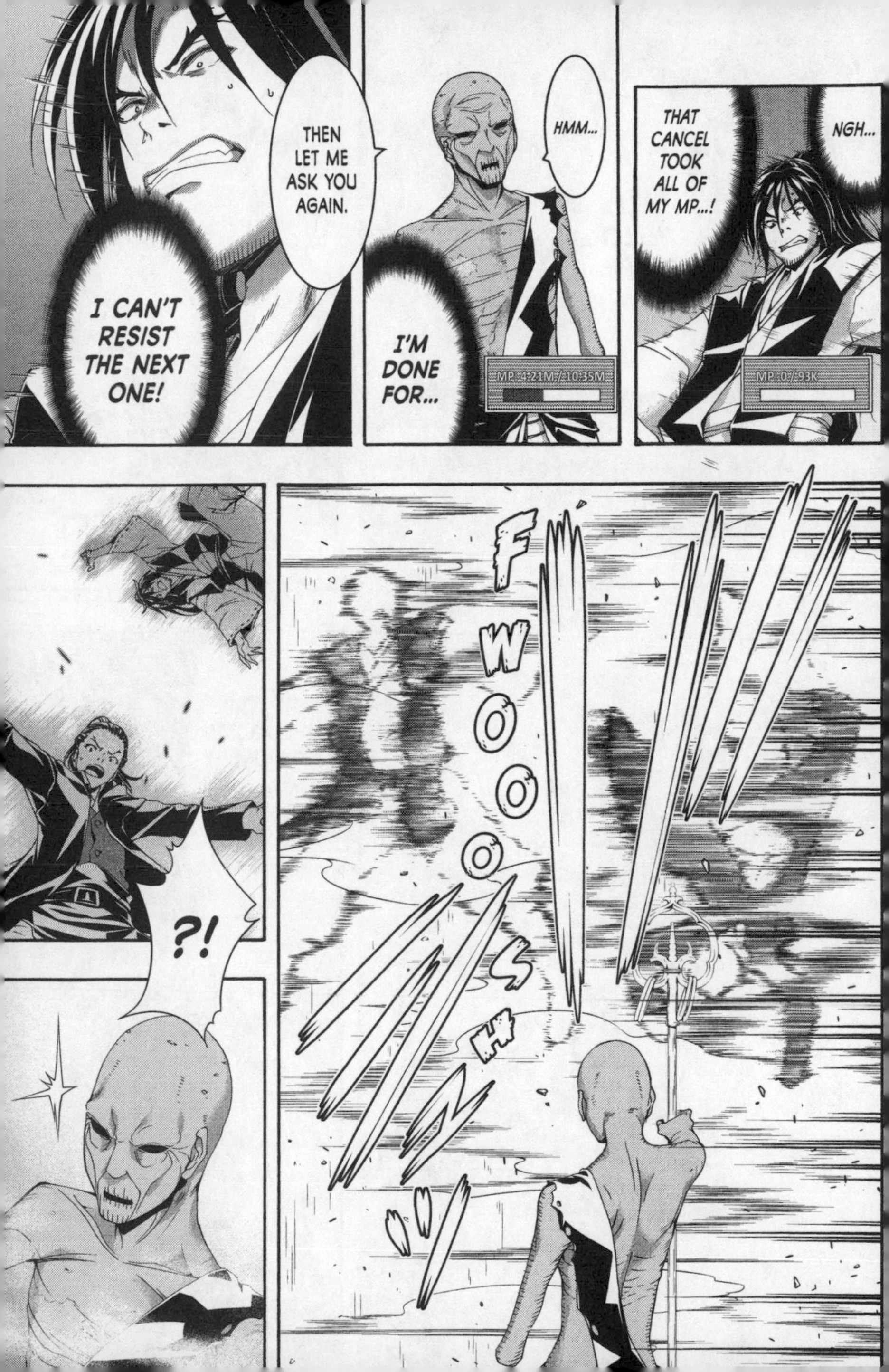
NGH...
THAT CANCEL TOOK ALL OF MY MP...!
MP: 0 / 93K
HMM...
I'M DONE FOR...
MP: 4.21M / 10.35M
THEN LET ME ASK YOU AGAIN.
I CAN'T RESIST THE NEXT ONE!
FWOOOOSH
?!

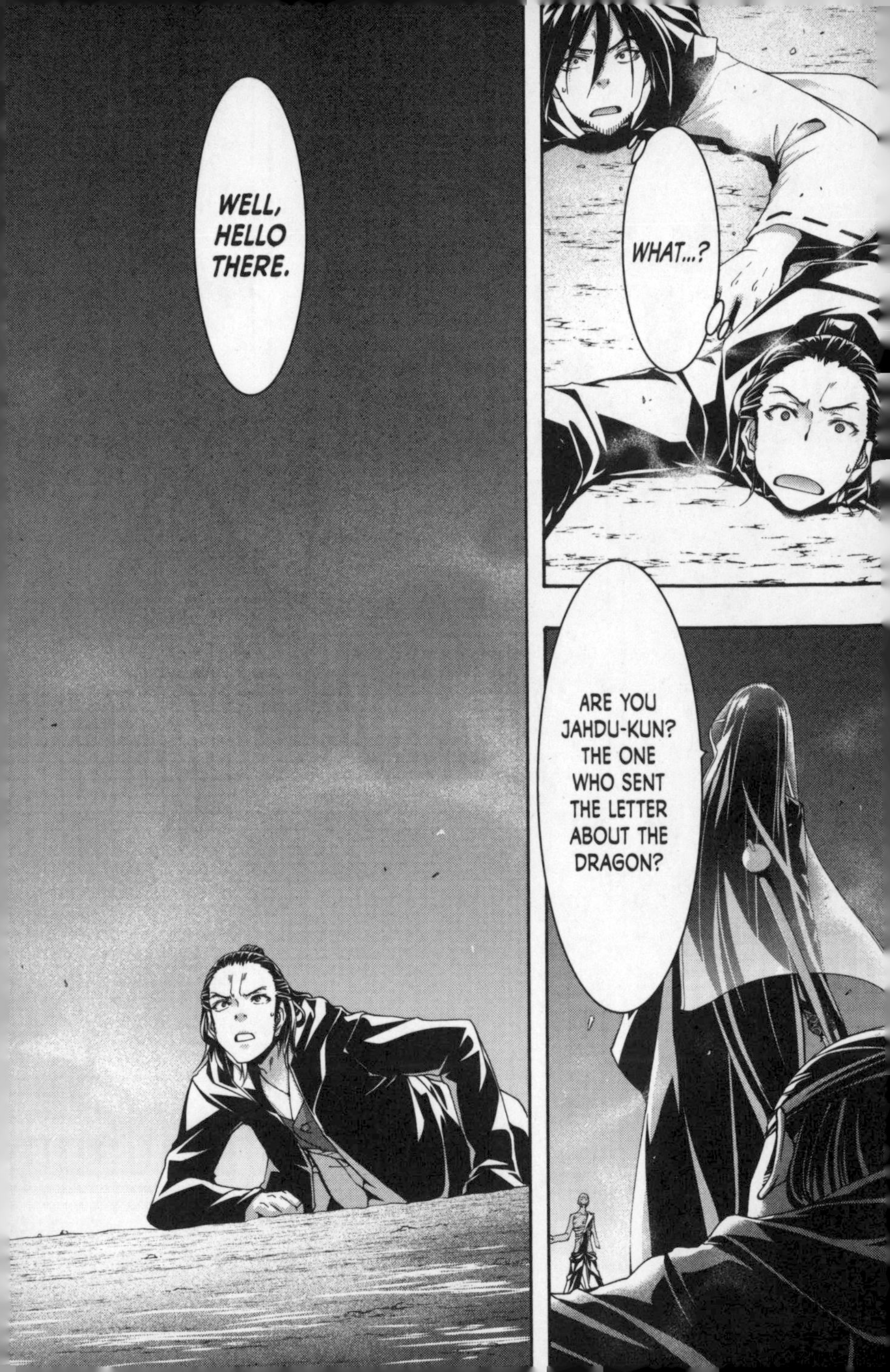
WHAT...?
ARE YOU JAHDU-KUN? THE ONE WHO SENT THE LETTER ABOUT THE DRAGON?
WELL, HELLO THERE.

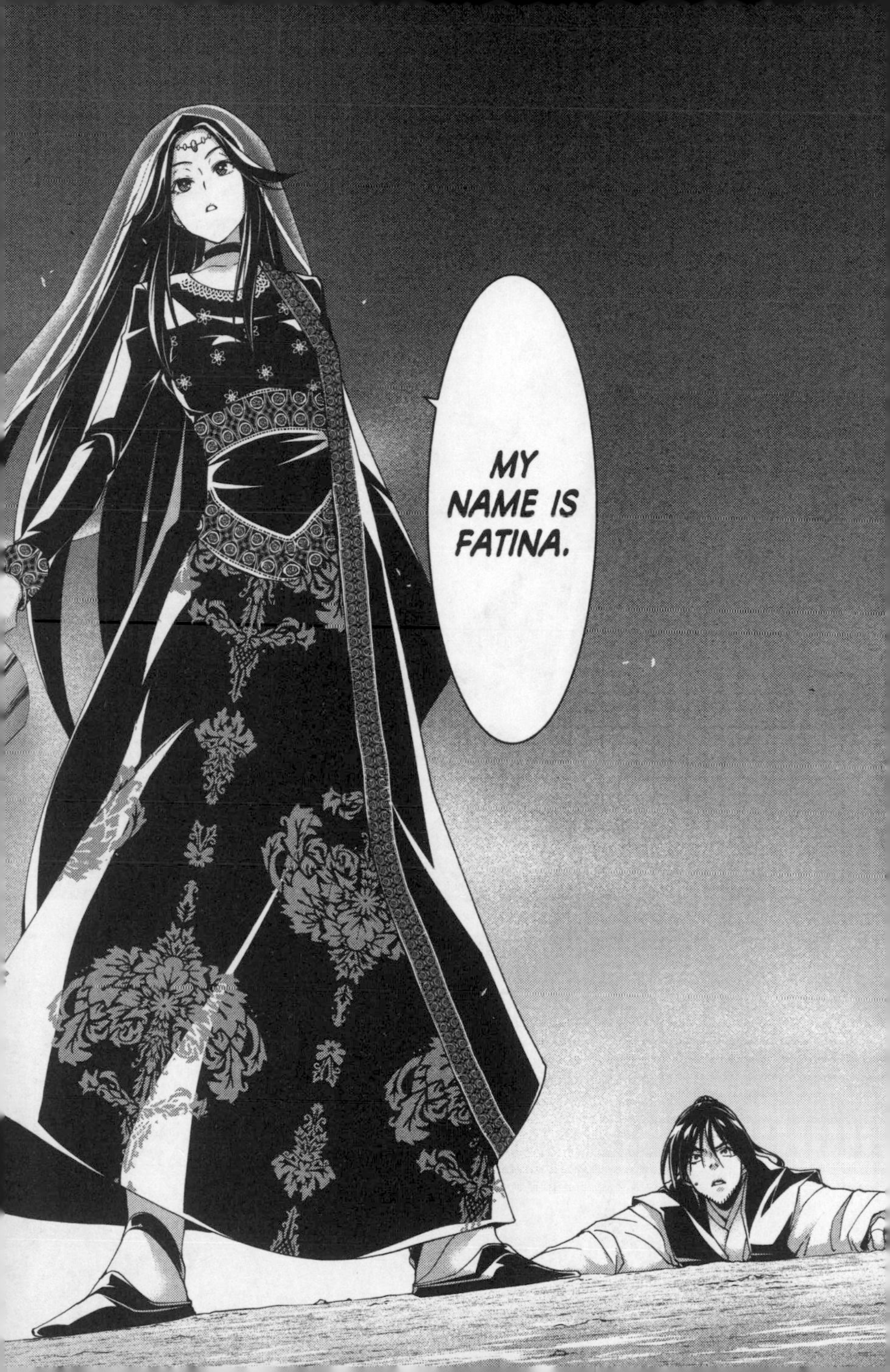
MY NAME IS FATINA.

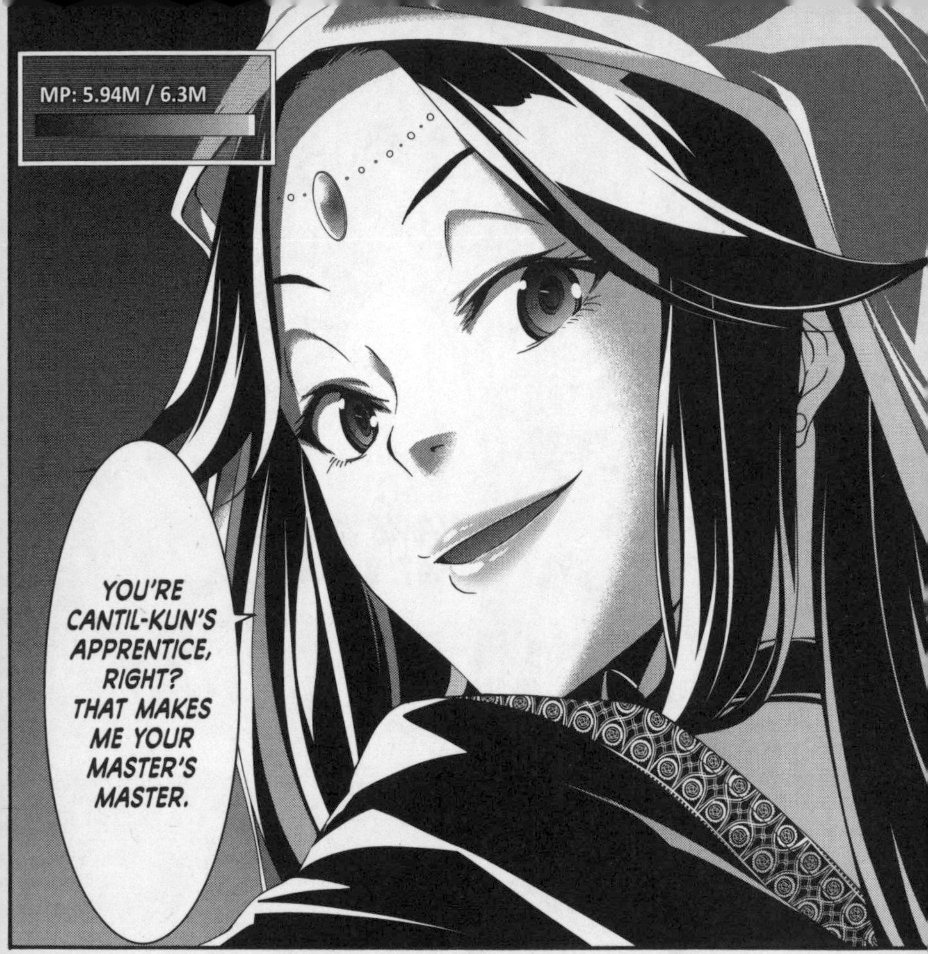
MP: 5.94M / 6.3M
YOU'RE CANTIL-KUN'S APPRENTICE, RIGHT? THAT MAKES ME YOUR MASTER'S MASTER.
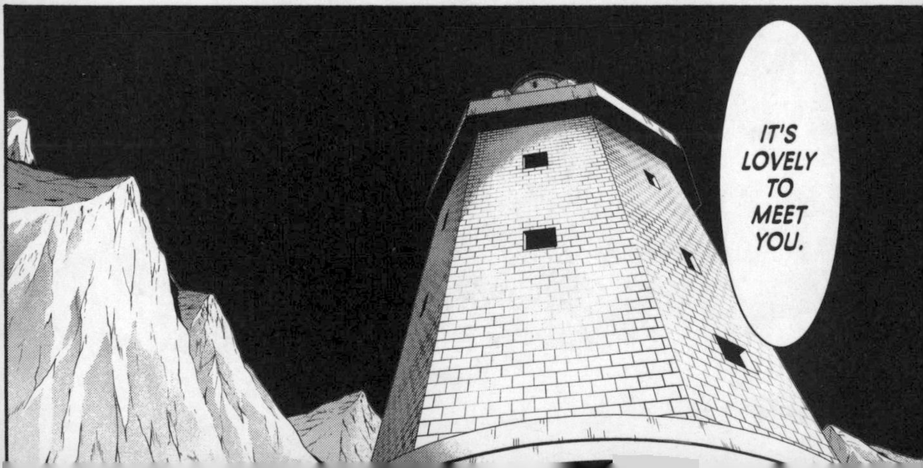
IT'S LOVELY TO MEET YOU.

I'M STANDING ON A MILLION LIVES

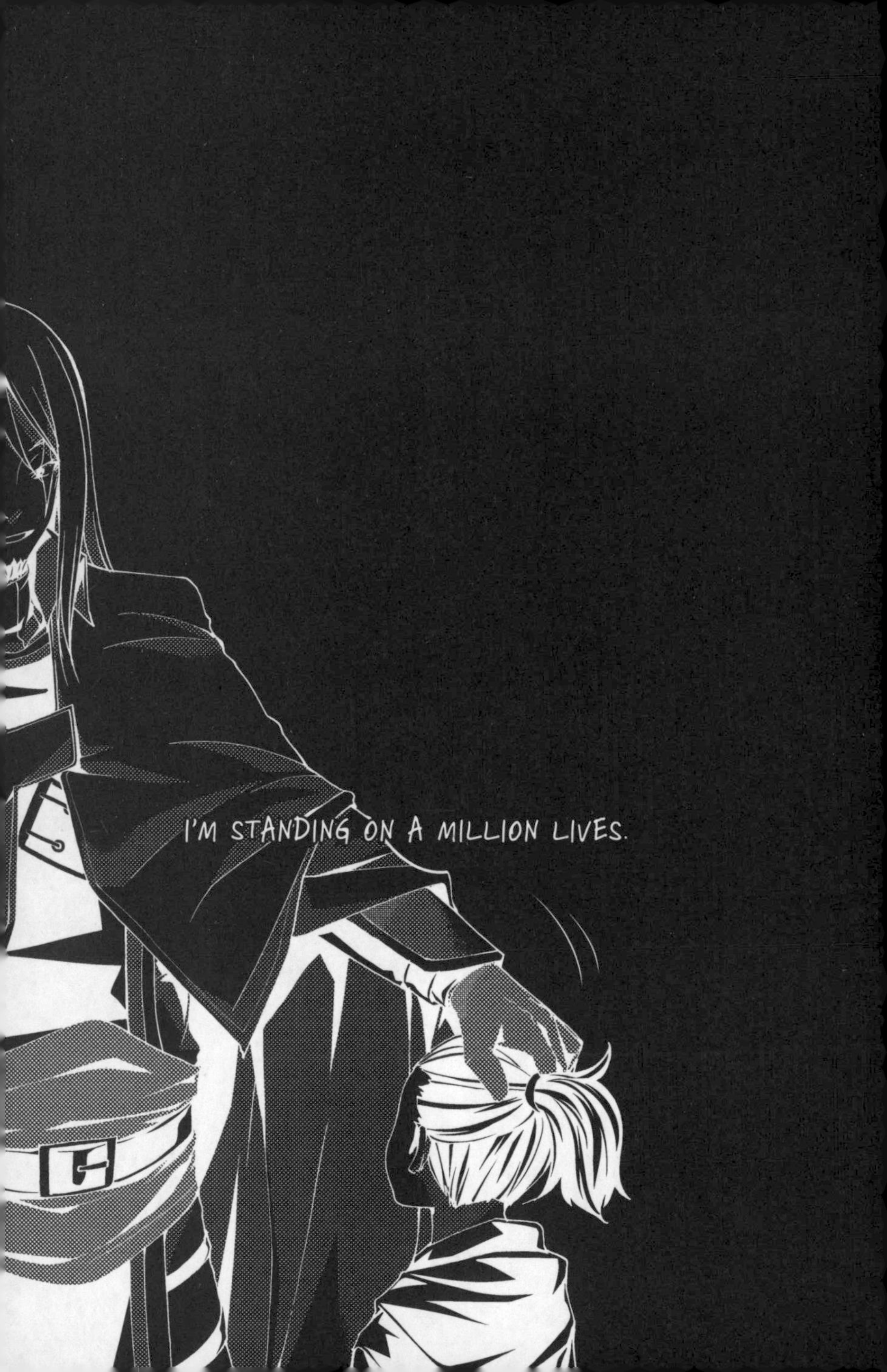
I'M STANDING ON A MILLION LIVES.

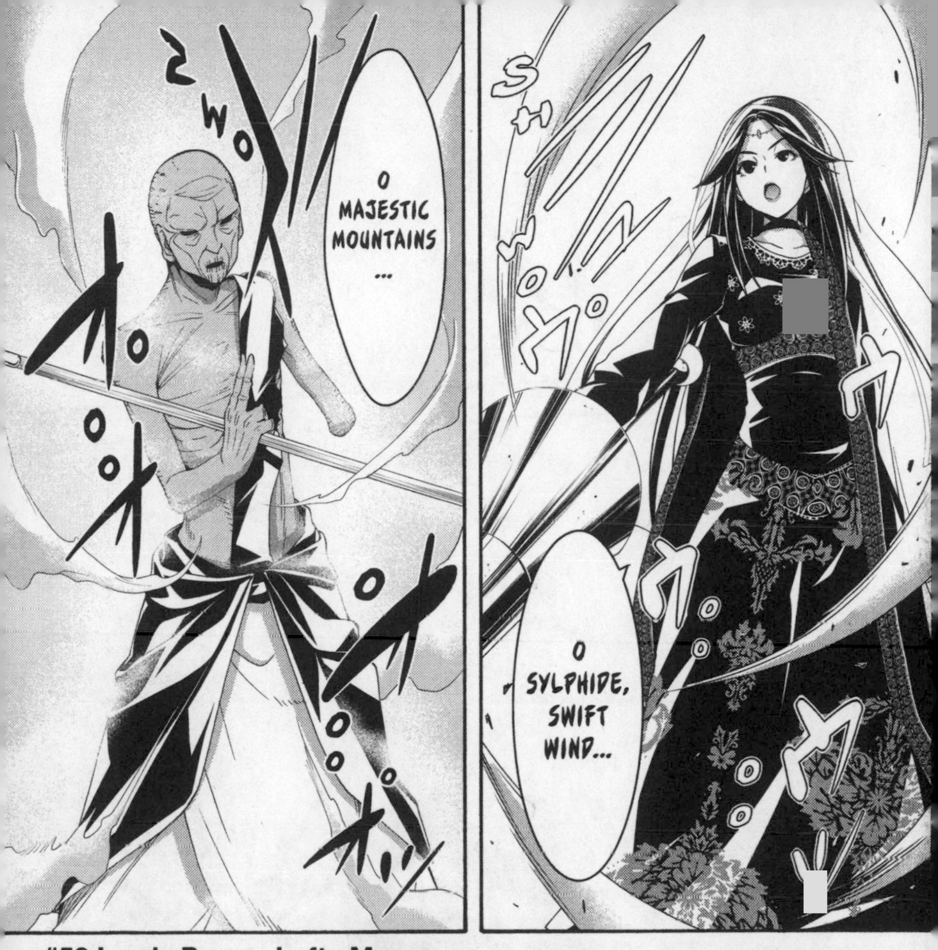
O SYLPHIDE, SWIFT WIND...
O MAJESTIC MOUNTAINS ...

#59 Lowly Peons, Lofty Managers

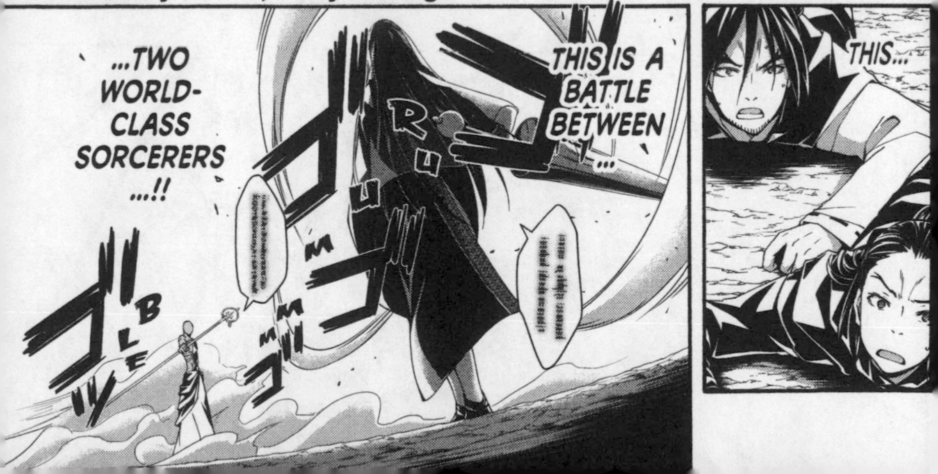
THIS...
THIS IS A BATTLE BETWEEN ...
...TWO WORLD-CLASS SORCERERS ...!!

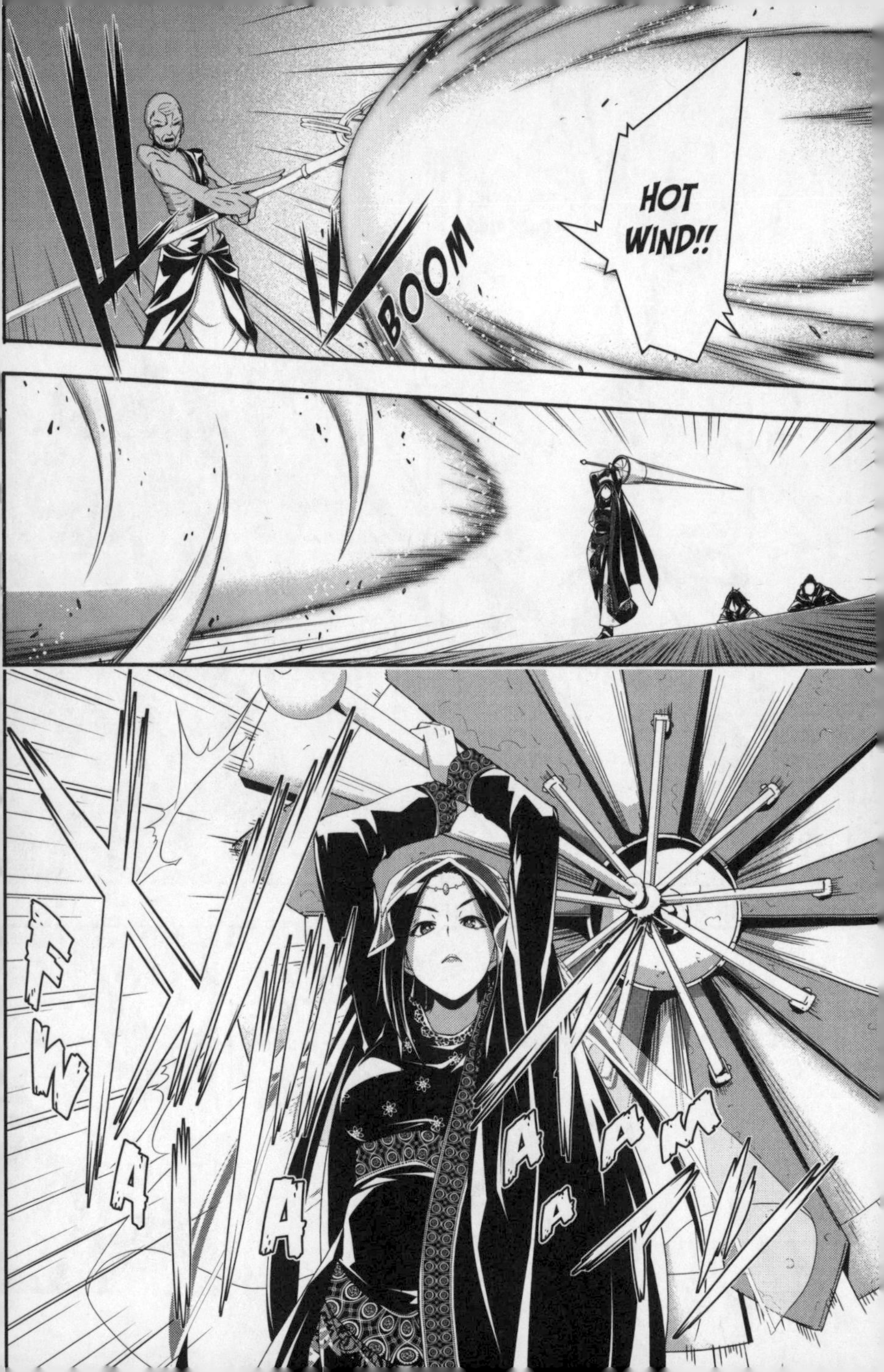
HOT WIND!!
BOOM
FWAAAAAM

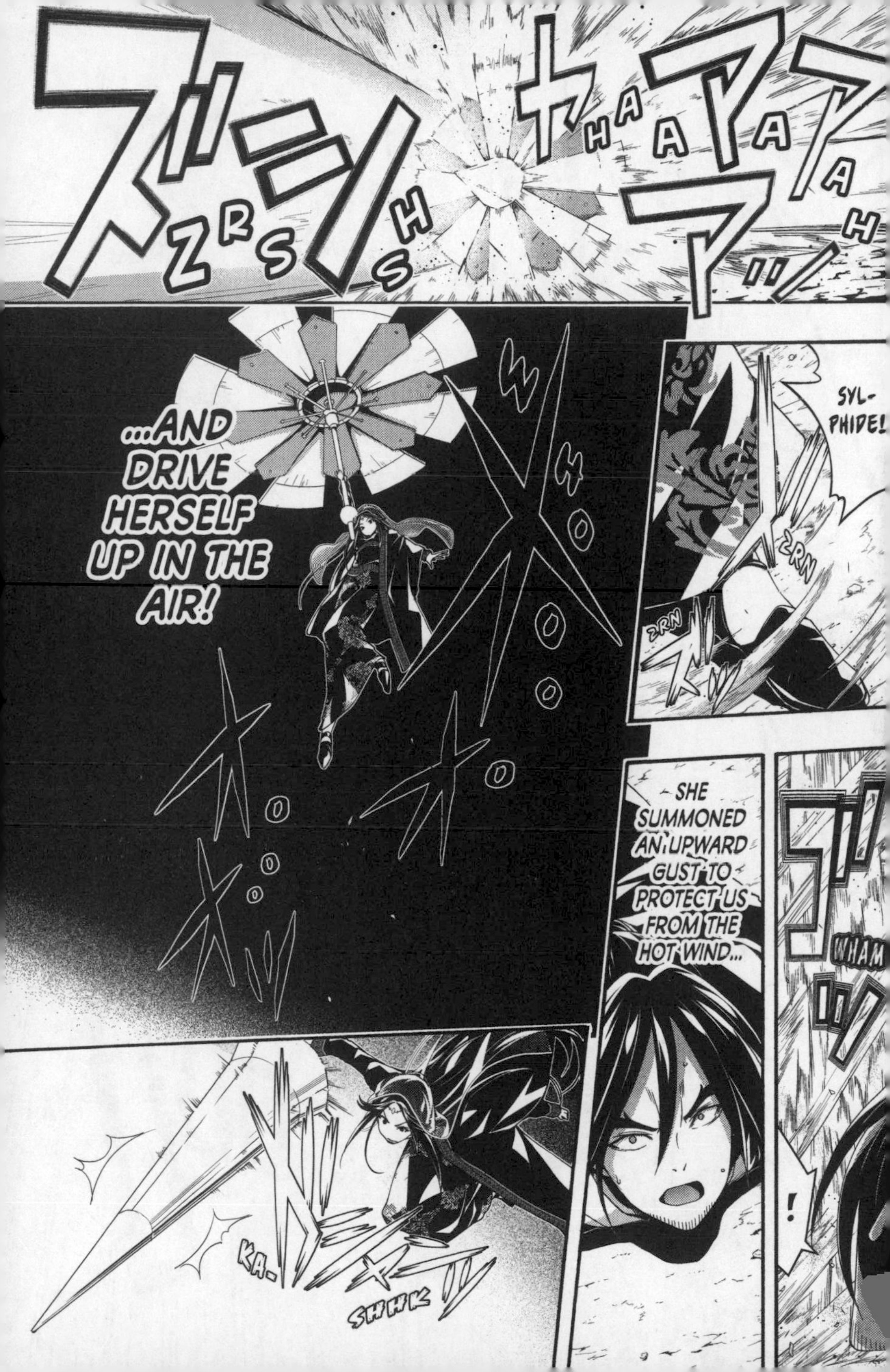
HAAAAH
ZRSSH
SYL-PHIDE!
ZRN
ZRN
...AND DRIVE HERSELF UP IN THE AIR!
WHOOOOOOOOO
WHAM
!
SHE SUMMONED AN UPWARD GUST TO PROTECT US FROM THE HOT WIND...
KA-SHHK

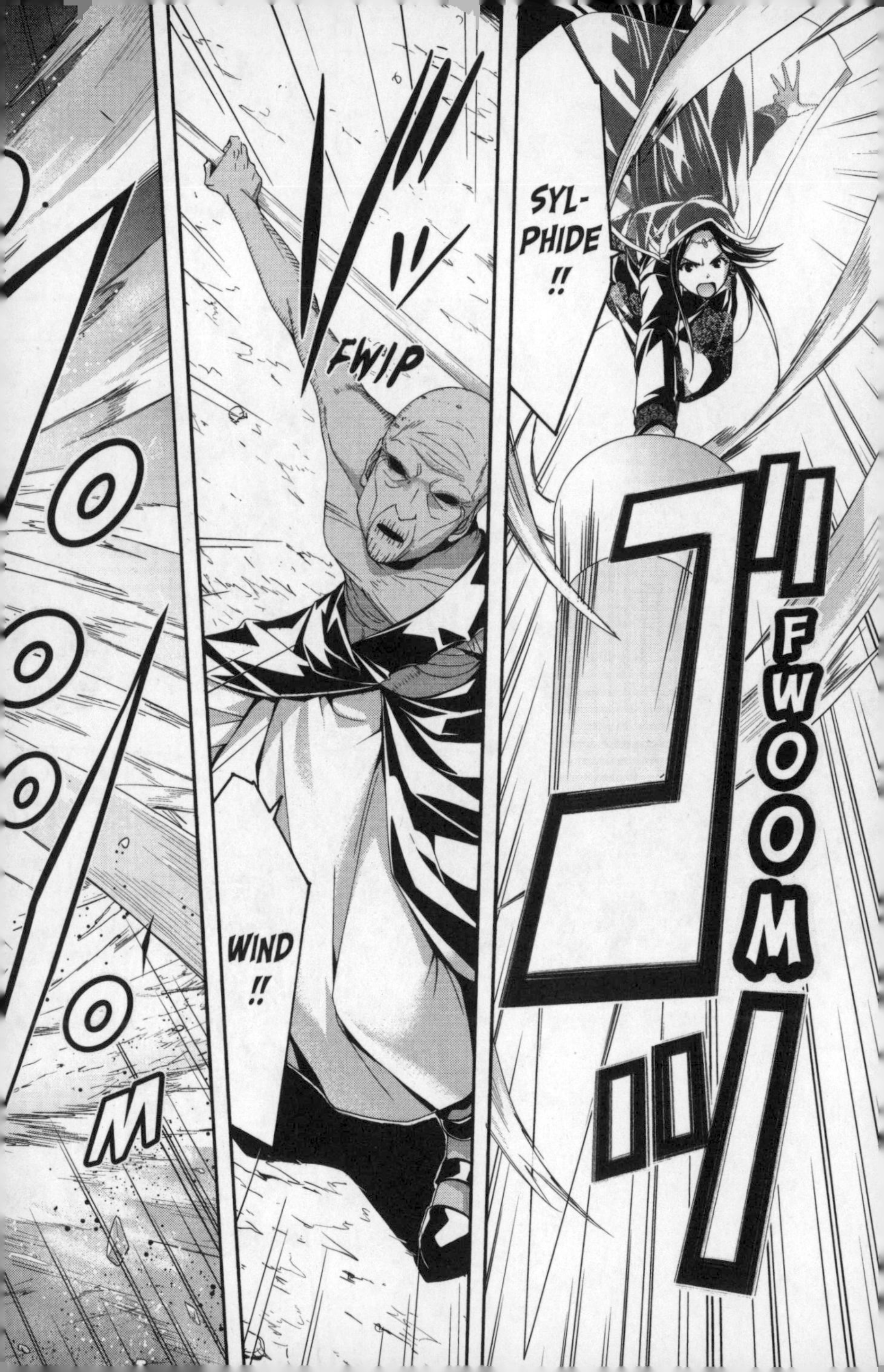
SYL-
PHIDE
!!
FWOOM
FWIP
WIND
!!
OOOOOM

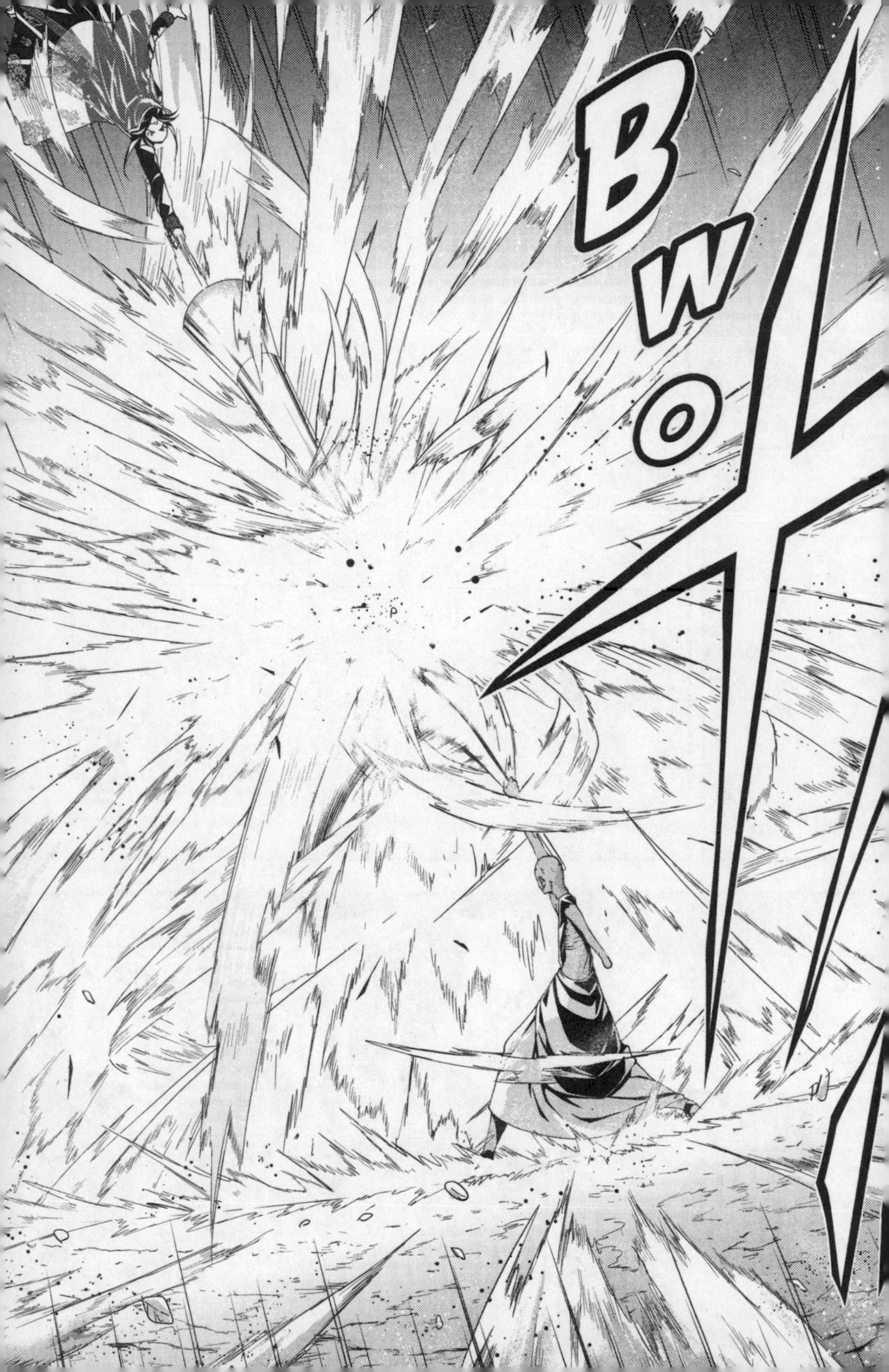
BWO

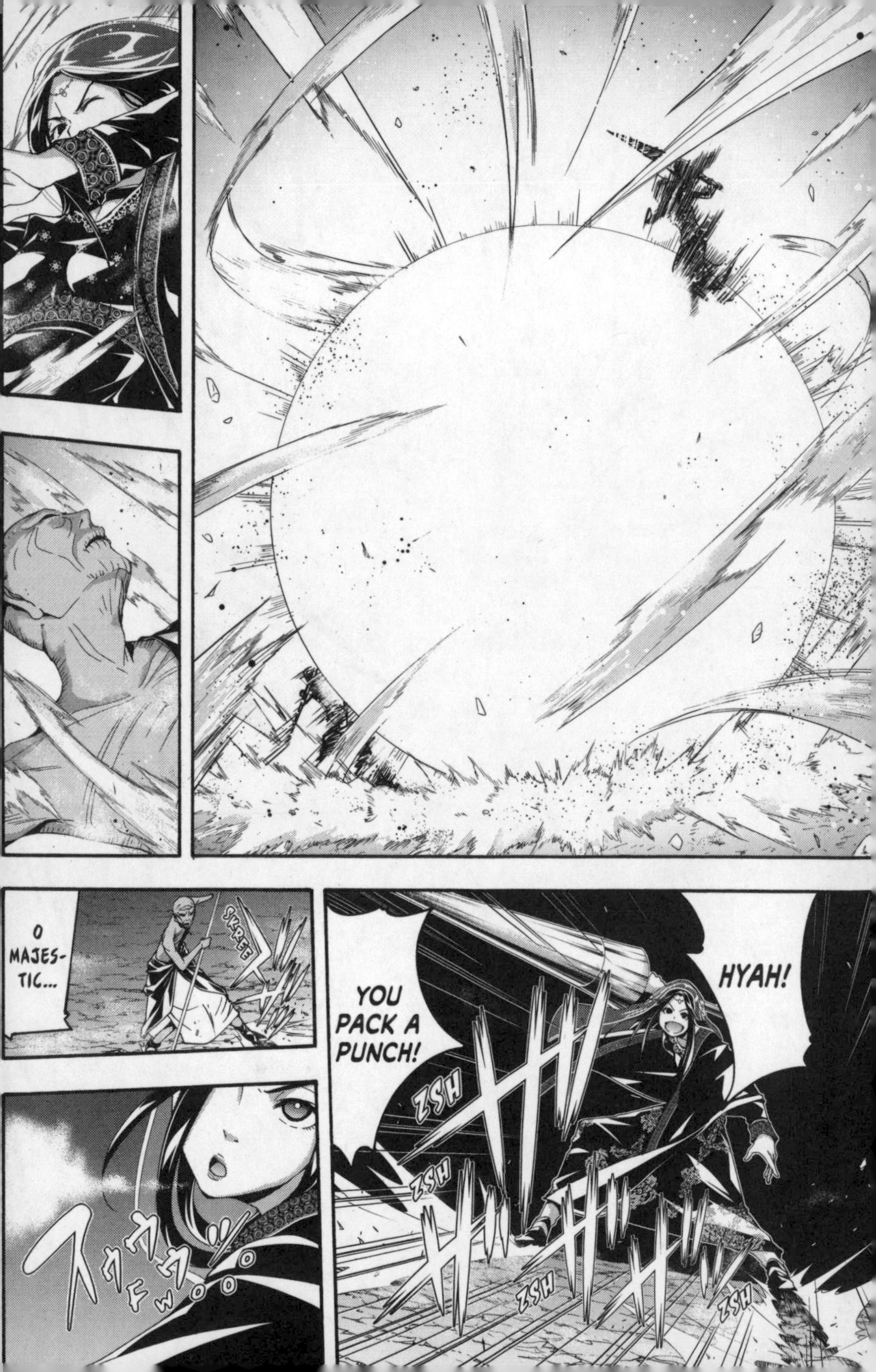
HYAH!
YOU PACK A PUNCH!
ZSH
ZSH
ZSH
ZSH
O MAJES-TIC...
SKREE
FWOOO

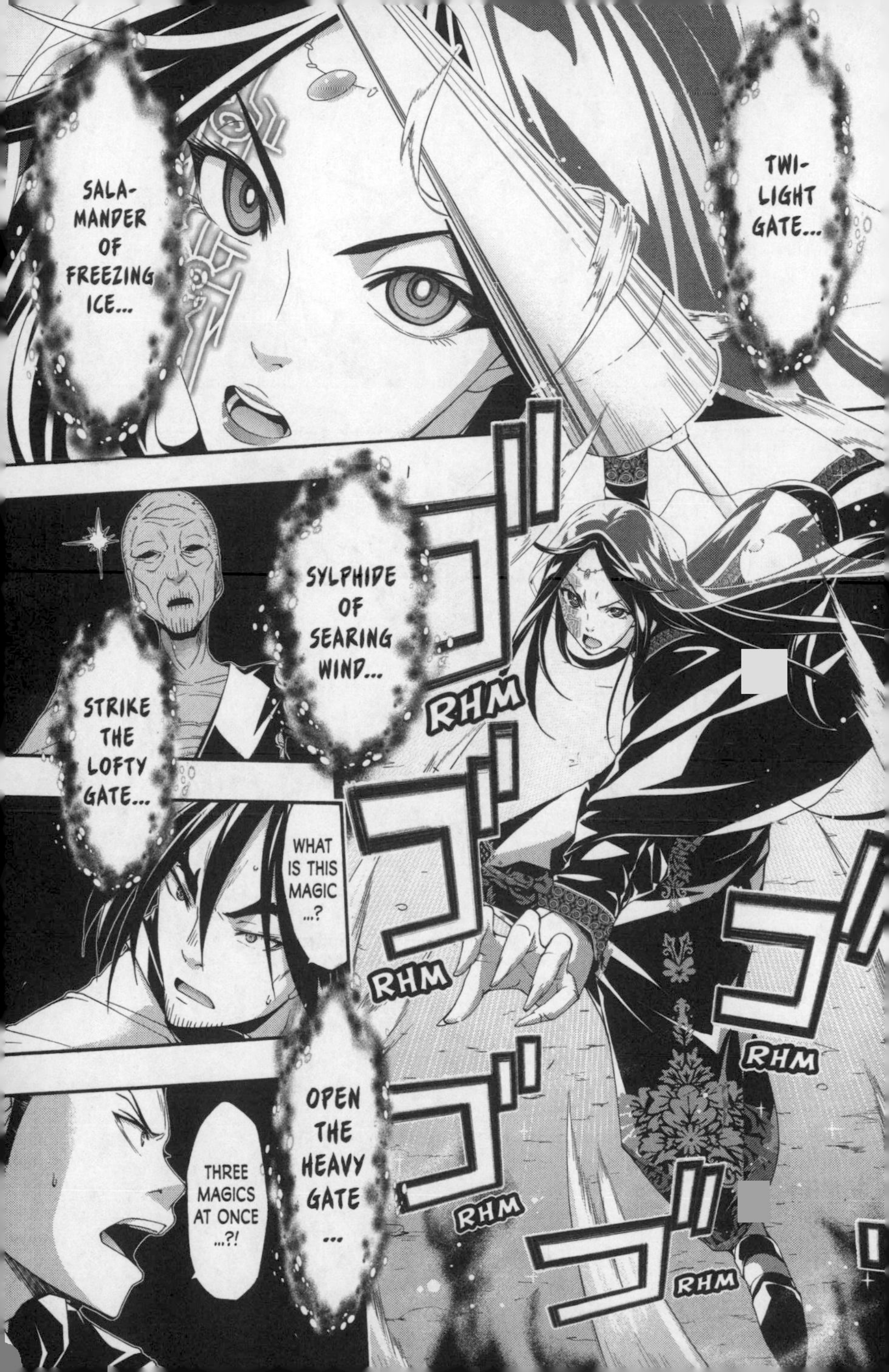
TWI-LIGHT GATE...
SALA-MANDER OF FREEZING ICE...
RHM
RHM
RHM
RHM
RHM
SYLPHIDE OF SEARING WIND...
STRIKE THE LOFTY GATE...
WHAT IS THIS MAGIC ...?
OPEN THE HEAVY GATE ...
THREE MAGICS AT ONCE ...?!

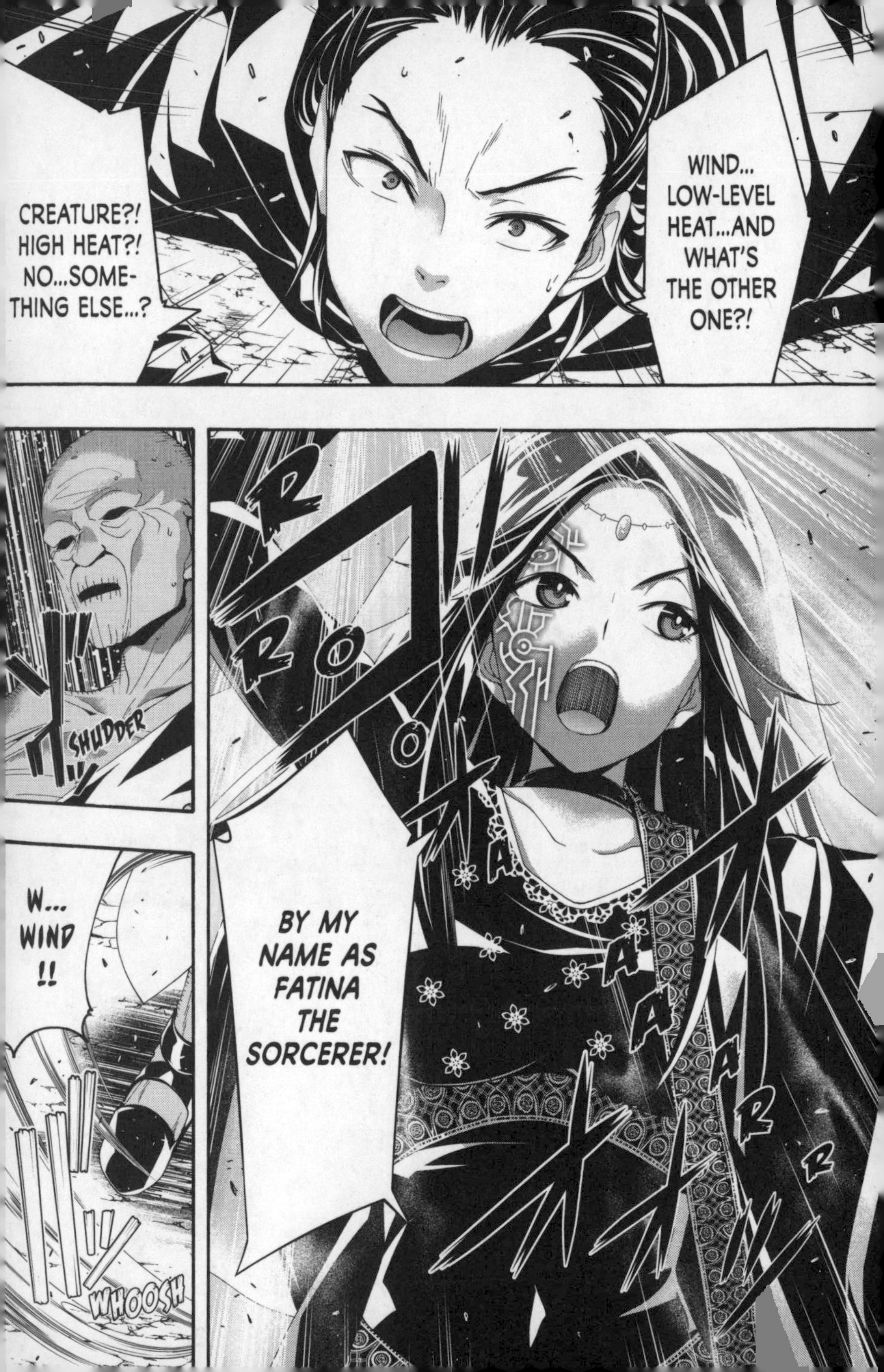
WIND... LOW-LEVEL HEAT...AND WHAT'S THE OTHER ONE?!
CREATURE?! HIGH HEAT?! NO...SOME-THING ELSE...?
RROOAAAARR
BY MY NAME AS FATINA THE SORCERER!
SHUDDER
W... WIND !!
WHOOSH

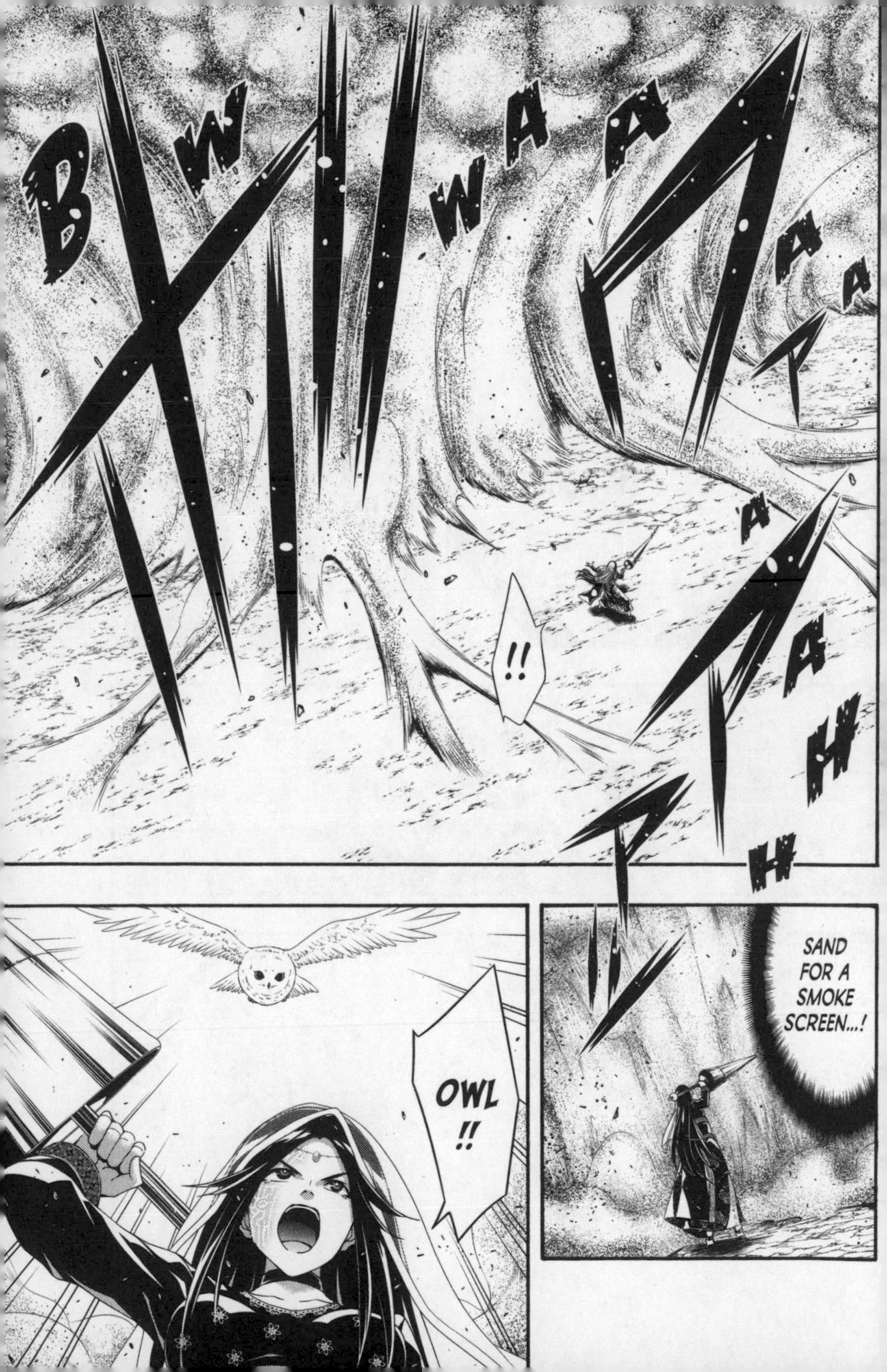
BWWAAAAAAAHH
!!
SAND FOR A SMOKE SCREEN...!
OWL!!

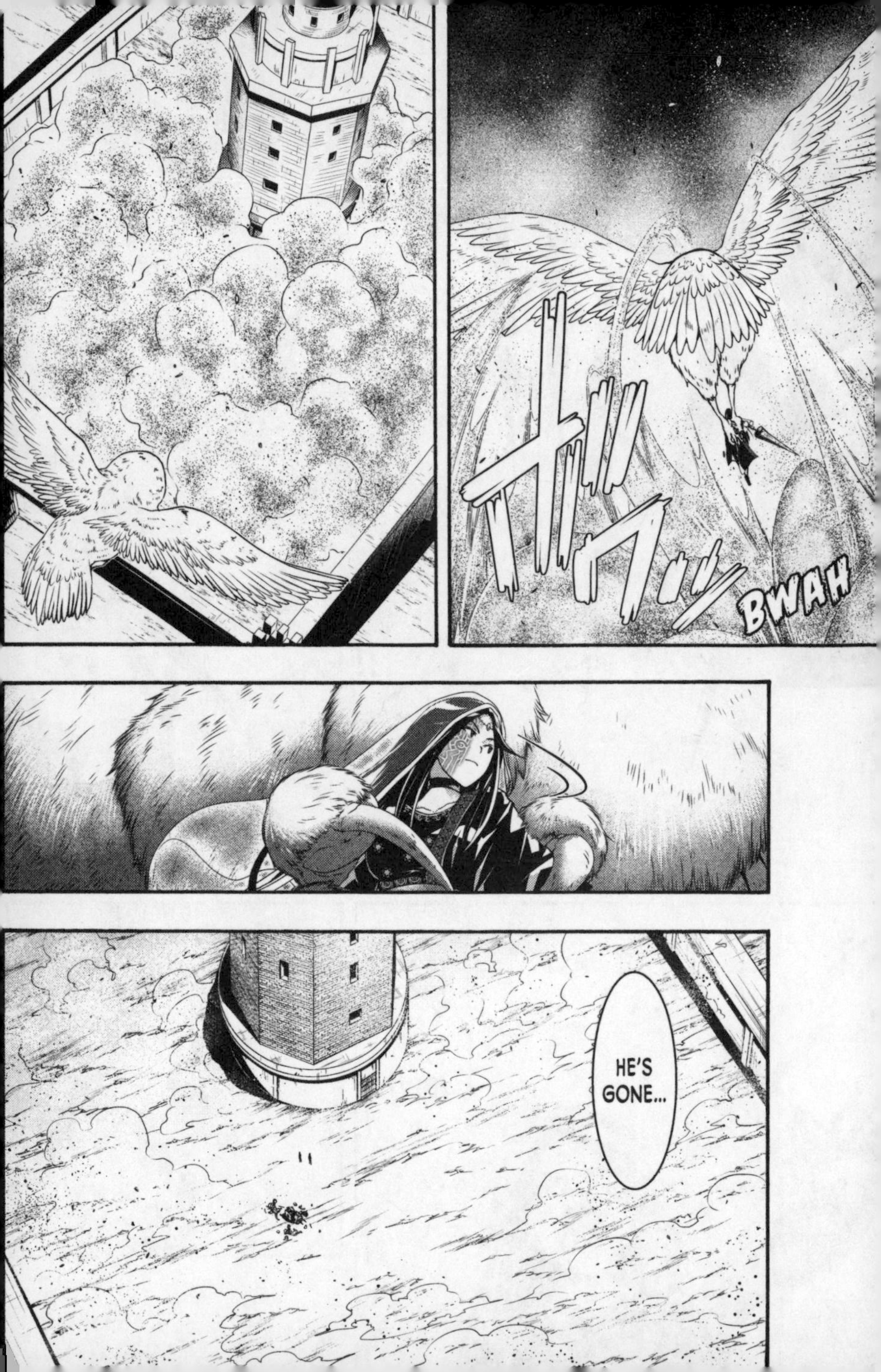
BWAH
HE'S GONE...

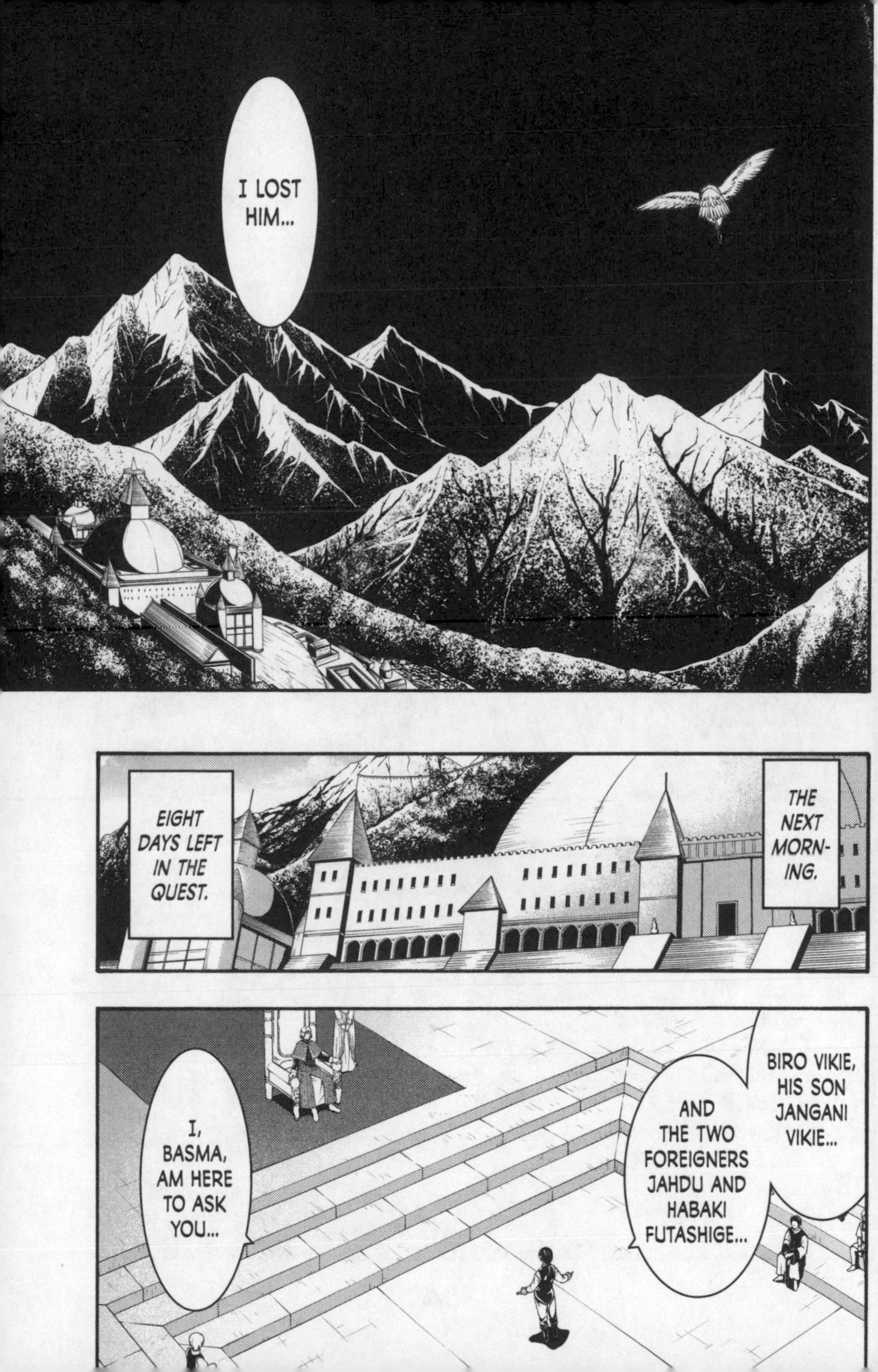
I LOST HIM...
THE NEXT MORNING.
EIGHT DAYS LEFT IN THE QUEST.
BIRO VIKIE, HIS SON JANGANI VIKIE...
AND THE TWO FOREIGNERS JAHDU AND HABAKI FUTASHIGE...
I, BASMA, AM HERE TO ASK YOU...

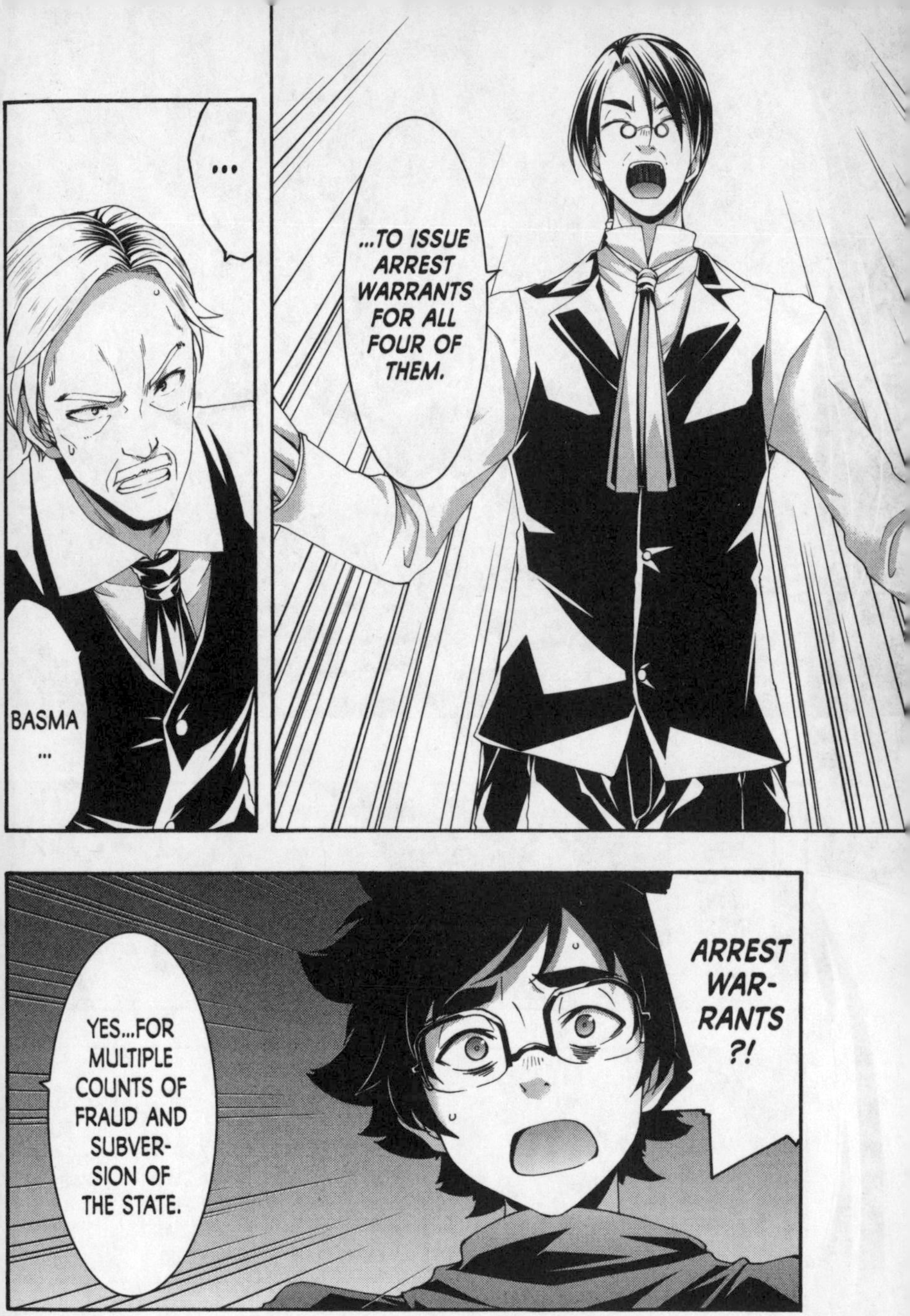
...TO ISSUE ARREST WARRANTS FOR ALL FOUR OF THEM.
...
BASMA ...
ARREST WAR-RANTS?!
YES...FOR MULTIPLE COUNTS OF FRAUD AND SUBVER-SION OF THE STATE.

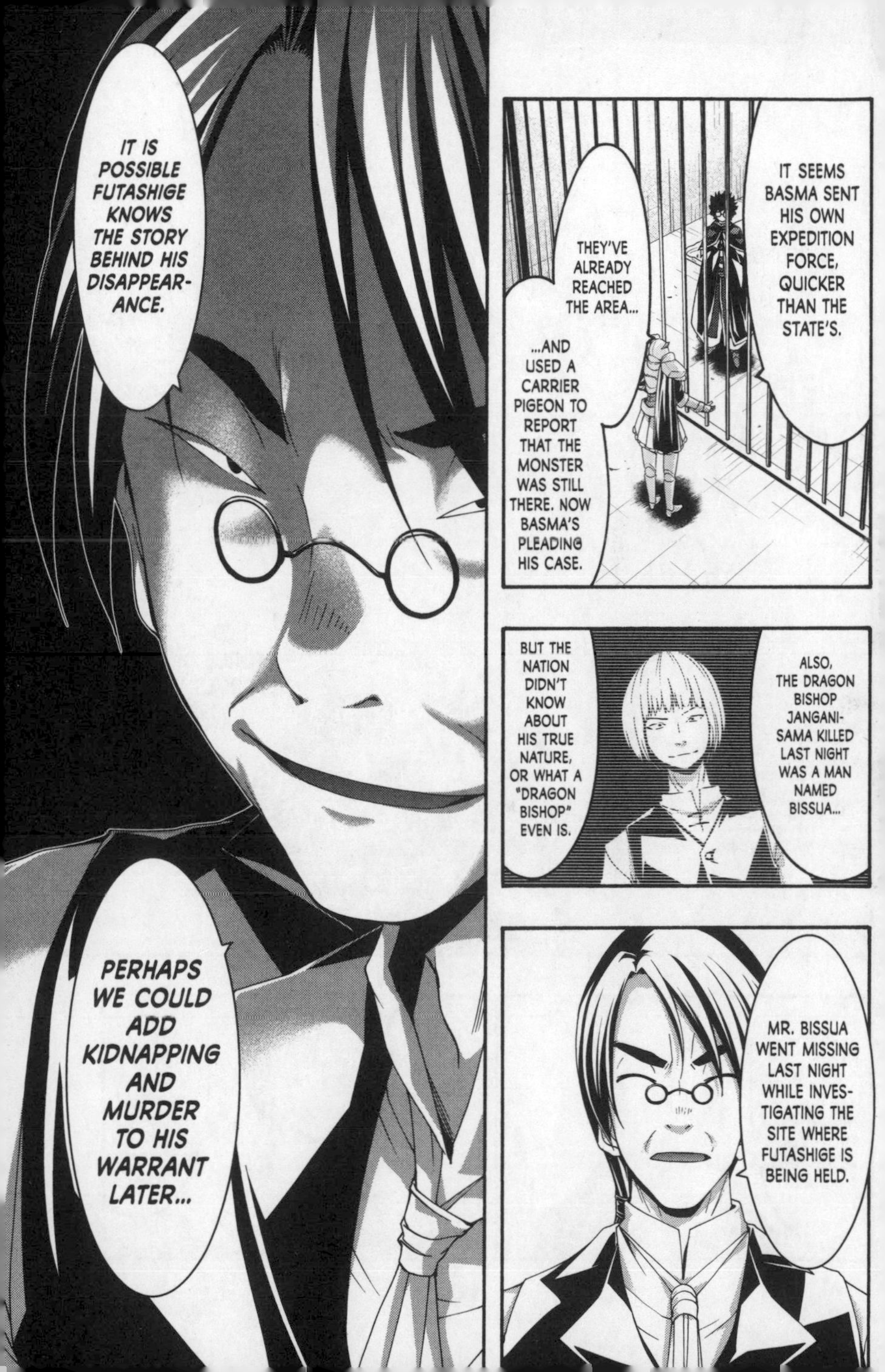
IT SEEMS BASMA SENT HIS OWN EXPEDITION FORCE, QUICKER THAN THE STATE'S.
THEY'VE ALREADY REACHED THE AREA...
...AND USED A CARRIER PIGEON TO REPORT THAT THE MONSTER WAS STILL THERE. NOW BASMA'S PLEADING HIS CASE.
ALSO, THE DRAGON BISHOP JANGANI-SAMA KILLED LAST NIGHT WAS A MAN NAMED BISSUA...
BUT THE NATION DIDN'T KNOW ABOUT HIS TRUE NATURE, OR WHAT A "DRAGON BISHOP" EVEN IS.
MR. BISSUA WENT MISSING LAST NIGHT WHILE INVES-TIGATING THE SITE WHERE FUTASHIGE IS BEING HELD.
IT IS POSSIBLE FUTASHIGE KNOWS THE STORY BEHIND HIS DISAPPEAR-ANCE.
PERHAPS WE COULD ADD KIDNAPPING AND MURDER TO HIS WARRANT LATER...

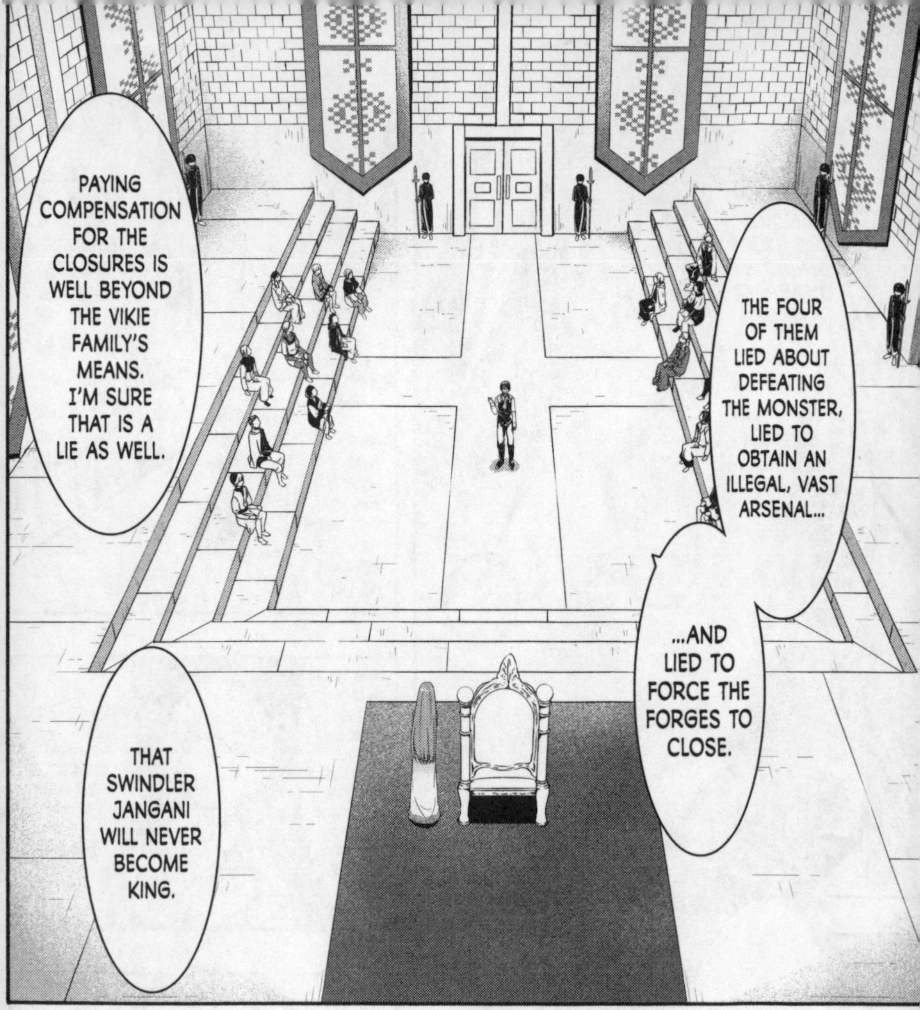
THE FOUR OF THEM LIED ABOUT DEFEATING THE MONSTER, LIED TO OBTAIN AN ILLEGAL, VAST ARSENAL...
...AND LIED TO FORCE THE FORGES TO CLOSE.
PAYING COMPENSATION FOR THE CLOSURES IS WELL BEYOND THE VIKIE FAMILY'S MEANS. I'M SURE THAT IS A LIE AS WELL.
THAT SWINDLER JANGANI WILL NEVER BECOME KING.

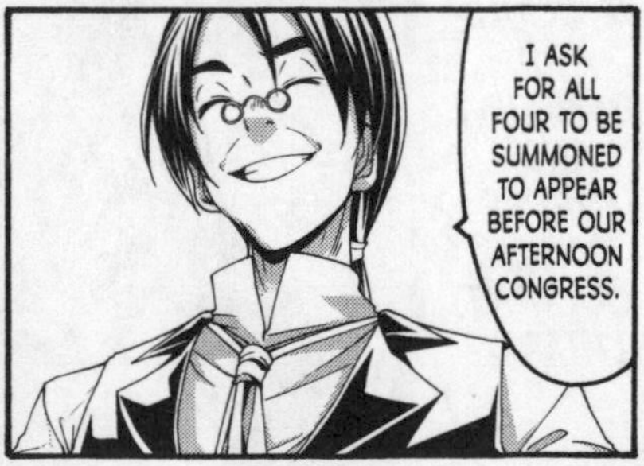
I ASK FOR ALL FOUR TO BE SUMMONED TO APPEAR BEFORE OUR AFTERNOON CONGRESS.

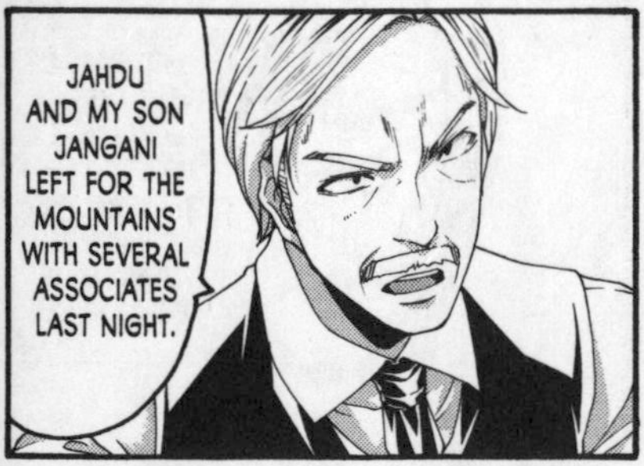
JAHDU AND MY SON JANGANI LEFT FOR THE MOUNTAINS WITH SEVERAL ASSOCIATES LAST NIGHT.

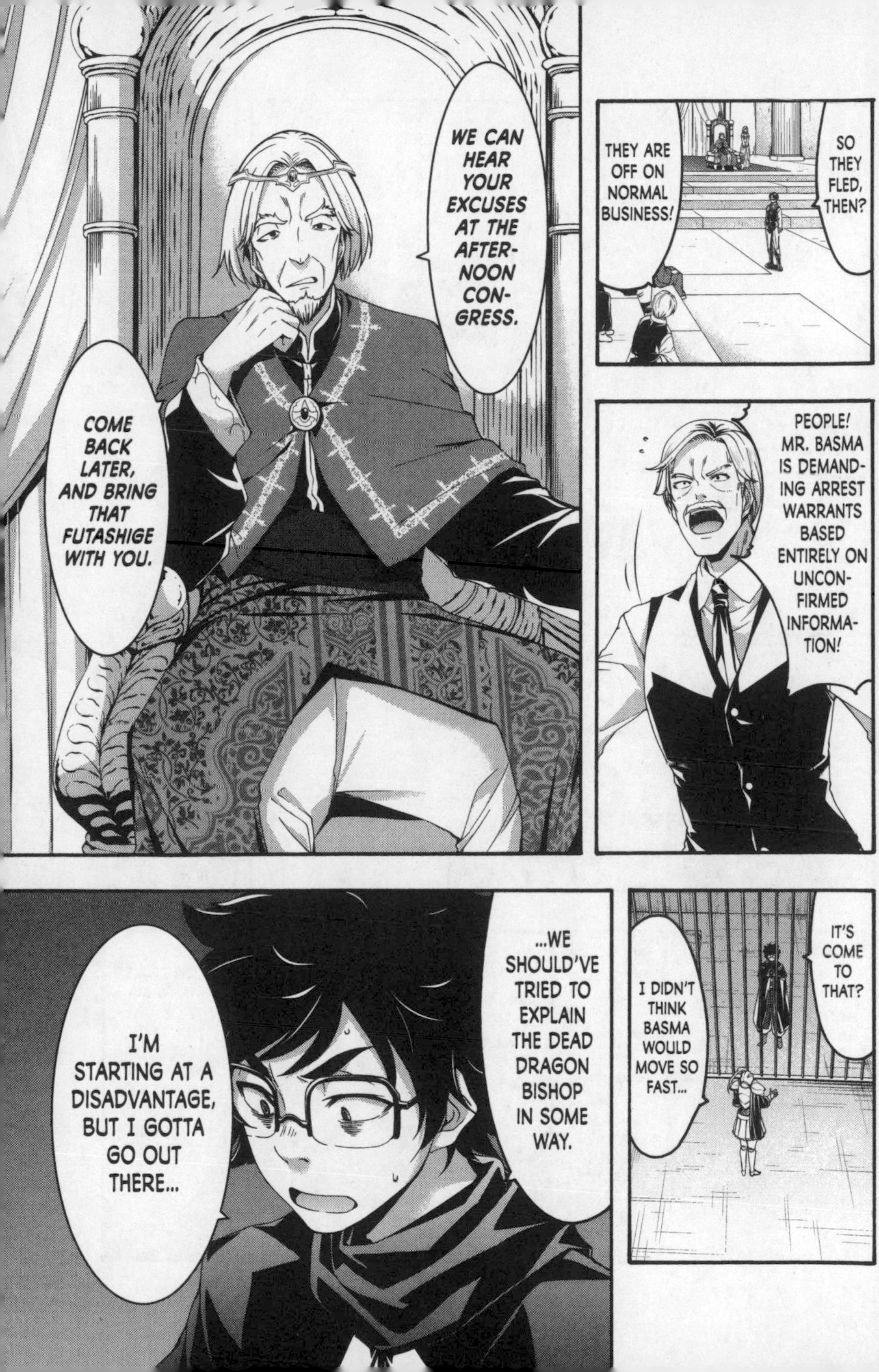
SO THEY FLED, THEN?
THEY ARE OFF ON NORMAL BUSINESS!
PEOPLE! MR. BASMA IS DEMANDING ARREST WARRANTS BASED ENTIRELY ON UNCONFIRMED INFORMATION!
WE CAN HEAR YOUR EXCUSES AT THE AFTERNOON CONGRESS.
COME BACK LATER, AND BRING THAT FUTASHIGE WITH YOU.
IT'S COME TO THAT?
I DIDN'T THINK BASMA WOULD MOVE SO FAST...
...WE SHOULD'VE TRIED TO EXPLAIN THE DEAD DRAGON BISHOP IN SOME WAY.
I'M STARTING AT A DISADVANTAGE, BUT I GOTTA GO OUT THERE...

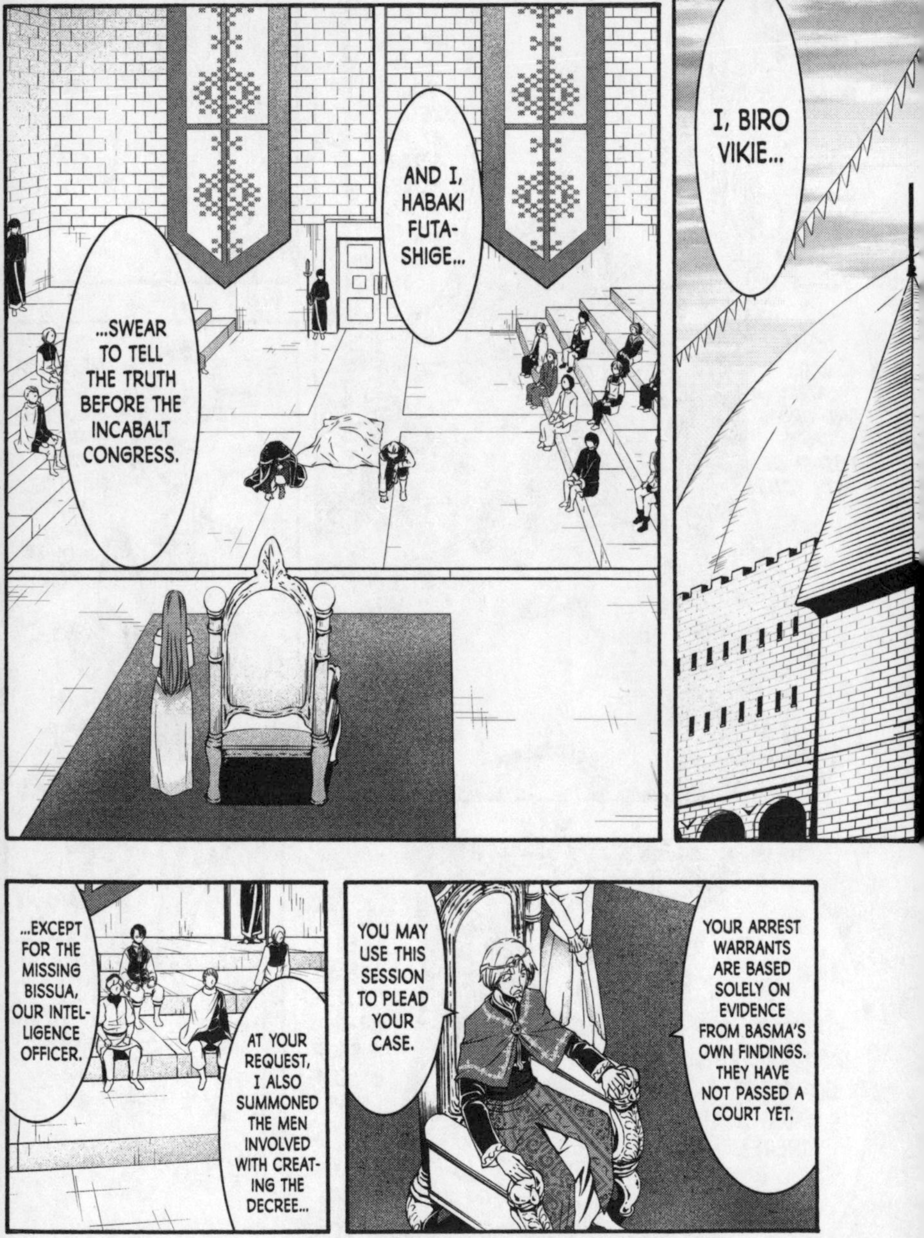
I, BIRO VIKIE...
AND I, HABAKI FUTA-SHIGE...
...SWEAR TO TELL THE TRUTH BEFORE THE INCABALT CONGRESS.
YOUR ARREST WARRANTS ARE BASED SOLELY ON EVIDENCE FROM BASMA'S OWN FINDINGS. THEY HAVE NOT PASSED A COURT YET.
YOU MAY USE THIS SESSION TO PLEAD YOUR CASE.
AT YOUR REQUEST, I ALSO SUMMONED THE MEN INVOLVED WITH CREAT-ING THE DECREE...
...EXCEPT FOR THE MISSING BISSUA, OUR INTEL-LIGENCE OFFICER.

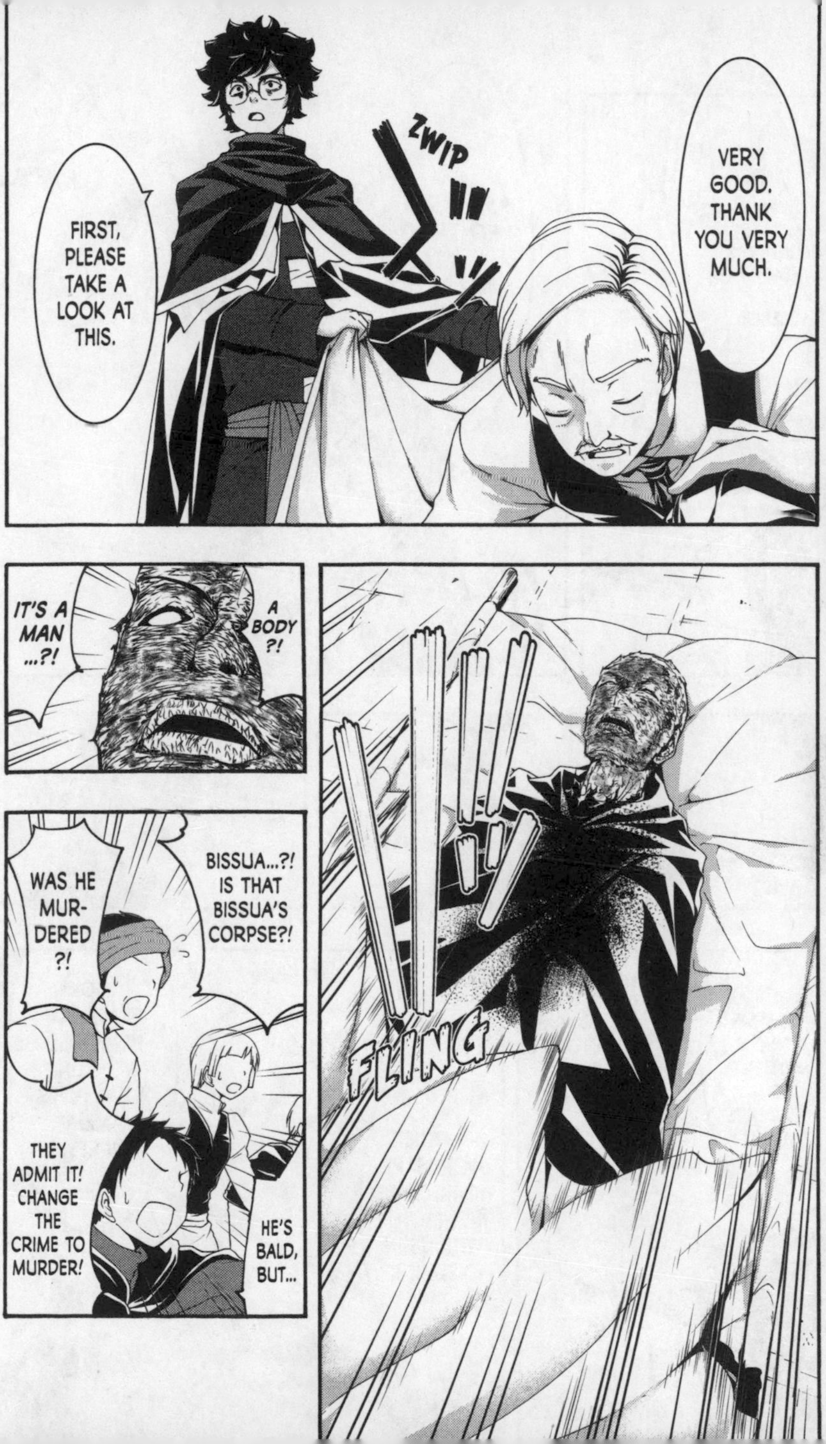
VERY GOOD. THANK YOU VERY MUCH.
ZWIP
FIRST, PLEASE TAKE A LOOK AT THIS.
FLING
A BODY ?!
IT'S A MAN ...?!
BISSUA...?! IS THAT BISSUA'S CORPSE?!
WAS HE MUR-DERED ?!
HE'S BALD, BUT...
THEY ADMIT IT! CHANGE THE CRIME TO MURDER!

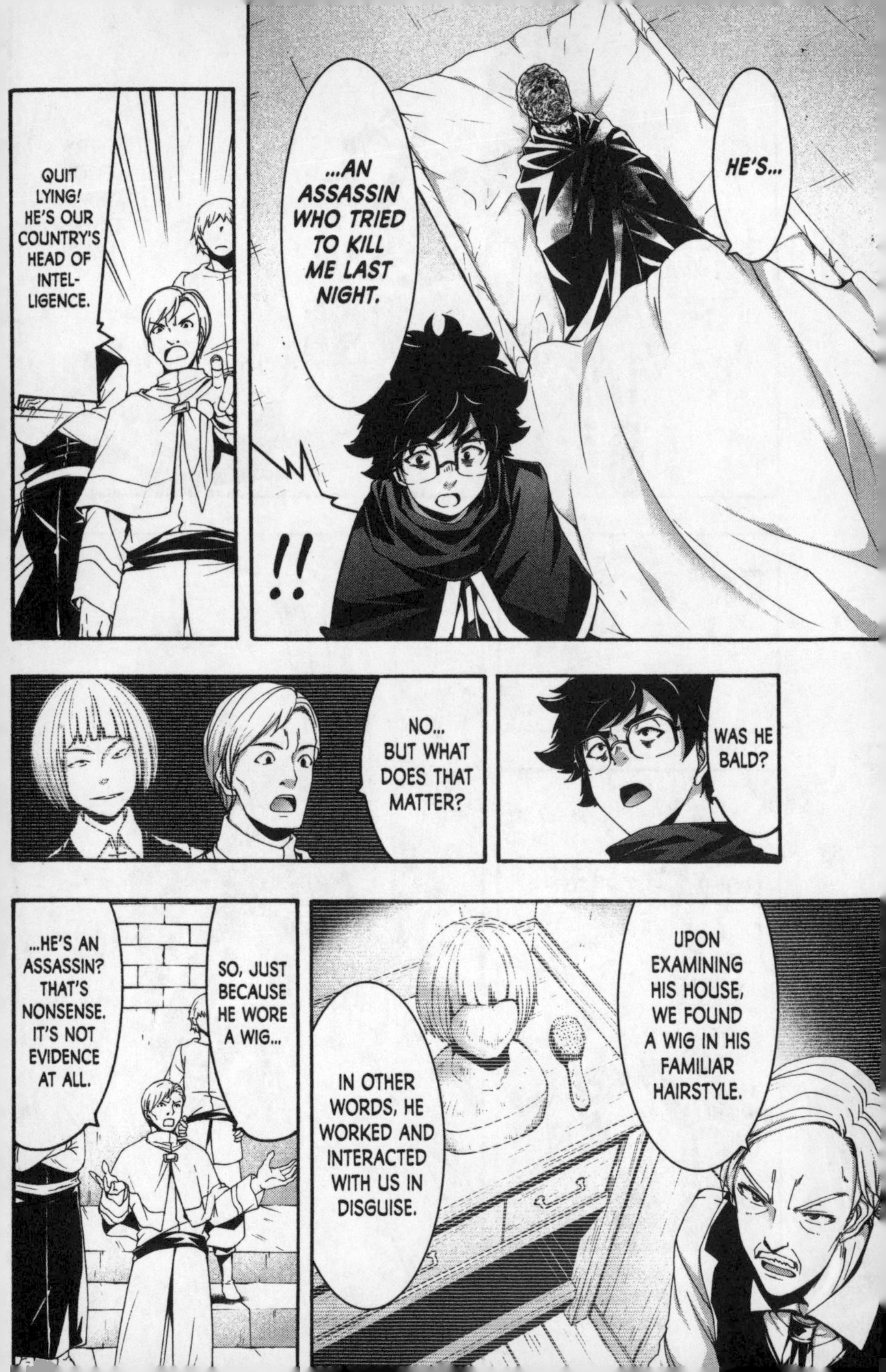
HE'S...
...AN ASSASSIN WHO TRIED TO KILL ME LAST NIGHT.
!!
QUIT LYING! HE'S OUR COUNTRY'S HEAD OF INTEL-LIGENCE.
WAS HE BALD?
NO... BUT WHAT DOES THAT MATTER?
UPON EXAMINING HIS HOUSE, WE FOUND A WIG IN HIS FAMILIAR HAIRSTYLE.
IN OTHER WORDS, HE WORKED AND INTERACTED WITH US IN DISGUISE.
SO, JUST BECAUSE HE WORE A WIG...
...HE'S AN ASSASSIN? THAT'S NONSENSE. IT'S NOT EVIDENCE AT ALL.

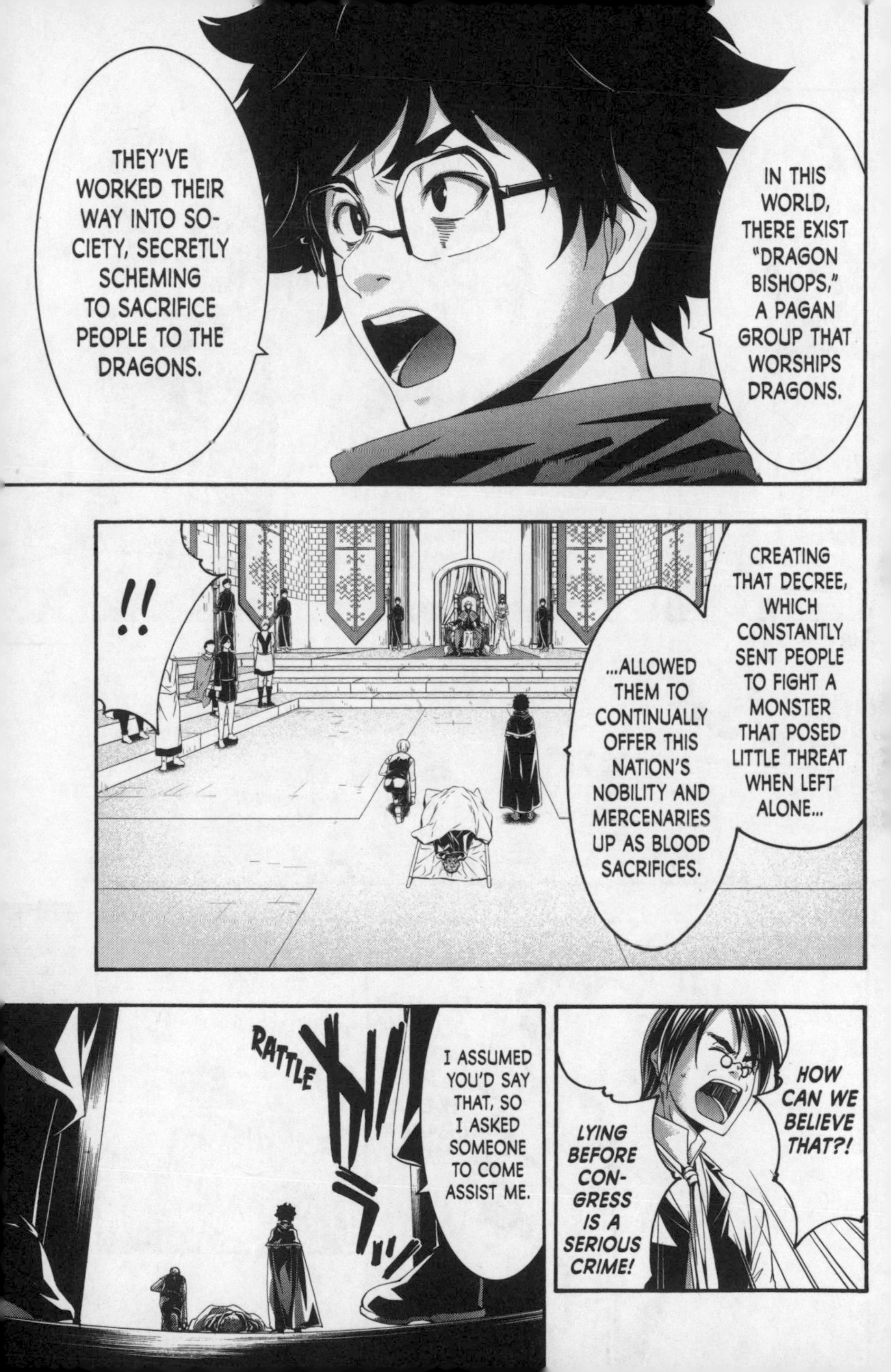
IN THIS WORLD, THERE EXIST "DRAGON BISHOPS," A PAGAN GROUP THAT WORSHIPS DRAGONS.
THEY'VE WORKED THEIR WAY INTO SOCIETY, SECRETLY SCHEMING TO SACRIFICE PEOPLE TO THE DRAGONS.
CREATING THAT DECREE, WHICH CONSTANTLY SENT PEOPLE TO FIGHT A MONSTER THAT POSED LITTLE THREAT WHEN LEFT ALONE...
...ALLOWED THEM TO CONTINUALLY OFFER THIS NATION'S NOBILITY AND MERCENARIES UP AS BLOOD SACRIFICES.
!!
HOW CAN WE BELIEVE THAT?!
LYING BEFORE CONGRESS IS A SERIOUS CRIME!
I ASSUMED YOU'D SAY THAT, SO I ASKED SOMEONE TO COME ASSIST ME.
RATTLE

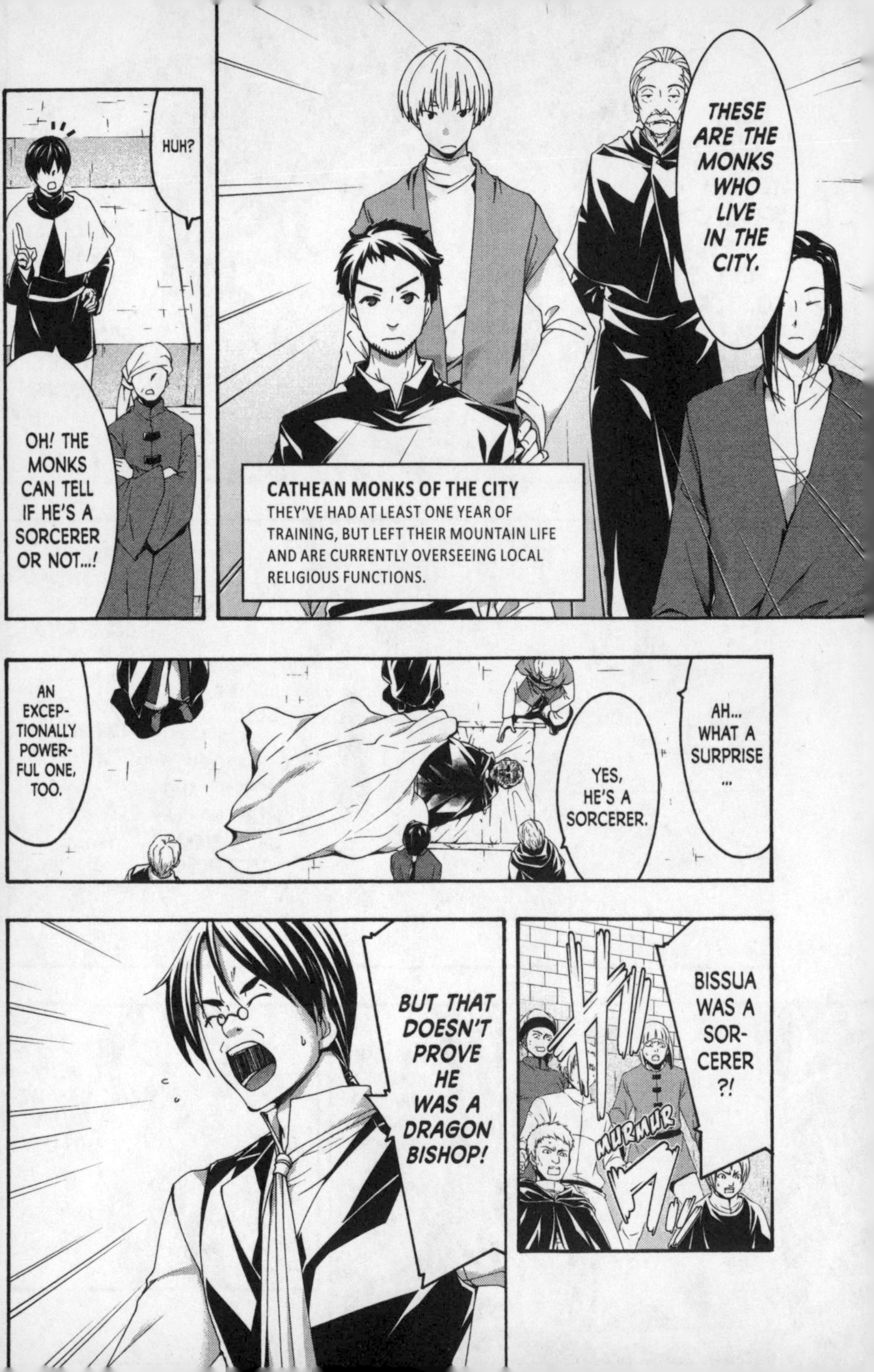
THESE ARE THE MONKS WHO LIVE IN THE CITY.
CATHEAN MONKS OF THE CITY
THEY'VE HAD AT LEAST ONE YEAR OF TRAINING, BUT LEFT THEIR MOUNTAIN LIFE AND ARE CURRENTLY OVERSEEING LOCAL RELIGIOUS FUNCTIONS.
HUH?
OH! THE MONKS CAN TELL IF HE'S A SORCERER OR NOT...!
AH... WHAT A SURPRISE ...
YES, HE'S A SORCERER.
AN EXCEPTIONALLY POWERFUL ONE, TOO.
BISSUA WAS A SORCERER?!
MURMUR
BUT THAT DOESN'T PROVE HE WAS A DRAGON BISHOP!

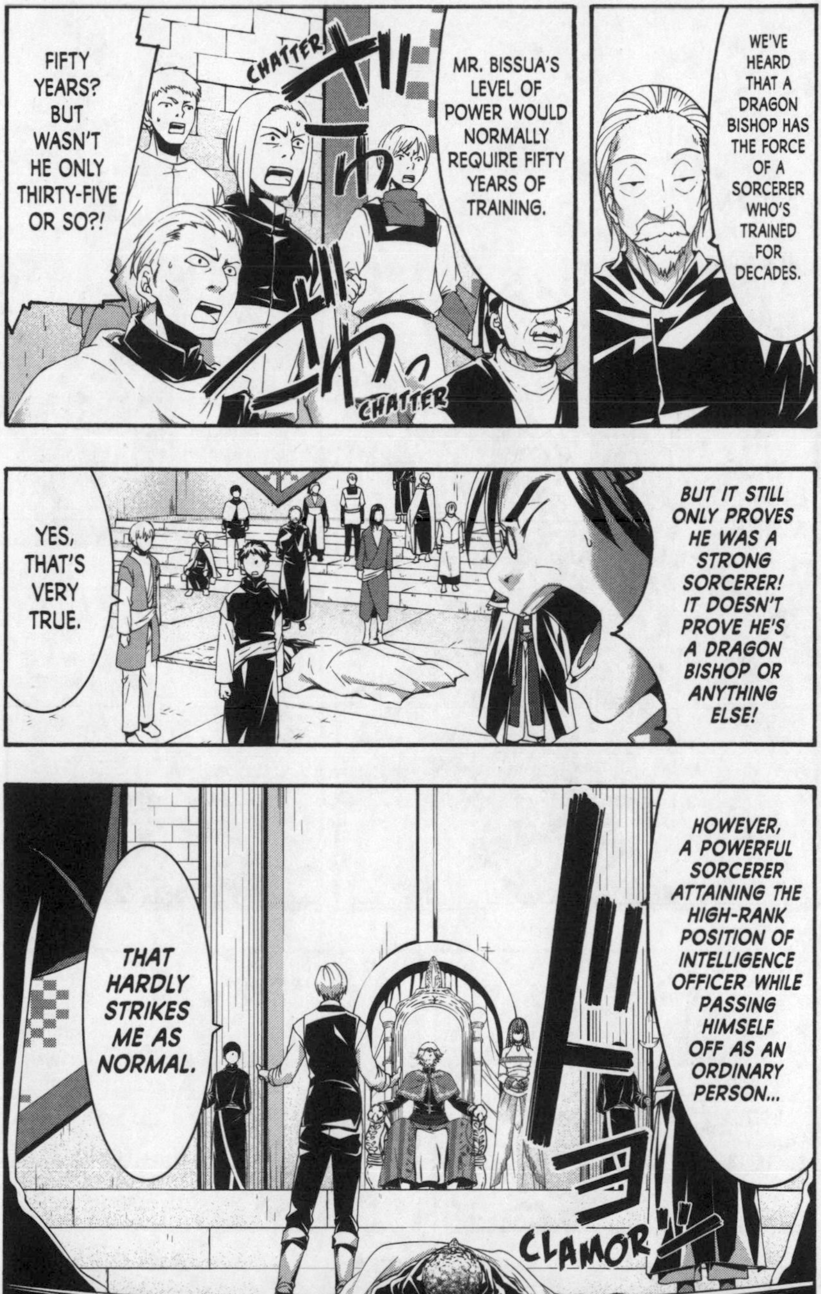
WE'VE HEARD THAT A DRAGON BISHOP HAS THE FORCE OF A SORCERER WHO'S TRAINED FOR DECADES.
MR. BISSUA'S LEVEL OF POWER WOULD NORMALLY REQUIRE FIFTY YEARS OF TRAINING.
CHATTER
FIFTY YEARS? BUT WASN'T HE ONLY THIRTY-FIVE OR SO?!
CHATTER
BUT IT STILL ONLY PROVES HE WAS A STRONG SORCERER! IT DOESN'T PROVE HE'S A DRAGON BISHOP OR ANYTHING ELSE!
YES, THAT'S VERY TRUE.
HOWEVER, A POWERFUL SORCERER ATTAINING THE HIGH-RANK POSITION OF INTELLIGENCE OFFICER WHILE PASSING HIMSELF OFF AS AN ORDINARY PERSON...
CLAMOR
THAT HARDLY STRIKES ME AS NORMAL.

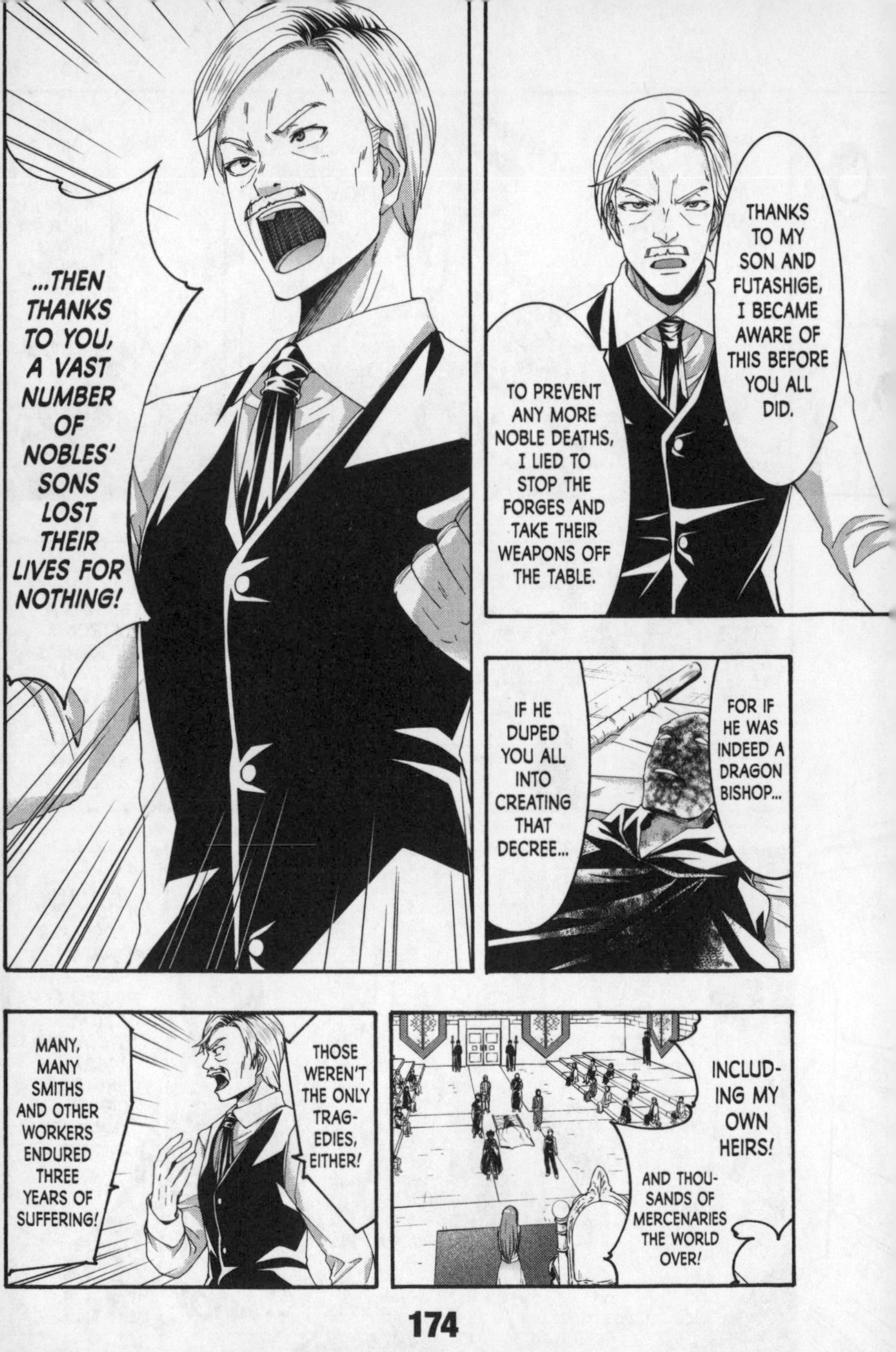
THANKS TO MY SON AND FUTASHIGE, I BECAME AWARE OF THIS BEFORE YOU ALL DID.
TO PREVENT ANY MORE NOBLE DEATHS, I LIED TO STOP THE FORGES AND TAKE THEIR WEAPONS OFF THE TABLE.
FOR IF HE WAS INDEED A DRAGON BISHOP...
IF HE DUPED YOU ALL INTO CREATING THAT DECREE...
...THEN THANKS TO YOU, A VAST NUMBER OF NOBLES' SONS LOST THEIR LIVES FOR NOTHING!
INCLUDING MY OWN HEIRS!
AND THOUSANDS OF MERCENARIES THE WORLD OVER!
THOSE WEREN'T THE ONLY TRAGEDIES, EITHER!
MANY, MANY SMITHS AND OTHER WORKERS ENDURED THREE YEARS OF SUFFERING!

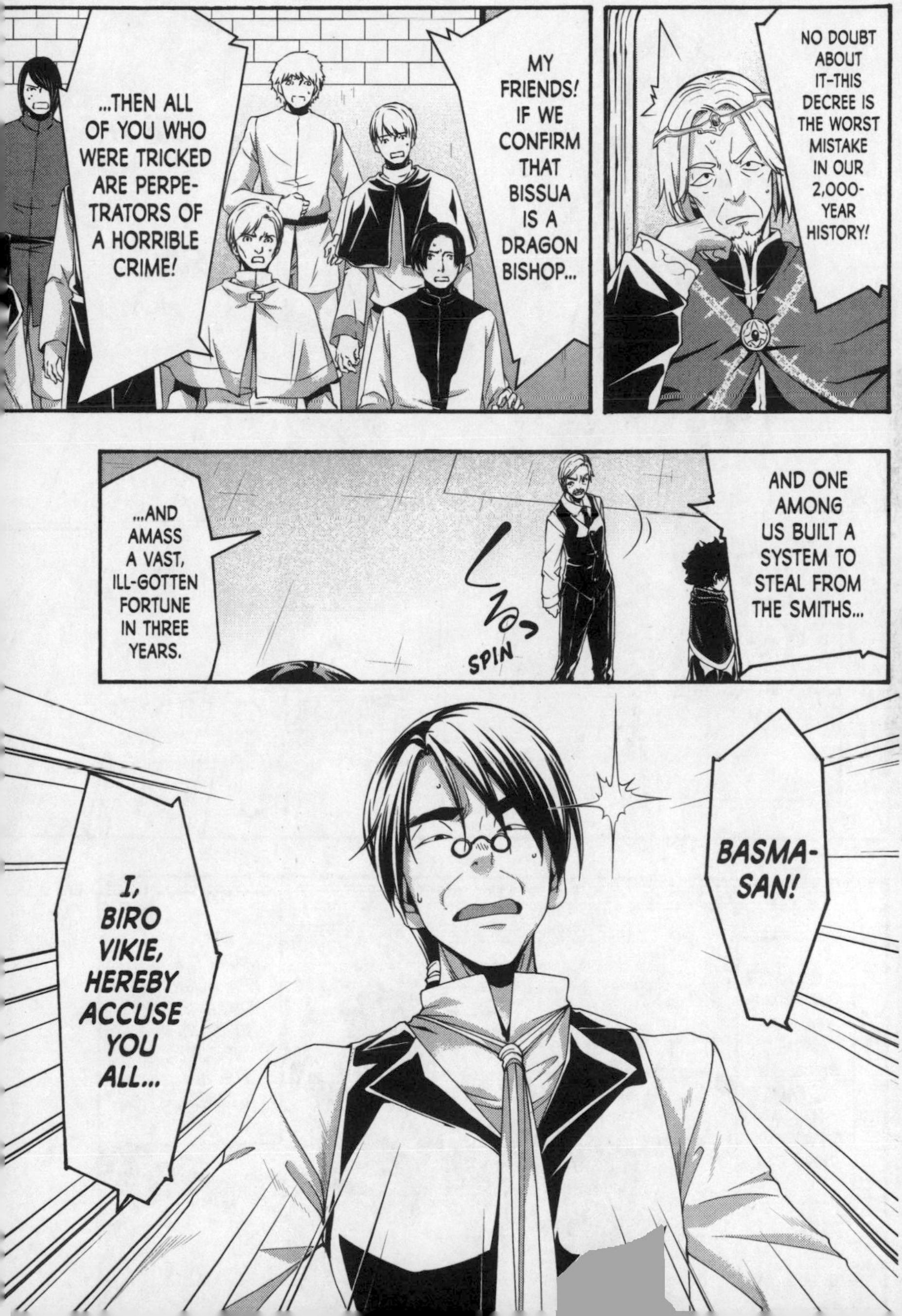
NO DOUBT ABOUT IT–THIS DECREE IS THE WORST MISTAKE IN OUR 2,000-YEAR HISTORY!
MY FRIENDS! IF WE CONFIRM THAT BISSUA IS A DRAGON BISHOP...
...THEN ALL OF YOU WHO WERE TRICKED ARE PERPE-TRATORS OF A HORRIBLE CRIME!
AND ONE AMONG US BUILT A SYSTEM TO STEAL FROM THE SMITHS...
SPIN
...AND AMASS A VAST, ILL-GOTTEN FORTUNE IN THREE YEARS.
BASMA-SAN!
I, BIRO VIKIE, HEREBY ACCUSE YOU ALL...

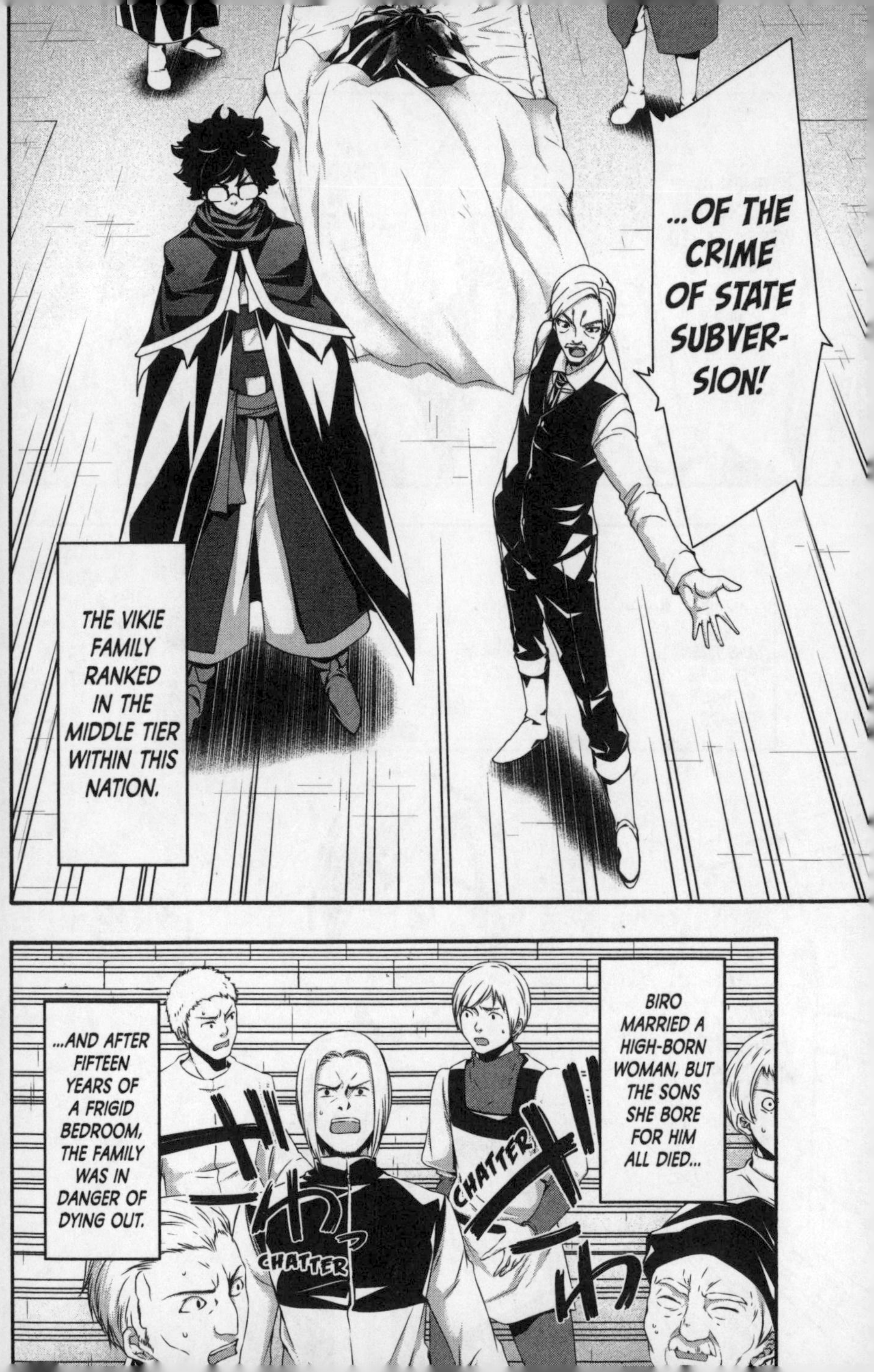
...OF THE CRIME OF STATE SUBVER- SION!
THE VIKIE FAMILY RANKED IN THE MIDDLE TIER WITHIN THIS NATION.
BIRO MARRIED A HIGH-BORN WOMAN, BUT THE SONS SHE BORE FOR HIM ALL DIED...
CHATTER
...AND AFTER FIFTEEN YEARS OF A FRIGID BEDROOM, THE FAMILY WAS IN DANGER OF DYING OUT.
CHATTER

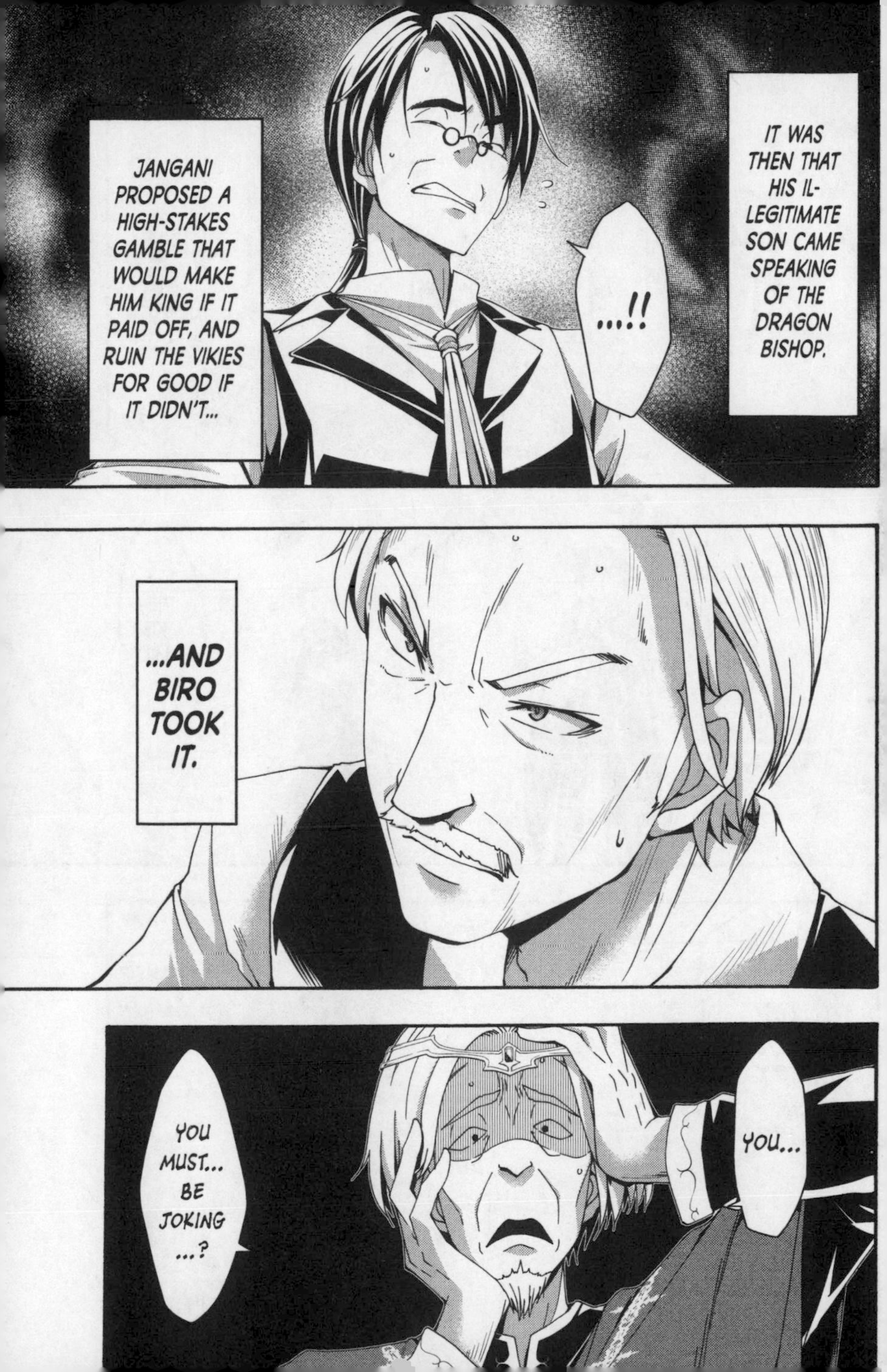
IT WAS THEN THAT HIS IL-LEGITIMATE SON CAME SPEAKING OF THE DRAGON BISHOP.
...!!
JANGANI PROPOSED A HIGH-STAKES GAMBLE THAT WOULD MAKE HIM KING IF IT PAID OFF, AND RUIN THE VIKIES FOR GOOD IF IT DIDN'T...
...AND BIRO TOOK IT.
YOU...
YOU MUST... BE JOKING ...?

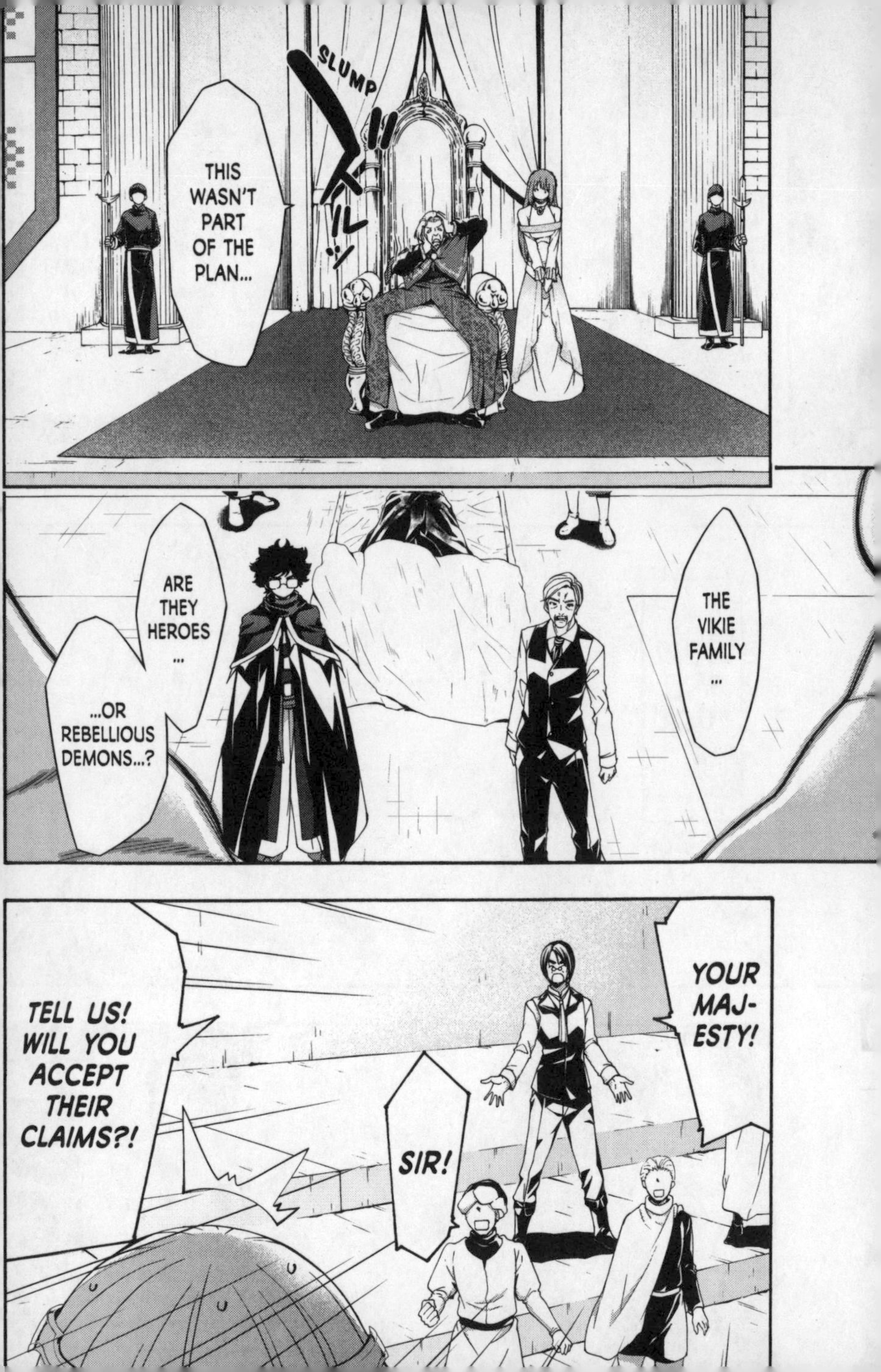
SLUMP
THIS WASN'T PART OF THE PLAN...
THE VIKIE FAMILY ...
ARE THEY HEROES ...
...OR REBELLIOUS DEMONS...?
YOUR MAJ-ESTY!
SIR!
TELL US! WILL YOU ACCEPT THEIR CLAIMS?!

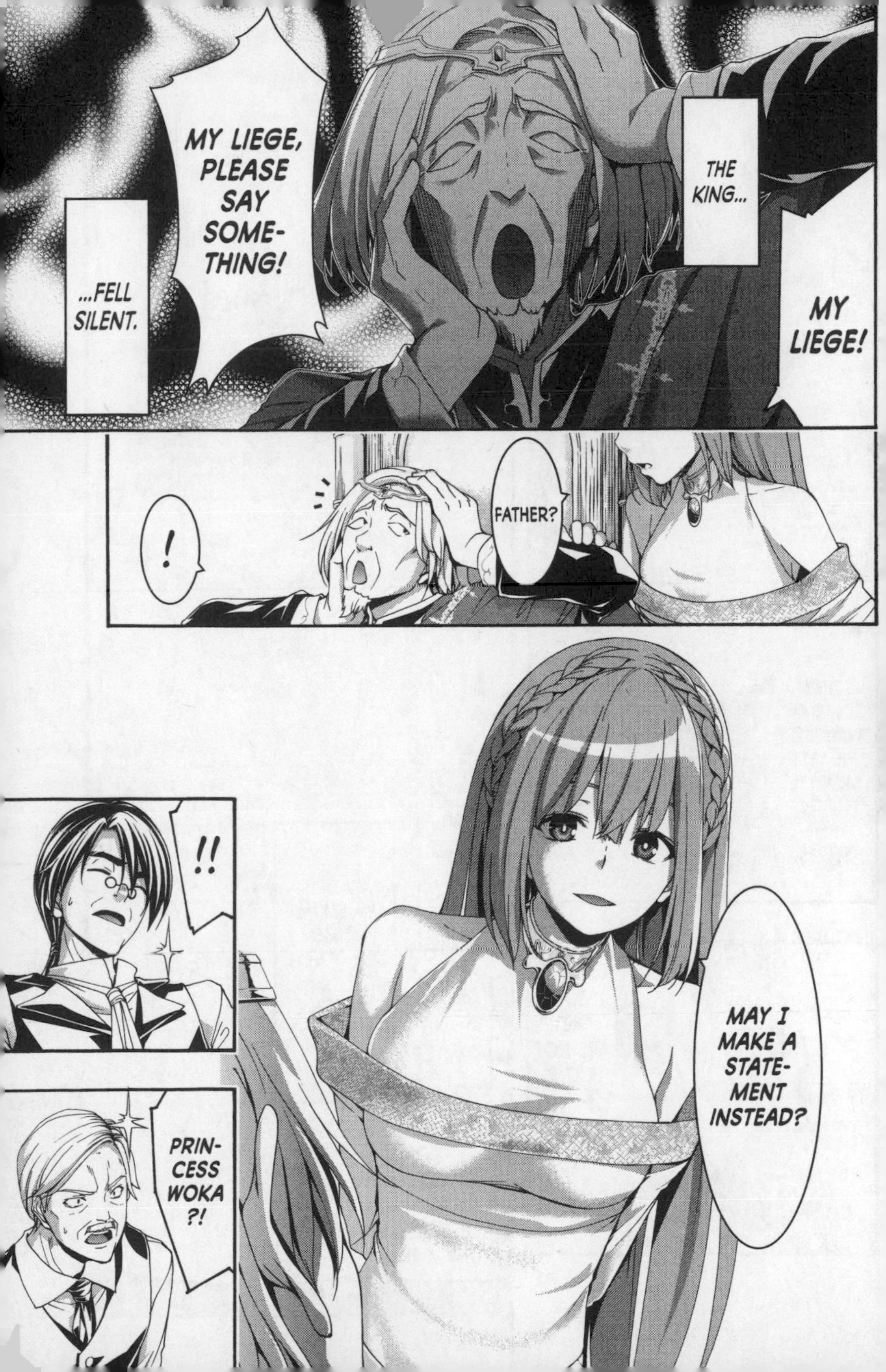
THE KING...
MY LIEGE!
MY LIEGE, PLEASE SAY SOMETHING!
...FELL SILENT.
FATHER?
!
MAY I MAKE A STATEMENT INSTEAD?
!!
PRINCESS WOKA?!

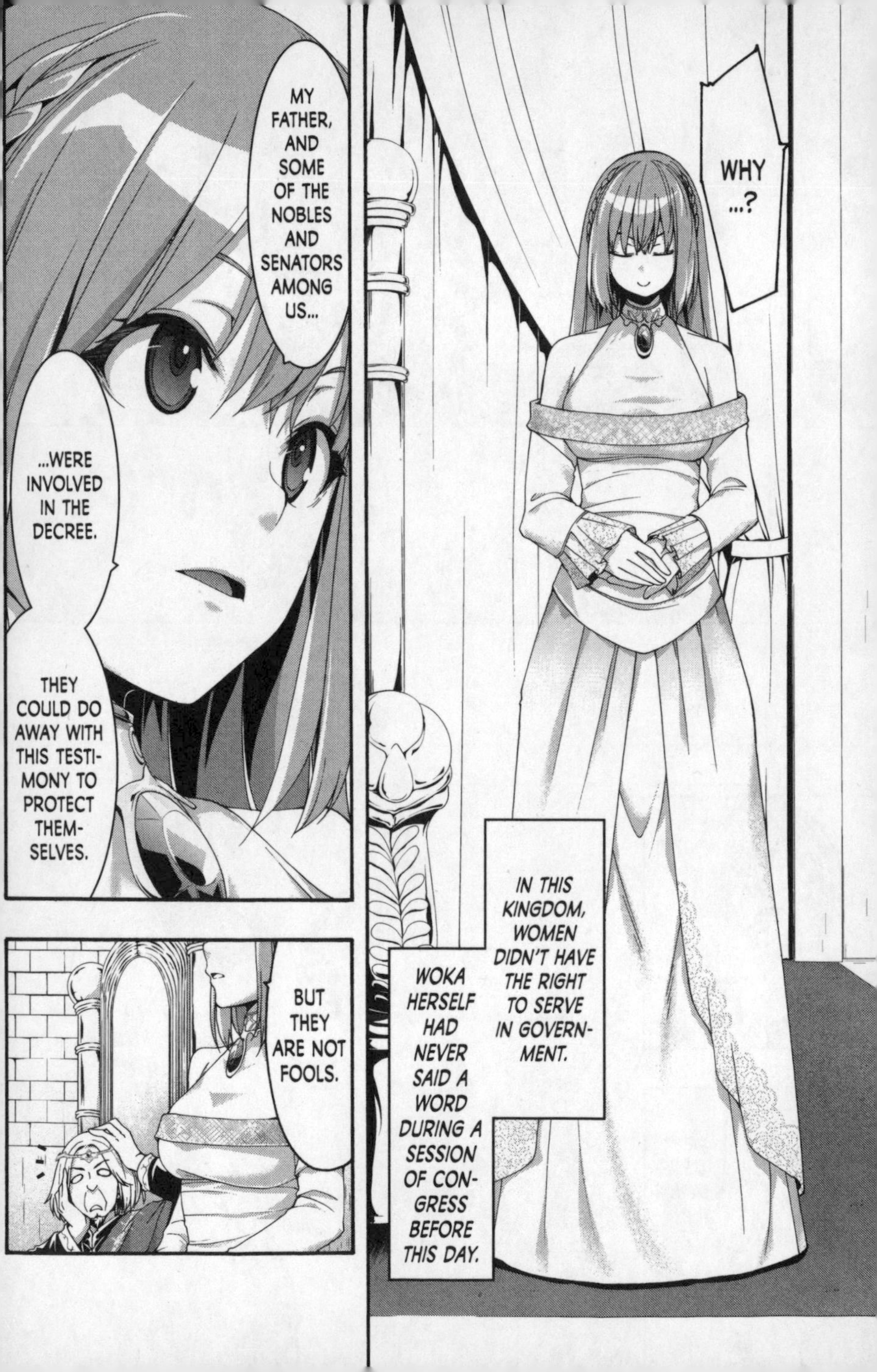
WHY ...?
IN THIS KINGDOM, WOMEN DIDN'T HAVE THE RIGHT TO SERVE IN GOVERN-MENT.
WOKA HERSELF HAD NEVER SAID A WORD DURING A SESSION OF CON-GRESS BEFORE THIS DAY.
MY FATHER, AND SOME OF THE NOBLES AND SENATORS AMONG US...
...WERE INVOLVED IN THE DECREE.
THEY COULD DO AWAY WITH THIS TESTI-MONY TO PROTECT THEM-SELVES.
BUT THEY ARE NOT FOOLS.

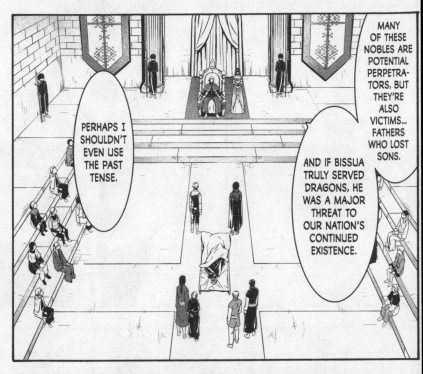

MANY OF THESE NOBLES ARE POTENTIAL PERPETRA-TORS, BUT THEY'RE ALSO VICTIMS... FATHERS WHO LOST SONS.
AND IF BISSUA TRULY SERVED DRAGONS, HE WAS A MAJOR THREAT TO OUR NATION'S CONTINUED EXISTENCE.
PERHAPS I SHOULDN'T EVEN USE THE PAST TENSE.
FOR THOUGH HE IS DEAD, OUR DECREE LIVES ON.
THIS IS NOT A MATTER WE CAN EASILY RESOLVE.
LET US EXAMINE THE TESTIMONY AGAIN AND CONVENE A COURT SESSION IN SIX DAYS.
BIRO VIKIE...
HABAKI FUTA-SHIGE...
...AND BASMA.

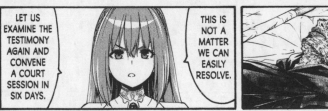

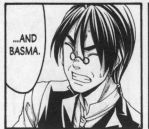

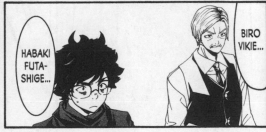

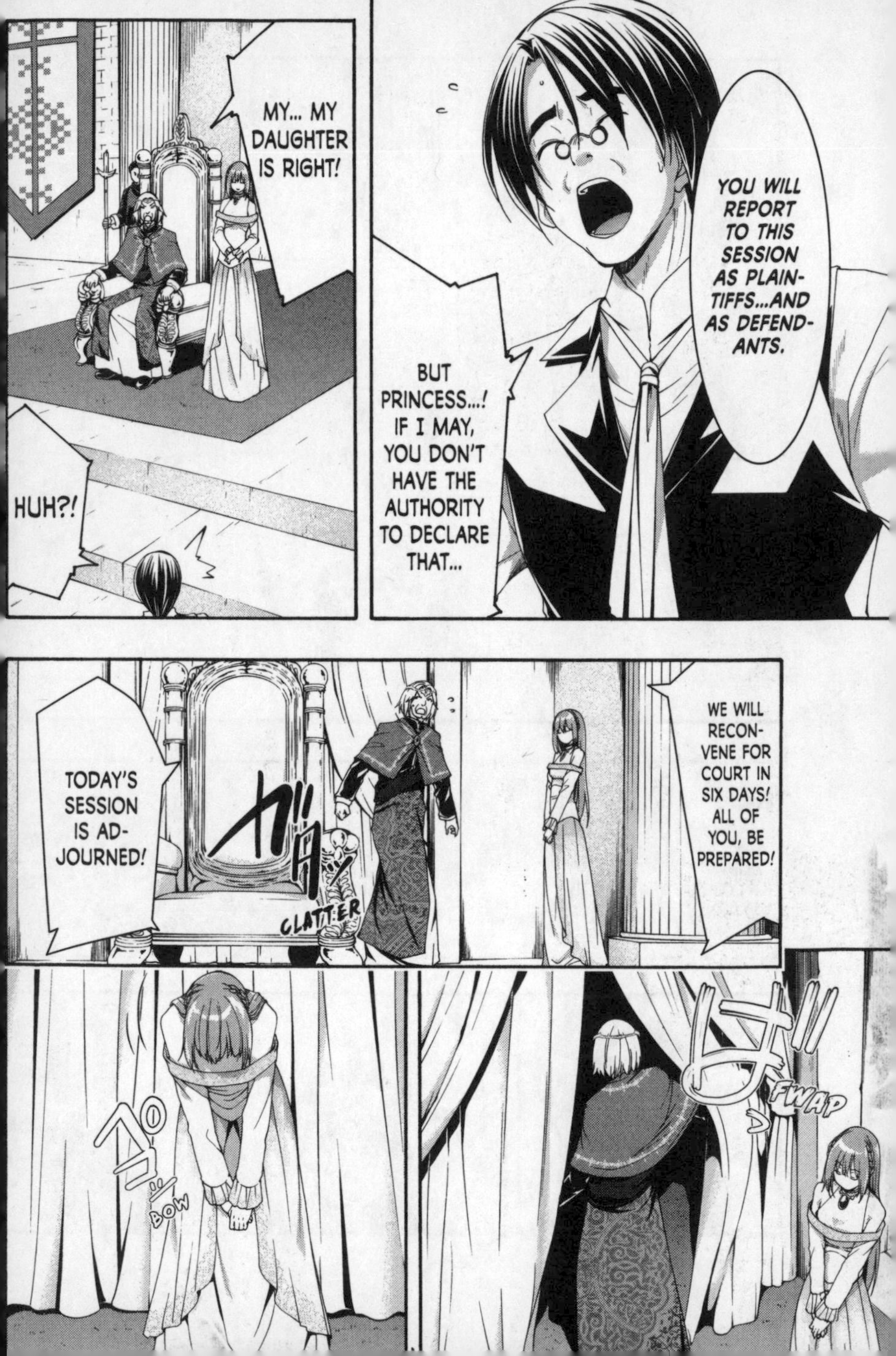
YOU WILL REPORT TO THIS SESSION AS PLAIN-TIFFS...AND AS DEFEND-ANTS.
BUT PRINCESS...! IF I MAY, YOU DON'T HAVE THE AUTHORITY TO DECLARE THAT...
MY... MY DAUGHTER IS RIGHT!
HUH?!
WE WILL RECON-VENE FOR COURT IN SIX DAYS! ALL OF YOU, BE PREPARED!
TODAY'S SESSION IS AD-JOURNED!
CLATTER
FWAP
BOW

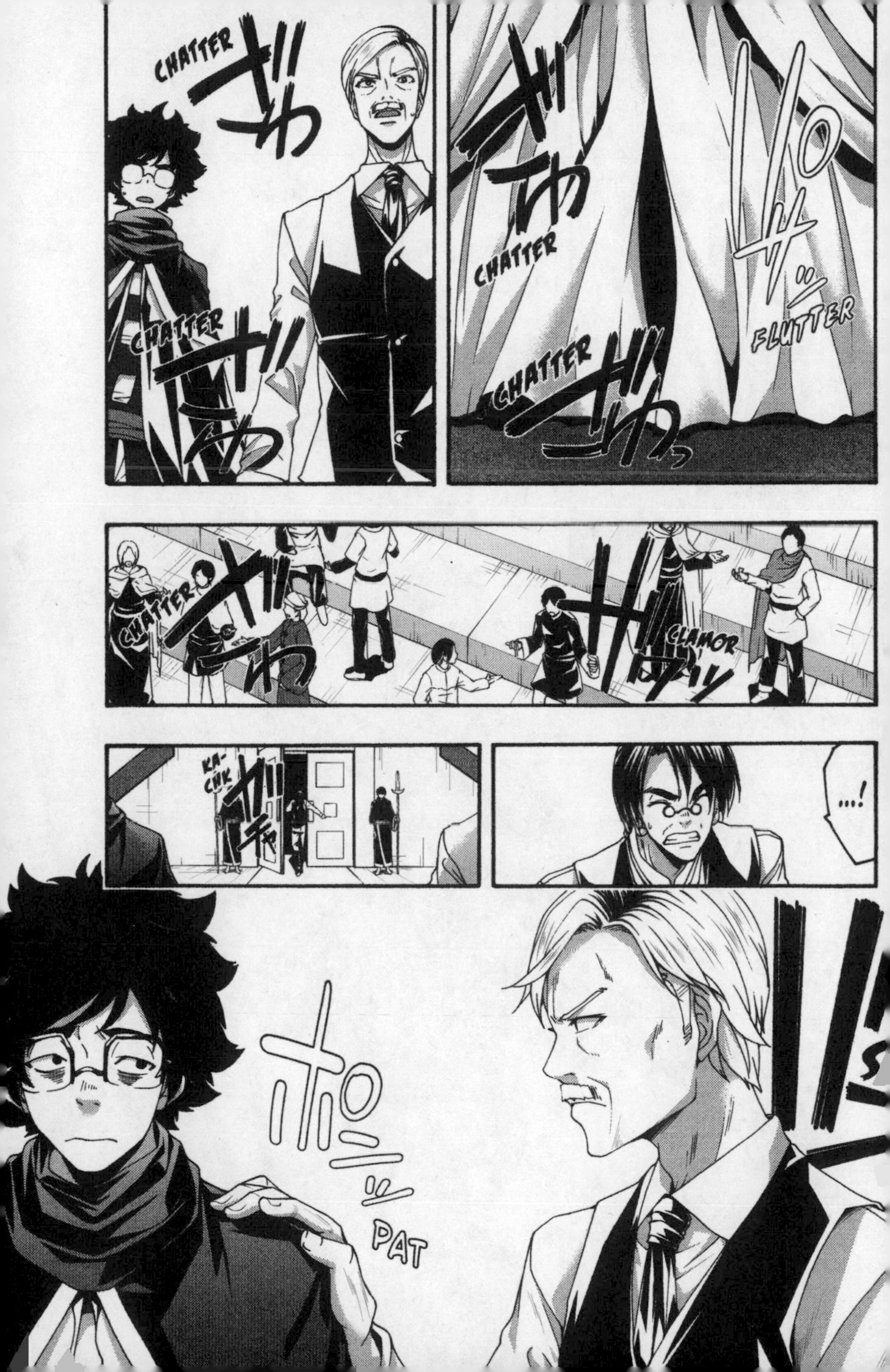
FLUTTER
CHATTER
CHATTER
CHATTER
CHATTER
CLAMOR
CHATTER
...!
KA-CHK
PAT

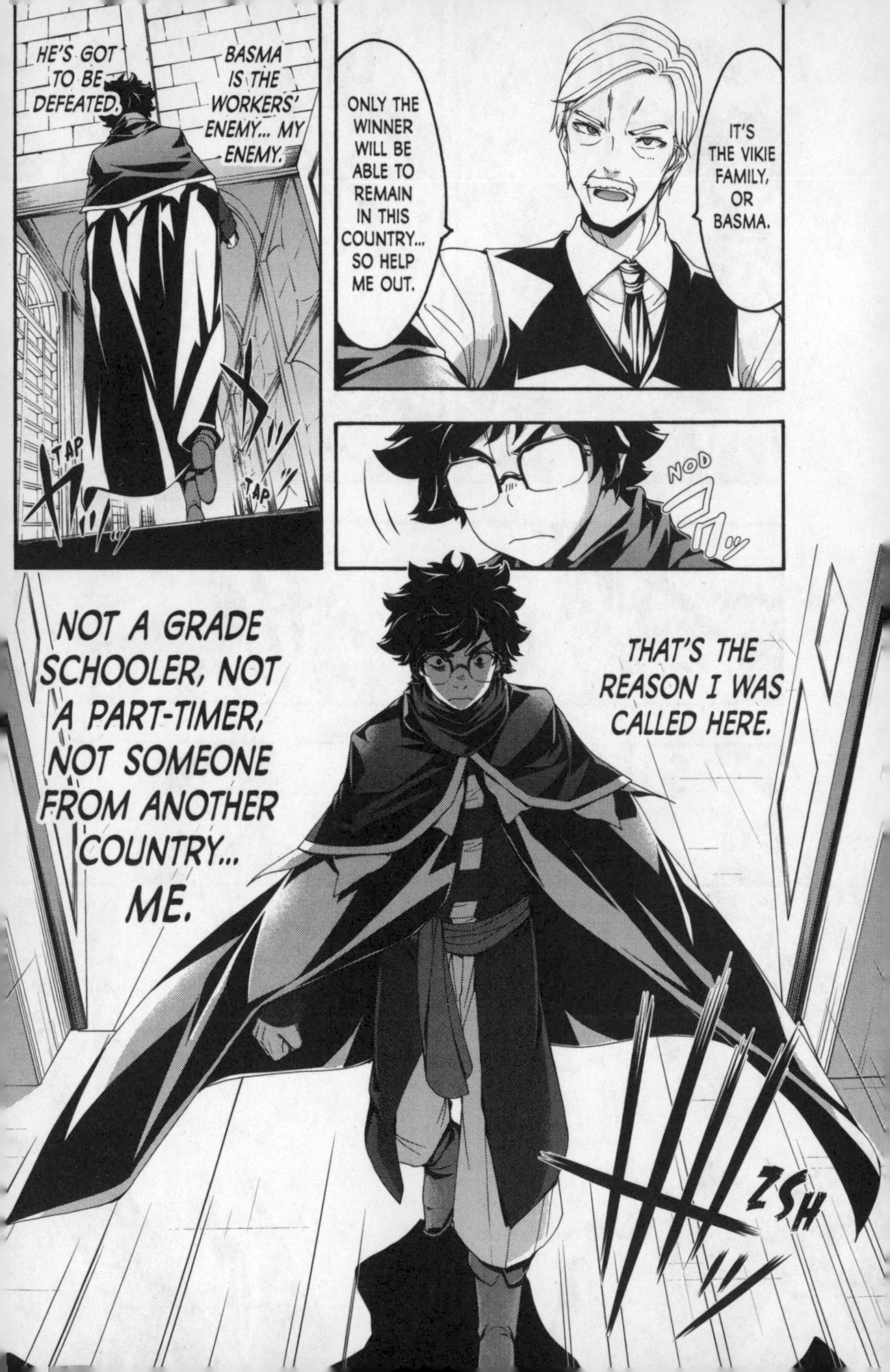
IT'S THE VIKIE FAMILY, OR BASMA.
ONLY THE WINNER WILL BE ABLE TO REMAIN IN THIS COUNTRY... SO HELP ME OUT.
NOD
BASMA IS THE WORKERS' ENEMY... MY ENEMY.
HE'S GOT TO BE DEFEATED.
TAP
TAP
THAT'S THE REASON I WAS CALLED HERE.
NOT A GRADE SCHOOLER, NOT A PART-TIMER, NOT SOMEONE FROM ANOTHER COUNTRY... ME.
ZSH

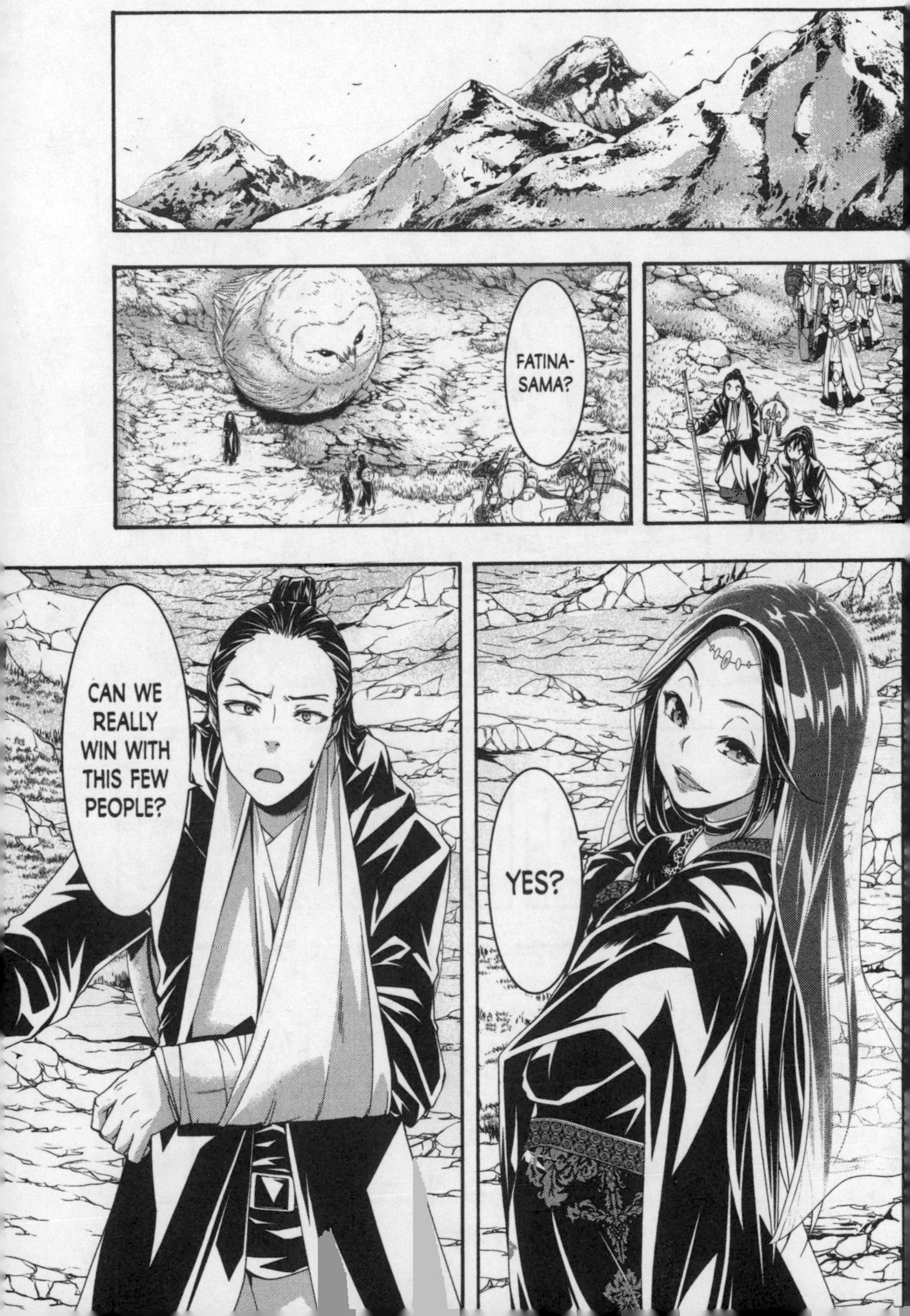
FATINA-SAMA?
YES?
CAN WE REALLY WIN WITH THIS FEW PEOPLE?

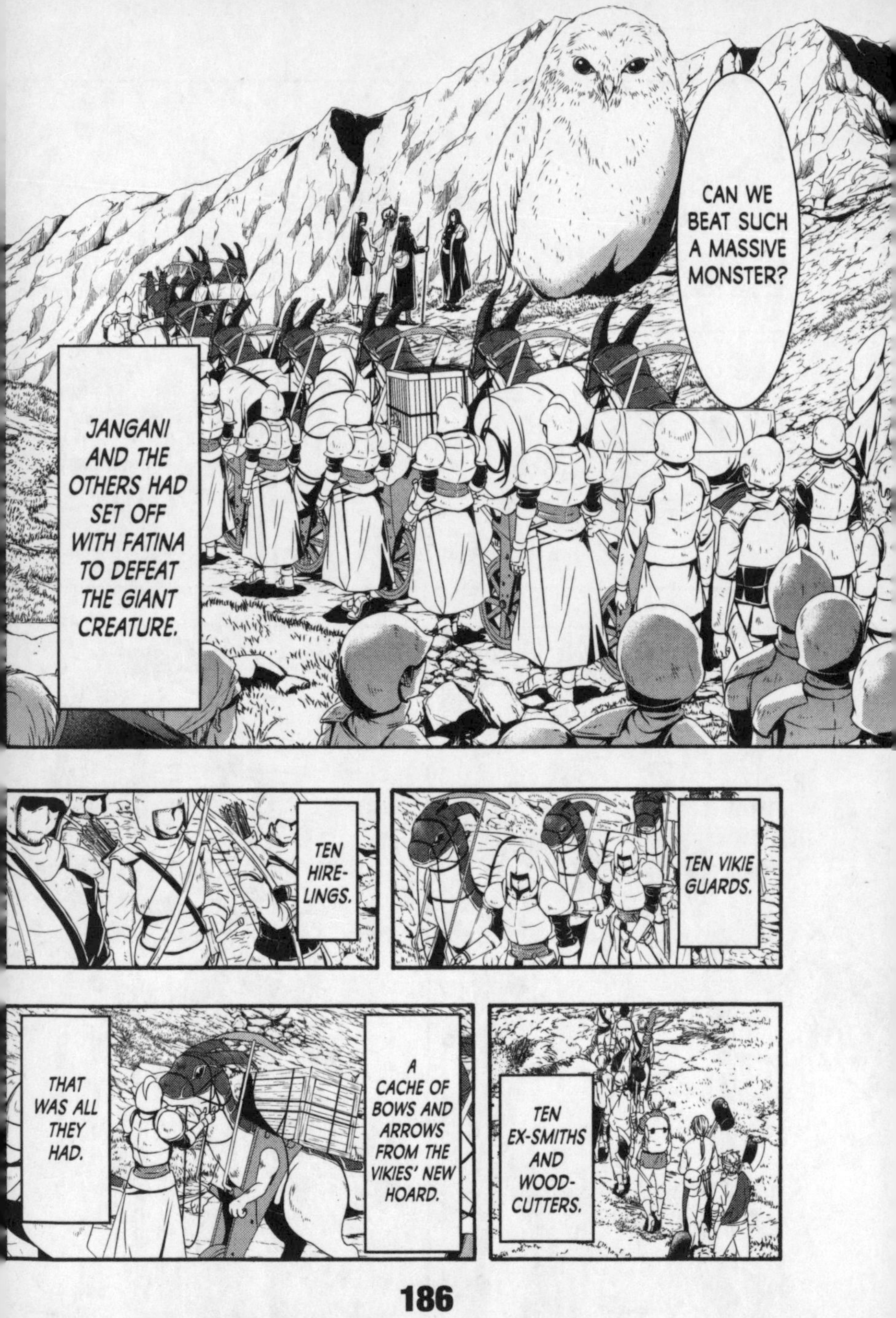
CAN WE BEAT SUCH A MASSIVE MONSTER?
JANGANI AND THE OTHERS HAD SET OFF WITH FATINA TO DEFEAT THE GIANT CREATURE.
TEN VIKIE GUARDS.
TEN HIRE-LINGS.
TEN EX-SMITHS AND WOOD-CUTTERS.
A CACHE OF BOWS AND ARROWS FROM THE VIKIES' NEW HOARD.
THAT WAS ALL THEY HAD.

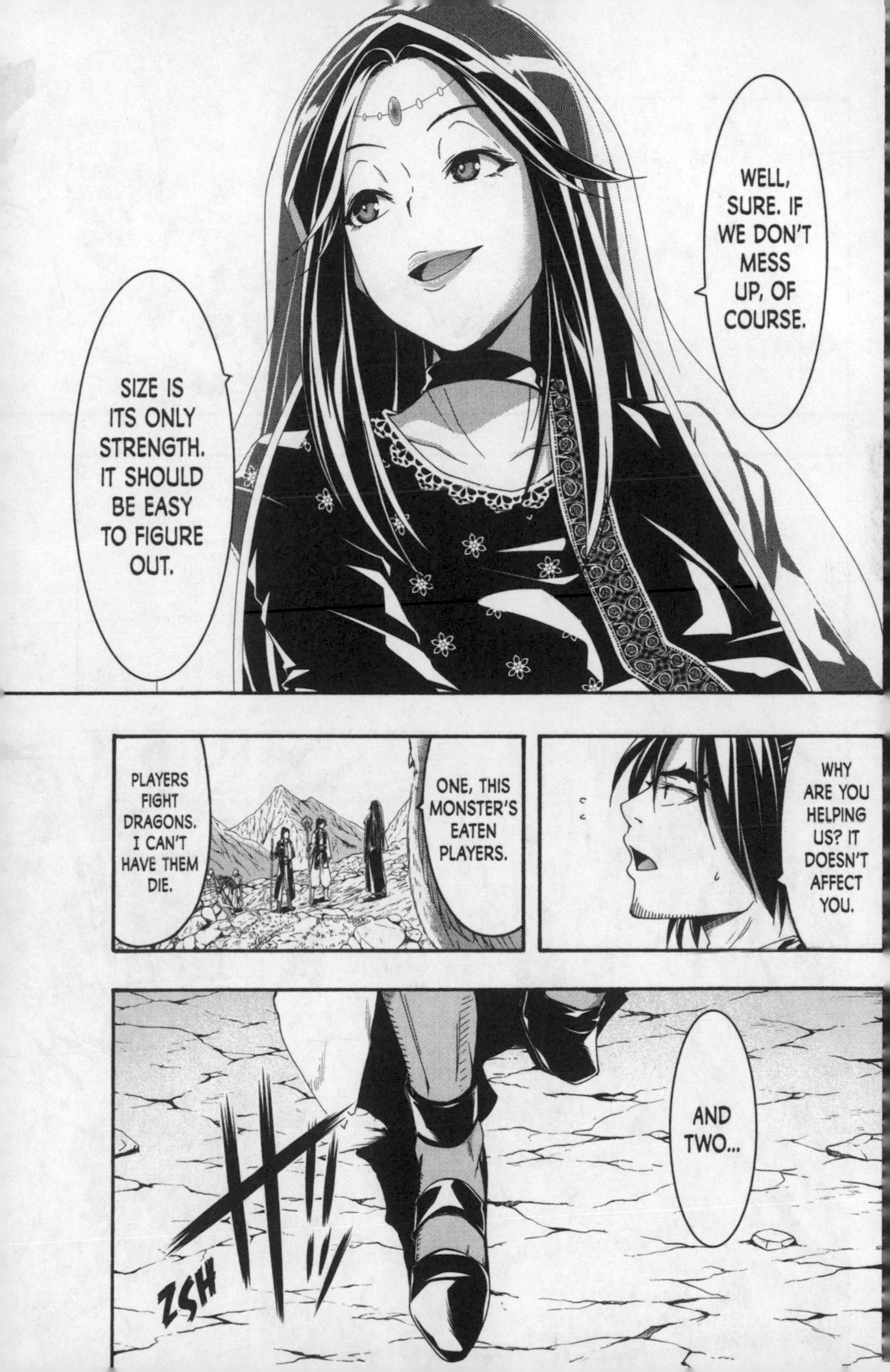
WELL, SURE. IF WE DON'T MESS UP, OF COURSE.
SIZE IS ITS ONLY STRENGTH. IT SHOULD BE EASY TO FIGURE OUT.
WHY ARE YOU HELPING US? IT DOESN'T AFFECT YOU.
ONE, THIS MONSTER'S EATEN PLAYERS.
PLAYERS FIGHT DRAGONS. I CAN'T HAVE THEM DIE.
AND TWO...
ZSH

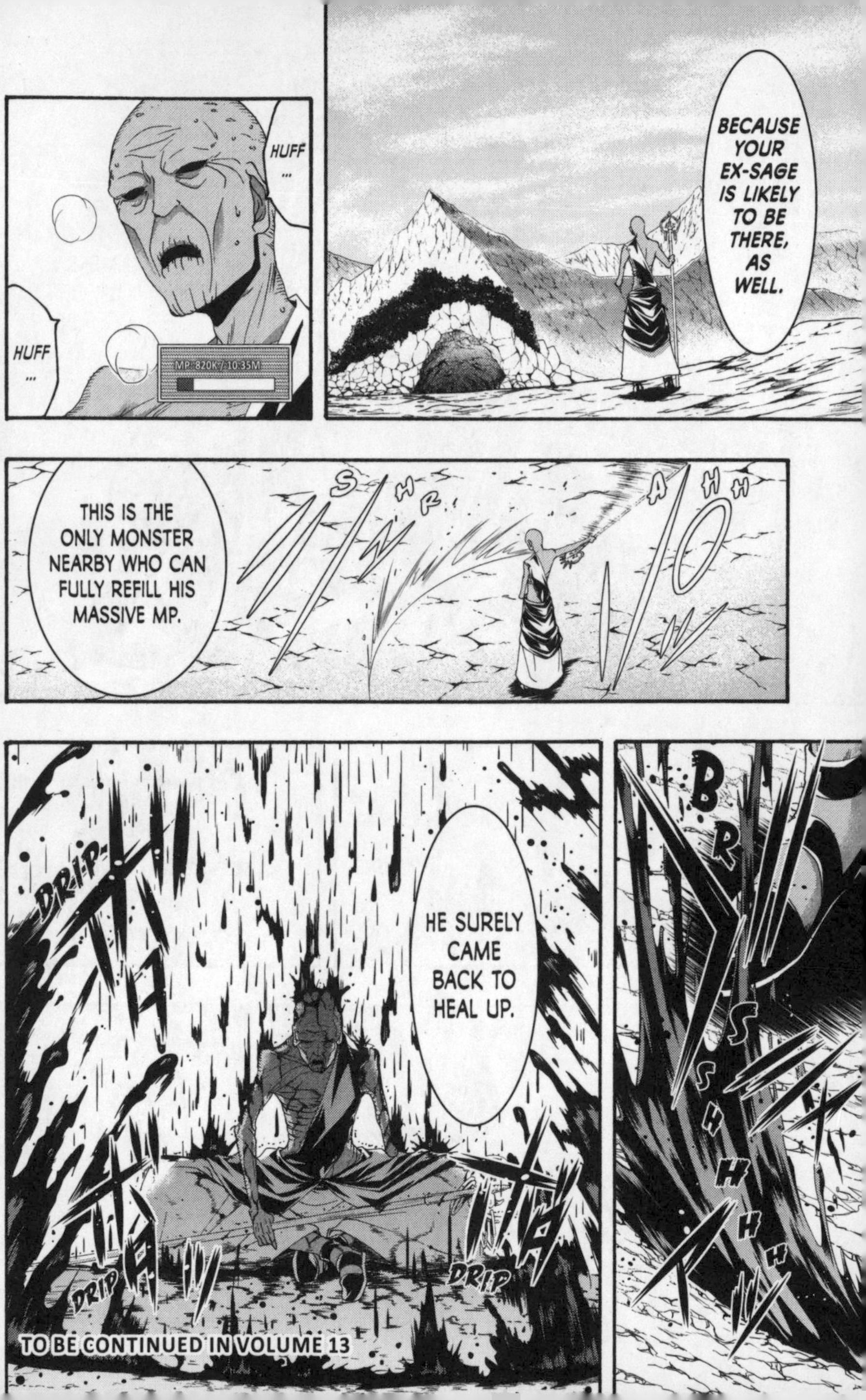
BECAUSE YOUR EX-SAGE IS LIKELY TO BE THERE, AS WELL.
HUFF ...
HUFF ...
MP: 820K / 10.35M
AHH
SHR
THIS IS THE ONLY MONSTER NEARBY WHO CAN FULLY REFILL HIS MASSIVE MP.
BR
SSHHHHH
HE SURELY CAME BACK TO HEAL UP.
DRIP-
DRIP
DRIP
TO BE CONTINUED IN VOLUME 13

Young characters and steampunk setting, like *Howl's Moving Castle* and *Battle Angel Alita*

Beyond the Clouds © 2018 Nicke / Ki-oon

A boy with a talent for machines and a mysterious girl whose wings he's fixed will take you beyond the clouds! In the tradition of the high-flying, resonant adventure stories of Studio Ghibli comes a gorgeous tale about the longing of young hearts for adventure and friendship!

The adorable new odd-couple cat comedy manga from the creator of the beloved *Chi's Sweet Home*, in full color!

Sue & Tai-chan

Konami Kanata

Sue is an aging housecat who's looking forward to living out her life in peace... but her plans change when the mischievous black tomcat Tai-chan enters the picture! Hey! Sue never signed up to be a catsitter! *Sue & Tai-chan* is the latest from the reigning meow-narch of cute kitty comics, Konami Kanata.

KC
KODANSHA
COMICS